SCHOLARS' GUIDE
TO WASHINGTON, D.C.
FOR
SOUTHEAST ASIAN STUDIES

THE WILSON CENTER

W

SCHOLARS' GUIDE

TO WASHINGTON, D.C.
FOR

SOUTHEAST ASIAN STUDIES

BRUNEI, BURMA, CAMBODIA, INDONESIA, LAOS, MALAYSIA,
PHILIPPINES, SINGAPORE, THAILAND, VIETNAM

PATRICK M. MAYERCHAK

Consultants
LOUIS A. JACOB
FRANK JOSEPH SHULMAN

Series Editor
ZDENEK V. DAVID

WOODROW WILSON INTERNATIONAL CENTER FOR SCHOLARS

SMITHSONIAN INSTITUTION PRESS
WASHINGTON, D.C.
1983

This work was developed under a grant from the U.S. Department of Education. However, the content does not necessarily reflect the position or Policy of that agency, and no official endorsement of these materials should be inferred.

Library of Congress Cataloging in Publication Data

Mayerchak, Patrick M.
Scholars' guide to Washington, D.C. for
Southeast Asian studies.

(Scholars' guide to Washington, D.C. ; no. 9)
Bibliography: p.
Includes index.
1. Asia, Southeastern—Library resources—Washington (D.C.)   2. Asia, Southeastern—Archival resources—Washington (D.C.)   3. Asia, Southeastern—Societies, etc.—Directories.   I. Jacob, Louis A.   II. Shulman, Frank Joseph, 1943–   III. Title.
IV. Series.
Z3221.M37 1983 [DS521]   016.959'0072073   82–19454
ISBN 0-87474-626-4
ISBN 0-87474-625-6 (pbk.)

Designed by Elizabeth Dixon.

CONTENTS

FOREWORD

This *Guide* is sponsored by the Woodrow Wilson International Center for Scholars, the nation's "living memorial" to its twenty-eighth president. It is the ninth in a series of reference works describing the scholarly resources of the Washington, D.C., area. These *Guides* were inspired, in part, by the accumulated lore about scholarly materials that was developing among fellows in the Wilson Center.

Southeast Asia represents a unique locus of interaction between the ancient cultural influences of China and of the Indian subcontinent. Commercial interests and technical assistance gave Americans a "presence" in Thailand during the nineteenth century. The Philippines were under American sovereignty from 1898 to 1946, and much of World War II in Asia was fought in the area ranging from Burma to Indonesia. Post–World War II tensions led to a major United States involvement in Indochina, culminating in the Vietnam conflict of 1961–1975. The Wilson Center, particularly through its East Asia Program since 1982, has shown increased interest in supporting research on Southeast Asian topics.

Taken as a whole, the series of *Guides* exemplifies the Wilson Center's "switchboard function" of facilitating connections between the vast resources of the nation's capital and those who have scholarly or practical needs—or simple curiosity. These *Guides*—like the Center's annual fellowship program—are designed to serve the national and international scholarly communities. At least 20,000 visiting scholars come each year to Washington from elsewhere in America and abroad to pursue serious research. The *Guides* are designed to inform scholars, many of them outside the major university research centers in the United States, about possibilities for engaging in research on particular topics in Washington. The *Guides* cover the metropolitan area of Washington, but they are not merely of local importance. In the city's libraries, archives, and data banks; its universities and research centers; and especially in the federal agencies and international organizations concentrated here, Washington holds resources that are of national—and even worldwide—significance.

The series of *Guides* is under the general editorship of Zdeněk V. David, the Wilson Center Librarian, who has devised the basic format. Elizabeth Dixon is largely responsible for the design and publication arrangements. Louis A. Jacob, Head of the Southern Asia Section in the Library of Congress, and Frank Joseph Shulman, Head of the East Asia Collection, McKeldin Library, University of Maryland, served as consultants in the preparation of this particular *Guide*. Wilson Center staff members providing advice and assistance were Prosser Gifford, George Liston Seay, and Peter Braestrup. The author of this volume, Patrick M. Mayerchak, is associate professor of political science at the Virginia Military Institute in Lexington, Virginia.

The Center thanks the United States Department of Education for its indispensable financial support of the *Guide's* preparation (under the authority of Title VI, Section 602, NDEA), as well as the Morris and Gwendolyn Cafritz Foundation of Washington, D.C., for additional support.

The Center has now prepared *Guides* for scholars in the fields of Russian/Soviet (1977), Latin American and Caribbean (1979), East Asian (1979), African (1980), Central and East European (1980), Middle Eastern (1981), and South Asian (1981) studies, as well as a *Guide* covering film and video collections (1980). All were published by the Smithsonian Institution Press, P.O. Box 1579, Washington, D.C. 20013). A forthcoming volume will survey resources in the Washington area for scholars interested in Northwest Europe. A revised edition of the *Guide* for the Russian/Soviet area is also under preparation, as well as a volume surveying audio resources.

James H. Billington, *Director*
Woodrow Wilson International Center for Scholars

Washington, D.C.
April 15, 1982

INTRODUCTION

Purpose: This volume is intended to be a basic reference aid for scholars interested in utilizing the diverse and often unique resources of the nation's capital for research in the field of Southeast Asian studies. Although this work is intended for the serious researcher, many readers with a more casual interest in Southeast Asia will also find much of value within its pages.

Washington, D.C., is an unsurpassed resource center for research on U.S.-Southeast Asian relations. Scholars, diplomats, technocrats, bureaucrats, politicians, and political activists with an interest in this region abound in Washington, D.C., and play a significant role in the decision-making process leading to the formulation of United States' Southeast Asia policy. In this city, diverse interest groups vie for the government's attention, and a multitude of consultants compete for its research and technical assistance contracts. The vehicle for many of these people is the variety of organizations listed in the pages of this *Guide,* and their documented results are often deposited in the many library and archival repositories described here.

Washington's massive library collections not only contain some of the largest holdings on Southeast Asia in the country, but also boast of specialized holdings on Vietnam, Indonesian textiles, and vast archival materials on this country's involvement in the Philippines. The capital city also features one of the largest and most comprehensive museum systems in the country, the Smithsonian Institution.

In Washington, D.C., history is both made and preserved. A scholar is able to study a foreign culture and meet it face-to-face. It is with this in mind that the present *Guide* was written. Its goal is to introduce the research possibilities of the Washington, D.C., area in the field of Southeast Asian studies by describing and exploring the many collections and organizational components that make up the capital city and surrounding area. While there are other fine academic centers for Southeast Asian studies outside of Washington, the nation's capital, taken as a whole, is unsurpassed as a resource center for the study of this interesting region of the world.

Learning how to find and use the various resources on Southeast Asia is not easy. It is hoped that this *Guide* will make the task easier.

Scope and Content: Over 400 collections, organizations, and agencies have been surveyed as part of the preparation for this volume. While providing the basic directory information (i.e., names, addresses, telephone numbers, and a variety of details about individual collections) the *Guide* is primarily a descriptive and evaluative survey of Washington's research resources. The body of the work is divided into two parts.

Part I examines Washington-area resource *collections:* libraries; archives and manuscript repositories; art, film, music, and map collections; and data banks. Each entry describes the size, content, and organizational format of a particular collection's Southeast Asia holdings and qualitatively evaluates the subject/country strengths and most unique materials within those holdings.

Part II is comprised of Washington-based *organizations,* public and private, which deal with Southeast Asia and are potential sources of information or assistance to researchers. Included in this part are: research centers and information offices; academic programs and departments at local universities; United States government agencies; Southeast Asian embassies and international organizations; private professional and cultural associations; cultural-exchange and technical-assistance organizations; places of worship and religious organizations; and media and publishing groups. Each entry describes the organization's Southeast Asia related functions, delineates its pertinent research activities, materials, and products (published and unpublished, classified and unclassified), and discusses the restrictions on access to unpublished and classified materials.

Brief introductions highlight special features of each section and provide related supplemental information. For example, the introductions explain library survey techniques (section A), Freedom-of-Information Act procedures (section K), and criteria used for selectively listing consultancy firms (sections H and N) and for including certain publications while omitting others (section Q). They also suggest places where visitors may see Southeast Asian films (section F) or purchase Southeast Asian music (section D).

At the back of the book, readers will find a series of appendixes—housing information; bookstores; libraries listed by size of Southeast Asia holdings; Vietnam war archives; standard entry formats—a bibliography, and indexes of personal-papers collections, library subject strengths and evaluation table, subjects, and names.

The *Guide's* topical coverage concentrates on the disciplines of the social sciences and humanities traditionally considered to fall under the rubric of Southeast Asian studies, although the fields of science and technology have been included where relevant. The volume's geographic scope encompasses Brunei, Burma, Cambodia (Kampuchea and Khmer Republic), Indonesia, Laos, Malaysia, the Philippines, Singapore, Thailand, and Vietnam. The time frame stretches from the ancient to the present.

Methodology: Preparation of the volume began with the compilation of a list of all Washington-area collections and organizations thought to be potential sources of information or assistance for scholarly research on Southeast Asia. The bibliography at the end of this volume contains the reference sources consulted in the compilation of this list. Each pertinent collection and organization was then investigated by the author in person or by telephone. Information was gleaned from on-site examination, printed materials, and discussions with staff members. Data should be considered current through early 1982. For possible future revisions of this work, suggestions by readers for additions, alterations, and improvements will be greatly appreciated. Please notify the Librarian, Woodrow Wilson International Center for Scholars, Smithsonian Institution Building, 1000 Jefferson Drive, S.W., Washington, D.C. 20560. The author also welcomes comments and inquiries.

Acknowledgments: The author wishes to express his appreciation to the U.S. Department of Education for the financial support (under the authority of Title VI, Section 602, NDEA), which made the preparation of this work possible; to Zdeněk V. David, Librarian of the Woodrow Wilson International Center for Scholars and editor of the Wilson Center's *Scholars' Guide* Series, for his limitless patience, valuable guidance and assistance; to Louis A. Jacob, Head, Southern Asia Section, Library of Congress, and to Frank Joseph Shulman for their consultation services;

and to the other authors of the *Guides* in this series whose labor in the same vineyard made the task of those who followed much easier: Steven A. Grant, Michael Grow, Hong N. Kim, Purnima M. Bhatt, Bonnie G. Rowan, Kenneth J. Dillon, Steven R. Dorr, James R. Heintze, and particularly Enayetur Rahim, whose *Guide* for South Asian studies was closest to this volume both in subject matter and in time of preparation. In addition, Mary Jane Wood Mayerchak provided valuable and timely research assistance for the museum, music, and film collections (sections C, D, and F). Janet Johnson Aldridge's typing was quick and efficient under difficult circumstances. Finally, the author extends his appreciation to the hundreds of men and women on the staffs of the institutions discussed below, who contributed their time and knowledge to this project. Many, but by no means all, of these individuals are mentioned in the pages that follow. Thanks go also to Y. B. Namahasarakam for his contribution of calligraphy on the half-title page.

HOW TO USE THE *GUIDE*

Format: The main body of this *Guide* is divided into seven collection sections and eight organization sections. Within each section, entries are arranged alphabetically by the name of the individual collection or organization. In the section containing United States government agencies (K), functional descriptors precede the generic name; e.g., *State Department* rather than *Department of State*. The Southeast Asia embassies (section L) are given their official titles as indicated in the *Diplomatic List* (February 1982) but are arranged alphabetically according to their geographic name and listed as a group before the international organizations.

Standard Entry Form: At the beginning of each section, a brief introductory paragraph follows a standard entry form (see also Appendix VII), which outlines the categories and sequence of information contained within each entry. The numbers of the entry form correspond to the numerical arrangement of each entry. If a particular number does not appear in an entry, that category of information was either not applicable or not available. If a single institution or organization has more than one entry in the *Guide,* references to all entries are gathered under the main entry and also in the Name Index.

Indexes: Four indexes provide access to information in the text from several perspectives. The Personal-Papers Index includes the names of individuals whose papers and manuscripts are located in libraries or other depositories in the Washington, D.C., area. The Library Subject-Strength Index ranks the major library collections in the metropolitan area by subject and country. The scale of evaluation used to rank these libraries is explained in the introduction to the library section and the Library Subject-Strength Index. The library ranking table used to evaluate the quantitative strength of the collections is also reproduced with this index. The Name Index contains the names of organizations and institutions, with subdivisions of highly differentiated agencies grouped under the main entry in the index. Names of individuals are not included in this index. The Subject Index covers rather broad categories and includes geographic headings. Most collections include information on the Southeast Asian region as a whole and, at least, representative materials on individual countries. The subject index indicates where certain countries are more prominently featured in a particular collection.

Names, Addresses and Telephone Numbers: These data are subject to frequent change, particularly for government agencies and highly differentiated organizations where reorganization and personnel changes occur often. All telephone numbers include area codes (202, for the District of Columbia; 301, for the Maryland Suburbs; and

703, for the Virginia suburbs) to assist those placing telephone calls from outside the Washington area. When dialing from within the Washington metropolitan area, the area codes should be ignored since these would all be local calls.

Transliteration: The transliteration system used in this book is essentially that of the Library of Congress. Certain inconsistencies are due to the author's attempt—for ease of retrieval—to spell names as they appear in the catalogs or other materials of the collection being described. Similarly, some organizations appear under names of their own transliteration. Anglicized geographic place names have been retained for most familiar locations.

Common Acronyms:
AID—Agency for International Development
ASEAN—Association of Southeast Asian Nations*
FBIS—Foreign Broadcast Information Service
FOIA—Freedom of Information Act
GPO—U.S. Government Printing Office
IBRD—International Bank for Reconstruction and Development (World Bank)
ICA—International Communication Agency**
IMF—International Monetary Fund
JPRS—Joint Publications Research Service
LC—Library of Congress
NARS—National Archives and Records Service
NTIS—National Technical Information Service
SEATO—Southeast Asia Treaty Organization
UN—United Nations

---

*Includes Indonesia, Malaysia, the Philippines, Singapore, and Thailand.
**As of September 1982, ICA reverted to its former name, United States Information Agency (USIA).

COLLECTIONS

A Libraries

Libraries Entry Format (A)

1. General Information
   a. *address; telephone numbers*
   b. hours of service
   c. conditions of access (including availability of interlibrary loan and reproduction facilities)
   d. name/title of director and heads of relevant divisions

2. Size of Collection
   a. general
   b. Southeast Asia

3. Description and Evaluation of Collection
   a. narrative assessment of Southeast Asian holdings—subject and area strengths/weaknesses
   b. tabular evaluation of subject strengths for holdings on Brunei, Burma, Cambodia, Indonesia, Laos, Malaysia, the Philippines, Singapore, Thailand, Vietnam, and Southeast Asia, giving the number of titles and a rating of A-D,* in the following subject categories:

   Philosophy and Religion
   History and Auxiliary Sciences of History
   Geography and Anthropology
   Economics

---

*A—comprehensive collection of primary and secondary sources (Library of Congress collection to serve as standard of evaluation).

B—substantial collection of primary and secondary sources sufficient for some original research (holdings equivalent to roughly one-tenth of those of the Library of Congress).

C—substantial collection of secondary sources with some primary materials, sufficient to support graduate instruction (holdings of roughly one-half those of the B collection).

D—collection of secondary sources, mostly in English, sufficient to support undergraduate instruction (holdings of roughly one-half those of C collection); collections rated below D are indicated by "D−."

Sociology
Politics and Government
International Relations
Law
Education
Art and Music
Language and Literature
Military Affairs
Bibliography and Reference

4.   Special Collections
   a. periodicals
   b. newspapers
   c. government documents
   d. miscellaneous vertical files
   e. archives and manuscripts
   f. maps
   g. films
   h. tapes

5.   Bibliographic Aids (catalogs, guides, etc.) Facilitating Use of Collection

━━━━━━━━━━━━━━━━━━━━━━━━━━━━━━━

Introductory Note

This *Guide* follows the evaluation methodology established for the series by Steven A. Grant's *Scholars' Guide to Washington, D.C. for Russian/Soviet Studies* (1977). Most large general collections and a number of smaller collections are evaluated on a scale of A through D to gauge the quality and quantity of library holdings in 13 subject categories and 11 geographic categories.

The Library of Congress's holdings were taken as the standard of evaluation for an A collection, which is defined as a comprehensive collection of primary and secondary source materials.

The B collection is defined as a substantial collection (approximately one-tenth the size of the Library of Congress collection) of primary and secondary sources, sufficient for some original research.

The C collection is considered to be a substantial collection (roughly one-half the size of the B collection) of secondary sources, with some primary materials, sufficient to support graduate instruction.

Finally, a D collection is defined as a collection (approximately one-half the size of a C collection) of predominantly secondary sources, sufficient to support under-graduate instruction. The table used to rank the measured library holdings is repro-duced with the Library Subject-Strength Index. It is based exclusively on the Library of Congress holdings and calculated according to the formula given above.

In most cases, the numbers of titles listed for the various subject and geographic categories were derived by measuring library shelflists and calculating 100 cards or 85 titles per inch of shelflist catalog cards. Only those call numbers with a geographic subsection devoted to the region and nations of Southeast Asia were measured. Numerical totals in geographic categories were calculated by combining the shelflist measurements of selected call numbers in the subject categories for each country or subregion. This method led to certain distortions in the impressions rendered of the relative strengths of various library holdings. Thus, the figures obtained by this measurement technique should be viewed as rough approximations only. In all cases they underestimate the numerical size of the collection.

Several particularly significant flaws in the measurement method just described should be noted. The Library of Congress classification system for Southeast Asian law remains incomplete, and, as a result, shelflist measurements for law produced meager findings. Since the philosophy and religion category used by the Library of Congress does not allow for easy differentiation of Southeast Asia specific materials, an effort was made to hand count entries relevant to our region. Results for this category may be considered reliable, though by no means absolute. History covers all periods from ancient to the modern; the language and literature category makes no distinction between Burmese, Lao, Malay, Thai, etc.; and the remaining categories are not readily amenable to geographic measurement.

In addition, the Library of Congress cataloging system for Southeast Asia will often place in the history category titles that could equally be classified under government and politics, international relations, or military subject headings. As a result, the number of titles listed under the latter categories may appear to be insubstantial even though rankings on the A to D scale have been assigned. The geographic category measurements must also be viewed with caution since language and literature have all been incorporated into the country figures. The Subject Index in the back of this *Guide* helps to clarify the distinctions blurred by the tabular system used in the text.

As for total library holdings, the measuring technique used in this *Guide* also leaves out the substantial amount of material on Southeast Asia found in works of collected essays, congresses, addresses, and serials, and in works on U.S. history and the history of American Foreign relations—which include much information about Southeast Asia without focusing primarily on the region (e.g., works about the Spanish-American War of 1898). Nevertheless, the figures do give the researcher an idea of where to begin a search for specialized literature on Southeast Asian topics. One should assume that, in those libraries where individual titles devoted to Southeast Asian topics are few, collected works with area themes included will also be limited.

Beyond these methodological considerations, a few generalized comments may allow the reader to use this *Guide* and the Southeast Asia related collections in Washington, D.C., to the best advantage. The Library of Congress (entry A27) is without a doubt the most important source of printed Southeast Asia resources in virtually every subject and geographic category. When combined with the holdings of the local major university libraries these resources (see section J) provide excellent support for the study of Southeast Asia. Finally, the specialized libraries of the U.S. government agencies offer valuable monograph and documentary resources in their fields of concentration, particularly in economics (see especially the National Agricultural Library, entry A30, and the specialized libraries maintained by the Department of Commerce, A9 and A10, and Health and Human Services, A33).

Academy for Educational Development—Clearinghouse on Development Communication See entry N1

A1 ACTION Library (Peace Corps Library)

1. a. *806 Connecticut Avenue, N.W.*
    Washington, D.C. 20526
    (202) 254-3307

b. 9:30 A.M.–4:00 P.M.   Monday–Friday

c. Open to the public for reference use only. Interlibrary loan service is available only when duplicate copies of titles are on hand. No photocopying is available.

d. Rita C. Warpeha, Chief Librarian

2. Much of the collection in this library consists of the holdings of the former Peace Corps library, which was assembled to support Peace Corps programs around the world, including Indonesia, Malaysia, the Philippines, and Thailand. The collection contains an estimated 38,000 books and reports of which 700 titles relate to Southeast Asia. The library currently receives approximately 400 periodicals, including *Asiaweek* and *Far Eastern Economic Review*.

3–4. While the Southeast Asia portion of this collection is small, it is relatively well developed in the foreign language subject area; e.g., 25 titles for the Philippines alone. Thai, Lao, Malay, and Indonesian language instruction materials are also plentiful.

The library holds extensive materials generated by the Peace Corps since 1961, when the international volunteer program was launched. Peace Corps documents to be found include: regional plans and analyses, training manuals, project reports, country program evaluations, news releases and volunteer newsletters, correspondence, memoirs, and journals. The pre-1970 program evaluations generally must be cleared before being made available to the public. The staff can assist you in gaining access to these evaluations. Post-1970 evaluations are open to the public.

The library maintains a vertical file arranged by country, which contains some foreign government documents, newspaper clippings on the country, and U.S. government documents. The file is designed to serve Peace Corps personnel preparing to travel abroad. Files for Malaysia, Indonesia, and the Philippines are included, though scholars will probably find little of significant research value.

To facilitate access, the library collection has been organized into three subdivisions: a general section including materials without a regional or country focus; a regional section containing materials which focus on Asia, Africa, or Latin America; and a country section where all materials are shelved by country.

5. A card catalog using the Library of Congress classification schedule serves the collection along with a periodical visible file. There is also a small card index for the vertical file.

It should be stressed that this library is not in a position to handle a large volume of public inquiries. Scholars with an interest in the Peace Corps will, however, find the staff very helpful.

A2 Agency for International Development (AID)—Development Information Center (DIC)

1. a. *Development Information Center*
Department of State Buiding
320 21st Street, N.W.
Washington, D.C. 20523
(202) 632-8571

Rosslyn Branch—DIC
1601 North Kent Street, Room 105
Arlington, Virginia 22209
(703) 235-8936

b. 9:00 A.M.–5:30 P.M.   Monday–Friday (both branches)

c. DIC's primary function is to serve AID personnel, AID contractors, and AID grantees. The facilities may be used by others for reference purposes. Interlibrary loan and photocopying services are available.

d. Joanne M. Paskar, Chief
Margaret Pope, Branch Head

2–3.   The DIC collection in both centers consists of approximately 125,000 items, over 4,400 of which relate to Southeast Asia. Much of this material consists of documents produced by AID or AID contractors and covers such areas as: agriculture and rural development, population and family planning, health and nutrition, urban development, technical assistance, administration and planning strategy for developing nations, and small industries development.

In addition to those materials generated by the agency and its contractors, the DIC acquires appropriate technical and methodological documentation produced by other non-AID sources, including government, professional organizations, and international agencies such as the Asian Development Bank and the International Monetary Fund.

Both the Rosslyn and main branch have on microfiche all reports contained in the two-volume *AID Catalog of Research Literature for Development,* 2 vols. (vol. 1: 1962–1976, published in 1976; vol. 2: 1976–1977, published in 1978), which covers the period from 1962 through 1976, and the quarterly *A.I.D. Research and Development Abstracts.*

The breakdown of items in the main DIC collection for the countries of Southeast Asia is as follows: Burma and Singapore less than 100 each, Malaysia 100, Cambodia 124, Indonesia 163, Laos 350, the Philippines 950, Thailand 1025, and South Vietnam 1613.

4.   The DIC has the 6,000-volume Population Reference Library at its Rosslyn Branch. This is a substantial collection of population-related studies and data.

5.   Since much of the material in the DIC is uncataloged, staff assistance is essential to locate and retrieve items. Card catalogs arranged by author, title, subject, geographical category, and contract number are available at both DIC locations. Also available is RANDO, AID's computerized bibliographic data base, which contains approximately 9,500 entries. In addition, the DIC has two project information data bases, PAISHIST and DIS. The former includes elementary information (titles, numbers, starting and completion dates) on all AID projects, while the latter contains summaries of active or completed projects from 1974.

American Association of University Women Library See entry M4

American Council on Education Library See entry M6

American Enterprise Institute for Public Policy Research Library
See entry H2

American Federation of Labor and Congress of Industrial Organizations (AFL-CIO) Library See entry N6

American Film Institute (AFI) Library See entry M7

A3 American Petroleum Institute (API) Library

1.   a. *Fifth Floor*
     2101 L Street, N.W.
     Washington, D.C. 20037
     (202) 457-7266

     b. 9:00 A.M.–5:00 P.M.   Monday–Friday

     c. Open to the public for on-site use only. Limited interlibrary loan service. Photoreproduction facilities available for a fee.

     d. Gladys E. Siegel, Librarian

2–3.   The largest portion of the collection, by far, is devoted to the domestic U.S. oil industry, as the library serves the reference needs of API, the American oil industry's trade association. Nevertheless, among its holdings of over 25,000 books and reports are a number of items relating to the world oil industry, including OPEC and the national oil companies of the various oil exporting countries, Indonesia among them.

4.   a. The library currently receives over 300 periodical titles, including *Petroleum Press Service, World Oil,* and annual reports from foreign oil companies.

5.   A dictionary card catalog to the collection is available, as is a list of periodicals.

American Public Health Association (APHA) Resource Center See entry M14

American Red Cross National Headquarters Library See entry N8

American Society of International Law (ASIL) Library See entry M16

A4 American University Library

1. a. *Massachusetts and Nebraska Avenues, N.W.*
       Washington, D.C. 20016
       (202) 685-2325 (Reference)

    b. Fall and Spring semesters:
       8:00 A.M.–Midnight   Monday–Friday
       9:00 –6:00 P.M.   Saturday
       11:00 A.M.–Midnight   Sunday

       Summer Sessions:
       9:00 A.M.–10:00 P.M.   Monday–Thursday
       9:00 A.M.–5:00 P.M.   Friday–Saturday
       For holiday and between sessions hours call 686-3839

    c. The library is open to the public for reference use. Interlibrary loan and photocopying services are available.

    d. Donald D. Dennis, University Librarian

2–3 a. The AU library collection exceeds 400,000 volumes. The library receives over 3,000 periodicals and some 50 newspapers. There are over 2,500 titles on Southeast Asian countries, 35 periodicals, and 3 newspapers: the *Bangkok Post, Straits Times,* and *Indonesia Times.* This collection is well developed and has benefited in the past from the presence of a Southeast Asian studies program in the School of International Service (see entry J1).

    b. Tabular evaluation of subject strengths:

	Brunei	Burma	Cambodia	Indonesia	Laos	Malaysia
Philosophy and Religion	—	13	4	9	—	6
History	5	110	23	399	20	146
Geography and Anthropology	—	3	2	12	1	7
Economics	—	26	9	62	5	52
Sociology	—	23	6	49	4	19
Politics and Government	—	21	3	71	4	22
International Relations	—	1	—	7	—	3
Law	—	—	—	—	—	1
Education	—	—	—	4	—	5
Art and Music	—	1	—	10	—	6
Language and Literature	—	2	1	34	—	7
Military Affairs	—	1	1	6	—	2
Bibliography and Reference	—	4	1	13	—	6
Total Country Evaluation:	5 B	205 D	50 D	676 C	34 C	282 C

	Philip-pines	Singa-pore	Thailand	Vietnam	Indo-china	SEA general
Philosophy and Religion	4	—	8	3	2	1
History	385	21	104	310	66	28
Geography and Anthropology	15	—	2	6	7	1
Economics	44	9	28	35	66	6
Sociology	26	2	18	24	4	—
Politics and Government	31	2	20	25	3	6
International Relations	4	—	1	22	—	—
Law	—	1	—	—	—	—

	Philip-pines	Singa-pore	Thailand	Vietnam	Indo-china	SEA general
Education	9	1	1	—	2	—
Art and Music	3	—	3	4	—	—
Language and Literature	7	—	4	3	—	—
Military Affairs	3	—	—	2	—	—
Bibliography and Reference	8	—	3	3	3	5
Total Country Evaluation:	539 D	36 D	192 D	437 C	153 B	47 D

Total Subject Evaluation:

Philosophy and Religion	50 D
History	1,617 C
Geography and Anthropology	56 D
Economics	342 D
Sociology	175 C
Politics and Government	208 C
International Relations	38 B
Law	2 D –
Education	22 D –
Art and Music	27 D –
Language and Literature	58 D –
Military Affairs	15 D
Bibliography and Reference	46 D
	2,656 D

5. The library follows the Library of Congress classification system. The collection is served by a card catalog in two parts: author/title and subject. A computer printout lists all periodicals and newspapers held by the library. A printed *Library Guide* is available.

Arms Control and Disarmament Agency (ACDA) Library See entry K4

A5 Army and Navy Club Library

1. a. *17th and Eye Streets*
    Washington, D.C. 20006
    (202) 628-8400

    b. The club library is primarily intended for members' use. Nonmembers should call ahead for an appointment. There is no interlibrary loan service or photocopying equipment available.

    c. John Mayfield, Director

2–3. The club library consists of some 10,000 items, covering a wide variety of subject matter. Within this collection, however, are a small number of items of potential interest to Philippine specialists including: *Under Dewey at Manila,* by Edward Stratemeyer, 1898; *The Expedition to the Philippines,* by Frank D. Millett, 1899; and *Myself and a Few Moros,* by Lt. Col. Sydney A. Cloman, 1923.

4. The collection does not have a comprehensive card catalog. However, the director can be of great help in locating specific items in the collection.

A6 Army Library (Army Department)

1. a. *The Pentagon, Room 1A 518*
   Washington, D.C. 20310
   (202) 697-4301 (Reference)

   b. 9:00 A.M.–4:00 P.M.   Monday–Friday

   c. Entrance to the Pentagon is restricted; a building pass is required, and a "no escort" policy exists. Interlibrary loan is available through established libraries only. Photoduplication service is not available to personnel outside of the Department of Defense.

   d. Mary L. Shaffer, Director

2–4. Within the Army Library collection of over 200,000 volumes are some 1,500 volumes on Southeast Asia, covering such fields as history, politics, international relations, and military affairs. The collection consists largely of English-language secondary literature. Approximately one-fourth of the Southeast Asia collection deals with Vietnam and Indochina. The library maintains a public card catalog and on-line access to the documents at the Defense Technical Information Center (DTIC) (entry G5). The library is a regular recipient of Rand Corporation studies, and takes some 20 periodicals related to Southeast Asia.

5. An author/title/subject card catalog serves the collection. The library publishes monthly acquisitions lists, special bibliographies, and an annual listing of periodical holdings.

A7 Association of American Railroads—Economics and Finance Department Library

1. a. *1920 L Street, N.W.*
   Room 523
   Washington, D.C. 20036
   (202) 293-4068/69

   b. 8:30 A.M.–5:15 P.M.   Monday–Friday

   c. Open to the public (stacks restricted). Interlibrary loan and photocopying facilities are available.

   d. John McLeod, Librarian

2–3. This specialized library contains only a few titles on railroads in Southeast Asia. The majority of the material dates from the late nineteenth century to the present, and includes a few railroad annual reports, plus a number of journal article offprints.

4. The annual and periodical collection may be of use to researchers for statistical information on railroads in Southeast Asia. Reference annuals and periodicals, such as *Railway Dictionary and Yearbook, Janes World Railways, International Railway Journal* (London), *Rail International* (Brussels), *Revue général des chemins de fer* (Paris), and the *Railway Gazette*

International (London), publish articles and current statistics on Southeast Asian railroads.

5. The dictionary card catalog contains over 1.5 million citations to railroad literature (books, periodical articles, government reports, legislation), some of which have been weeded from the library collection. This catalog remains a useful bibliographic tool despite the limited number of Southeast Asia titles remaining in the collection.

Association of Former Intelligence Officers (AFIC) Library See entry M26

Brookings Institution Library See entry H9

A8 Catholic University of America—Mullen Library

1. a. *620 Michigan Avenue, N.E.*
    Washington, D.C. 20064
    (202) 635-5070

    b. 9:00 A.M.–10:00 P.M. Monday–Thursday
    9:00 A.M.–6:00 P.M. Friday
    9:00 A.M.–5:00 P.M. Saturday
    1:00 P.M.–10:00 P.M. Sunday
    Call for holiday and summer hours.

    c. Open to serious readers for on-site use. Temporary borrowing privileges may be obtained through the office of the director (202/635-5055). Interlibrary loan and photocopying facilities are available.

    d. Fred M. Peterson, Director

2–3 a. The library collection exceeds 1 million volumes, including fewer than 600 titles for Southeast Asia. The library has 11 periodicals and 2 newspapers (on microfilm) from the region out of a total of over 6,000 such items that it receives. The collection's strongest subject areas are theology, philosophy, and history. This is a relatively small collection when compared with other Southeast Asia collections in the area.

    b. Tabular evaluation of country strengths:

	Brunei	Burma	Cambodia	Indonesia	Laos	Malaysia
Philosophy and Religion	—	—	—	—	—	—
History	—	22	12	24	14	22
Geography and Anthropology	—	2	4	6	1	12
Economics	—	8	—	7	2	9
Sociology	—	3	—	1	1	1
Politics and Government	—	4	—	2	—	6
International Relations	—	—	—	—	1	—
Law	—	—	—	—	—	—
Education	—	—	—	—	—	—
Art and Music	—	—	—	—	1	—
Language and Literature	—	—	1	2	—	5

	Brunei	Burma	Cambodia	Indonesia	Laos	Malaysia
Military Affairs	—	—	—	1	—	1
Bibliography and Reference	—	1	—	1	—	
Total Country Evaluation:	—	40 D –	17 D –	44 D –	20 D –	56 D –

	Philip-pines	Singa-pore	Thailand	Vietnam	Indo-china	SEA general
Philosophy and Religion	23	—	2	9	—	—
History	101	12	15	86	5	6
Geography and Anthropology	12	4	6	—	—	—
Economics	15	10	3	6	—	—
Sociology	10	4	5	3	—	—
Politics and Government	14	7	7	9	—	—
International Relations	5	—	—	17	—	—
Law	—	—	—	—	—	—
Education	4	—	—	—	—	—
Art and Music	1	—	—	1	—	—
Language and Literature	10	—	—	—	—	—
Military Affairs	—	—	—	4	—	—
Bibliography and Reference	5	—	—	—	—	—
Total Country Evaluation:	200 D –	37 D –	38 D –	135 D –	5 D –	6 D –

Total Subject Evaluation:

Philosophy and Religion	34 D –
History	319 D –
Geography and Anthropology	47 D –
Economics	60 D –
Sociology	28 D –
Politics and Government	49 D –
International Relations	23 C
Law	—
Education	4 D –
Art and Music	3 D –
Language and Literature	18 D –
Military Affairs	6 D –
Bibliography and Reference	7 D –
	598 D –

4. The library has a number of impressive special collections. Two should be noted for our purposes. The 10,000-volume Clementine Collection (202/ 635-5091) is comprised of a third of the libraries of Pope Clementine XI and the Albani family for the years 1453–1850. Much of the contents focuses on Europe's view of Islam. A description of this collection can be found in "A Pope's Library is Brought to Light After 200 Years," by Michael Olmert, *Smithsonian*, January 1978, pp. 70–77.

    Another notable collection is the Oliveira Lima Library, which contains over 50,000 printed items and thousands of manuscripts, photographs, and memorabilia focusing upon Brazil, Portugal, and their present and former territories or spheres of influence (including Timor in the case of Portugal). This collection is open to scholars for on-site use; however, it is advisable to make an advance appointment with the curator, Manoel Cardozo (202/ 635-5059).

5. The general collection is served by a large dictionary card catalog located on the second floor of the Mullen Library. The library uses the Library of

Congress classification system for its collection, with variations for materials on ecclesiastical literature, theology, canon law, and church history. For current periodicals, mimeographed lists for the humanities, social sciences, and theology-philosophy are available.

A9 Census Bureau Library (Commerce Department)

1. a. *Federal Office Building 3*
   Wing 4, Room 2451
   Suitland and Silver Hill Roads
   Suitland, Maryland
   (301)763-5042 (Reference)

   Mail: *Washington, D.C. 20233*
   A shuttle-service (van plus subway) operates between the Main Commerce Building (entry K8) in Washington, D.C., and the Census Bureau.

   b. 8:00 A.M.–5:00 P.M. Monday–Friday

   c. Open to the public. Interlibrary loan and photoreproduction services are available.

   d. Betty Baxtresser, Chief of the Library Branch

2. Holdings now exceed 250,000 volumes, and approximately 3,400 periodical titles are currently received. The bulk of the collection is made up of U.S. and foreign materials (censuses, yearbooks, bulletins) and monographs on statistics and demography.

   The Census Bureau Library has complete census reports for the following countries and years: Philippines, 1918, 1939, 1948, 1970; Thailand, 1947, 1960, 1970; and Malaysia, 1947, 1957, 1970. Unlike the Commerce Department Library, the Census Bureau Library maintains recent and retrospective census documentation as well as foreign trade bulletins and central bank reports. Although many current items are on loan either to the Census Bureau's International Demographic Analysis Branch or the Foreign Demographic Analysis Division (see entry K8), materials can be recalled for private researchers.

5. The dictionary card catalog is divided into three sections, one covering acquisitions up to March 1976 and the other for the period since that date. The catalog has been published as the *Catalogs of the Bureau of the Census Library* 20 vols. (Boston: G. K. Hall and Co., 1977) and *Supplement* (1979) complete through January 1979 (5 vols.).

Center for Defense Information (CDI) Library See entry H13

Center for National Security Studies (CNSS) Library See entry H15

Center for Naval Analysis (CNA) Library See entry H16

Central Intelligence Agency Library See entry K6

Church of Jesus Christ of the Latter Day Saints (Mormon Church)—Genealogical Libraries See entry B4

A10 Commerce Department Library

1. a. *Main Commerce Building*
    Room 7046
    14th Street and Constitution Avenue, N.W.
    Washington, D.C. 20230
    (202) 377-2161

    b. 10:00 A.M.–4:45 P.M.   Monday–Friday

    c. Open to the public for on-site use; proper identification required. Interlibrary loan and photoduplication services are available.

    d. Stanley J. Bougas, Library Director

2–3.   The library houses and services a collection of over 300,000 volumes, arranged mostly by Library of Congress classification, of current and contemporary interest to the department. Primary focus in the collection is in the areas of economic theory and history, agricultural economics, industries and commerce, technology and marketing, and political science and history. The holdings contain an extensive collection of official foreign trade reports and official and nonofficial publications from more than 100 foreign countries, one-third of which are in foreign languages.

   Southeast Asia related materials consist of some 495 titles. The country breakdown is as follows: Burma, 50; Cambodia, 20; Indonesia, 20; Laos, 5; Malaysia, 10; Philippines, 250; Singapore, 65; Thailand, 35; Vietnam, 35; and Southeast Asia general, 5.

   The library's extensive collection of some 1,350 periodicals includes approximately 50 Southeast Asian government serials and statistical abstract. Some of these are: *Annual Economic Report* (1963–1972, Bank of Thailand); *Monthly Digest of Statistics for Singapore; Foreign Trade Statistics of the Philippines; Statistical Bulletin* (Central Bank of the Philippines); and *Monthly Statistical Bulletin, Peninsular Malaysia.*

   The reference room (Room 7043) contains an extensive collection of abstracts, indexes, business services, and commercial and business directories in addition to reference books in the fields of economics and business. Of interest to the Southeast Asianist are the Hong Kong based weekly *Business Asia,* and the daily, *Asian Wall Street Journal.*

4.   The law branch of the library, located in Room 1894, consists of some 50,000 volumes of legal materials and congressional and governmental documents on microforms. The branch maintains the same hours as the main library; visitors and general public are admitted by permission.

   The library's maritime collection of approximately 50,000 volumes covers a wide variety of subjects, including shipping, shipbuilding, navigation, marine engineering, nuclear propulsion, and technical periodicals.

5.	Two dictionary card catalogs provide access to the collection: entries for publications received prior to 1975 are listed in the 1914–1974 catalog; entries for publications received in 1975 and after are listed in the 1975— catalog. The library provides data base access for computerized information retrieval through several commercial and government systems. Professional reference assistance is provided to the general public and visitors. Users may request reference staff to conduct outline information retrieval searches from approximately 150 data bases.

The library distributes the monthly *Commerce Library Bulletin* that lists new accessions, bibliographies compiled by the staff, and other research activities. A series of business information seminars on topics of current interest is conducted from time to time by the library. A descriptive pamphlet, the *Department of Commerce Library,* is a useful guide to the library and contains a list of other commerce libraries in the metropolitan Washington area.

A11 Congressional Quarterly (CQ), Inc.—Editorial Reports Library

1.	a. *1414 22nd Street, N.W.*
Washington, D.C. 20037
(202) 887-8569

	b. 9:30 A.M.–5:30 P.M. Monday–Friday

	c. Closed to the public; however, researchers may be able to obtain special permission from the librarian to use the collection. Limited interlibrary loan and photoreproduction services are available.

	d. Edna M. Frazier-Cromwell, Librarian

2–3.	The library's collection of over 18,000 volumes (including the *Congressional Record*), 5,000 microfilm reels, and 200 periodicals and serials emphasizes current events, domestic politics, and international relations. Items on Southeast Asia are included, usually within the context of U.S.-Southeast Asia relations.

4.	Out of the more than 200 periodicals and serials in the collection, possibly the most valuable are the complete sets of the organization's own *Congressional Quarterly Weekly Report* (a digest of information on Congress, government, and politics) and the *Editorial Research Reports* (weekly, single issue reports). Both have carried information on Southeast Asian domestic politics, the Vietnam-Cambodia crisis, and U.S. aid and arms sales to various countries in the region. In addition the library subscribes to a number of U.S. newspapers, and has an extensive collection of the *Congressional Record*. The library maintains a useful set of vertical files, which contain newspaper clippings, periodical articles, government documents, and White House releases. Both the subject and biographical files include folders on current Southeast Asian events, countries, and personalities.

5.	The publication, *Congressional Quarterly Weekly Reports,* appears quarterly and is cumulated annually.

Defense Department—Defense Intelligence Agency Reference Library See entry K11

Dibner Library—National Museum of American History See entry C5

A12 Dominican College Library (Dominican House of Studies)

1.   a. *487 Michigan Avenue, N.W.*
   Washington, D.C. 20017
   (202) 529-5300

   b. 8:30 A.M.–4:30 P.M. and 7:00 P.M.–10:00 P.M.   Monday–Thursday
   9:00 A.M.–Noon   Saturday

   c. Open to the public. Interlibrary loan and photoduplication services available.

   d. Rev. Raymond Vandegrift, P.O., Librarian

2–3.   The library maintains 50,000 volumes, 250 periodical subscriptions, and a sizable rare-book collection to support the program of instruction at the Dominican House of Studies. The library collects books by Dominical authors and about the Dominican Order. In addition, the thought and works of St. Thomas Aquinas and the works of his commentators form an important element in the holdings. The number of titles on Southeast Asia is quite small (approximately 100 volumes) but does include some histories and biographies of early Dominican activities and personnel in the Philippines.

Embassy of Malaysia Library See entry L4

Embassy of the Philippines Library See entry L5

Embassy of the Republic of Singapore Library See entry L6

A13 Energy Library (Department of Energy)

1.   a. *Department of Energy (DOE)*
   Interstate 270 and Route 118
   (Germantown, Maryland)
   Washington, D.C. 20545
   (301) 353-4301

   b. 8:30 A.M.–5:00 P.M.   Monday–Friday

    c. The library is open to the public for on-site use. Researchers should call in advance. Photocopying and local interlibrary loan services are available.

    d. C. Neil Sherman, Director

       Forrestal Branch Library
       Room GA-138, Forrestal Building
       1000 Independence Avenue, S.W.
       Washington, D.C. 20585
       Mary Vignone, Chief
       (202) 252-9534

       Germantown Branch Library
       Room G-042 GTN
       Washington, D.C. 20545
       Denise B. Diggin, Chief
       (301) 353-2855

       North Capitol Branch Library
       825 North Capitol Street, N.E.
       Room 8502
       Washington, D.C. 20426
       Robert F. Kimberlin, Chief
       (202) 357-5479

2–3.   The Energy Library consists of three branch libraries as indicated above. The library holds over 30,000 cataloged titles, a number of which concern one or more parts of Southeast Asia and include petroleum matters. In addition, the library subscribes to over 2,000 professional journals. Basic reference materials are available at each branch library.

4.   The library's various collections include over 660,000 uncataloged technical reports, many of which are available through the National Technical Information Service (entry Q19), 20,000 reels of microfilmed congressional hearings from the Eighty-second to the Eighty-sixth Congress, and microfiche holdings of all reports and documents from the Sixty-ninth through the Ninety-fifth Congress, comprising over 3,000 items. In paper copy the library has selected hearings for the pre-1970 period and, on microfiche, all hearings after 1970.

5.   The Energy Library book catalog is available to the public through touch terminals at each branch library that access the Users Online Catalog and also through File Power on Systems Development Corporation's ORBIT, an online bibliographic data retrieval system.

Environmental Fund Library See entry H19

A14 Export-Import Bank (Eximbank) Library

1.   a. *811 Vermont Avenue, N.W.*
      Washington, D.C. 20571
      (202) 566-8897

    b. 8:15 A.M.–4:45 P.M. Monday–Friday

c. Open to the public. Interlibrary loan services available.

d. Theodora McGill, Librarian

2–4. The Eximbank Library holds over 20,000 books and nearly 1,000 periodical titles. The periodicals collection contains approximately 20 titles on or from Southeast Asia and includes various trade newsletters, bulletins of central banks, and a few English language weekly, monthly, and quarterly periodicals covering Southeast Asian economics. Items are retained for approximately two years and then transferred to the Library of Congress.

5. A *Periodicals* list is available upon request.

Note: Also see entry K14.

Federal Aviation Administration Library See entry K35

Federal Reserve Board—Research Library of the Board of Governors See entry K16

A15 Folger Shakespeare Library

1. a. *201 East Capitol Street, S.E.*
Washington, D.C. 20003
(202) 544-4600

b. 8:45 A.M.–4:30 P.M.   Monday–Saturday

c. Designed to be an advanced research facility, the collection is open to serious scholars for on-site use. Proper identification is required. Photoduplication and microfilming services are available, but there is no interlibrary loan.

d. O. H. Hardison, Jr., Director
Nate Krivatsy, Reference Librarian

2–3. Housed in an elegant building that is classical in approach and Tudor in interior decorative details, the carefully selected collection exceeds 200,000 volumes and 40,000 manuscripts on the theme of Elizabethan England and Renaissance Europe. Within the collection, popularly known as "Shakespeareana," are to be found only a handful of Southeast Asian titles on early European descriptions and travels, maps, trade, settlements and missionary accounts of fifteenth- and sixteenth-century China, Dutch East Indies, Siam, and Laos.

   Some titles include: Borri, Christoforo, *Cochin China* (1633); Huet, Pierre Daniel, *Le Grand Trésor Historique et Politique du Florissant Commerce des Hollandois,* (1712); Marini, Giovanni Filippe de', *Histoire Nouvelle et Curieuse des Royaumes de Tunquin et de Lao* (Tonkin and Laos), (1666); and La Loubere, Simon de, *A New Historical Relation of the Kingdom of Siam,* (1693).

5. The library follows LC classification schedules. Finding aids include a dictionary card catalog; *Catalog of Printed Books of the Folger Shakespeare Library,* 28 volumes, 1970, a volume *Supplement,* 1976; and a 3-volume *Catalog of Manuscripts of the Folger Shakespeare Library,* 1971.

Food and Agriculture Organization (FAO) of the United Nations— Office for North America Library See entry L8

A16 Foreign Service Institute Library (Department of State)

1. a. *1400 Key Boulevard*
   Room 300
   Arlington, Virginia 22209
   (703) 235-8717

   b. 8:15 A.M.–5:00 P.M.   Monday–Friday

   c. Although the library is designed to service the institute's language and area studies program, its facilities are open to the public for on-site use. Interlibrary loan and photoduplication services are available.

   d. William W. Bennett, Librarian

2. The library's collection consists of about 42,000 very selective volumes, including 310 periodical titles that emphasize political science, economics, history, and social problems. Special collections have been established to support such programs as the Executive Seminar in National and International Affairs and the School of Area Studies.

3. Southeast Asian materials in the library are conservatively estimated at 2,500 titles, including several periodicals from the region. This modest but very solid collection includes Southeast Asia series publications from Cornell University; the Center for International Studies, Ohio University; and the Center for Southeast Asian studies in Singapore.

5. A card catalog using LC classification schedules is available. There is also a separate periodical list.

Freer Gallery of Art (Smithsonian Institution) Library See entry C3

General Accounting Office (GAO) Library See entry K17

A17 Geological Survey Library (Interior Department)

1. a. *12201 Sunrise Valley Drive, Fourth Floor*
   Reston, Virginia 22092
   (703) 860-6671 (Reference)

b. 7:15 A.M.–4:15 P.M.   Monday–Friday

c. Open to the public. Interlibrary loan services and photocopying facilities are available. Shuttle service from the Interior Department building in Washington runs daily.

d. George H. Goodwin, Jr., Chief Librarian

2.   The library contains over 600,000 monographic and serial titles and government publications, of which over 1,000 are on Southeast Asia. The library also holds approximately 300,000 pamphlets and reprints, doctoral dissertations, and maps. Over 100,000 album prints, lantern slides, transparencies, and negatives are located in the survey's Denver library.

3.   The collection is primarily concerned with various aspects of the geosciences with emphasis on geology, paleontology, petrology, mineralogy, geochemistry, geophysics, ground and surface water, cartography, and mineral resources. In recent years, the Geological Survey's additions have reflected a greater interest in the environment, earth satellites and remote sensing, geothermal energy, marine geology, land use, lunar geology, and the conservation of natural resources. The strength of the Southeast Asia portion of the collection conforms generally to the strengths of the library. Holdings for Southeast Asia are as follows:

Country/Region	Number of Titles
Brunei	4
Burma	40
Cambodia	22
Indonesia	122
Laos	3
Malaysia	128
Philippines	160
Singapore	5
Thailand	80
Vietnam	15
Indochina	95
Southeast Asia General	36

4.   a. The library receives approximately 9,500 serial titles which are organized into four major categories: (000–999) official geological survey publications; (G) nonofficial geological publications; (P) nongeological official publications; and (S) science serials other than geology. A hand count of entries in the serials shelflist revealed that there are some 225 serials currently being received from Southeast Asian countries. The vast majority of these come from Indonesia, Malaysia, and the Philippines. Other countries have less than 5 titles each.

5.   The library's collection is served by a large card catalog and a serials file. Without a specific title for a serial, however, the serials shelflist should be consulted to locate an item from Southeast Asia. The card catalog is available in printed form: *Catalog of the United States Geological Survey Library* (Boston: G. K. Hall, 1964). In addition, there is an on-going supplement to this work (21 additional volumes thus far). The brochure, *U.S. Geological Survey Library* (1977) is available without charge. For a description of the Survey's map collection, see entry E3.

A18 George Washington University (GWU) Library

1. a. *2130 H Street, N.W.*
    Washington, D.C. 20052
    (202) 676-6558

    b. 8:30 A.M.–Midnight   Monday–Friday
    10:00 A.M.–Midnight   Saturday–Sunday
    For holidays and between session hours, call (202) 676-6845

    d. James B. Alsip, University Librarian

2–3 a. Library holdings are in excess of 500,000 volumes. The Southeast Asia holdings amount to more than 800 titles. The library takes no Southeast Asian newspapers but has 3 periodicals from the region. There are some 15 periodicals that deal with Asia in general, which have a partial subject focus on our region. The collection, though not well developed, is adequate, owing to GWU's extending its efforts toward Sino-Soviet studies. The small collection does have census data for almost all of the Southeast Asian countries for the 1950s and 1960s.

b. Tabular evaluation of country strengths:

	Brunei	*Burma*	*Cambodia*	*Indonesia*	*Laos*	*Malaysia*
Philosophy and Religion	—	1	—	—	—	—
History	4	35	16	70	16	67
Geography and Anthropology	—	2	—	—	—	5
Economics	—	6	—	29	1	18
Sociology	—	1	—	—	1	4
Politics and Government	—	5	—	13	1	12
International Relations	—	—	—	2	1	—
Law	—	—	—	—	—	—
Education	—	—	—	—	—	1
Art and Music	—	—	—	1	—	—
Language and Literature	—	—	—	—	—	10
Military Affairs	—	—	—	3	—	3
Bibliography and Reference	—	—	—	2	—	3
Total Country Evaluation:	4 B	50 D –	16 D –	120 D –	20 D –	123 D –

	Philip- *pines*	*Singa-* *pore*	*Thailand*	*Vietnam*	*Indo-* *china*	*SEA* *general*
Philosophy and Religion	6	1	2	—	—	—
History	116	13	34	125	32	2
Geography and Anthropology	4	—	—	1	3	—
Economics	28	9	21	17	3	—
Sociology	3	4	5	3	—	—
Politics and Government	17	—	11	4	3	—
International Relations	4	—	4	26	—	—
Law	—	—	—	1	—	—
Education	1	—	—	—	—	—
Art and Music	—	—	—	1	—	—
Language and Literature	—	—	—	—	1	—
Military Affairs	—	—	—	2	—	—
Bibliography and Reference	12	3	4	2	—	—
Total Country Evaluation:	191 D –	30 D	81 D –	182 D –	42 C	2 D –

Total Subject Evaluation:

Philosophy and Religion	10 D –
History	530 D
Geography and Anthropology	15 D –
Economics	132 D –
Sociology	21 D –
Politics and Government	66 D –
International Relations	37 C
Law	1 D –
Education	2 D –
Art and Music	2 D –
Language and Literature	11 D –
Military Affairs	8 D
Bibliography and Reference	26 D –
	861 D –

4.	The Special Collections Division (202/676-7497) has several items of interest to the Southeast Asianist. Of considerable interest are the papers of Frederick Kuh (1924–1967), a foreign correspondent for the *Chicago Sun-Times*. The collection consists of diaries, biographical information, correspondence, articles, speeches, subject files, notebooks, scrapbooks, and working papers. Kuh wrote a number of articles on Laos in the early 1960s, and 30 to 40 pieces on the Indochina war in the mid-1950s, including the Geneva Conference. These articles, with accompanying materials, may contain some valuable new information for those interested in Indochina.

Also of interest are the papers of Congressman Gilbert Gude (1967–1976). Within this collection are a number of file folders on Vietnam and Southeast Asia, which the congressman accumulated as a member of the House Armed Services Committee. Materials cover the Ninetieth through the Ninety-fourth Congress.

The George Washington University Library is the Washington, D.C., Consortium of Universities' depository library for Defense Mapping Agency Topographic Center maps. The library keeps a small number (under 50) of current maps, which cover Southeast Asia, produced by the agency.

5.	The collection is served by a card catalog that lists entries by author, subject, and title. The library uses the Library of Congress classification system. A current periodicals list is available at the reference desk on the ground floor.

A19 Georgetown University—Lauinger Library

1.	a. *37th and O Streets, N.W.*
Washington, D.C. 20057
(202) 625-4173 (Information)

b. 8:30 A.M.–Midnight   Monday–Thursday
8:30 A.M.–10:00 P.M.   Friday
10:00 A.M.–10:00 P.M.   Saturday
11:00 A.M.–Midnight   Sunday
For summer and between session hours call (202)625-3300

c. Open to scholars for on-site use. Interlibrary loan and photocopying facilities are available.

d. Joseph E. Jeffs, University Librarian

2–3 a. The Lauinger Library collection totals over 814,000 volumes. Southeast Asian titles exceed 1,600. There are very few periodicals from the region in the library's 3,500 serials, and no Southeast Asia newspapers.

b. Tabular evaluation of country strengths:

	Brunei	Burma	Cambodia	Indonesia	Laos	Malaysia
Philosophy and Religion	—	8	—	3	—	—
History	3	80	43	102	34	108
Geography and Anthropology	—	2	—	3	—	2
Economics	—	11	3	38	7	36
Sociology	—	2	1	8	1	5
Politics and Government	—	7	1	22	—	31
International Relations	—	—	—	2	4	—
Law	—	—	—	—	—	1
Education	—	—	—	1	—	—
Art and Music	—	—	—	—	—	—
Language and Literature	—	22	4	37	2	19
Military Affairs	—	—	—	1	—	1
Bibliography and Reference	—	7	1	5	1	5
Total Country Evaluation:	3 B	139 D	53 D	222 D –	49 C	208 D

	Philip-pines	Singa-pore	Thailand	Vietnam	Indo-china	SEA general
Philosophy and Religion	—	—	2	4	—	—
History	185	40	90	265	13	20
Geography and Anthropology	1	—	—	4	—	—
Economics	52	20	35	61	7	4
Sociology	15	9	5	6	—	1
Politics and Government	35	7	9	20	4	10
International Relations	10	—	3	6	—	—
Law	—	1	—	—	—	—
Education	—	—	—	—	—	—
Art and Music	—	—	—	—	—	—
Language and Literature	29	3	1	40	3	—
Military Affairs	—	—	—	2	1	—
Bibliography and Reference	20	1	5	8	4	6
Total Country Evaluation:	347 D –	81 C	150 D –	416 C	32 D	41 D –

Total Subject Evaluation:

Philosophy and Religion	17 D –
History	983 D
Geography and Anthropology	12 D –
Economics	274 D
Sociology	53 D
Politics and Government	146 D
International Relations	25 B
Law	2 D –
Education	1 D –
Art and Music	—
Language and Literature	160 C
Military Affairs	5 D –
Bibliography and Reference	63 D
	1,741 D

4.   The library is a selective depository library for United States government documents. The collection is primarily from the post-1969 period and includes more than 75,000 government publications. Within this collection may be found the Department of the Army's multi-volume *Vietnam Studies,* which dates from the 1970s. The collection also includes Joint Publication Research Service and Foreign Broadcast Information Service documents, both of which contain materials related to Southeast Asia. No foreign government documents are included in this collection, though the library has such materials scattered throughout the general collection. For further information, contact Rachel Van Winger, Government Documents Librarian (202/625-4213).

The Woodstock Theological Center Library (202/625-3120), at Georgetown University, has a small collection of church documents, dating from 1633 up through the nineteenth century, which deal with the church in Cochin China and Vietnam. Included are materials written by Alexander Rhodes (1650).

5.   The collection is served by a standard author, title, subject card catalog. There is also a *Guide for Users of the Government Documents Depository,* which is available without charge in the reference section.

A20 House of Representatives Library

1.   a. *Cannon House Office Building, Room B 18*
New Jersey and Independence Avenues, S.E.
Washington, D.C. 20515
(202) 225-0462

b. 9:00 A.M.–5:30 P.M.   Monday–Friday

c. Open to the public for on-site use only. Photocopying and interlibrary loan services are not available. Researchers should call or write before visiting the library if extensive research is contemplated.

d. Emanuel R. Lewis, Librarian.

2–5.   The collection exceeds 200,000 volumes and contains House and Senate Reports, documents, and journals, as well as the *Congressional Record, House Bills and Debates, House Committee Hearings, Supreme Court Reports,* and other materials including U.S. treaties and international agreements, globes, annals, and directories.

This collection may be particularly important for those with an interest in U.S.-Southeast Asian relations. Materials generated by the House Foreign Affairs Committee contain a substantial amount of material related to the Vietnam conflict, U.S.-Thai relations, U.S.-Philippine relations, and perhaps U.S.-Indonesian relations. The multi-volume *Congressional Information Service* is useful for locating congressional materials. Staff assistance is required to obtain items. A brief flyer, the *House Library,* is available on request.

Housing and Urban Development (HUD) Department Library See entry K19

A21 Howard University—Founders Library

1. a. *500 Howard Place, N.W.*
      Washington, D.C. 20059
      (202) 636-7253 (Reference)

   b. Academic year:
      8:00 A.M.–Midnight   Monday–Friday
      8:00 A.M.–5:00 P.M.   Saturday
      Noon–Midnight Sunday
      Founders Library also offers limited service
      Midnight–8:00 A.M.   Sunday–Friday

   c. Open to serious researchers for on-site use. Standard interlibrary loan and photocopying facilities are available.

   d. Binford H. Conley, Director of University Libraries

2–3 a. The Founders Library, the general library of the university, houses the general collection. With the 13 other branch libraries and units, the total collection exceeds 1 million volumes, including some 7,000 serials. The library collection is classified under the Library of Congress and the older Dewey Decimal system, which makes difficult the quantification of Southeast Asian materials. The holdings for our region can be conservatively estimated to exceed 1,300 titles, excluding the Bernard Fall Collection described below. The periodicals holdings include over 40 titles for Southeast Asia, but no newspapers from the region.

   b. Tabular evaluation of country strengths:

	Brunei	Burma	Cambodia	Indonesia	Laos	Malaysia
Philosophy and Religion	—	1	—	4	—	6
History	—	38	26	68	38	57
Geography and Anthropology	—	3	—	6	—	9
Economics	—	8	9	10	3	12
Sociology	—	—	1	5	2	10
Politics and Government	—	7	4	9	2	7
International Relations	—	1	—	—	4	—
Law	—	—	—	—	1	—
Art and Music	—	—	—	—	—	—
Language and Literature	—	—	3	2	—	6
Military Affairs	—	—	—	1	1	1
Bibliography and Reference	—	2	—	3	3	10
Total Country Evaluation:	—	60 D –	43 D	108 D –	54 C	118 D

	Philip-pines	Singa-pore	Thailand	Vietnam	Indo-china	SEA general
Philosophy and Religion	3	—	1	3	3	—
History	107	14	64	187	80	36
Geography and Anthropology	4	—	—	4	10	—
Economics	26	4	6	38	19	6
Sociology	7	—	3	10	4	2
Politics and Government	15	2	6	29	13	3
International Relations	2	—	1	29	—	—
Law	—	—	—	—	—	—

	Philip-pines	Singa-pore	Thailand	Vietnam	Indo-china	SEA general
Education	1	—	—	—	—	—
Art and Music	—	—	—	6	—	—
Language and Literature	—	—	—	10	6	—
Military Affairs	1	—	—	4	—	—
Bibliography and Reference	5	2	2	11	2	10
Total Country Evaluation:	171 D –	22 D –	83 D –	331 C	137 B	57 D –

Total Subject Evaluation:

Philosophy and Religion	21 D –
History	715 D –
Geography and Anthropology	36 D –
Economics	141 D –
Sociology	44 D –
Politics and Government	97 D –
International Relations	37 B
Law	1 D –
Education	1 D –
Art and Music	6 D –
Language and Literature	27 D –
Military Affairs	8 D –
Bibliography and Reference	50 D
	1,184 D –

The Founders Library houses the Bernard B. Fall collection (Room 300, 202/636-7261, 8:30 A.M.–5:00 P.M., Monday–Friday). This collection of Southeast and East Asian materials, assembled in memory of Bernard Fall—journalist, scholar, and author of numerous articles and several books on the Indochina and Vietnam conflicts—is a must for those with a research interest in Indochina, Vietnam, and related subjects. The collection contains over 5,000 cataloged titles in English and French and an undetermined number of uncataloged books. A computer printout indicates that 3,000 titles have been cataloged since 1976. The following is indicative of the subject strengths of the holdings:

Philosophy and Religion	160t
History	2,400t
Geography and Anthropology	80t
Economics	350t
Sociology	120t
Politics and Government	260t
International Relations	100t
Law	45t
Education	40t
Art and Music	50t
Language and Literature	340t
Military Affairs	80t
Bibliography and Reference	100t
TOTAL	4,125t

The collection also includes a small number of titles for medicine and cooking.

In addition to the fine monograph collection, a number of other items hold potential for the interested researcher. The collection contains over

200 Southeast Asian periodicals, 50 of which deal with Vietnam. Many of these are discontinued or broken, but still are significant research materials.

The collection also contains a substantial vertical file with over 500 folders of clippings, documents, and other reports and materials related to the Vietnam war and Southeast Asia in general. Some of the headings that can be found in this file are: anti-war protests, atrocities, chemical warfare, films, and the Geneva Accord Conference. There are 12 folders for Indochina, 19 for Laos, 10 for Cambodia, and 100 or more for South Vietnam, as well as a large number of folders on U.S. foreign policy.

The file contains a substantial number of unpublished conference papers written by Fall as well as some 100 Joint Publication Research Service (JPRS) documents on North Vietnam.

The collection also has a substantial number of Bernard Fall's published articles, and a large file (restricted to staff use) of correspondence, memos, and reports. There are several large file drawers of unindexed newspaper clippings covering the Vietnam conflict from the mid-1950s to 1964.

The newspaper collection is not large but will be of considerable value for those interested in Vietnam. Included are: *Réalités Cambodgiennes, Vietnam Daily News, The Times of Vietnam, Saigon Post, N.L.F. Bulletin d'Information, Le Courrier,* and *Bulletin du Vietnam* (Democratic Republic of Vietnam). These papers span the period 1962–1972 with a few items having earlier dates.

This outstanding collection is served by a subject catalog, author/title catalog, a shelflist, periodical card file, a computer printed list of titles cataloged since 1976, and a small paperback collection catalog file.

The collection was without a curator in 1981 and 1982. Researchers should call or write ahead for an appointment to use the collection.

5.   The general collection is served by an author, title, subject catalog. A computer printout of serials is available at the reference desk.

A22 Interior Department—Natural Resources Library

1.   a. *Department of the Interior*
   C Street between 18th and 19th Streets, N.W.
   Washington, D.C. 20240
   (202) 343-5815 (Reference)

   b. 7:45 A.M.–5:00 P.M.   Monday–Friday

   c. Open to the public for on-site use only. Interlibrary loan and photocopying facilities available.

   d. Philip Haymond, Director

2.   The library possesses over 1,000,000 volumes and currently receives 4,000 periodicals and 8,000 serials. The collection includes approximately 500 titles on Southeast Asia.

3.   Specializing in literature on conservation, and the development of natural resources, energy, power, land use and recreation, fish and wildlife management, parks and recreation, mines and minerals, the library holds approximately 500 items for Southeast Asia, with 200 on the Philippines. The collection does include, in addition to the secondary materials, some government documents and reports.

5. The library staff has issued the following guides: *Abstracting and Indexing Services Received in the Department Library* (1968); *Abstracting and Indexing Services in the Office of Library Services* (rev. ed 1970); a *Bibliography Series* (over 30 titles) including No. 9, *Natural Resources in Foreign Countries;* and *A Contribution Toward a Bibliography of Bibliographies* (1968) by Mary Anglemyer. The card catalog has been published as *Dictionary Catalog of the Departmental Library,* 37 volumes (1967), 4 supplements (1969–75).

International Association of Chiefs of Police (IACP) Library See entry M40

International Center for Research on Women (ICRW) Library See entry H26

A23 International Communication Agency (ICA) Library*

1. a. *1750 Pennsylvania Avenue, N.W., Room 1011*
    Washington, D.C. 20547
    (202) 724-9126

    b. 8:45 A.M.–5:30 P.M. Monday–Friday

    c. The ICA (formerly the United States Information Agency) Library serves the reference and research needs of agency personnel and, as such, does not open its facilities to the general public. However, permission to use the collection may be obtained upon application to the agency office of Congressional and Public Liaison (202/724-9103). Interlibrary loan and photocopying facilities are available.

    d. Jeanne R. Zeydel, Agency Librarian

2–3 a. This collection focuses on international relations, American communications, and area studies, and consists of approximately 61,000 titles, 425 current periodicals and 72,750 microforms. The Southeast Asian portion of the collection numbers less than 1,000 titles. In addition, there are some 20 periodicals that deal with the region to some degree.

    The above collection is composed essentially of general reference works and contains little special interest for the Southeast Asia scholar. The breakdown of titles by country is given in the table below.

    b. Tabular evaluation of country strengths:

	Brunei	Burma	Cambodia	Indonesia	Laos	Malaysia
Philosophy and Religion	—	4	—	1	—	3
History	—	58	21	51	21	35
Geography and Anthropology	—	1	1	2	—	—
Economics	—	4	1	9	2	7

---

*As of September 1982, the ICA reverted to its former name, United States Information Agency (USIA).

	Brunei	Burma	Cambodia	Indonesia	Laos	Malaysia
Sociology	—	1	1	6	2	1
Politics and Government	—	10	—	11	2	6
International Relations	—	—	—	1	1	—
Law	—	—	—	—	—	—
Education	—	—	—	1	—	—
Art and Music	—	—	—	—	—	—
Language and Literature	—	—	—	3	1	4
Military Affairs	—	—	—	1	—	—
Bibliography and Reference	—	1	1	—	—	—
Total Country Evaluation:	—	79 D−	25 D−	86 D−	29 D−	56 D−

	Philip-pines	Singa-pore	Thailand	Vietnam	Indo-china	SEA general
Philosophy and Religion	—	—	1	2	—	—
History	70	20	40	170	—	13
Geography and Anthropology	1	—	—	4	—	—
Economics	5	1	10	22	—	—
Sociology	2	1	2	14	—	—
Politics and Government	2	4	4	20	—	—
International Relations	3	—	4	29	—	—
Law	—	—	—	—	—	—
Education	—	—	1	2	—	—
Art and Music	—	—	—	—	—	—
Language and Literature	1	—	1	8	—	—
Military Affairs	7	—	—	—	—	—
Bibliography and Reference	1	—	3	8	—	—
Total Country Evaluation:	92 D−	26 D−	66 D−	279 D−	—	13 D−

Total Subject Evaluation:

Philosophy and Religion	11 D−
History	499 D−
Geography and Anthropology	9 D−
Economics	61 D−
Sociology	30 D−
Politics and Government	59 D−
International Relations	38 B
Law	
Education	4 D−
Art and Music	
Language and Literature	18 D−
Military Affairs	8 D−
Bibliography and Reference	14 D−
	751 D−

4. The Documents Branch (202/724-9364) manages the General Documents Collection of the library, which is in effect a current information file. This collection of some 770 file drawers is located in the main library room and contains newspaper clippings from the national press and recent documents including U.S. government materials, U.S. reports, "think-tank" studies, and annual reports from foundations, associations, interest groups, and corporations. These materials are arranged in chronological order, by subject, in file folders within the drawers. Country names are affixed to each drawer. There is an index card file of subject headings for the documents. A separate biographical file covers approximately 25,000 prominent persons, including a number of persons from Southeast Asia.

There are 14 drawers of Southeast Asia material in this collection. Subjects covered are diverse and sometimes offbeat. If your interests coincide with those of the ICA, you may well find something of interest here.

5.   The ICA Library follows the LC classification system. A card catalog lists books by author, subject, and title. There is also a list of periodicals (black binder) in the library. The library has access to the automated bibliographic data bases of the New York Information Bank, the Lockheed/DIALOG, and Systems Development Corporation/ORBIT, and NEXIS. The library distributes bi-weekly acquisition lists of *New Books,* and *New Documents* for agency use.

International Food Policy Research Institute (IFPR) Library See entry H28

International Institute for Environment and Development (IIED)— Washington Office Library See entry H29

A24 International Labor Office (International Labor Organization)— Washington Branch Office Library

1.   a. *1750 New York Avenue, N.W.*
Washington, D.C. 20006
(202) 376-2315

       b. 8:30 A.M.–5:00 P.M.   Monday–Friday

       c. Open to the public. Photocopying facilities are available but there is no interlibrary loan. Publications are on sale.

       d. Patricia S. Hord, Librarian

2–4.   The International Labor Office (ILO) Library collection holds some 16,850 volumes. In addition to a good selection of materials in the categories of labor legislation, trade unionism, social security, industrial relations, unemployment, labor statistics, labor welfare, migration, cooperatives, occupational safety and health, women and children as working force, and other related fields, the library also contains numerous ILO publications and documents since the inception of the organization. Particularly valuable are the relevant reports and studies prepared by the World Employment Programme (WEP) and the Asian Regional Team for Employment Promotion (ARTEP). Recent WEP studies and working papers include: "Poverty in West Malaysia," "Rural Poverty in Indonesia: With Special Reference to Java," and *Internal Migration in Developing Countries.* Some examples of ARTEP studies are: *Labour Absorption in Asian Agriculture, Women Workers in Asian Countries, Manpower and Related Problems in Indonesia, Strategy for Educational Development in Laos, Training for Employment in Thailand,* and "Building and Development in Southeast Asia" (working paper). Numerous other studies and papers on Southeast Asia, and the developing countries in general, are available.

The library's extensive serial collection includes current and retrospective runs of the *Official Bulletin of the ILO, International Labour Review, Bulletin of Labor Statistics, Cooperative Information, Women at Work,* and the annual *ILO Yearbook of Labor Statistics.*

The documents collection maintained in the library includes the Legislative Series of national laws and regulations on labor and social security. Within this collection may be found files on most of the countries of Southeast Asia, excluding Cambodia and Vietnam. Though these country files are not extensive, they do contain documents on social security and labor codes for some of the countries of the region. The documents collection also includes: publications of the International Social Security Association and documents from the International Conference of Labor Statiticians; ILO Conference documents; minutes of the ILO Governing Body; reports, resolutions, and proceedings of ILO regional conferences (including Asian Regional Conferences) and industrial conferences (e.g., mining, petroleum, steel, textiles, and transportation); and numerous ILO studies and reports on international labor conditions, trade unions, labor-management relations, social security, and occupational health and safety.

In addition the library maintains a small film and photograph collection devoted primarily to the operation of the ILO. This photo collection has been drawn from the much larger photo library at the ILO headquarters in Geneva, Switzerland. An inventory of the Geneva collection, *ILO Photo Library: Catalogue,* is available in the Washington office, along with a film catalog.

5. There is no comprehensive card catalog for this collection. Several useful guides to ILO publications are available: ILO Catalog of Publications in Print (1980–1981); Subject Guide to Publications of the International Labor Office (1919–1964) (Geneva, 1967); International Labor Documentation, a 12-volume cumulative index to the holdings of the ILO Central Library in Geneva, and an on-going monthly supplement of the same title with information on new books cataloged by the ILO Geneva Library, major new ILO publications, and labor-related abstracts from about 1,000 international journals.

Note: See also entry F11.

International Religious Liberty Association (IRLA) Library See entry M41

A25 International Trade Commission (ITC) Library

1. a. *701 E Street, N.W.*
    Washington, D.C. 20436
    (202) 523-0013

    b. 8:45 A.M.–5:15 P.M.   Monday–Friday

    c. Open to the public. Interlibrary loan is possible, and photoreproduction facilities are available for a fee.

    d. Dorothy J. Berkowitz, Chief, Library Division

2–3. The ITC Library (formerly U.S. Tariff Commission Library) holds approximately 80,000 volumes plus 2,200 serial titles. In addition to collecting foreign trade serials and statistical yearbooks from Southeast Asian countries, the library maintains a full set of International Customs Journal translations of tariff laws—past, present and future—which includes laws for Southeast Asian countries extending back several decades.

4. The ITC library's vertical files contain some Southeast Asia country files with pamphlets and newspaper clippings. These materials are weeded every two to three years. A portion of the library's periodical holdings has been transferred to microform, and the serials may also be microfilmed in the future.

5. The author-subject-title dictionary card catalog contains geographic entries. The library also publishes irregularly a *Selected Current Acquisitions List*.

Islamic Center Library See entry M42

A26 Joint Bank-Fund Library (Library of the International Bank for Reconstruction and Development, and the International Monetary Fund)

1. a. *700 19th Street, N.W.*
    Washington, D.C. 20431
    (202) 477-3167

    b. 9:00 A.M.–5:00 P.M.   Monday–Friday

    c. Open to researchers for on-site use. Interlibrary loan and photocopying facilities are available.

    d. Maureen M. Moore, Librarian

2–3. The library contains over 180,000 cataloged volumes, 3,000 current periodicals, and 200 daily newspapers. With particular emphasis on materials from the 143 member countries, the collection represents some 30 languages, although English predominates. The focus of the collection is on the areas of banking, public finance, planning, development, economics, international economics, and international monetary systems.

There are some 3,500 titles for Southeast Asia in the library collection. In addition, the library receives 112 periodicals and 11 newspapers from the region. Figures for individual countries are given below:

Country/Region	Books	Periodicals	Newspapers
Brunei	21	14	—
Burma	200	3	2
Cambodia	71	4	—
Indonesia	550	18	2
Laos	80	1	—
Malaysia	850	23	2
Philippines	700	25	1
Singapore	250	16	2
Thailand	500	8	2
Vietnam	250	—	—

5. The Library has a dictionary card catalog—based on the Dewey Decimal classification preceded by a numerical letter designator for the country— and a geographic catalog, arranged alphabetically by country. In addition, a printed catalog, *The Developing Areas, A Classified Bibliography of the Joint Bank-Fund Library,* in 3 volumes (1976), and *Economics and finance: index to periodical articles* in 4 volumes (1972), plus supplements, provide access to the collection. A serials file provides access to periodicals and newspapers. Also available is the monthly *List of Recent Periodical Articles,* the monthly *List of Recent Additions* of books and monographs, and a *Guide to the Joint Bank-Fund Library.*

Justice Department Library See entry K23

Labor Department Library See entry K24

A27 Library of Congress (LC)

1. a. *10 First Street, S.E.*
    Washington, D.C. 20540
    (202) 287-5000

    b. General Reading Rooms: Jefferson Building (Main), First Floor, and Adams Building (Annex), Fifth Floor
    8:30 A.M.–9:30 P.M.   Monday–Friday
    8:30 A.M.–5:00 P.M.   Saturday
    1:00 P.M.–5:00 P.M.   Sunday
    Stack service usually ends one hour before closing. Closed on all holidays except Washington's Birthday, Columbus Day, and Veterans' Day, when the hours are: 8:30 A.M.–5:00 P.M.
    Hours of other divisions and services are noted below.

    c. For on-site use, LC's facilities and services are available at no charge to all scholars. The Loan Division makes LC's resources available through the interlibrary loan service. Photoreproduction equipment for public use is available near the reading room. LC provides a number of related services through its Photoreproduction Service, which is located in Room G-1009 of the Adams Building (202/287-5640).

    d. Daniel J. Boorstin, The Librarian of Congress

2–3 a. The Library of Congress is the largest library of the United States. Items in the library now total almost 76 million. The Southeast Asia collection numbers over 100,000 titles. While some university library collections approach or equal LC's holdings for one particular country, none can match LC for the region as a whole. LC holds in excess of 500 Southeast Asian newspapers, 53 of which are currently received, and has over 2,000 periodical titles related to Southeast Asia. Walking through the Southeast Asia stack area—with the proper clearance, of course— can be awe-inspiring. It can also be dangerous, as most floor space is cluttered with stack overflow (a move to more spacious quarters was planned for 1982).

Before describing in more detail LC's holdings, a few comments on how to approach the library are in order. Size has its drawbacks. Materials are often dispersed among various divisions and special collections; therefore it may be difficult to identify and retrieve materials on a given topic quickly. In addition, many acquisitions remain uncataloged or available only through a special custodial division. It should be pointed out that this latter, less than ideal state of affairs, is not the fault of LC's overloaded personnel so much as it is the consequence of congressional preference to spend money on dams instead of the nation's library.

Another problem is that no comprehensive catalog or finding aid exists for the entire collection, though given its size, one can readily see why. More annoying is the frequent "not on shelf" response to requests for materials. Even worse, one often waits an hour before a negative response arrives. This problem, for the most part, resulted from the crowding of too many books into too small a space and was remedied when the new Madison building was fully occupied in 1982. Unfortunately, the Southeast Asia collection remains in its old quarters.

After ordering books in the reading rooms, you can obtain from the issue desk a printed form stating that you will return, put it at your place, and use the waiting line for other scholarly errands. This greatly decreases the anxiety associated with long waits. If you plan to use LC for an extended period, ask the Research Facilities Office in Alcove 8 of the Main Reading Room (202/287-5211) for a study shelf where you can keep your books. You can also request a desk in the stacks from the office if you have the type of project to justify stack access. There is a long waiting list for the above services, so you are advised to write ahead, noting your research interest, qualifications, and giving the date of your arrival.

You may also obtain a Stack Pass, from the Research Facilities Office, which allows you to enter the stacks at your leisure. If you are planning to spend a good chunk of time on a serious research project, this is the way to go. Once familiar with the area containing materials on your subject, you may discover resources you never knew existed. Then too, being able to flip back and forth and through related items is greatly preferred to scanning catalog cards that often reveal little if any information about an item.

Man cannot live on scholarly pursuits alone. Thus, you may want to visit the snack bar in the main building. The Madison Building offers three very nice and moderately priced eateries, practicing different degrees of culinary arts. A limited cafeteria is located on the basement level only a few steps from the tunnel to the main building. On the sixth floor are two very pleasant facilities with good food and a view.

b. The following table, compiled from shelflist measurements, reflects relative strengths at best rather than the actual numerical strength in each category. Readers should note that the table includes only cataloged monographs accessible through the main catalog. Pamphlets, many titles in microform, are averages, and titles not accessible through obvious classification schedules are not included. Readers are also reminded of the remarks in the "How to Use the Guide" section, concerning the significance of the numerical strength of the geographic categories. Atlases and maps of the Geography and Map Division are not included in the tabulations, but are described separately in entry E4.

	Brunei	Burma	Cambodia	Indonesia	Laos	Malaysia
Philosophy and Religion	—	380	53	669	24	149
History	7	2,045	706	5,798	598	1,800
Geography and Anthropology	4	380	75	1,150	63	180
Economics	5	1,211	211	3,639	121	937
Sociology	—	300	85	250	53	224
Politics and Government	8	286	73	1,396	86	294
International Relations	—	10	8	40	13	21
Law	—	700	25	2,500	11	1,200
Education	—	140	50	380	10	130
Art and Music	—	85	132	383	39	58
Language and Literature	—	370	60	1,200	33	492
Military Affairs	—	40	6	98	1	60
Bibliography and Reference	6	64	48	210	21	110
Totals	30	6,011	1,532	17,713	1,073	5,655

	Philip-pines	Singa-pore	Thailand	Vietnam	Indo-china	SEA general
Philosophy and Religion	137	52	280	198	—	396
History	4,988	573	1,786	4,873	—	1,999
Geography and Anthropology	498	54	132	533	—	173
Economics	4,344	415	763	1,710	—	927
Sociology	473	84	173	421	—	368
Politics and Government	588	108	331	909	—	682
International Relations	41	26	31	37	—	51
Law	2,400	500	2,600	300	—	—
Education	1,260	87	173	316	—	187
Art and Music	201	19	154	241	—	93
Language and Literature	798	32	340	254	—	205
Military Affairs	209	4	14	63	—	—
Bibliography and Reference	433	74	119	255	—	929
Totals	16,370	2,028	6,896	10,110	—	6,010

4.   ASIAN DIVISION (formerly Orientalia Division)

Adams Building, First Floor, Room A 1024
(202) 287-5420

Richard Howard, Acting Chief

Southern Asia Section
Adams Building, Room 1018
(202) 287-5600, (202) 287-5428

Louis Jacob, Head
A. Kohar Rony, Southeast Asia Specialist
William Tuchrello, Reference Librarian

8:30 A.M.–5:00 P.M.   Monday–Friday
8:30 A:M.–12:30 P.M.   Saturday

The Asian Division consists of three sections: Chinese and Korean Section, Japanese Section, and Southern Asia Section, the last of which covers both South Asia and Southeast Asia. The Southeast Asia collection is unique in that it is relatively strong for all countries in the region. As such, this collection is unequalled by any of the several noted university libraries which have substantial collections for one or several countries in Southeast Asia; e.g., Cornell and Ohio University.

The Southeast Asia unit should be the first point of contact for Southeast Asia specialists. Staff members can save you precious time in locating materials, and, in general, acquainting you with the collection. The Southeast Asia unit, in conjunction with the Asian Division, takes an active role in the development of national library resources for research and the study of Southeast Asia. Its facilities are used by United States government agencies and research and educational institutions, as well as by individual scholars. The unit handles reference inquiries by phone, by correspondence, and in person.

The Southeast Asia unit maintains a substantial reference collection for use by visiting scholars. Space considerations do limit the size of the collection. Included in the reference collection are a substantial number of books not usually considered reference works. These are primarily the "classics" in a particular field, which tend to be heavily used. The unit attempts to stock the shelves with items that have a track record of use.

In general, reference materials are in English. Included are yearbooks, handbooks, and a fairly complete set of phone directories for many of the major cities in Southeast Asia, including a complete directory for all of Thailand. In addition, there are substantial numbers of bibliographic works on the shelves, organized by country. Indonesia and the Philippines are best represented, while fewest references are on hand for Laos, Cambodia, and Brunei. The Southeast Asia unit also keeps a current service copy of major Southeast Asia language newspapers from most of the countries in the region.

The unit strives to provide a quick and convenient reference facility oriented to interdisciplinary studies, and to the generalist. However, it should be stressed that if you are conducting heavy research, the staff can provide you with expert advice and help you locate that one crucial government pamphlet or journal article. To be sure, materials are available for the most advanced work. The unit's reference collection is served by a card catalog.

The Asian Division has custody of all vernacular materials relating to Southeast Asia, with the exception of those in the Law Library. All non-Western newspapers and other serials will eventually be in the division.

There is a substantial collection of non-Western language newspapers for researchers to investigate. The coverage is, however, somewhat uneven. For example, there are in excess of 75 newspapers from Indonesia, but there are far fewer than that for some other countries in the region. A few examples of these primarily post–World War II publications are as follows:

Country	Title	Period
Burma	*Hanthawaddy*	April 1950–to date
	Myanna Alin	May 1945–May 1962
Cambodia	*Nek Chiat Niyom*	January 1962–Feb. 1967
Indonesia	*Merdeka*	January 1961–to date
	Kompas	January 1965–to date
Malaysia	*Berita Harian*	January 1962–to date
	Utusan Melayu	January 1960–to date
Thailand	*Siam Nikorn*	June 1947–September 1969
Vietnam	*Nhan Dan*	January 1954–to date

There is also a large quantity of publications that go way back: e.g., *Primary Gazette and Straits Chronicle,* 1833–1941 (broken); and *British North Borneo Herald,* 1883–1940 (broken).

To locate specific publications, a number of finding aids are available and, in fact, must be consulted, as no one aid is complete in itself. *Newspapers in Microfilm* (1973) and succeeding volumes through 1975 are very good starting points. A second aid consists of a card index that lists microfilmed newspapers by country and city. There is also a set of loose-leaf binders that has listings of newspapers by country. Together, the above mentioned aids provide very good coverage of the newspaper holdings.

For newspapers currently received, consult *Newspapers Received Currently in the Library of Congress*. The Serials Division, where current English language publications are kept, is discussed below.

The Southeast Asia unit also has a substantial collection of Southeast Asian vernacular periodicals. This collection is served by a unique main entry file, which lists periodicals (no newspapers included) for each country in the region including Brunei. The file includes current and discontinued entries. The unit is actively collecting periodicals produced by, or relating to, Southeast Asian minorities living outside the region. There is at present no aid that lists only currently received periodicals. However, a count of these items by this researcher and Southeast Asia unit personnel indicates the unit currently receives over 600 unbound serials. The unit also has a large pamphlet collection that researchers may find of interest.

In addition to those finding aids relating to papers and periodicals, the Southeast Asia unit has several other aids that will be very helpful to the serious researcher. The unit maintains a subject catalog that includes English and vernacular titles after 1969. This is actually two catalogs in one, consisting of a "major" catalog containing entries for individual Southeast Asian countries, and a "minor" catalog with entries on Southeast Asia. The unique feature of this two-part catalog is its use of specialized headings, which are updated as conditions or events in Southeast Asia, meriting recognition, occur. For example, the refugee crisis has spawned a heading in the catalog already containing over 1,000 entries. The catalog includes non-LC materials as well as items in the LC collection—both cataloged and uncataloged. Periodical entries are included. This catalog is ideal as a research tool for the development of bibliographies on subjects of current interest, and is the result of the dedicated and creative work of the unit personnel.

The unit also maintains an author file of cataloged and uncataloged vernacular materials. The file covers Burma, Cambodia, Laos, and Thailand. Items in this file are not yet in the custody of the Asia Division. This file contains items not found in the other aids. Shelflists for the Philippines, Thailand, Burma, and Vietnam are also open for use by visiting scholars. These shelflists contain entries for books and monographs in vernacular languages. Shelflists for Cambodia and Laos are in progress.

Also useful is the *Southeast Asia Subject Catalog*. This multivolume set lists all Southeast Asia materials (including articles appearing in some periodicals) in LC up to 1972. This aid will be useful for those who wish to locate a number of titles on a specific topic for one or more countries; e.g., religion in Thailand or foreign relations of Malaysia. Readings are limited to traditional library entries: economics, foreign relations, language, literature, and trade, among others. Specific items cannot be located through the subject catalog.

Of greater significance has been the computerization of Southeas Asia book and monograph entries beginning in 1968. While not open to everyone, serious researchers use a nearby computer terminal to generate bibliographic information on the country and topic of their choice from the more than 2,000 "legitimate" headings to which the machine can respond. For example, one might ask for listings on revolution or rice agriculture in Thailand. Appropriate entries will appear on the screen in front of the keyboard; an additional command will print the viewed material. Eventually, it is hoped, the entire Southeast Asia collection will be accessible through the computer.

All of the above finding aids are available through the Southern Asia Section, Adams Building, room 1018.

FAR EASTERN LAW DIVISION

Madison Building, Room 235
(202) 287-5085

Dr. Tao-tai Hsia, Chief
Mya Saw Shin, Senior Legal Specialist
Phuong Khan Nguyen, Legal Specialist

8:30 A.M.–4:30 P.M. Monday–Friday

The Far Eastern Law Division is one of five divisions of the Law Library and has custody of materials dealing with Southeast Asia, excluding the Philippines, which is under the jurisdiction of the Hispanic Law Division. As of mid-1982, the division's holdings on Southeast Asia totaled some 7,900 volumes. In addition, there are periodicals in the division that deal with Southeast Asia. The following figures were derived from shelflist measurements and information supplied by the division personnel:

Country	No. of Titles	Languages
Burma	700	Burmese and English
Cambodia	25	Mostly French
Indonesia	2,500	Indonesian, some Dutch
Laos	11	French
Malaysia	1,200	English and Malay
Singapore	500	English
Thailand	2,600	English and Thai
Vietnam	300	French, Vietnamese, and some English

It is anticipated that holdings for Vietnam will be substantially increased over the next several years. The division is working to establish regularized contacts with in-country sources, some of which were disrupted during the 1970s.

Copying equipment is available along with microform reader-printers located next to the library's reading room. The Far Eastern Law Division does make materials available to scholars through the interlibrary loan program.

The division's non-Southeast holdings, cataloged during the 1958–1971 period, are included in the LC's *Far Eastern Language Catalog* (Boston: G. K. Hall, 1972). There is, however, no separately published catalog of the division's collection. No LC classification schedule has as yet been devised for East and Southeast Asian legal materials. The division's holdings, through 1980, are available through a dictionary catalog maintained in the Law Library and in the public catalog of the Library of Congress. From January 1981, the holdings are accessible only through LC's automated data bases. Entries for the division's microfilm materials, which number approximately 1,000 reels, have been made in the Law Library's microtext shelflist. The Far Eastern Law Division also has a shelflist that scholars may use. A useful introduction to the entire Law Library is *The Law Library of the Library of Congress: Its History, Collections, and Services*, edited and compiled by Kimberly W. Dobbs and Kathryn A. Haun, (1978). This publication is available at the Library or through the Government Printing Office.

HISPANIC LAW DIVISION

Madison Building, Room 235
(202) 287-5070

Rubens Medina, Chief
Armando Gonzalez, Assistant Chief

8:15 A.M.–4:15 P.M.   Monday–Friday

The Hispanic Law Division maintains the most complete collection of Iberian and Latin American legal materials in the world, with holdings exceeding 160,000 volumes. The Division has custody over legal materials related to the Philippines, owing to that country's long relationship with Spain as a colonial possession. The Philippine holdings number some 2,500 titles, which constitutes the best collection for the Philippines in this country. Included are all statutes passed in the Philippines from the beginning of the colonial period, and all Philippine Supreme Court reports. There is also a good collection of legal periodicals, though many from the World War II period were never received.

SERIAL AND GOVERNMENT PUBLICATIONS DIVISION

Newspaper and Current Periodical Reading Room
Madison Building, Room 133
(202) 287-5690

Donald F. Wisdom, Chief
Robert W. Schaaf, Senior Specialist in the United Nations and International Documents

The Western language newspapers from Southeast Asia are extensive in this division, to say the least. This is a prime resource unmatched in the United States and probably the world. There are 53 papers currently being received from Southeast Asia. The breakdown is as follows:

Brunei	1t
Burma	5t
Indonesia	19t
Malaysia	8t
Philippines	6t
Singapore	3t
Thailand	9t
Vietnam	2t

The strength of this collection, however, does not rest entirely on the number of current newspapers in the division, for a few of the better university research libraries may approximate in number the division's holdings. What is staggering is the number of primarily post–World War II, but noncurrent, newspapers in the collection. To make the point, here are a few gems from Thailand: *Bangkok Daily Mail,* 1927–1931, scattered; *Bangkok Post,* 1946–1955, microfilmed after 1955; *Bangkok Times,* 1923–1928, 1941–1942; *Bangkok Tribune,* 1952–1957, partial; *Bangkok World,* 1959–1961; *Democracy,* 1945–1946, partial; and *Liberty,* 1945–1956, partly on microfilm. As one can see, some of these papers run for decades, while others cover only a few years. Based on the author's own experience, however, it seems safe to say that if you have an interest in one Southeast Asian country, which focuses on a particular period, it will be worth your time to search for relevant newspapers in this division.

Currently received newspapers are listed in the LC publication, *Newspapers Received Currently in the Library of Congress,* available in the Newspaper and Current Periodical Room. There is no comprehensive newspaper card catalog for older holdings. The best aid is *A Check List of Foreign Newspapers in the Library of Congress* (1929) and the looseleaf supplements through the 1960s. Newspapers acquired since 1962 are on microfilm and are accessible through a card catalog; the LC publication, *Newspapers in Microfilm: Foreign Countries, 1948–1972* (1973); and the annual supplement, *Newspapers in Microform.* Eventually the pre-1962 newspaper collection will be microfilmed. Microfilmed newspapers are available for purchase.

The Newspaper and Current Periodical Room maintains a large current periodical collection, including government serials. There are approximately 700 Western language periodicals from Southeast Asia. The largest number of these, about 280, are from the Philippines. Indonesia, Malaysia, and Singapore each has approximately 100 titles, and each of the remaining countries in the region has 30 or fewer titles. Periodicals are transferred to LC's main collection anywhere from six months to two years after being received. There are many Western language periodicals from Southeast Asia in the LC collection but not in the Newspaper and Current Periodical Room because some were discontinued or ceased publication.

Periodicals may be located through the periodical card catalog in the general reading rooms; the five-volume *Union List of Serials,* 1965, and its supplement, *New Serials Titles;* and the periodical card catalog in the room that has entries arranged by country.

If you are coming from out of town for serious research, it may be wise to phone ahead to make sure the materials you need are available.

MUSIC DIVISION

Jefferson Building, Room G 146
(202) 287-5507

Donald L. Leavitt, Chief

8:30 A.M.–5:00 P.M. Monday–Saturday

This division contains a collection of music and music literature, international in scope, which spans many centuries. The collection includes books, periodicals, sound recordings, pieces of music, scores, sheet music, libretto, and miscellaneous items. These holdings are overwhelmingly Western oriented, with the Southeast Asia materials—regrettably—being few and far between.

To make matters worse, much of the music collection is not indexed or cataloged and is identifiable only with the assistance of the reference staff of the division. Still more confounding, some of the cataloged materials under the custody of the division are not in the main card catalog.

In all, several hundred titles related to Southeast Asia were located, but undoubtedly there are many more. The most significant items consist of recordings of folk and national music. There are approximately 50 titles for the Philippines, with other countries in the region having fewer entries. In addition, there is a separate collection of some 60 songs related to the Vietnam conflict, 1961–1975. Some of these are commercial recordings made in America.

Division holdings also include a stack of sheet music from Southeast Asia: less than 50 items in all. There is a similarly small collection of literature on Southeast Asian music, Indonesia and Bali, in particular, being the best represented.

The following may be helpful: *Music, Books on Music, and Sound Recordings,* and its predecessor, *Library of Congress Catalog: Music and Phonorecords—a Cumulative List of Works Represented by Library of Congress Printed Cards.* Both are available as volumes of the *National Union Catalog.* The division also distributes a leaflet containing information on its collections and services.

Photoduplication services and microfilm readers are available in the reading room. Most of the collection is available for interlibrary loan.

RARE BOOK AND SPECIAL COLLECTIONS DIVISION

Jefferson Building, Second Floor, Room 256
(202) 287-5434

William Matheson, Chief

8:30 A.M.–5:00 P.M.   Monday–Friday

The Rare Book Room has a collection of over 300,000 volumes and 200,000 broadsides, pamphlets, theater playbills, title pages, prints, manuscripts, posters, and photographs.

Should you discover there is little of interest here for your research tastes, you may still want to linger a while, as the Rare Book Room is on the plush side in contrast to other LC facilities. The division has a fairly comprehensive card catalog containing over 600,000 cards that provide access to the collection. Country headings in this catalog facilitate finding a fair amount of Southeast Asia materials.

Two LC leaflets are worth noting as finding aids: *Some Guides to Special Collections in the Rare Books,* and *Special Collections in the Library of Congress.* It should be noted that some items in the collections do not appear in the general card catalog or the LC computerized card catalog. It is therefore advisable to approach the professional staff on hand when you think your luck has run out. Requests for photoduplication, since equipment is not available in this division, can be handled through the LC's Photoduplication Service. None of the division's holdings are available through interlibrary loan. Scholars are required to show identification and register prior to commencing research in the Rare Book Room.

There is no special collection related to Southeast Asia in the division's holdings. There are, however, several hundred books, collections of personal papers, and other items that deal with the area. Many of these items are in Dutch, French, Spanish, and even Latin, while the majority are in English. The collection includes several works by Sir Thomas Stanford

Raffles (1781–1826), including his *History of Java* (London: Black, Parbury, and Allen, 1817). There are a number of language-oriented materials, including the "Comparative Vocabulary of the Burma, Malaya and T'hai Languages," compiled in 1810 by John Leyden. Personal papers constitute a good many of the entries. For example, the papers of William Griffith, 1810–1845, bequeathed to the East India Company, contain journals of his travels in Burma.

MICROFORM READING ROOM SECTION

Jefferson Building, First Floor, Room 140-B
(202) 287-5471

Robert V. Gross, Head
Pablo A. Calvan, Reference Librarian

8:30 A.M.–9:30 P.M.   Monday–Friday
8:30 A.M.–5:00 P.M.   Saturday
1:00 P.M.–5:00 P.M.   Sunday

This section's growing microfilm collections are currently estimated to exceed 1.5 million items. The reading room is equipped with several microfilm and microfiche readers and printers. Materials not otherwise restricted can be obtained through interlibrary loan, which is processed by the LC Loan Division (202/287-5441).

Generally the materials in the collection are not included in the Main Card Catalog or the computerized catalog and can be accessed primarily through specialized guides and indexes prepared for the collections by the micropublishers, and through the assistance of the reference staff of the section. Scholars should also consult the subject-title-author card catalog located in the reading room and the mimeographed preliminary reference guide, *Selected Microfilm Collections in the Microfilm Reading Room* (1978). This reference guide details all major collections that the section has acquired. Entries indicate the scope and format of each collection. There is also a card file in the reading room for periodical holdings in microfilm.

The section's Southeast Asia holdings are small, about 250 titles. There are however a number of unique items included. Of the 40 titles on Burma, a good many are for government financial reports, gazetteers, and army publications. There are also some census data. All from the early 1900's.

Another noteworthy, if small, part of this collection is the inclusion of 20 or so titles on Indochina. Most of these are in French and deal with Indochina in the pre–World War II period.

There are also a few description and travel titles for Laos that date back to the 1860s.

For Malaysianists, the most interesting items will be the *Malay States, Federated Council Proceedings,* 1910–1940.

Materials on the remainder of the region seem to be of lesser interest.

Other items of general importance include the following: materials from the U.S. Foreign Broadcast Information Service (FBIS); U.S. Joint Publication Research Service (JPRS), Inter Documentation Company (Zug, Switzerland); Human Relations Area Files (HRAF), documents and official reports of the League of Nations and the United Nations, House of Commons (Great Britain) Sessional Papers; New York Times Information Bank, and twentieth-century economic development plans for selected developing countries in Africa, Asia, and Latin America. A fairly comprehensive collection of U.S. doctoral dissertations microfilmed by University Microfilm International (Ann Arbor, Michigan), as well as many filmed by the University of Chicago Library photoduplication service, are also available in the section. Dissertations can be identified by using the monthly volumes of *Dissertation Abstracts International* (Ann Arbor, Michigan-University Microfilms International). Also very useful, because they include the University Microfilms International order numbers, which are identical with the LC Microfilm Reading Room's call numbers, are the following publications by Frank Joseph Shulman: the Southeast Asia sections of his periodical, *Doctoral Dissertations on Asia: An Annotated Bibliographical Journal of Current International Research* (published since 1975 by the Association for Asian Studies); "Doctoral Research on Malaya and Malaysia, 1895–1977: A Comprehensive Bibliography and Statistical Overview," in *Malaysian Studies: Present Knowledge and Research Trends,* pp. 250-436, edited by John A. Lent (Dekalb, Illinois: Center for Southeast Asian Studies, Northern Illinois University, 1979); and *Doctoral Dissertations on Southeast Asia: An Annotated Bibliography of International Research* (Ann Arbor, Michigan Center for South and Southeast Asian Studies, University of Michigan, forthcoming).

SCIENCE AND TECHNOLOGY DIVISION

Adams Building, Fifth Floor, Science Reading Room
(202) 287-5639

John W. Price, Chief

The Science and Technology Division maintains the same service hours as the general reading rooms. This division is responsible for LC's holdings on science and technology. It manages the Science Reading Room, and provides a variety of bibliographic and reference services. The reading room is equipped with a computer terminal and has a reference and microfilm collection.

The division maintains no separate catalogs or indexes on LC holdings in science and technology. A computer-generated catalog, *Science and Technology Room Collection, Books and Serials* (1979), is available in the reading room. The division's holdings do contain materials on the social sciences, which may be of interest to Southeast Asia scholars.

NATIONAL REFERRAL CENTER

Adams Building, Fifth Floor
(202) 287-5670 (referral services)
(202) 287-5680 (registration of information resources)

Edward MacConomy, Chief
Monica Bowen, Referral Specialist for Humanities
John Hass, Referral Specialist for Social Sciences

8:30 A.M.–4:30 P.M.   Monday–Friday

National Referral Center is a free referral service that directs those who have questions, concerning any subject, to organizations that can provide the answer. The referral center is not equipped to furnish answers to specific questions or to provide bibliographic assistance. Its purpose is to direct those who have questions to resources that have the information and are willing to share it with others. Some of these resources exist within LC itself.

The referral service uses a subject-indexed, computerized file of 13,000 organizations, called "Information Resources." A description of each resource includes its special fields of interest and the types of information service it provides.

An information resource may be any organization, institution, group, or individual with specialized information in a particular field.

The center will accept requests for referral services on any topic. When a subject is not covered in the data file, the center will attempt to locate new information resources from extensive contacts. In each case, responses to requests are individually tailored to the specific inquiry.

The center occasionally compiles directories of information resources covering a broad area. These are published by the Library of Congress under the general title *A Directory of Information Resources in the United States* with subtitles. Some of these volumes are: *Social Sciences,* rev. ed., Washington, D.C.: GPO, 1973; and *Federal Government, With a Supplement of Government Sponsored Information Analysis Centers,* rev. ed., Washington, D.C., Government Printing Office, 1974. See also the center's guide, *Directory of Federally Supported Information Analysis Centers,* which is distributed by the National Technical Information Service.

PHOTODUPLICATION SERVICE

Adams Building, Room G-1009
(202) 287-5654

Norman J. Shaffer, Chief
8:30 A.M.–4:15 P.M.   Monday–Friday

For all scholars, especially those with time constraints, the Photoduplication Service provides invaluable assistance. For a fee, individuals and institutions may obtain photoreproductions in different formats of materials excluding those restricted by copyright or by other restrictions.

The Document Expediting Service receives, duplicates and sells materials from government agencies, including unclassified CIA reports. The service also maintains the LC Master Negative Microfilm Collection, numbering more than 150,000 reels, which includes selections from the Manuscript Division, U.S. and foreign government documents, and periodicals and newspapers. Some of these items are on sale. Information about the holdings of the division may be found in the *National Register of Microfilm Masters, Newspapers in Microfilm, Microfilm Clearinghouse Bulletin,* and *Guides to Microfilm in Print.* An information brochure describing the facilities, a price list, and a flyer listing the catalogs of available materials are available from the Photoduplication Service without charge. Requests for photoduplication should be made in person or by mail.

LOAN DIVISION

Jefferson Building, Room G-155
(202) 287-5441

Olive James, Chief

8:00 A.M.–5:15 P.M.   Monday–Friday

As a research library, LC extends the use of its collections outside its facilities through an interlibrary loan provided by the Loan Division. The service is intended to aid scholarly research by making available unusual materials that are not readily accessible elsewhere. The service is available to most U.S. libraries as well as any major library of the world. All loan requests must originate from libraries and not from individuals. Loan requests are entertained only when such requests do not conflict with LC's internal needs and its primary service obligation to the Congress. Rare books, manuscripts, newspapers, periodicals, collected sets, sheet music, librettos, motion picture films, and easily available books do not circulate.

GENERAL READING ROOMS DIVISION

Jefferson Building
(202) 287-5530

Ellen Z. Hahn, Chief

Reference staff members of this division are on duty in Alcoves 4 and 5 of the Main Reading Room and can provide reference assistance during evenings and weekends when the specialized divisions are closed. For reference assistance by telephone, call (202) 287-5522. The Division's Union Catalog Reference Section (202/287-6300), on Deck 33 off the Main Reading Room, can provide bibliographic reference assistance for both the published and "in preparation" portions of LC's *National Union Catalog*. The section's hours are 8:00 A.M.–4:30 P.M., Monday–Friday.

The General Reading Room Division also maintains a list of private, local, freelance researchers who can be hired for library searches and research assistance in any field or language. For further information call (202) 287-5515.

5.   The traditional access tool for the LC collection is its 20-million card main catalog, an author-title-subject dictionary file located in the Main Reading Room. However, this catalog was frozen December 31, 1980. Cataloging by computer was inaugurated for English language titles in 1968. Since that time, romanized entries for non-English languages have been added gradually. Entries for titles in Southeast Asian languages were introduced about 1978. As of January 4, 1981, the automated record became LC's official record of holdings from that date forward.

The Library of Congress Information System (LOCIS) is accessible through SCORPIO (Subject-Content-Oriented-Retriever-for-Processing-Information-On-Line) and MUMS (Multiple-Use-MARC-System) commands. Both access the MARC (Machine-Readable-Cataloging) data base, a comprehensive catalog record—available on tape for purchase from LC's Cataloging Distribution Service—which serves now as the basis for the *National Union Catalog*.

SCORPIO can be used to access post-1968 LC holdings by subject (LC subject headings), legislation information files for recent Congresses, bibliographic citations to current literature on public policy issues from periodicals, U.N. and U.S. government documents published in recent years, referrals to organizations that are information sources on a wide variety of topics, information from the *Congressional Sourcebook,* and certain restricted files. MUMS provides author, title, and component-word access to LC records of holdings cataloged since 1963 or in process, and LC's name authority files.

LC's computer catalog center (202/287-6213), located off the Main Reading Room, contains public computer terminals. The staff will instruct researchers in the use of terminals, which then may be used free of charge. For a fee, the staff will perform bibliographic searches. Data output is available in a variety of forms.

As for published reference works the reader is reminded of those listed under the appropriate divisions above. The publications that follow are of a more general nature, of use not only to Southeast Asianists but to all scholars who come to LC or otherwise employ its services. Unless contrary indication is given, these publications are for sale by the Superintendent of Documents, U.S. Government Printing Office, Washington, D.C. 20402, or by LC itself.

Major LC publications—catalogs:

The National Union Catalog, Pre-1956 Imprints. Currently published by the Mansell Company in England, this catalog supersedes the following two titles: 754 v.

A Catalog of Books Represented by Library of Congress Printed Cards Issued (from August 1898 through July 1942), 167 v. Supplement: cards issued August 1, 1942–December 31, 1947, 42 v.

The Library of Congress Author Catalog; A Cumulative List of Works Represented by Library of Congress Cards, 1948–52, 24 v.

The National Union Catalog; A Cumulative Author List Representing Library of Congress Printed Cards and Titles Reported by Other American Libraries. Cumulation for 1953–57, 28 v., available in reprint from Rowman and Littlefield; cumulation for 1958–62, 54 v., o.p.; cumulation for 1963–67, 72 v., available from J. W. Edwards; cumulative for 1956–67, 125 v., available from Rowman and Littlefield; cumulative for 1968–72, available from J. W. Edwards; cumulation for 1973–77 available from Rowman and Littlefield; cumulations for recent years available from LC Cataloging Distribution Service. Currently published in nine monthly and three quarterly issues with an annual cumulation, the catalog covers some 1,100 U.S. and Canadian libraries.

Monographic Series, an aid to locating works published as a series but with various titles, is published in three quarterly issues and an annual cumulation.

Library of Congress—Books: Subjects, A Cumulative List of Works represented by Library of Congress Printed Cards, for 1945 and later imprints, is arranged alphabetically by LC subject headings and by author under subject headings. Cumulation for 1950–54, 20 v., available in reprint from Rowman and Littlefield; cumulation for 1955–59, 22 v., available from Rowman and Littlefield; cumulations for 1960–64, 25 v., and for 1965–69, 42 v., available from J. W. Edwards; cumulations for 1970–74, 100 v., available from Rowman and Littlefield. From 1975 this catalog is no longer being published under the title above but is continued by the following title.

Subject Catalog continues the preceding work, published in three quarterly issues and an annual cumulation, available from LC Cataloging Distribution Service.

National Register of Microfilm Masters is an annual; 1969 and later years are available from LC Cataloging Distribution Service.

Other major publications, including both LC and non-LC:

New Serial Titles; A Union List of Serials Commencing Publication After December 31, 1949 is based on reports from some 800 U.S. and Canadian libraries; cumulation for 1950–70, four v., available from R. R. Bowker Co.; cumulation for 1971–75 and 1976–80, available from LC Cataloging Distribution Service. Currently published in eight monthly and four quarterly issues with an annual cumulation (annuals cumulate up to 5- or 10-year periods). This work is a supplement to:

Union List of Serials in Libraries of the United States and Canada, five v., ed. Edna B. Titus (3d ed., 1965).

Combined Indexes to the Library of Congress Classification Schedules, 15 v., comp. Nancy Olson (Washington, D.C.: U.S. Historical Documents Institute, 1974—) is an aid to locating call numbers for materials by authors, names, geographic areas, subjects, and keywords.

Library of Congress Publications in Print, a biennial, is available free from the LC Cataloging Distribution Service.

Annual Report of the Librarian of Congress.

Quarterly Journal of the Library of Congress is particularly useful for the description of acquisitions of the various divisions.

Library of Congress Information Bulletin is a weekly.

Note: See also entries B5, D3, D4, D5, E4, F12, and F13.

A28 Martin Luther King, Jr., Memorial Library (District of Columbia Public Library)

1. a. *901 G Street, N.W.*
    Washington, D.C. 20001
    (202) 727-1111 (Information)

    b. 9:00 A.M.–9:00 P.M.   Monday–Thursday
    9:00 A.M.–5:30 P.M.   Friday–Saturday
    (Hours vary during the summer.)

    c. Open to the public, Interlibrary loan and photoreproduction services are available.

    d. Kathleen Wood, Librarian, Martin Luther King

2. The total library collection exceeds two million bound volumes, including books and periodicals. Southeast Asia related holdings number nearly 1,200 items.

3. This library maintains a good general collection on Southeast Asia. The History field is by far the largest part of the collection. Nevertheless, other fields, such as art, culture, and economics, reflect attention on the part of the staff to provide basic coverage. The country breakdown is as follows: the Philippines, 310; Indonesia, 235; Malaysia, 185; Thailand, 110; Burma, 65; Laos, 37; Singapore, 35; and Southeast Asia general, 250.

4. The library curently receives some 300 periodical titles and maintains specialized collections of films, slides, tapes, records, and art reproduction. Each division of the library maintains its own vertical file collection. Researchers will find scattered materials on Southeast Asia throughout. The

Audio-visual Division, Room 226, has over 20 films related to Southeast Asia (see entry F15). The Music and Recreation Division and the Art Division also have a few Southeast Asia holdings.

5. The library maintains a card catalog that combines title, subject and author listings. The library uses the Dewey Decimal system of classification. Free brochures describing special library programs and events are available to visiting patrons.

A29 Maryland University Libraries at College Park

1. a. *McKeldin Library*
   College Park, Maryland 20742
   (301) 454-5704
   Undergraduate Library
   (301) 454-4737
   Architecture Library
   (301) 454-4316
   Art Library
   (301) 454-2065
   Music Room (McKeldin)
   (301) 454-3036

   b. Academic year:
   8:00 A.M.–11:00 P.M.   Monday–Thursday
   8:00 A.M.–6:00 P.M.   Friday
   10:00 A.M.–6:00 P.M.   Saturday
   Noon–11:00 P.M.   Sunday
   The above hours are for McKeldin Library only. Call above numbers for other schedules.

   c. Libraries are open to the public for on-site use. Interlibrary loan and photocopying facilities are available.

   d. H. Joanne Harrar, Director of Libraries

2–3 a. The university's libraries contain an estimated 1.3 million volumes, with Southeast Asian holdings of approximately 1,400 titles. Out of the 15,800 serials currently received, 21 are from Southeast Asia. However, no newspapers from the region are currently received by the library.
   While the Southeast Asia collection is relatively small, it does contain a few items in the fields of art and music not found in most other collections in the Washington, D.C., area.

   b. Tabular evaluation of country strengths:

	Brunei	Burma	Cambodia	Indonesia	Laos	Malaysia
Philosophy and Religion	—	—	1	1	—	2
History	5	44	34	120	31	78
Geography and Anthropology	—	5	—	—	1	4
Economics	—	13	32	31	—	20
Sociology	—	3	2	10	1	3
Politics and Government	—	10	1	23	—	15
International Relations	—	1	—	2	2	—
Law	—	—	—	—	—	—

	Brunei	Burma	Cambodia	Indonesia	Laos	Malaysia
Education	—	1	—	—	—	—
Art and Music	—	11	1	2	—	1
Language and Literature	—	—	—	11	—	17
Military Affairs	—	—	—	1	—	—
Bibliography and Reference	1	2	2	4	3	6
Total Country Evaluation:	6 B	90 D–	44 D	205 D	38 D	146 D

	Philip-pines	Singa-pore	Thailand	Vietnam	Indo-china	SEA general
Philosophy and Religion	2	1	8	3	—	—
History	113	34	70	150	38	24
Geography and Anthropology	10	—	4	—	1	—
Economics	32	6	10	17	14	3
Sociology	12	3	3	4	4	—
Politics and Government	18	4	15	4	6	2
International Relations	6	—	3	20	—	—
Law	—	—	—	—	—	—
Education	1	—	—	—	—	—
Art and Music	—	—	—	—	—	—
Language and Literature	9	—	—	—	—	—
Military Affairs	6	1	3	1	—	—
Bibliography and Reference	19	6	10	3	8	11
Total Country Evaluation:	228 D	55 D	126 D	202 D	71 C	40 D

Total Subject Evaluation:

Philosophy and Religion	18 D–
History	741 D
Geography and Anthropology	25 D–
Economics	149 D–
Sociology	45 D
Politics and Government	98 D
International Relations	34 B
Law	—
Education	2 D–
Art and Music	15 D–
Language and Literature	37 D–
Military Affairs	12 D
Bibliography and Reference	75 C
	1,251 D–

4.   McKeldin Library is a regional depository for United States government documents. Holdings exceed 500,000 items, and are virtually complete from 1925 with substantial holdings of earlier series. Documents and reports of the League of Nations, United Nations, and other international organizations and agencies are also available in the library. Much of this material does not appear in the main card catalog but can be located with the help of finding aids in the Government Documents/Map Room on the third floor. There are a substantial number of Southeast Asia maps in the room.

Phonograph holdings of Southeast Asian music are serviced through the Music Room on the fourth floor of McKeldin Library (301/454-3036). The collection consists of a small but interesting group of commercially produced recordings, many from Indonesia. No field recordings from the region are in the collection.

5. The author/title and subject catalogs are located on the second floor of McKeldin Library. These catalogs are not comprehensive for all materials on the College Park campus. Reference assistance is available at the information desk. There is also a computer assisted research service (301/ 454-5704) available for a small fee. Computer printouts of serial holdings are available throughout the library system. No printed bibliographic aid is available for the main collection.

National Aeronautics and Space Administration Libraries See entry K25

A30 National Agricultural Library (U.S. Department of Agriculture)

1. a. *Main Library*
    U.S. Route 1 and I-495 (Beltway Exit 25 North)
    Beltsville, Maryland 20705
    (301) 344-3756 (Reference)
    (301) 344-3755 (Information)
    D.C. Branch and Law Library
    U.S. Department of Agriculture
    South Building
    Independence Avenue and 14th Street, S.W.
    Room 1052
    Washington, D.C. 20250
    (202) 447-3434

    b. Main Library:
    8:00 A.M.–4:30 P.M.   Monday–Friday

    D.C. Branch:
    8:30 A.M.–5:00 P.M.   Monday-Friday

    c. Open to the public. Interlibrary loan services and photoduplication facilities available.

    d. Richard A. Farley, Acting Director

2. The National Agricultural Library collection contains more than 1.7 million volumes and 23,000 serials and periodicals. There are over 130,000 items in the NAL's microfilm collection. Library holdings fall mainly in the subject category of agriculture and related fields such as botany, forestry, economics, statistics, entomology, food and nutrition, natural and water resources, and rural health care.

3. This library is a major resource for those with an interest in the agriculture of the countries of Southeast Asia. A computer search of the collection revealed that there are approximately 8,000 items listed for those countries. Totals for each country and the region are as follows:

Country/Region	*No. of Items*
Burma	171
Cambodia	108

Country/Region	No. of Items
Indonesia	1,532
Laos	84
Malaysia	2,182
Philippines	1,846
Singapore	190
Thailand	996
Vietnam	371
Southeast Asia general	364

4. NAL's collection includes 169 serials from Southeast Asia.

5. An extremely useful bibliographic tool is NAL's computerized information retrieval system, AGRICOLA. There are over 700,000 book and periodical article entries in this data base. AGRICOLA contains all items cataloged and indexed by the library since 1970.

    AGRICOLA can be used to conduct searches by using key words such as geographic names, language, subject headings, author name, and more. The database can be accessed through Bibliographic Retrieval Services (BRS), Systems Development Corporation (SDC), and Lockheed Information System (DIALOG). The printed version of the AGRICOLA database is the monthly *Bibliography of Agriculture*, 1941—, published by Oryl Press.

    The *Dictionary Catalog of the National Agricultural Library, 1862–1965*, in 73 volumes, contains records for all publications cataloged by the library to 1965. Catalog records for all publications acquired and processed after 1965 are published in the monthly *National Agricultural Library Catalog*.

    Users should consult *Guide to Services . . . Technical Information Systems/National Agricultural Library* (April 1980) for information and guidance on utilizing resources of the library.

National Defense University (Defense Department) Library See entry K11

National Endowment for the Humanities (NEH) Library See entry K26

A31 National Geographic Society Library

1. a. *1146 16th Street, N.W.*
    Washington, D.C. 20036
    (202) 857-7787 (Reference Librarian)

    b. 8:30 A.M.–5:00 P.M.   Monday–Friday

    c. Open to visitors for on-site use. There is no interlibrary loan or photocopying service available to the public. Readers may place materials on the reserve shelf for three days.

    d. Virginia Carter Hills, Head Librarian

2.   The collection is designed to serve primarily the needs of the society's staff. Holdings total some 70,000 volumes and cover a wide variety of subjects, including geography and allied sciences, natural history, travel, ethnography, wildlife, and the society's research and exploration materials.

3.   The collection contains some 550 titles on Southeast Asia: Brunei, 4; Burma, 60; Cambodia, 20; Indochina, 35; Indonesia, 60; Laos, 20; Malaysia, 61; the Philippines, 200; Singapore, 28; Thailand, 70; and Vietnam, 70. The small Indochina collection contains a number of titles from the late 1800s and early 1900s, mostly in the area of History.

4.   The periodical holdings of the library exceed 1,800 titles. There are eight periodicals from Southeast Asia including: *Philippine Quarterly of Culture and Society, Philippine Development, Journal of the Siam Society, Southeast Asia,* and *Indonesian Journal of Geography.* The periodical collection is served by a card file located at the circulation desk and the periodical indexes located in the Bibliographies Room (Room 115).

    The library maintains a complete file of National Geographic Society publications: *National Geographic, World,* books, maps, and news service releases.

    The Society's Clipping Service (202/857-7053) offers a unique source of information. Contained in its 68 files and 340 drawers are newspaper clippings from 13 U.S. newspapers, foreign magazines, government publications, and several hundred unindexed periodicals, newsletters, and ephemera on a variety of topics such as animals, cyclones, festivals, population, railroads, religion, and transportation. Some of the newspapers from which clippings are taken include: *Christian Science Monitor, Financial Times, London Times, Los Angeles Times, New York Times,* and *Washington Post.* The collection is weeded periodically. Nevertheless, a significant amount of material from the 1940s and 1950s can be found. Clippings are arranged alphabetically by geographic categories and main headings. The service has approximately five drawers on Southeast Asia. Over half of this collection relates to Vietnam. Serious researchers should call at least one day in advance before visiting the service. The clippings files are very well organized and, as such, are a useful research tool.

    The Society's Map Library (Cartographic Division) located in the Membership Center Building, Gaithersberg, Maryland 20760 (301/857-7000, extension 1401) maintains an extensive collection of maps and atlases (see entry E6). Its services, however, are restricted to society members and authorized visitors for on-site use.

5.   The principal finding aid for the collection is the card catalog in the main reading room; the catalog is in dictionary form with author, title, and subject access. The library also maintains a very detailed separate reference card index to the articles published in the *National Geographic* since 1883. This index lists every geographic area, country, city, or village that has ever appeared in the magazine. Also useful to researchers is the *National Geographic Index,* which has been cumulated for 1888–1946, 1947–1976, and 1977–1981. The pamphlet, *National Geographic Society Library,* may be helpful to those intending to use the collection.

A32 National Institute of Education (Education Department)— Education Research Library

1.   a. *1832 M Street, N.W.*
6th Floor
Washington, D.C. 20208
(202) 254-5060
Branch Library:
400 Maryland Avenue, S.W.
Room A-039
Washington, D.C. 20202
(202) 245-8853

b. 10 A.M.–4:00 P.M.   Monday–Friday

c. Open to the public. Interlibrary loan and photoduplication services available.

d. Charles Missar, Supervisory Librarian

2–3.   The library contains approximately 150,000 books and bound periodicals. In 1973 large portions of what was then the Health, Education and Welfare (HEW) Department Library were transferred to the National Institute of Education (NIE) facilities including all education titles. As a result the collection is particularly strong in educational psychology, history of education, and urban education issues related to U.S. education. Holdings on Southeast Asia are limited. However, books dealing with international and comparative education may contain occasional information on the area.

4.   Currently, the library subscribes to over 1,200 periodicals, but the collection does not include any Southeast Asian publications. Library holdings also include a large microfilm collection drawn from these periodicals, plus other documents and special collections. Both branches of the library have access to the ERIC data system (see entry G6).

5.   An author/subject card catalog is available. Researchers may also consult the *Author/Title Catalog of the Department Library* (Boston: G. K. Hall, 1965) in 20 volumes with a 7-volume supplement (1973), and the *Subject Catalog of the Department Library* (Boston: G. K. Hall, 1965), 20 volumes plus a 4-volume supplement (1973), prepared for the former HEW Department Library; included here are references to those items transferred to NIE's library facilities in 1973. The *Periodical Holdings List* (3d ed., 1978) is also available on request.

A33 National Library of Medicine (U.S. Department of Health and Human Services) (NLM)

1.   a. *8600 Rockville Pike*
Bethesda, Maryland 20209
(301) 496-6095 (Reference)
(301) 496-5511 (Interlibrary Loan)
(301) 496-5405 (History of Medicine Division)

b. Reading Room (Labor Day to Memorial Day)
8:30 A.M.–9:00 P.M.   Monday–Thursday
8:30 A.M.–6:00 P.M.   Friday
8:30 A.M.–5:00 P.M.   Saturday
Summer Hours (Memorial Day to Labor Day)
8:30 A.M.–5:00 P.M.   Monday–Saturday
History of Medicine Division
8:30 A.M.–4:45 P.M.   Monday–Friday

c. The NLM facilities are open to serious scholars. First-time users are required to obtain a registration number at the reader service desk. Users are also required to sign a daily log. Interlibrary loan and coin-operated copying machines are available.

d. Martin M. Cummings, Director

2–3.   Established in 1836 as the Library of the Army Surgeon General's Office, the library was renamed in 1956 as the National Library of Medicine by an act of Congress. The mission of the NLM is to collect, preserve, disseminate, and exchange information important to the progress of the health services.

The library is the world's largest research library in a single scientific and professional field. It collects materials exhaustively in some 40 biomedical areas, and to a lesser degree in other related subjects. The holdings exceed 2.5 million items in more than 70 languages. The NLM's collection is predominantly technical in nature, but a fair amount of material, especially in the History of Medicine Division, is significant for study and research in the fields of history and the social sciences.

The NLM's collection of Southeast Asia related materials seems to be substantial, numbering over 5,200 items. This collection includes technical medical data, government documents, and statistics; private and institutional publications dealing with health, sanitation, nutrition, population control, and mortality; and literature produced by various international organizations.

The major part of the holdings of the NLM are arranged by subject, which is in turn broken down by geographic area. The library does not follow the usual LC classification system. Consequently, it is not possible to give an accurate assessment of the numerical strength of the collection. A search of the name catalog did produce a total of 788 monograph titles: Philippines, 240; Malaysia, 120; Singapore, 90; Indonesia, 80; Thailand, 70; Burma, 60; Vietnam, 50; and Southeast Asia, 40. Remaining countries in the region have fewer than 20 titles each. A computer search of the MEDLINE file revealed over 3,500 journal articles indexed in the collection. This search covered only the last three years and consists of journal articles published in Southeast Asia, and articles published elsewhere, dealing with the region or one or more countries therein. An NLM Literature Search, *Medicine in Vietnam,* contains 337 citations on Vietnam entered into the computer files from January 1969 through June 1972. Given the numbers cited above, it is likely that the more extensive, and more expensive computer search, which is possible back to 1966, would produce a significantly larger amount of materials for the interested Southeast Asianist.

4.   The Documents Collection of the library contains over 7,000 selected serials and monographs, mainly health-related reports and statistics of U.S. foreign and international agencies. These documents are arranged geographically

on the lower level of the library. However, the majority of the collection is scattered throughout the library, particularly in the stacks with the general collection.

The History of Medicine Division has some scattered materials relating to Southeast Asia. These are not easily located. The *Bibliography of the History of Medicine* and the Index-Catalog should be consulted. See point 5.

5. The NLM has two catalogs for locating books: a name catalog (author and title), and a subject catalog. The *National Library of Medicine Current Catalog*, a computerized book catalog published quarterly with annual and five-year cumulations, can be used instead of the card catalogs for items entered since 1965.

    The NLM offers several computerized search services for a fee ranging from approximately $4.00 to $14.00.

    MEDLARS (Medical Literature Analysis and Retrieval System) contains more than 4.5 million references to journal articles and books in the health sciences published since 1965. This information is made available through a network of centers at universities, medical schools, hospitals, government agencies, commercial organizations, and international affiliates.

    MEDLINE (MEDLARS Online) contains some 600,000 references to biomedical articles drawn from 3,000 periodicals published in the United States and 70 foreign countries, and a limited number of chapters and articles from selected monographs. From time to time a Literature Search (a bibliography produced by MEDLARS) on a specific topic felt to be of wide interest will be reprinted and made available free of charge. One such item of interest to Southeast Asianists is Literature Search No. 72-18, *Medicine in Vietnam.*

    CATLINE (Catalog Online) contains references to nearly 335,000 books and serials cataloged at NLM since 1965.

    SERLINE (Serials Online) contains bibliographic information for about 38,000 serial titles, including all journals that are on order or cataloged for the NLM collection.

    HISTLINE (History of Medicine Online) contains about 48,000 references to articles, monographs, symposia, and other publications dealing with history of medicine and related sciences drawn from NLM's *Bibliography of the History of Medicine.*

    AVLINE (Audiovisuals Online) contains citations to some 10,000 audiovisual teaching packages used in health sciences education.

    Of the published bibliographic tools available, the *Index Catalogue of the Library of the Surgeon General's Office* is the most important for materials in the History of Medicine Division. Researchers may also wish to consult the *Periodical Locator* in the Reading Room.

National Museum of Natural History (Smithsonian Institution)— Anthropology Branch Library See entry C6

National Science Foundation Library See entry K27

A34 Navy Department Library

1. a. *Washington Navy Yard, Building 220*
   11th and M Streets, S.E.
   Washington, D.C. 20374
   (202) 433-4131

   b. 10:00 A.M.–4:30 P.M.   Monday–Friday

   c. Open to the public for on-site use only. Interlibrary loan and photocopying facilities are available.

   d. Stanley Kalkus, Director

2. The library collection contains some 150,000 volumes, with 300 periodicals currently being received. About a dozen of these deal with Asia. A search of the card catalog revealed 815 titles for Southeast Asia.

3. Major subjects covered in the library collection are: naval history, exploring expeditions, warfare with emphasis on naval and combined operations, naval architecture and shipbuilding, and naval customs and tradition. Over half of the titles for Southeast Asia are on Vietnam, placing this part of the collection in the "C" category. Other countries in the region are poorly represented. Worth noting is the fact that many titles written by military personnel and official Navy publications are within this collection. Most of these items are not available in other library collections.

4. The library has a number of important special collections including approximately 5,000 rare books, some of them unique, dating from the sixteenth through the twentieth century. This collection includes many narratives of voyages of the eighteenth and nineteenth centuries. Most works are in English. There are some twenty items on Southeast Asia. For example, Edmund Roberts' *Embassy to the Eastern Courts of Cochin-China, Siam and Muscat in the U.S. Sloop-of-War Peacock . . . During the Years 1832-3-4* (New York: Harper & Brothers, 1837). There are approximately 70 monographs in Japanese that deal with the history of the Pacific War. A number of these concern the Philippines and the Dutch East Indies.

5. Two dictionary card catalogs must be consulted: an inactive catalog (pre-1968 acquisitions), and an active catalog of subsequent acquisitions. A descriptive pamphlet, *Navy Department Library,* is available.

Population Crisis Committee (PCC) See entry M52

Population Reference Bureau, Inc. (PRB) Library See entry H33

Rand Corporation—Washington Office Library See entry H34

A35 School of Advanced International Studies (SAIS) (Johns Hopkins University)—Mason Library

1.   a. *1740 Massachusetts Avenue, N.W.*
     Washington, D.C. 20036
     (202) 785-6296

   b. Academic year:
   8:30 A.M.–10:00 P.M.   Monday–Thursday
   8:30 A.M.–6:00 P.M.   Friday
   10:00 A.M.–5:00 P.M.   Saturday
   Noon–9:00 P.M.   Sunday

   When classes are not in session:
   8:30 A.M.–5:00 P.M.   Monday–Friday

   c. Open to serious researchers for reference use for a limited time. A fee is charged for borrowing privileges and for visiting privileges beyond one month. Interlibrary loan and photocopying facilities are available.

   d. Peter J. Promen, Director

2.   The Mason Library collection totals approximately 80,000 volumes. There are about 1,000 titles on Southeast Asia. The library takes some 900 periodicals. Only two are from Southeast Asia. No newspapers from the region are currently subscribed to.

3   a. Although small, the collection is stocked with essential titles, and tends to be best developed in the field of comparative politics and modernization, international economics, international relations, and area studies.

   b. Tabular evaluation of country strengths:

	Brunei	Burma	Cambodia	Indonesia	Laos	Malaysia
Philosophy and Religion	—	—	—	—	—	—
History	—	104	20	92	15	104
Geography and Anthropology	—	1	—	—	—	—
Economics	—	22	4	22	4	20
Sociology	—	2	4	5	1	—
Politics and Government		8	2	11	—	7
International Relations	—	—	—	2	1	1
Law	—	2	—	2	—	—
Education	—	2	—	2	—	—
Art and Music	—	—	—	1	—	—
Language and Literature	—	1	—	8	—	—
Military Affairs	—	4	1	2	1	—
Bibliography and Reference	—	1	—	4	1	—
Total Country Evaluation:	—	147 D –	31 D	149 D –	22 D	133 D

	Philippines	Singapore	Thailand	Vietnam	Indochina	SEA general
Philosophy and Religion	—	—	—	—	—	—
History	82	16	68	98	39	25
Geography and Anthropology	3	—	1	—	2	—
Economics	24	11	13	4	4	—
Sociology	7	1	3	12	—	—
Politics and Government	9	13	6	8	—	—

	Philip-pines	Singa-pore	Thailand	Vietnam	Indo-china	SEA general
International Relations	3	—	33	16	1	—
Law	—	1	—	—	—	—
Education	—	1	—	—	1	—
Art and Music	—	—	1	—	—	—
Language and Literature	1	—	—	—	1	—
Military Affairs	1	1	1	1	2	—
Bibliography and Reference	4	1	2	3	2	—
Total Country Evaluation:	134 D –	45 D	98 D –	142 D –	52 D	25 D –

Total Subject Evaluation:

Philosophy and Religion	–
History	663 D
Geography and Anthropology	7 D –
Economics	128 D –
Sociology	35 D –
Politics and Government	64 D –
International Relations	27 B
Law	3 D –
Education	6 D –
Art and Music	2 D –
Language and Literature	11 D –
Military Affairs	14 D
Bibliography and Reference	18 D –
	978 D –

5.   The library follows the Library of Congress classification. The collection is served by a card catalog arranged by subject, title, and author. A separate periodical card catalog is available in the periodical reading room.

A36 Senate Library

1.   a. *Capitol Building*
Room S 332
Washington, D.C. 20510
(202) 224-7106

b. 9:00 A.M.–5:00 P.M.   Monday–Friday

c. The library is restricted to the use of senators, Senate staff, House members, their staffs, and select other persons. Scholars may use the library with a letter of introduction from a senator. No interlibrary loan services are available but the library provides photoduplication facilities.

d. Roger K. Haley, Librarian

2–5.   This 300,000-volume reference collection of congressional legislative history is of potential value to the scholars dealing with U.S. relations with Southeast Asia. Holdings include Senate and House bills and resolutions, reports, hearings, debates, and other publications. The library prepares bibliographies, chronologies, digests of legislation, and the *Index of Congressional Committee Hearings.* The library has a dictionary card catalog. A descriptive brochure, *General Information and Services of the Senate Library,* is available.

A37 State Department Library

1. a. *State Department Building*
   2201 C Street, N.W., Room 3239
   Washington, D.C. 20520
   (202) 632-0535

   b. 8:15 A.M.–5:00 P.M. Monday–Friday

   c. The collection primarily serves the staff needs for the personnel of the Department of State, the Agency for International Development, and the Arms Control and Disarmament Agency. Scholars may obtain prior permission for on-site use of the collection for materials not available elsewhere in the metropolitan area. Limited photocopying facilities are available.

   d. Conrad Eaton, Librarian

2. The library collection contains in excess of 650,000 volumes with over 4,700 titles on Southeast Asia. The collection is growing by about 16,000 volumes per year, of which 30–40 percent are acquired from foreign countries. As one might imagine, the collection is particularly strong in such fields as economics, government, history, and international relations.

   The library has a considerable collection of foreign government documents including official gazettes from 100 countries. There is also a wealth of diplomatic materials probably unavailable elsewhere. The library is a depository for United States Government documents.

3. a. The Southeast Asia holdings in this library constitute one of the largest collections in the area, exceeded only by the Library of Congress and Bernard Fall collections.

	Brunei	Burma	Cambodia	Indonesia	Laos	Malaysia
Philosophy and Religion	—	—	—	3	—	3
History	—	192	55	441	71	247
Geography and Anthropology	—	4	2	10	2	4
Economics	—	60	19	139	30	47
Sociology	—	20	4	24	4	8
Politics and Government	—	25	11	101	18	60
International Relations	—	6	4	21	3	11
Law	—	—	—	—	—	—
Education	—	2	—	4	—	7
Art and Music	—	—	—	3	—	2
Language and Literature	—	—	3	13	—	10
Military Affairs	—	4	5	10	4	8
Bibliography and Reference	—	7	10	31	8	14
Total Country Evaluation:	—	320 C	113 B	800 C	140 B	421 B

	Philip-pines	Singa-pore	Thailand	Vietnam	Indo-china	SEA general
Philosophy and Religion	10	—	12	12	8	—
History	440	140	203	560	57	71
Geography and Anthropology	15	10	10	20	10	6
Economics	171	32	100	178	36	331
Sociology	20	7	25	13	7	4
Politics and Government	81	15	70	101	17	20

	Philip-pines	Singa-pore	Thailand	Vietnam	Indo-china	SEA general
International Relations	13	2	23	39	4	—
Law						
Education	8	11	10	7	—	—
Art and Music	5	—	5	6	1	—
Language and Literature	11	—	9	15	—	—
Military Affairs	9	2	6	21	3	3
Bibliography and Reference	32	18	4	36	14	10
Total Country Evaluation:	815 C	237 B	477 C	1,008 B	157 B	445 D

Total Subject Evaluation:

Philosophy and Religion	48 D
History	2,477 B
Geography and Anthropology	93 D
Economics	1,143 B
Sociology	136 C
Politics and Government	519 B
International Relations	126 A/B
Law	—
Education	49 D
Art and Music	22 D −
Language and Literature	61 D
Military Affairs	75 B
Bibliography and Reference	184 B
	4,933 C

4. The library receives over 1,000 periodicals including 25 from Southeast Asia. There is also a much larger number of journals on Asia, often including articles on the region: e.g., *Asian Recorder, Asian Survey,* and *Pacific Community,* among others. The library does not take any Southeast Asian newspapers.

5. The collection is served by two card catalogs. The first is a dictionary catalog arranged alphabetically by author, title, and subject. The second is a geographic catalog arranged by country, region and continent.

    For periodicals, a geographically arranged list is available at the information desk. An informative brochure, the *Department of State Library* (1978), is available without charge. The library also publishes a monthly *Acquisitions* list of selected titles added to the collection during the month.

A38 Textile Museum Library

1. a. *2320 S Street, N.W.*
    Washington, D.C.
    (202) 667-0441

    b. 10:00 A.M.–5:00 P.M.   Tuesday–Friday
       10:00 A.M.–1:00 P.M.   Saturday

    c. The Arthur D. Jenkins Library is open free to members, and to interested visitors for a $2.00 daily user's fee. Students having letters of introduction from their professors can make arrangements with the librarian to waive the user's fee.

    d. Katherine Freshley, Librarian

2–3.   The library has over 7,000 volumes relating to the textile arts. This is one of the largest libraries specializing in textiles in the world. Southeast Asia holdings consist of approximately 250 volumes with Indonesia and the Philippines the best represented countries in the collection. The library subscribes to some 144 journals and newsletters, including a number of foreign publications.

The Indonesian collection consists of approximately 100 volumes on textiles, 42 in the field of anthropology, and 2 on art.

4.   The library has a copy of James M. Andres, *Notes on the Siamese Collection Purchased in Siam for the Peabody Museum in 1934–35*. Some of the textiles from this collection now belong to the Textile Museum in Washington, D.C.

5.   A card catalog serves the collection. Items may be located by subject and geographic location.

A39 Transportation Department Library

1.   a. *Transportation Department Headquarters Building*
400 7th Street, S.W.
Room 2200
Washington, D.C. 20591
(202) 426-2565 (Director)
(202) 426-1792 (Reference)

Branch (Air Transportation and Aeronautics)
800 Independence Avenue, S.W.
Room 930
Washington, D.C. 20590
(202) 426-3611 (Reference)

b. Both libraries:
8:30 A.M.–5:00 P.M.   Monday–Friday

c. Open to the public for on-site use. Interlibrary loan and photoreproduction services are available.

d. Lucile E. Beaver, Library Director

2.   The combined holdings of the libraries exceed 300,000 hard copy documents, 125,000 microform items, and 2,170 journal titles.

3.   Although total holdings in the general collection on Southeast Asian transportation do not exceed several hundred titles, the international railway and highway periodicals and the various international statistical handbooks and reference works, plus a number of U.S. government documents, contain useful information on Southeast Asian railroad, road, sea, airline, and local urban mass-transportation systems.

4.   The library maintains an extensive card index to periodical literature on transportation from the 1920s to the present, with some 815 entries for transportation in Southeast Asia. There are approximately 350 entries for the Philippines, 165 for Malaysia, and 100 entries for Thailand. The remaining countries in the region are represented by less than 50 entries each. The bibliographic literature file, now containing well over 800,000 citations,

has been microfilmed as the Transportation Masterfile, 1921–71, in 140 reels and a supplement covering 1971–74 in seven reels.

5. The main dictionary card catalog for the collection is broken down by transportation mode (highways and railroads, for example), each of which is sub-divided geographically.

Publications of the library include *Transportation: Current Literature* (semi-monthly) and *Selected Library Acquisitions* (monthly).

Treasury Department Library See entry K36

A40 United Nations Information Centre

1. a. *2101 L Street, N.W.*
      Washington, D.C. 20037
      (202) 296-5370

   b. 9:00 A.M.–1:00 P.M.   Monday–Friday

   c. Open to the public. Interlibrary loan and photoduplication facilities are available.

   d. Helen MacSherry, Librarian
      Willard Hass, Information Officer

2–4. The U.N. Information Centre in Washington maintains a 15,000-volume reference library of U.N. documents, official records, and U.N. sales publications dealing with economic, statistical, financial, international trade, legal and social questions, and human rights. Documents generated by U.N. specialized or regional agencies are not available here. The center also maintains a small collection of U.N. photographs and films, which may be borrowed by individuals and institutions without charge (see entry F21). For general reference inquiries, the center maintains a collection of pamphlets on varying subjects such as decolonialization, disarmament, economic and social questions, human rights, and background materials on upcoming major U.N. conferences. These materials are available free of charge upon request. No publications are sold at the center in Washington.

5. For reference assistance, the library maintains a complete set of *U.N. Documents: Index* (monthly with an annual cumulation) and a catalog of *U.N. Publications in Print* (1979–80). Interested individuals may request to be placed on the mailing list to receive the *Weekly News Summary, Objective: Justice* and *U.N. Monthly Chronicle*.

Note: See also entries F21 and H36.

University of Maryland Libraries (College Park Campus) See entry A29

A41 Wesley Theological Seminary Library

1. a. *4400 Massachusetts Avenue, N.W.*
      Washington, D.C. 20016
      (202) 363-0922

b. 8:00 A.M.–10:00 P.M. Monday–Thursday
8:00 A.M.–4:30 P.M. Friday
10:00 A.M.–3:00 P.M. Saturday
6:00 P.M.–10:00 P.M. Sunday

c. The library is open to the public, but borrowing privileges are limited to the faculty, staff, students, and alumni of the seminary, faculty and seminarians of the Washington Theological Consortium, and faculty and graduate students of American University. There is a limited interlibrary loan service, and a self-service, coin-operated photocopier is available.

d. Roland E. Kircher, Director

2–3. Wesleyana, early British and American Methodism, and historical records of the former Methodist Protestant Church are of special note in this theological library of 85,000 monograph volumes and 550 periodical subscriptions. There are less than 200 titles—these being primarily on religious topics—which fall within the purview of Southeast Asian studies. There are a few general works on the Philippines, dating from the early 1900s. Holdings for other countries in the region are insignificant.

4. a. The periodical collection includes only a few titles of interest to Southeast Asianists.

5. The library employs the Dewey Decimal System of classification and a subject/author title card catalog is available. Periodical titles are not part of the catalog but may be found in the *Wesley Theological Seminary Library Periodical List,* edited by Claudia J. Steinbruchner (Washington, D.C., 1978).

Woodrow Wilson International Center for Scholars (WWICS) Library See entry H37

A42 Private Collection

1. a. Frank Joseph Shulman
College Park, Maryland
Mailing Address:
East Asia Collection, McKeldin Library
University of Maryland
College Park, Maryland 20742
(301) 454-2819

2–3. As part of a rapidly growing personal library collection on Asia as a whole, Shulman (Head of the University of Maryland Library's East Asia Collection) owns over 1,000 books and periodicals dealing with Southeast Asia. Areas of particular strength include: Western language bibliographies and other types of reference works on Southeast Asia, and publications on modern Southeast Asian history in English, French, and German. In addition, Shulman maintains very extensive archives (over 400 titles) of Western language newsletters and information bulletins published during the 1960s and the 1970s in the area of East, Southeast, and South Asian studies (e.g., *Kabar Angin/Antara Kita, Philippine Studies Bulletin,* and *Southeast*

Asian Research Materials Group Newsletter) and comprehensive bibliographical files for completed worldwide doctoral research on Asia. An unpublished card catalog (arranged alphabetically by author) exists for the book collection. Many of the newsletters have been listed in Shulman's "Newsletters and Association Bulletins on Asia; An Annotated Guide to Current Academic Resources" (*Asian Studies Professional Review,* vols. 4 [1974–75] and 5 [1975–76]. A revised and greatly expanded version of the guide is gradually being prepared for publication through the University of Michigan. The dissertation files, in turn, form the basis for the magazine, *Doctoral Dissertations on Asia; An Annotated Bibliographical Journal of Current International Research,* as well as for Shulman's "Doctoral Research on Malaya and Malaysia, 1895–1977: A Comprehensive Bibliography and Statistical Overview" in *Malaysian Studies,* edited by John A. Lent (DeKalb, Ill.: Center for Southeast Asian Studies, Northern Illinois University, 1979) and his forthcoming bibliographies *Doctoral Dissertations on Southeast Asia,* for 1968–1975 and 1976–1980. The entire collection is available by appointment for scholarly use at Shulman's home in College Park.

B Archives and Manuscript Repositories

Archives and Manuscript Repositories Entry Format (B)

1. General Information
    a. *address; telephone numbers*
    b. hours of service
    c. conditions of access
    d. reproduction services
    e. name/title of director and heads of relevant divisions

2. Size of Holdings Pertaining to Southeast Asia

3. Description of Holdings Pertaining to Southeast Asia

4. Bibliographic Aids (inventories, calendars, etc.) Facilitating Use of Collection

Introductory Note

The most valuable archival material in the Washington area relates to United States relations with the countries of Southeast Asia. For these materials, the National Archives and Records Service (entry B7) is unsurpassed. Particularly important is the archival material dealing with the Philippines. Also of significance is the vast amount of material dealing with Vietnam to be found not only in the National Archives, but in the Air Force History Office (entry B1), the Army Center of Military History (entry B3), the Marine Corp Archives (entry B6), and the Naval History Center/Operations Archives (entry B9). See also Appendix III.

B1 Air Force History Office

1. a. *Bolling Air Force Base*
        Washington, D.C. 20332
        (202) 767-5746

    b. 9:00 A.M.–5:00 P.M.   Monday–Friday

c. Open to the public. Visitors must have prior visitation clearance, which can be arranged by phone.

d. Photoduplication equipment available.

e. Stanley L. Falk, Historian

2–4.   Staff historians prepare historical studies of the U.S. Air Force; however, many of these are classified. The staff may be of assistance in locating Air Force records. This office also possesses microfilm copies of Air Force archival materials located at the Albert F. Simpson Historical Research Center, Maxwell Air Force Base, Alabama. Most of these materials are classified. The office also maintains a small reference library that contains a collection of mostly classified Air Force historical studies and a collection of selected statements by principal Air Force and Defense Department officials since 1958. Two publications by the office may be of interest to researchers: *United States Air Force History: A Guide to Documentary Sources* (1973), and *United States Air Force History: An Annotated Bibliography,* which is periodically updated. Also useful in working with classified materials is the *Air Force Historical Archives Documentation Classification Guide* (1971).

B2 American Red Cross Archives

1.   a. *431 18th St. N.W.*
Washington, D.C. 20006
(202) 857-3712

b. 8:30 A.M.–4:45 P.M.   Monday–Friday

c. Open to scholars for on-site use.

d. Photoduplication facilities are available.

e. Odette Binns, Archivist

2–3.   Materials in the archives deal with American Red Cross (ARC) activities both in the United States and abroad. Archival materials in the collection are arranged by subject within chronologically determined record groups. The first three record groups: RG1 (1881–1916), RG2 (1917–1934), and RG3 (1935–1946) have been transferred to the National Archives and Records Service. A list of folder captions of these three record groups is available at the American Red Cross Archives. RG4 (1947–1964) and RG5 (1965–present) are located at the ARC archives. Included in some of these record groups are files on numerous disaster-relief operations in Southeast Asia, especially in the Philippines, the Indochina states, and, to a lesser extent, other countries in the region.

4.   Unpublished indexes to all the record groups are available. Information Research Specialist Rudolf A. Clemen, Jr. (202/857-3647) may assist scholars in locating Southeast Asia related materials.

Note: See also entry F3.

B3 Army Center of Military History

1. a. *Pulaski Building*
   20 Massachusetts Avenue, N.W.
   Washington, D.C. 20314
   (202) 272-0317

   b. 8:00 A.M.–4:30 P.M.   Monday–Friday

   c. U.S. citizens may examine unclassified documents and published works without prior permission. Unofficial researchers must have an unofficial researcher's security clearance to examine classified documents. Foreign nationals should obtain permission to visit the center from the Assistant Chief of Staff for Intelligence, Department of the Army, Washington, D.C. 20310.

   d. Photoduplication services are available through the Library of Congress, Washington, D.C. 20540.

   e. Brigadier General James L. Collins, Jr., Chief of Military History
   Dr. David F. Trask, Chief Historian
   Hannah M. Zeidlik, Chief, Historical Records Branch

2–3.   The U.S. Army Center of Military History has custody of approximately: 5,000 unpublished histories dealing with U.S. Army activities, worldwide, 1940–1981; 600 linear feet of reference materials dealing with the U.S. Army, 1776–1981; 600 linear feet of medical records, 1950–1981; 400 linear feet of unpublished sources dealing with Colonial Militia and U.S. Army units, 1631–1981; 37,000 published works and Department of the Army publications, 1776–1981; and 14,000 paintings, drawings, sketches, and cartoons related to military topics.

   Following is a brief description of the materials contained in the collections that deal with Southeast Asia:

   a. About 500 unpublished manuscripts, including a series of histories of the China-Burma-India Theater during World War II, Allied and Japanese operations in World War II, annual histories dealing with U.S. Army operations in the Far East and Pacific Areas, U.S. Military Advisory Group Vietnam, and 184 Japanese monographs covering the World War II period, prepared by former Japanese officers.

   b. 1,480 separate interviews on the Vietnam War, 1965–1973.

   c. Approximately 100 linear feet of historical source materials that include situation reports, reports on U.S. operations in Vietnam and Thailand, U.S. casualty and strength figures for the Vietnam War period, Allied and Japanese operations during World War II, historical background information on the war in Vietnam, Military Advisory Group monthly reports, lessons learned in Vietnam, the Vietnamization program, Pentagon papers, and the U.S. Army historical program in Vietnam.

   d. U.S. Army unit histories and unit history information.

   e. Medical records that cover operations in Vietnam.

   f. The personal papers of General Samuel Williams, chief, M.A.G., 1955–1960 (these papers cannot be made available to researchers without General Williams's permission); copies of the papers of General William C. Westmoreland, commander, U.S. Military Assistance Command, Vietnam, 1964–1968, and commander, U.S. Army, Vietnam; and the papers of Thomas

Thayer, who served as director of the Southeast Asia (SEA) Intelligence and Force Effectiveness Division of the SEA Programs Office under the assistant secretary of defense for systems analysis.

g. A large amount of source materials in the form of working papers accumulated by official historians assigned to write the volumes on the war in Vietnam.

h. Approximately 2,000 paintings, drawings, sketches, and cartoons produced by U.S. Army artists in Vietnam, 1966–1972.

4. There is a card index file to the major collections. It is relatively easy to locate Southeast Asia related materials through the use of this index. There is also the *Guide to Japanese Monographs and Japanese Studies on Manchuria, 1945–1960,* and two volumes of a proposed five-volume series entitled *Catalog and Index to Historical Manuscripts, 1940–1966.* Volume 1 covers histories prepared by Headquarters, War Department and Department of the Army, and Volume 2 covers studies prepared by the Army Service Forces. When completed, Volume 3 will cover the technical services; Volume 4, overseas operations; and Volume 5, the Armies, Army Ground Forces, and Army Air Forces. A guide to the Vietnam interviews is also being prepared. Requests concerning the guides and catalogs should be directed to the U.S. Army Center of Military History, Washington, D.C. 20314.

The brochure "Publications of the U.S. Army Center of Military History" contains information on the official histories published by the center. Requests for copies of this brochure should be directed to the U.S. Army Center of Military History, Washington, D.C. 20314.

The U.S. Army Military History Institute, Carlisle Barracks, Pennsylvania 17013, a principal part of the center, is also a custodian of historical source materials on Southeast Asia. Inquiries concerning its holdings should be directed to that agency.

B4 Church of Jesus Christ of the Latter Day Saints (Mormon Church)—Genealogical Libraries

1. *Annandale Branch Genealogical Library*
   3900 Howard Street
   Annandale, Virginia 22033
   (703) 256-5518

   9:30 A.M.–10:00 P.M.   Tuesday, Wednesday, Friday
   Marge Bell, Librarian

   Oakton Branch Genealogical Library
   2719 Hunter Mill Road
   Oakton, Virginia 22124
   (703) 281-1836

   9:30 A.M.–2:00 P.M.   Monday, Wednesday, Friday
   7:00 P.M.–10:00 P.M.   Wednesday
   Mimi Stevenson, Librarian

Silver Spring Branch Genealogical Library
500 Randolph Road
Silver Spring, Maryland 20904
(301) 622-0088

9:00 A.M.–5:00 P.M.   Monday, Wednesday
7:00 P.M.–10:00 P.M.   Tuesday, Wednesday, Thursday
9:00 A.M.–5:00 P.M.   first and third Saturday of each month
Barton Howell, Librarian

c. Open to the public. The Genealogical Society of the Church of Jesus Christ of the Latter Day Saints is headquartered at 50 East North Temple, Salt Lake City, Utah 84150, (801) 531-2323. The records collected and maintained there can be obtained on loan by researchers through any of the church's three genealogical libraries in the Washington, D.C., area for the price of mailing and handling. Delivery can take up to six weeks.

d. Microfilm readers and reader-printers are available.

2–3.   The Genealogical Society has undertaken a massive program of microfilming religious and civil records in archives throughout the world. The collection totals well over 1 million rolls of film and is growing at the rate of 5,000 rolls per month. Southeast Asian holdings are small but include some nineteenth- and early-twentieth-century data from Indonesia, Malaysia, Philippines, and Vietnam.

4.   No comprehensive index to the microfilm collection is available. A computerized catalog was under development in 1982.

Folklife Program (Smithsonian Institution)—Music and Recorded Sound Collection See entry D2

Howard University—Founders Library—Bernard B. Fall Collection See entry A21

International Communication Agency—Archive See entry K21

B5 Library of Congress—Manuscript Division

1.   a. Madison Building, First Floor
Library of Congress
Washington, D.C. 20540
(202) 287–5383

b. 8:30 A.M.–5:00 P.M.   Monday–Saturday

c. Open to serious researchers with proper identification. Registration is required. Restrictions have been placed on certain materials.

d. Excepting those materials under restriction, most manuscripts may be photocopied for research. The room is equipped with a copy machine and a microfilm reader-printer. The LC's Photoduplication Service (202/287-5654) provides a full range of copying services. Permission is required to use cameras in the reading room. Microfilm reproductions of most manuscripts are available through interlibrary loan. Publication of manuscripts requires prior clearance. The division provides an explanatory leaflet on copying and publication on request.

e. Paul T. Heffron, Acting Chief
David Wigdor, Specialist in 20th Century Political History

2–3. The division's holdings consist of approximately 10,000 collections, some of which number more than a million items. Included are presidential papers and papers of other government officials, family papers, and records of some nongovernmental organizations. Materials on Southeast Asia are few and far between. Given the fact that no geographic or subject headings are available to assist the researcher in locating items, some digging will be required.

Scholars will want to search the following obvious categories for Southeast Asia materials: presidential papers, papers of the secretaries of state, diplomats, officers of the armed forces, scholars, journalists, and missionaries. Here, specific names will be required.

In addition to the above, there are undoubtedly other collections that hold materials of interest to Southeast Asianists. The Naval Historical Foundation collection is one of these. Included in this collection are the following:

Belknap, George E., paper for 1857–1903, subject: the Asiatic fleet.
Carpenter, Dudley Newcomb, papers, 1897–1901, battle of Manila Bay and materials on Singapore.
Julian, Charles, papers, 1897–1899, battle of Manila Bay.
Kaiser, Louis Anthony, papers, 1899–1901, the Philippine insurrection.
Konter, Richard W., 1920, article, "Sinking of the USS Charleston in the Philippines (1899)."
Manila Bay Society, records, 1901–1933, correspondence, minutes, financial records, programs, and photos.
Strauss, Joseph, 1881–1922, correspondence on the defense of the Philippines.
Taussig, Edward, 1867–1900, includes description of battle with insurgents in the Philippines (1900).
Welsh, George R., 1771–1851, includes journals for 1843–1845, with extensive commentary on negotiations, and visits of special agent Joseph Balestier in Cochin, China, Siam, and Borneo.

4. The following finding aids are available in the Manuscript Reading Room: *Catalog of Collections*—a two part catalog: "old catalog" and "new catalog"—which provides basic descriptive information for cataloged collections, including broad subject content; *Master Record of Manuscript Collections,* providing current bibliographic data on all collections in the Manuscript Division; published registers that provide detailed information for approximately 1,000 collections; and special printouts from the division's Master Record of Manuscript Collections, listing collections under a variety of areas of specialization, including Hispanic, where Philippine materials may be found.

Additional aids are described in the division's leaflet of catalogs, indexes, and finding aids. Scholars should be advised that no cases or papers are allowed into the reading room. The guard will direct you to a locker where personal items can be stored while you are working in the reading room.

B6 Marine Corps Historical Center

1. a. *Washington Navy Yard, Building 58*
   9th and M Streets, S.E.
   Washington, D.C. 20374
   (202) 433-3439 (Archives Section)

   b. 8:00 A.M.–4:30 P.M. Monday–Friday

   c. Open to researchers. Some buildings are classified or otherwise restricted.

   d. Photoreproduction facilities are available.

   e. E. H. Simmons, Director, 433-3574
   Henry I. Shaw, Jr., Chief Historian, 433-3839
   Benis M. Frank, Director, Oral History Program, 433-3840
   Joyce E. Bonnett, Head, Archives Section, 433-3439
   Charles A. Wood, Head, Collections Section, 433-3396

2. Southeast Asia related holdings are to be found in three subdivisions of the Historical Center, including the Archives, the Oral History Collection, and the Personal Papers Collection. While it is not possible to specify the quantity of materials to be found, holdings are substantial.

3. The Archives Section is the repository for official Marine Corps operational records. The record inventory comprises approximately 4,000 cubic feet, consisting chiefly of combat operational reports, plans, command diaries and chronologies, after-action reports, and related records dating from the early 1900s. Materials for World War II and Vietnam are considerable. Records are on a continuous basis, transferred to the Government Services Administration's Washington National Records Service at Suitland, Maryland, and eventually go to the National Archives in Washington.

   The Marine Corps Oral History Collection consists of over 6,000 interviews conducted for the Marine Corps Oral History Program. The collection includes both bound transcripts of in-depth interviews and the tapes of those interviews, as well as classified and unclassified interview tapes relating to Marine Corps operations in the Vietnam War, debriefings, presentations, and press conferences.

   Classified and unclassified Vietnam related tapes are held by the Archives Section, but may be audited on tape recorders in the Oral History office, where an index of all interviews in the collection is available for use by researchers.

   The Personal Papers Collection contains some Philippine and Vietnam related materials, the most noteworthy being as follows:

   PC 1: Henry Clay Cochrane papers (1863–1905). This collection contains about 86 correspondence files, including one file on the Philippine Expedition. Cochrane served as District Commander of Peninsula of Cavite, Philippines (1900).

   PC 93: Robert W. Huntington papers (1861–1900). A collection of holograph letters and a voluminous scrapbook of printed materials dealing with Huntington's action in the Spanish American War (Philippine materials) comprise this collection.

PC 331: Harold Kinman papers (1898–1903). Thirty-one holographic letters written by Private Kinman are contained here. The letters chronicle his participation in the Marine action against the insurgent Aguinaldo in the Philippines.

PC 464: Keith B. McCutcheon (1937–1971). This is a significant collection that provides insight into the role and mission of Marine Corps aviation during the Korean and Vietnam conflicts. Many top policy proposals and decisions pertaining to these two areas of Marine Corps involvement are explored.

PC 486: Victor H. Krulak (1934–1968). Some 160 xerographic copies of letters, reports, memoranda, speeches, transcripts, and newspaper articles dating from November 1952 to May 1977, are included here. Dealing primarily with General Krulak's far-ranging activities during the Vietnam War, a small portion of the early entries record the general's views of the role of the Marine Corps, while a similar portion of the more recent entries reflect his position as editor-journalist for the Copley News Service.

PC 511: Wallace M. Greene, Jr. (1930–1967). This large collection of a former Commandant of the Marine Corps contains over 26 linear feet of official and personal correspondence, daily journals, subject files, speeches, trip itineraries, and other documentary materials. The bulk of the materials reflect General Greene's tenure as Commandant of the Marine Corps from 1964 to 1967. The collection contains significant Vietnam materials.

PC 593: Barbara J. Dulinsky. The personal recollections of the first woman Marine to serve on active duty in Vietnam during the period of hostilities, 1967–1968, form the basis for this collection.

The Marine Corps Art Collection is discussed under entry C5.

The Still Photographic Archives is discussed under entry F14.

4. Researchers should consult the *Guide to the Marine Corps Historical Center* (1979), *Marine Corps Personal Papers Collection Catalog* (1980), and *Marine Corps Historical Publications in Print 1978.*

B7 National Archives and Records Service (NARS) (General Services Administration)

1. a. *8th and Pennsylvania Avenue, N.W.*
  Washington, D.C. 20408
  (202) 523-3218 (General Information)
  (202) 523-3232 (Central Research Room)
  (202) 523-3285 (Microfilm Research Room)

 b. Central Research Room and Microfilm Reading Room:
  8:45 A.M.–10:00 P.M. Monday–Friday
  8:45 A.M.–5:00 P.M. Saturday

 Branch Research Rooms:
 Hours vary, although most rooms are open 8:45 A.M.–5:00 P.M. Monday–Friday

 c. Open to all serious researchers with a National Archives researcher identification card, obtainable from the Central Reference Division, Room 200-B.

 d. Extensive photocopying and microfilming services are available.

 e. Robert M. Warner, Archivist

2–3.   For the researcher interested in modern Southeast Asia, the National Archives and Records Service offers a wealth of material resources. Regardless of one's discipline, the Archives is sure to hold something of interest. Not only is it one of the major centers in the world of source materials on the world wars, but it contains hundreds of thousands of reports and other documents created by United States Government agencies filled with information on the politics, economy, society, and culture of every part of Southeast Asia over the past century. As the official respository for the records of the United States Government, NARS has collected more than 3 billion records (over 1 million cubic feet of material). The sheer volume of material dictates that the scholar devote careful attention to research design before ever setting foot in the archives. The following comments may be helpful.

It should be stressed that the National Archives is not a library: that is, most materials cannot be located in an item-index or catalog. The holdings are organized into over 450 "record groups" (RGs), each stemming from the records of an individual unit of the United States government, or in a few cases, from other sources pertinent to American civilization. To conduct research intelligently, one should first investigate the administrative history of those United States government departments and agencies that deal with one's research subject.

The National Archives issues a host of published finding aids to assist in research investigations. These aids should be used together for greatest effect:

(1) *Guide to the National Archives of the United States (1974).* A new edition was in preparation in 1982. For $12.50, the *Guide* is a real steal and something any social science department could well afford to have on its reference shelf. The *Guide* provides indispensable information of many kinds, including a thumbnail sketch of the administrative history of each United States government unit; data on the quantity, dates, and formats of the records; and applicable restrictions. It also has an index and a list of record groups arranged by record group number. It is constantly being updated in looseleaf-binder form for the archivists' use. This binder copy can be consulted in the NARS Library.

(2) Published finding aids (inventories, preliminary inventories, and special lists) to some record groups are available free upon request in room 6-G. For some record groups, these aids will be out of print, while for other record groups will be unavailable. The finding aids are listed in the *Select List of Publications of the National Archives and Records Service,* also available free upon request in Room G-6. All existing finding aids are available for consultation in Room 200-B. The researcher is advised first to pick up whatever aids are of interest from Room G-6. Those needed but not available can be consulted in Room 200-B. A fourth aid, the *Reference Information Paper,* provides a subject-oriented guide to materials in various record groups. These are also listed in the *Select List* (SL).

(3) The publication *National Archives Microfilm Publications (1974)* gives essential information on the thousands of microfilm publications now for sale or available from the Archives. These include all of the Department of State's central file up to 1910 (and many later items), as well as vast quantities of Japanese records—many relating to Southeast Asia—captured at the end of World War II. It should be noted that NARS microfilm can

be ordered by interlibrary loan from the NARS regional archives and that with each body of microfilm comes a pamphlet describing the material. Unfortunately, these pamphlets are not listed anywhere.

By shuttling back and forth between the above-mentioned publications, you can bring your research into sharp focus before ever setting foot in the Archives. On the spot, you should begin in Room 200-B to determine whether there are any pertinent finding aids that were unobtainable through the mail. From there, proceed next door to Room 200-C to speak with an archivist, from whom you may learn that certain record groups, containing valuable material for your purposes, were overlooked in your initial planning. From Room 200-C, proceed to the appropriate division or branch that has charge over the record group in which you are interested. Here, an archivist will assist you with your research. Many of these individuals know the record groups extremely well and can be of tremendous help. Often the archivist can provide you with unpublished finding aids such as card files and special indexes. Be prepared to wait for an archivist, as they are often in short supply if several researchers descend on the division at once. Mondays and Fridays seem to be the busiest days; therefore, bring along some related work to occupy the waiting time, and when the archivist is available, be ready with specific and direct questions.

Although most of the records in the National Archives are open to researchers, some materials are restricted. In addition to general restrictions pertaining to security-classified nuclear energy, business, personal, medical, and investigatory matters, agencies and donors put specific restrictions on materials. In case of doubt, an inquiry in writing or by telephone to the appropriate branch can save much time traveling to study restricted materials. A useful, general discussion on restrictions can be found in the introduction to the *Guide to the National Archives of the United States*.

The comments on Freedom-of-Information (FOI) requests preceding the United States Government Agencies section "K" can be supplemented here by noting that the Freedom-of-Information Act does not apply to records of the legislative and judicial branches. A scholar should check whether a document has already been released under another FOI request. Here, as elsewhere, researchers should maintain lists of dates, file numbers, and authors of withheld documents to make their FOI requests as detailed as possible. A researcher may also request NARS to return a document or group of materials to the originating government unit for clearance. The chances are that the records will be cleared. Both of the above processes can be lengthy.

To summarize, do as much of the preliminary work as possible outside the Archives. Once in the National Archives, proceed to the appropriate branch(es) only when you have developed specific objectives.

Research cards and access to the holdings of the NARS are obtainable without reference to nationality. Those who do not speak English fluently would do well to bring along an interpreter.

Below are summaries of some of the record groups that contain materials relating to Southeast Asia, categorized according to the archival division or branch that has administrative authority over them. The descriptions that follow should in no sense be considered comprehensive; they may, however, suggest avenues of inquiry for the interested scholar.

CIVIL ARCHIVES DIVISION

Daniel Goggin, Director
(202) 523-3108

Diplomatic Branch
Milton Gustafson, Chief
(202) 523-3174

RG 11: General Records of the United States Government. The files on international treaties, executive agreements and related records, 1942–1969, contain documents related to Southeast Asia. See Preliminary Inventory (PI) 159.

RG 43: Records of International Conferences, Commissions and Expositions. Some materials dealing with Southeast Asia may be located in the records of post–World War II conferences (1945–1953), records relating to international expositions and exhibitions (1856–1963). Most records in this group dated after 1949 are restricted and may be used only with the permission of the Department of State. See PI 76 (1955) and its 1965 Supplement.

RG 59: General Records of the Department of State. This is the principal archival source for documentation of United States diplomatic history and foreign relations. Southeast Asia related materials are substantial.

One of the potentially more interesting subgroups of materials within RG 59 is the one concerning Records of the Philippine and Southeast Asia Division, 1944–1952. The Philippine Affairs Division and Division of Southeast Asia Affairs were under the Office of Far Eastern Affairs and were responsible for the conduct of United States relations with the Republic of the Philippines, Thailand, all American controlled islands in the Pacific, and—jointly with the appropriate divisions in the Office of European Affairs—all British, Dutch, French, and Portuguese possessions (including those that subsequently became independent) in Southeast Asia. The two divisions were consolidated into the Philippine and Southeast Asia Division in 1940. The primary function of the division was to effect, through long-range and day-to-day action, the plans and over-all policies formulated by the Office of Far Eastern Affairs.

The records consist of memoranda, notes of conversations, draft addresses, correspondence, position papers, policy statements, telegrams and staff studies. There is a considerable amount of material relating to nationalist and anti-colonial resistance movements in Indochina, Indonesia, and Malaya. Of particular interest is the documentation pertaining to Ho Chi Minh and communist activities in Indochina. Most of the records are in the 1944–1953 period. However, a few scattered documents date back to 1929. The material is contained in 20 archives boxes. Total volume equals 8.6 cubic feet. Box lists are the only finding aids.

RG 59 contains the Records of the Joint Preparatory Committee on Philippine Affairs (entries 729–735). The purpose of this committee was to study United States–Philippine trade relations after the granting of independence. Records began in April 1943 and consist of minutes and memoranda of the committee's meetings.

Of interest to scholars of the Philippines are the Records of the U.S. Commission to the Philippine Islands. These records began circa January 1899 and consist of minutes, dispatches, letters, telegrams to and from the commission, and instructions from the Secretary of State. The commission records also contain the manuscript, "El Archipielago Filipino, 1899," prepared by the Society of Jesus in the Philippine Islands. This 1,740-page volume (in Spanish) relates general conditions in the islands.

RG 59 contains a staggering number of foreign-service inspection reports, lists of diplomatic instructions and dispatches, lists of notes to and from foreign missions, and consular dispatches. The following is in no way a complete listing, but is intended only as an illustration of the nature of this material.

Consular Dispatches:

Bangkok (June 30, 1856–June 26, 1906) 11 vols.; Brunei (June 27, 1856–March 5, 1868) 1 vol.; Batavia (September 25, 1818–July 23, 1906) 13 vols.; Manila (March 21, 1817–September 7, 1899) 13 vols.; Padang (August 23, 1853–April 20, 1898) 2 vols.; Saigon (March 10, 1889–July 6, 1906) 1 vol.; Singapore (October 31, 1833–July 20, 1906) 26 vols.

Foreign Service Inspection Reports, 1906–1939:

Burma—Rangoon 1907, 1909, 1915, 1917, 1921, 1923, 1925, 1930, 1935.

French Indochina—Saigon (Consulate) 1907, 1909, 1911, 1913, 1915, 1921, 1923, 1925, 1935.

Union of Malaya—Penang (Consulate) 1909, 1911, 1912, 1915, 1921, 1925, 1932, 1935; Singapore (Consulate) 1907, 1909, 1911, 1912, 1915, 1921, 1922, 1926, 1930, 1935.

British North Borneo—Sandarkan (Consulate) 1907, 1909, 1911, 1913.

Siam—Bangkok (Legation) 1926, 1935; Bangkok (Consulate) 1907, 1909, 1911, 1913, 1915, 1921, 1925, 1935.

Netherlands East Indies—Batavia 1907, 1909, 1911, 1913, 1915, 1921, 1926, 1935; Makassar (Consulate) 1909, 1911, 1913, 1915, 1921; Medan 1921, 1922, 1925, 1930, 1935; Padang 1909, 1911, 1913, 1915; Samarang 1909, 1911, 1913; Surabaja 1922, 1926, 1930, 1935, 1938, 1939.

These reports often contain commentary on social, political, and economic conditions within the country or territory served by the consulate. In addition, a good many of these reports are accompanied by maps of various types. These are described in the finding aids for this record group.

Finally, mention should be made of the large number of intelligence and research reports prepared by the Office of Strategic Services (OSS), which are held in RG 59. The following provides some examples of the types of reports included.

Burma: "Burma's Leaders Concern for the Future" (July 1945) 3 p.; "Biographies of Persons in Burma" (May 1946) 67 p.; "The Communist Party's Declining Influence in Burma's Anti Fascist League" (October 1946).

Indochina: "Biographical Information on Prominent Nationalist Leaders in French Indochina" (October 1945), 91 p.; "The Potential of World Communism: Indochina" (August 1949), 23 p.; "Brief on Issues in Dispute Between France and Vietnam" (March 1947), 5 p.

Indonesia: "Political Parties and Movements in the Netherlands East Indies" (February 1945) 206 p.; "The Cabinets of the Republic of Indonesia" (November 1945), 66 p.; "Sumatra in the Indonesian Crisis" (May 1946), 55 p.

Malaya: "British Malaya: A Social Political Economic Survey" (June 1942), 108 p.; "Programs of Japan in Malaya" (October 1945), 202 p.; "Singapore Water Supply" (n.d.), 6 p.

Philippines: "Philippine Agriculture Under Japanese Control" (August 1942), 37 p.

Thailand: "Trends Toward Democracy in Thailand" (October 1944), 17 p.; "Extent of Economic Recovery in Siam" (January 1948), 122 p.; "Biographical Information on Key Individuals in Present Day Thailand" (July 1945), 138 p.

Reports after 1947 are classified. Clearance may be requested, but it could take up to a year for it to be completed.

For RG 59, see the finding aids PI 157 and SL 37.

RG 84: Records of the Foreign Service Posts of the Department of State. This record group duplicates to a large extent RG 59, but is not identical. RG 84 contains some dispatches and instructions missing from RG 59 and also has substantial amounts of correspondence with local governments, businesses, and individuals—material not sent to the department. Very often the consuls dealt with matters far beyond their defined responsibilities; therefore, wading through this material can be an enlightening endeavor, though substantial effort is required. The following covers foreign-service posts in the Southeast Asia region.

Records of Consulates by Country:

Burma—Rangoon (1891–1912) 9 shelf feet.

French Indochina—Saigon (1889–1940) 40 shelf feet.

Union of Malaya—Penang (1885–1921) 2 shelf feet; Singapore (1849–1935) 56 shelf feet.

Siam—Bangkok (1856–1941) 45 shelf feet.

British North Borneo—Sandarkan (1904–1912) 2 shelf feet.

Netherlands East Indies—Batavia (1830–1942) 71 shelf feet; Makassar (1917–1922) 1 shelf foot; Medan (1919–1942) 2 shelf feet; Padang (1893–1915) 3 shelf feet; Semarang (1885–1913) 2 shelf feet; Surabaja (1865–1941) 6 shelf feet.

For RG 84, see the findings aids PI 60 and SL9.

RG 256: Records of the American Commission to Negotiate Peace. This record group contains material pertaining to the effects of World War I on various regions and countries of the world, including Southeast Asia. Included are brief papers dealing with the Netherlands East Indies, French Indochina, Siam, and Singapore. Entry 22 consists of 14 annotated maps of the Pacific islands, showing the colonial status of various islands (1880–1919), American interests in the Pacific, and communications lines in the region. Also included is a photostat map with an accompanying legend that shows areas dominated by the various naval powers. For RG 256 see finding aids PI 68 and PI 89.

Industrial and Social Branch
Franklin Burch, Chief
(202) 523-3119
8:45 A.M.–5:00 P.M. Monday–Friday

RG 14: Records of the United States Railroad Administration 1917–

1945. The files of the director general contain some material on railroads in French Indochina and the Dutch East Indies.

RG 20: Records of the Office of the Special Adviser to the President on Foreign Trade. The following entries may contain information on Southeast Asian countries. Entry 16 holds records for the period 1934–1935, relating to commodity production and trade information; included are published reports of the Bureau of Agricultural Economics, Department of Agriculture, and the Bureau of Foreign and Domestic Commerce, Department of Commerce. Entry 17, which has records relating to country trade information, contains lists of trade tables used in country studies; trade bulletins and circulars; consular reports and commercial attaché reports on economic conditions abroad; analysis of proposed trade agreements, copies of trade agreements, and newspaper clippings. Material is arranged alphabetically by country.

RG 23: Records of the Coast and Geodetic Survey. Reports on earthquake and seismological registers from foreign countries (1899–1948), are contained here. There seems to be little material relating to Southeast Asia, though the Survey did assign a number (Cutter's list of Geographic Numbers) to the Philippines.

RG 28: Records of the Post Office Department. This RG includes information on the postal service in the Philippines, 1900–1901; material on postal agreements with Southeast Asian countries; and records on international congresses and conventions, 1857–1929.

For RG 28, see finding aid PI 128.

RG 29: Records of the Bureau of the Census. The alphabetic subject file of the geographic division contains a significant amount of material on Filipino naturalization, covering the period, 1898–1940.

The subject file of the chief clerk (changed to Administrative Service Division) contains material on the Philippine census for the period 1900–1953 and measures four shelf feet.

General Subject File, 1935–1942, is made up of material related to the compiling, editing, and tabulation of census data for the territories and island possessions of the United States, and to the collection of supplementary information on racial characteristics and citizen status of territorial population.

Entry 254, Miscellaneous Records Relating to Territorial Census, 1900–1938, includes an index to occupations for the Philippines census of 1900 and instructions for the Philippine census of 1938.

RG 32: Records of the United States Shipping Board. This record group contains material on steamship lines operating between the United States and various parts of Southeast Asia, commercial shipping records, and trade routes in the region.

RG 40: General Records of the Department of Commerce. The correspondence files of the Secretary of Commerce may contain material on commercial activities and trade with Southeast Asian countries.

RG 81: Records of the United States Tariff Commission. Entry four contains some printed reports on foreign tariff laws, correspondence concerning discrimination in tariffs, copies of consular reports, and foreign tariff laws.

RG 90: Records of the Public Health Service. Within this record group are some reports on diseases such as cholera, plague, smallpox, malaria, leprosy, and dysentery. Also included is some information on sanitation and water supply.

RG 151: Records of the Bureau of Foreign and Domestic Commerce. The records are comprised of reports and other communications from commercial attachés, foreign offices, and trade commissioners. Records of the Office of International Trade include some material of interest. Monthly reports of trade commissioners attached to U.S. consulates contain data that include statistics on foreign trade in the Southeast Asia region. There is also a map of the Dutch East Indies and Borneo, issued by the Petroleum Division, showing proven oil fields, prospective fields, and facilities for handling petroleum.

RG 178: Records of the United States Maritime Commission. Material relating to merchant shipping and trade with Southeast Asia—including information on trade routes, merchant-marine casualties during World War II, freight tariffs and rates, exports-imports, and the movement of vessels and cargo—can be found in these records.

RG 234: Records of the Reconstruction Finance Corporation. Included are records of United States businesses acquiring strategic and critical materials throughout the world during World War II.

RG 262: Records of the Foreign Broadcast Intelligence Service. This record group contains a number of translations of monitored foreign-radio broadcasts. The following is a list of radio stations in Southeast Asia under which transcripts are filed.

Bandung (October 1945–December 1946), Bangkok (September 1941–December 1944), Batavia (September 1941–December 1946), Djakarta (May–July 1943 and December 1943), Hanoi (January–May and November–December 1946), Indonesia, Voice of Free (November–December 1946), Makassar (March–November 1943 and May–December 1946), Malaya (August 1946), Manila (March 1942–January 1945 and July–December 1946), Philippines, Voice of the New (May 1942), Rangoon (November 1943, September–October 1945, and April–October 1946), Saigon (September 1940–December 1946), Samakki (June 1943), Singapore (January 1942–December 1946), Suva (November 1943), Voice of Leyte (October 1944–January 1945), Voice of Luzon (January–February 1945).

Judicial and Fiscal Branch
Clarence Lyons, Chief
(202) 523-3059
8:45 A.M.–5:00 P.M.   Monday–Friday

RG 36: Records of the Bureau of Customs. Among other records are those of the collector of customs (1789–1954). These document the sailings of vessels from Southeast Asian ports to the United States, and include cargo manifests, crew and passenger lists, import books, and information concerning the entrance and clearance of vessels.

RG 39: Records of the Bureau of Custom Accounts. Included may be Treasury Department correspondence concerning fiscal conditions in Southeast Asian countries and diplomatic and consular reports on financial conditions, local currency, commerce, industries, and other subjects.

RG 56: General Records of the Department of Treasury. Correspondence and monthly deposit lists for the Philippine Islands and Puerto Rico can be found here, as well as information on tariff funds for the 1900–1907 period.

RG 60: General Records of the Department of Justice. Files accumulated by the Assistant Attorney General in adjudicating 542 Spanish treaty claims cases in 1901, many of which relate to the Philippines, comprise this record group.

RG 85: Records of Immigration and Naturalization Service. The general immigration files (1882–1952) contain the personal records of Southeast Asians applying for naturalization and the decisions in these cases. The records may contain other scattered information on Southeast Asia.

RG 104: Records of the Bureau of the Mint. Reports on the value of foreign currency and on gold and silver in foreign countries—including Southeast Asia for some periods—are to be found here.

RG 216: Records of the Office of Censorship. Within the administrative subject files is a box of material relating to censorship in liberated and occupied territories (Philippines). Also included are some Asia-Pacific program reports. Material on Burma, Malaya, and Singapore may be found in the British censorship materials.

RG 217: Records of the United States General Accounting Office. One can find some correspondence and reports on customs regulations in Southeast Asia.

RG 220: Records of Presidential Committees, Commissions and Boards. Material relating to Southeast Asia may be found in the numerous classified group, which includes records of: the President's Committee on Foreign Aid, 1947–1948; the President's Commission on Foreign Economic Policy, 1953–1954; the President's Commission on Immigration and Naturalization, 1952–1953; the President's Commission on International Trade and Investment Policy; the President's Committee to Study the United States Military Assistance Program, 1958–1959; and the President's Task Force on International Developments, 1969–1970.

Legislative and Natural Resources Branch
Trudy H. Peterson, Chief
(202) 523-3238
8:45 A.M.–5:00 P.M.   Monday–Friday

RG 7: Records of the Bureau of Entomology and Plant Quarantine. Correspondence files may contain documents and reports relating to insect control and prevention of plant diseases in Southeast Asian countries.

RG 16: Records of the Office of the Secretary of Agriculture. Materials relating to agriculture in Southeast Asia, 1893–1966, are here.

RG 46: Records of the United States Senate. Included are records of the Senate Committee on Immigration, the Senate Commerce Committee and Foreign Relations Committee, and the Territories and Insular Affairs Committee, 1933–1940.

RG 48: Records of the Office of the Secretary of the Interior. This is one of several RGs in this branch with significant material on the Philippines. The central classified files contain 22 files on the Philippines covering the period 1937–1953. Some of the titles are: administration, bonds, suits, duties and taxes, roads, postage stamps, aviation, commerce, lands, and inquiries concerning residence. A smaller amount of material is located in the records of patents and miscellaneous division. This small file deals with the Philippines prior to 1907.

RG 54: Records of the Bureau of Plant Industry, Soils and Agricultural Engineering (1881–1953). Within this RG are materials relating to plant pathology, agricultural technology, tropical plants, crop diseases, and plant nutrition; some of the materials may deal with Southeast Asia.

RG 70: Records of the Bureau of Mines. Included are materials on petroleum and fuel (1905–1945), foreign activities (1913–1945), and reports of the Bureau of Foreign and Domestic Commerce (1920–1925).

RG 83: Records of the Bureau of Agricultural Economics. Contains records relating to international organizations, committees and conferences on postwar foreign relief requirements. Also included in this RG is the atlas, *Geography of the World Agriculture,* which includes several maps of Java and the Philippines prior to 1919.

RG 126: Records of the Office of Territories. Included are the records of the U.S. High Commissioner to the Philippine Islands, which functioned from November 1935 to July 1946. The records of the Manila Office, 1935–1946 (6 feet) include letters, memoranda, radiograms, directives, reports, and other documents pertaining to the initiation, planning, administration, and management of all phases of the operation of the office. Records relate primarily to budgetary matters, office personnel, and public relations. Some of the correspondence is with Philippine officials.

Records of the Washington (Commission) Office, 1942–1948 (5 feet) include letters, memoranda, directives, orders, instructions, plans, reports, and other records pertaining to the operation of the Office in Washington, D.C., after its evacuation from Manila. Included are files concerning the Alien Property Custodian, the sugar industry, immigration, postwar planning, claims, rehabilitation, and reoccupation.

Another interesting subset of data within the records of the commissioner is the set of records concerning persons interned in the Philippine Islands by the Japanese military government during World War II. Included are correspondence and form reports concerning internees, form letters from internees, and some material giving information about living conditions in the internment camps (3 feet). See PI 151 for more information.

RG 233: Records of the United States House of Representatives. Materials concerning Southeast Asia are to be found in the bills, resolutions, records, and documents, as well as in the proceedings and hearings of the various committees. In addition to the obvious committees such as Foreign Affairs, those interested in the Philippines should investigate the records of the Committee on Territories, 1825–1947, and its successor committees—the Committee on Public Lands, 1805–1951, and the Committee on Interior and Insular Affairs, 1951—.

RG 350: Records of the Bureau of Insular Affairs. A large part of the bureau's records concern the Philippine Islands, which represented its one continuous responsibility and were a large island group with many and complex problems. The administrative powers of the bureau were primarily to gather information, for the secretary of war, to advise him, and to formulate, recommend, and execute policies. The bureau purchased and shipped supplies for the Philippines, appointed persons in the United States to the Philippine Civil Service, gathered statistics on insular imports and exports, shipping, and immigration, disbursed all Philippine funds in the United States, handled matters relative to the sale of Philippine bonds, reviewed the receipts and expenditures of the Philippine government, and performed numerous other tasks.

This is a "monster" record group of 1,632 cubic feet, having two main, numerically arranged, series of files. The shorter of these series—the customs files—contains something over 2,000 files and the larger—the general classified files—consists of some 28,000 files. It should be pointed out that one large file may contain up to 1,000 entries. However, more important than the quantity of Philippine related material is the fact that this record group is a truly unique resource, containing materials found nowhere else in the world.

In addition to the above mentioned files, which contain material related to more than one island possession, a large number of files deal specifically with the Philippines. Some examples follow:

Proclamations of the Governor General of the Philippine Islands, 1925–1935 (2 feet); Acts of the United States Philippine Commission, 1900–1907 (3 feet); Acts of the Legislature of the Philippine Islands, 1907–1935 (5 feet); House and Senate Bills of the Philippine Legislature, 1928–1935 (20 feet); Customs Acts Relating to the Philippine Islands, 1897–1935 (1 foot); Galley Proofs of Manuscript "Philippine Insurrection against the United States," 1906 (2 feet); "Manifesto" of Apolinario Mabini Regarding American Occupation of the Philippines, 1916 (2 inches); Photographic Prints: Philippine Islands, 1898–1935 (20 feet) (Subject index in separate file); Lantern Slides: Philippine Islands, 1898–1939 (5 feet); Manuscript Reports of the Philippine Commission, 1900–1915 (108 vols., 36 feet); Manuscript Reports of the Governor General of the Philippines, 1916–1940 (118 vols., 39 feet).

In addition to the above-mentioned files, the record group also contains the records of the Philippine Exposition Board (4 files) and the records of the Manila Railroad Company (3 files).

The general classified files are served by a set of record cards that contain abstracts of each of the 28,000 files. The cards give cross references to the subjects. In addition, consult SL 2 and PI 130.

MILITARY ARCHIVES DIVISION

Gary Ryan, Acting Director
(202) 523-3340

Modern Military Branch
Robert Wolfe, Chief
(202) 523-3340
8:45 A.M.–5:00 P.M.   Monday–Friday

RG 18: Records of the Army Air Force. This record group contains security-classified "foreign files" of World War II for the China, Burma, India theater. Materials deal with air transport, supply of equipment and spare parts, lend-lease supplies, strategies, and training. Two documents of interest are a "Signal Plan, U.S. Army Forces, China, Burma, and India," which outlines methods of procedures for communication, code transmission, and maintenance, and "Shipments of Aircraft to the China, Burma, India Theater," accompanied by photos.

Included are several binders of material dealing with the Philippines, including one on air fields in the Philippines. There is a smaller amount of material on airfields in the Netherlands East Indies and New Guinea.

RG 77: Records of the Office of the Chief Engineer. Records of World War II army mapping activities—some of which may deal with Southeast Asia—are located here.

RG 107: Records of the Office of the Secretary of War. Records of the War Department, covering World War II to 1947, including special reports of the Joint and Combined Chiefs of Staff (1940–1945) and miscellaneous speeches, statements, and newspaper clippings (1940–1945), can be found in this group. Also included are records relating to policy and general administration of the military units in the island possessions, including the Philippines, as well as correspondence received and sent concerning representatives there, civilian personnel records, and records of the planning branch.

RG 160: Records of Headquarters Army Service Forces. These contain Southeast Asia material related to intelligence planning and logistics and supply operations for overseas theaters, 1941–1946.

RG 165: Records of the War Department General and Special Staffs. This is a very large body of material that merits serious attention by scholars of Southeast Asia. Of interest are the records of the Military Intelligence Service, Far East Branch, 1926–1946 (3 feet); materials included in the general records of the Office of Director of Intelligence with subject, organization and geographic index, 1906–1948; and security classified registers of communications received from military attachés, 1900–1944. Also not to be overlooked is the security-classified intelligence reference-publication "Regional File," (1225 feet) arranged by country, 1933–1944.

Some examples of materials found in the registers of communications received from military attachés for the World War II period are as follows:

Dutch actions in Timor; Rank operations in Java and Outer Islands; Hospital facilities in the Netherlands East Indies; Japanese minor tactics in Malaya; Notes on communications—Malaya; Report on Inter-Allied conference at Singapore, December 18–20th, 1941; Directory of Bangkok and Thailand, 1941.

RG 179: Records of the War Production Board. Materials in this RG relate to the control of raw materials at the international level during World War II. Of particular interest may be the classified correspondence, reports, and charts relating to the allocation of materials to liberated areas, 1944–1945, by name of country.

RG 218: Records of the United States Joint Chiefs of Staff. The Geographic files (1942–1953) contain a number of reports of interest to Southeast Asianists. Some examples are as follows:

"Japanese strength in Burma in the Fall of 1944" (September 27, 1944); "Withdrawal of Chinese Divisions from North Burma" (November 6, 1944); "Request for Mediation by the U.S. in Indochina" (February 12, 1945); "Administration of Civil Affairs in the Netherlands East Indies" (October 24, 1944); "Psychological Warfare Plan for the Netherlands East Indies" (October 24, 1944); "Commercial Communications Facilities between the U.S. and the Philippines" (September 2, 1944); "Plan for Subdividing the Japanese in Thailand" (December 22, 1945).

Also available are the files of the chairman of the Joint Chiefs of Staff for the period 1949–1957. Country material is arranged in boxes. There seems to be a good amount of material on Burma, Cambodia, Indo-China, the Philippines, the Moluccas, and Thailand.

This record group also has the four-volume unpublished *History of the Joint Chiefs of Staff,* by Walter S. Poole (available on microfilm for about $15.00 as of this writing). Southeast Asianists will be interested in Chapter 14, Vol. II (1947–49), which covers the topic of Philippine base rights, and Chapter 12, Vol. IV (1950–52), "The Far East, Nationalism, Communism, and Containment," particularly the section on the Indochina Quagmire and Insurgency in the Philippines.

RG 226: Records of the Office of Strategic Services (OSS). This is one of the more important record groups for those with an interest in Southeast Asia. The holdings, primarily consisting of research and analysis reports, are superior to similar materials in RG 59 for the World War II period. A two-part index, spanning the period 1941–1946, serves these records. Cards are arranged under a country title into eight categories: general, political intelligence, economic intelligence, military intelligence, naval intelligence, aviation, religion-public opinion and population, and subversive activities. Notes cannot be taken from the cards, though the reports themselves are open. There may be upwards of 20 thousand cards under the Southeast Asian country headings.

RG 238: World War II War Crime Records. This record group contains the records of the International Military Tribunal for the Far East. Included is material on the war-crimes trials of 28 Japanese officers, many of whom served in Burma, Indochina, the Philippines, or Singapore. See PI 180.

RG 243: U.S. Strategic Bombing Survey. Holdings within this record group include the Pacific Survey, 1928–1947, and textual records with material on North Borneo, Burma, Indochina, the Malay states, Netherlands East Indies, the Philippines, and Thailand.

RG 263: Records of the Central Intelligence Agency. Included are reports of the Foreign Broadcast Information Branch, consisting of daily transcripts and summaries in English of monitored foreign radio broadcasts, 1947–1948, daily teletypes of materials selected for transmission to government agencies, and daily reports of these broadcasts.

RG 330: Records of the Office of the Secretary of Defense (OSD). The office files of the Secretary of Defense contain approximately 100 items related to Southeast Asia. Some examples are as follows:

"United States Policy Toward the Philippines: Payment of Claims" (July 7, 1949); "Review of Jurisdictional Problems in the Philippines" (May 10, 1948); "Disquieting Military Developments in Indonesia Since the Recent Cease Fire Orders" (September 8, 1949).

The record group also contains the general records of the OSD subject correspondence file relating to foreign military aid programs, 1949–1951. Other as-yet classified materials include the monthly reports on activities of the Army, Navy, and Air Force sections of Military Assistance Advisory Groups in various countries, 1950–1955, and the country files containing correspondence reports, memoranda, and other papers relating to shipments of military and civilian supplies to countries participating in the Mutual Defense Assistance Program, 1950–1955.

RG 407: Records of the Adjutant General's Office: This record group contains military attaché's reports from Southeast Asian countries.

Navy and Old Army Branch
Gary Ryan, Chief
(202) 523-3229
8:45 A.M.–5:00 P.M.   Monday–Friday

RG 24: Records of the Bureau of Naval Personnel. This record group contains some materials dealing with the Philippines from 1903–1943, and is mainly classified under general correspondence.

RG 38: Records of the Office of the Chief of Naval Operations. Included are records of the Office of Naval Intelligence, within which is material on French Indochina, including maps and country reports, 1936–1945. Reports of naval attachés, 1886–1922, are contained in the Foreign Intelligence Branch, Far Eastern Theater Section. Also of interest are the reports of

Naval attachés, 1886–1922, which contain information on political, social, and economic conditions in Siam and the Dutch East Indies. A small file on confidential news summaries of conditions in the Far East, 1938–1941, is also of minor interest.

RG 94: Records of the Adjutant General's Office. Files on military units in the Philippines are included here.

RG 98: Records of the United States Army Commands. This group contains records on territorial commands in Cuba and the Philippine Islands, 1898–1901.

RG 120: Records of the American Expeditionary Forces. This RG contains documentation on medical organizations in the Philippine Islands, 1917–1921.

RG 153: Records of the Judge Advocate General (Army). Included are records of the Insular Affairs Section, 1915–1939, concerning legal matters arising from the administration of the insular possessions, including the Philippines.

RG 159: Records of the Office of the Inspector General. Files of the Inspector General Department, Philippine Division, 1899–1912, are included.

RG 127: Records of the United States Marine Corps. These records contain materials relating to the Marine Corps activities in the Philippines, 1900–1904.

GENERAL ARCHIVES DIVISION

Washington National Records Center
4205 Suitland Road
Suitland, Maryland
Mail: Washington, D.C. 20409
Daniel T. Goggin, Director
(301) 763-7410

Daily shuttle service is available from the main Archives Building.

This division contains parts of record groups listed elsewhere as well as records not in the Main Archives building.

RG 131: Records of the Office of Alien Property Custodian. Within this record group are records of the Division of Insular Possessions relating to aliens and their property, 1917–1921 (material on the Philippines).

RG 192: Records of the Office of the Commissary General of Subsistence. Included are materials related to rations issued to Philippine Scouts, 1900–1911.

RG 319: Records of the Army Staff. This is a massive record group with substantial material of interest to Southeast Asianists. Records of the attaché branch contain materials relating to activities of military attaché officers, 1939–1949, (20 feet). The huge "Regional File" (1144 feet) contains intelligence documents for the 1939–1944 period. This is followed by a numeric series of intelligence documents, the "ID File," which covers the period, June 1944–1955. The latter is only partially declassified .

4.   In addition to the bibliographic aids mentioned above, the following finding aids may be of assistance to researchers: *Catalog of National Archives Microfilm Publications* (1974) and its supplement; *The National Archives and Foreign Relations Research* (1974), edited by Milton O. Gustafson; *Commerce Data among State Department Records* (Reference Information

Paper No. 53, 1973); *List of Record Groups of the National Archives and Records Service* (1976); *Federal Records of World War II* in 2 vols. (1951); *Cumulative Subject Index to the Declassified Documents Reference System* (1975), edited by Annadel Wile; and the Department of State's on-going *Foreign Relations of the United States* series.

General information leaflets available include: *A Researcher's Guide to the National Archives* (1977); *Regulations for the Public Use of Records Service* (1972); *Select List of Publications of the National Archives and Records Service* (1977); *Location of Records and Fees for Reproduction Services in the National Archives and Records Service* (1979); *General Restrictions on Access to Records in the United States* (1976); and *Suggestions for Citing Records in the National Archives of the United States* (1972).

For recent accessions in the National Archives, contact the Central Reference Division, Room 200-B, or the respective divisions. Scholars may also wish to consult *Prologue: The Journal of the National Archives;* the American Historical Association's newsletter; *The Historian,* published by Phi Alpha Theta; and the newsletter of the Society for Historians of American Foreign Relations. Information on the latest archival accessions may also be obtained from the Central Reference Division, Room 200-B, or from the respective divisions.

Note: See also entries D5, E5, F16, F17, G10, and Q16.

B8 National Museum of Natural History (Smithsonian Institution)— National Anthropological Archives

1.   a. *Natural History Building, Room 60-A*
     Constitution Avenue and 10th Street, N.W.
     Washington, D.C. 20560
     (202) 357-1986

     b. 9:00 A.M.–5:00 P.M.   Monday– Friday

     c. Open to the public. Appointments in advance are requested.

     d. Photoduplication facilities are available.

     e. Herman Viola, Director
        James R. Glenn, Archivist

2–3.   The archives are concerned primarily with American Indians, but non-Indian cultures are included in the purview of the archives. Southeast Asia related materials are limited and consist of some ten archive boxes of representative photos from Southeast Asia, the majority of which are from the Philippines. As these materials have not yet been catalogued, collection registers are unavailable; however, the staff will help serious researchers interested in this collection. There seem to be no significant manuscript materials related to Southeast Asia in the National Anthropological Archives.

4.   See the four-volume *Catalog to Manuscripts at the National Anthropological Archives* (Boston: G. K. Hall, 1975).

B9 Naval Historical Center (Navy Department)—Operational Archives Branch

1. a. *Washington Navy Yard, Building 210*
    9th and M Street, S.E.
    Washington, D.C. 20374
    (202) 433-3171

    b. 7:30 A.M.–4:30 P.M.   Monday–Friday

    c. Most of the pre-1955 archival materials are open to the public for on-site use. Some post-1955 materials are also open. The staff may be able to assist serious researchers in obtaining declassification of needed materials. Researchers should call ahead.

    e. Dean C. Allard, Director
    Edward J. Marolda and G. Wesley Pryce, Vietnam Section

2. The Naval Historical Center, with custody over the operational archives of the U.S. Navy, was created in 1942 to centralize and organize the basic records documenting the combat activities of the naval fleet units. The Operational Archives Branch continues to collect documents on fleet operations as well as official records of the Office of the Chief of Naval Operations and other operational headquarters of the U.S. Navy. The records contain some 200,000 items, totaling approximately 10,000 feet. These materials date from 1940 to the present, with more than half pertaining to the Pacific region (western, central, and southern).

3. Of particular interest to Southeast Asianists is the mountain of material relating to the U.S. Navy in Vietnam. Though most documents are classified and not fully organized, serious researchers are invited to contact the Archives personnel with their requests. These Vietnam materials are currently being used to produce the multi-volume *United States Navy and the Vietnam Conflict*. Volume one, *The Setting of the Stage to 1959*, by Vice Admiral Edwin B. Hooper, Dean C. Allard, and Oscar P. Fitzgerald, appeared in 1976.

    In addition, there are numerous collections covering World War II in the Pacific, which may be of interest to Southeast Asianists.

4. Various finding aids and indices exist to facilitate research in the Operational Archives. Two publications may be especially useful: *Declassified Records in the Operational Archives,* and *Information for Visitors to the Operational Archives.* Both are available without charge from the Archives. The staff can also be of considerable assistance in helping to acquaint you with the holdings.

Note: See also entries A34, C8, F19, and F20.

B10 Smithsonian Institution Archives (SIA)

1. a. *900 Jefferson Drive, S.W.*
    Washington, D.C. 20560
    (202) 357-1420

b. 9:00 A.M.–5:00 P.M.   Monday–Friday
Researchers wishing to use the archives before 10:00 A.M. should make special arrangements.

c. Open to the public. Researchers should make arrangements in advance to insure service from the archivist best acquainted with the records to be consulted.

d. Photoduplication facilities and microfilm viewers are available. Permission and proper acknowledgment are required to quote from any SIA documents.

e. Richard H. Lytle, Archivist

2. This archive is the official depository for the institution's records and some private papers that document the growth of the institution and the growth of science and art in the United States. Current holdings in the archives exceed 5,500 cubic feet. Southeast Asia related materials are, however, very limited. The following Record Units (RU) may contain materials pertaining to Southeast Asia. Some of the SIA records are marked "restricted," which indicates that some staff review is necessary before the records could be made available to researchers.

3. RU 45: Office of the Secretary (Charles D. Walcott), 1907–1924. Records about the founding of the Freer Gallery, including Freer's gifts, are contained here.
RU 91: Office of International Activities, 1964–1967. These records include correspondence, memoranda, and other information about the activities of the office, which establishes cooperative research programs with institutions of higher learning in other countries and fosters programs for the international exchange of persons in those fields of science and humanities related to Smithsonian interest.
RU 104: Assistant Secretary for History and Art, 1965–1972. Contained here are records related to the Freer Gallery.
RU 145: Assistant Secretary for Public Service, 1961–1974. Some records of the Office of International Activities are included in this unit.
RU 150: Assistant Secretary for Science, 1965–1971. This RU contains research award proposals, awards, and contracts.
RU 158: United States National Museum, 1881–1964. Curator's Annual Reports. Reports of the departments, divisions, and sections, which were not reproduced in their entirety in the published *Annual Report,* can be found here along with more information than is to be found in the published version.
RU 180: Office of International Activities, Foreign Currency Program, 1965–1973. Files include grants proposals, awards, project status reports, and correspondences related to Smithsonian Excess Foreign Currency Programs (PL 480) in Burma.
RU 189: Assistant Secretary in Charge of the United States National Museum, 1860–1908. Incoming correspondence records chiefly document museum accessions and Smithsonian expeditions and field collecting trips.
RU 192: United States National Museum, 1877–1975. Some of these permanent administrative files document museum accessions and Smithsonian expeditions and field trips.
RU 218: Office of International and Environmental Programs, 1962–1975. These records include fiscal information relating to the Foreign Cur-

rency Program and environmental information relating to marine, ecology, specific fauna, and other scientific projects.

RU 223: Division of Plants, 1899–1947. This RU contains correspondences with foreign botanists and expeditions to Asia.

RU 6999T: Registrar, 1834–1958 (accessions to 1976). Records include accession documents.

4. A comprehensive and detailed record of the archives is contained in the *Guide to the Smithsonian Archives* (1978) which supersedes the 1971 *Preliminary Guide to the Smithsonian Archives*. Separate unpublished finding aids for some of the Record Units are also available.

C Museums Galleries, and Art Collections

Museums, Galleries, and Art Collections Entry Format (C)

1. General Information
   a. *address; telephone numbers*
   b. hours of service
   c. conditions of access
   d. reproduction services
   e. name/title of director and heads of relevant divisions

2. Size of Holdings Pertaining to Southeast Asia

3. Description of Holdings Pertaining to Southeast Asia

4. Bibliographic Aids (Inventories, calendars, etc.) Facilitating Use of Collection

Introductory Note

The outstanding batik collection of the Textile Museum (entry C9) is a must for the museum-goer with a Southeast Asia interest. For philatelists, the stamp collection of the National Museum of American History (entry C5) will be of considerable interest. This museum also possesses a good numismatic collection of Southeast Asian items. The National Museum of Natural History (entry C6) has the W. L. Abbott mammal collection from the East Indies, which includes the world's largest collection of orangutan specimens. For the military scholar or buff, the Navy Memorial Museum (entry C8) will be of more than passing interest. In sum, Southeast Asianists will have no difficulty in finding something of interest in the museums of Washington, D.C.

C1 Air Force Art and Museum Branch

1. a. *The Pentagon*
   Room 4A-120
   Washington, D.C. 20330
   (202) 695-6983

b. 8:30 A.M.–5:00 P.M.   Monday–Friday

c. Open to the public. Because access to the Pentagon is restricted, researchers must telephone the branch from the Pentagon entrance. An escort will be sent to accompany the visitor.

d. Photoduplication is available according to a schedule of fees.

e. Alice B. Price, Chief, Art and Museum Branch

2–3. This collection of over 5,300 paintings includes the work of freelance artists; members of the Societies of Illustrators in New York, Los Angeles, and San Francisco; and the Artists Guild of Chicago; plus the work of several foreign artists. The collection includes a small but interesting number of paintings that depict Vietnam during the war as well as other parts of mainland Southeast Asia, including several striking views of the Southeast Asian landscape. Unfortunately, the paintings are not easily accessible. The Air Force Art and Museum Branch has color slides of more than 90 percent of the items in the collection. Photographic reprints from the slides are also available for some items.

4. Computer-generated inventory rosters of the collection may be used by researchers.

Army Center of Military History See entry B3

C2 Division for Performing Arts (Smithsonian Institution)

1. a. *2100 L'Enfant Plaza, S.W.*
Washington, D.C. 20560
(202) 287-3420

b. 8:45 A.M.–5:15 P.M.   Monday–Friday

c. Open to the public.

d. Reproduction services are available.

e. James R. Morris, Jr., Director

2–3. The division organizes public concerts, releases records, and explores the history of the American musical theater. The division's World Explorer series periodically sponsors performances by artists from abroad. Several Southeast Asian performances have been sponsored by the division and the Asia Society in the last several years—among them, Javanese and Balinese dancing. For additional information, contact Shirley E. Cherkasky (202/287-3420). The division publishes *Notes on the Arts,* which features art criticism, interviews, and a calendar of art events for the Washington area. At $5 a year, *Notes* is a real bargain!

C3 Freer Gallery of Art (Smithsonian Institution)

1. a. *12th Street and Jefferson Drive, S.W.*
Washington D.C. 20560
(202) 357-2104

b. 10:00 A.M.–5:30 P.M. every day except Christmas Day.

c. Open to the public. Scholars wishing to review objects not on display should make special arrangements in advance. No objects from the museum's permanent collection are lent outside the building.

d. Prints and slides of major objects in the collection are available for purchase. Objects on exhibition may be photographed, but special permission must be obtained to use tripods.

e. Thomas Lawton, Director

2. The Freer Gallery of Art houses one of the world's most renowned collections of oriental art. Over 10,000 objects in the oriental section represent the arts of the Far East, the Near East, and Southeast Asia and include paintings, manuscripts, scrolls, screens, pottery, metalwork, glass, jade, lacquer ware, and sculpture. Unfortunately, items relating to Southeast Asia are very limited. The international reputation of the Freer Gallery rests in part on the significant contributions to oriental studies made by its staff in the areas of art history and conservation. Members of the curatorial staff spend considerable time studying objects in, or related to, the collection and publishing results in scholarly journals and books. Furthermore, they regularly serve as advisors to students, scholars, and the general public on matters pertaining to their areas of expertise. The gallery also presents each year six or seven free public lectures by distinguished scholars in oriental art.

    Like the gallery, the library has few items related to Southeast Asia. It has an excellent card index, organized by medium and location, to the gallery collection. Ellen Nollman, librarian, is very knowledgeable about the collection and can be of considerable assistance to serious scholars. The gallery also maintains a conservation laboratory and an oriental picture mounting studio.

    A proposed new Asian Art Gallery, an adjunct to the Freer, will provide room for expansion and will enable the Freer to increase its programs for exhibitions, research, and public service.

3. The Freer collection contains only a few Southeast Asian objects. Items of interest from Cambodia include an Angkor period stone sculpture, and a Khmer (twelfth century) bronze Buddha. Items of interest from Indonesia include a ninth- to tenth-century stone sculpture of a Hindu goddess from Java, and a Sailandre period (eighth to ninth century) stone Buddha from Java. The collection also includes six statuettes in ivory from Thailand (n.d.), and two pieces of Celadonware (pottery) from Swankhalok (Thailand) which date from the fourteenth to fifteenth century. The gallery also has four pieces of Annamese pottery (n.d.).

4. The Freer Gallery of Art occasionally publishes illustrated catalogs and guides to its collection or special exhibitions. The gallery also publishes, with the University of Michigan, the *Ars Orientalis*, previously *Art Islamica*, a journal devoted to the arts of the Near and Far East. An illustrated booklet, the *Freer Gallery of Art*, is available at modest cost.

C4 Marine Corps Historical Center—Art Collection

1. a. *Washington Navy Yard, Building 58*
   9th and M Streets, S.E.
   Washington, D.C. 20374
   (202) 433-2820

   b. 8:00 A.M.–4:30 P.M.   Monday–Friday

   c. Open to the public.

   e. Jack Dyer, Art Curator

2–3.   The art collection was organized in 1966 and now contains over 5,000 exhibitary works, which include paintings, drawings, sketches, sculptures, woodblocks, silk-screen prints, and some cartoons. There are also recruiting posters dating from the early 1900s, salon quality photographs, and contemporary prints.

   Southeast Asianists should note that the bulk of this collection stems from artists' coverage of Marines in the Vietnam War. There are also a few pictures covering the World War II period that may be of interest.

   For a description of the Historical Center's Archives, see entry B6. For a description of the still photographic collection, see entry F14.

4.   Researchers should consult the *Guide to the Marine Corps Historical Center* (1979).

C5 National Museum of American History (Smithsonian Institution)

1. a. *14th Street and Constitution Avenue, N.W.*
   Washington, D.C. 20560
   (202) 357-2510

   b. Public Exhibits:
   10:00 A.M.–5:30 P.M.   every day except Christmas Day
   Departmental offices and research facilities:
   8:45 A.M.–5:15 P.M.   Monday–Friday

   c. Exhibit areas are open to the public. Prior appointments are recommended for visiting research facilities and viewing items not on display.

   d. Exhibits may be photographed, but permission is required for publication. Photoreproduction facilities are available through the departmental offices. Color transparencies and prints of some exhibits are available for sale in the museum gift shop.

   e. Roger G. Kennedy, Director

2–3.   Being a museum of American experience, the collection primarily focuses on the growth of the United States; therefore, materials on foreign areas are limited. Items of interest to Southeast Asian scholars are discussed below under appropriate divisions or units. The museum's curators, specialists, and technicians command professional knowledge and skills that are basic to the exhibits. The staff publishes widely, and some of its exhibits, catalogs, and research monographs are available in the museum bookstore.

NATIONAL PHILATELIC COLLECTIONS

Robert G. Tillotson, Director
(202) 357-1796

This unit manages a philatelic collection of over 15 million objects. While the Southeast Asia collection is not large, there are some substantial and interesting holdings for parts of the region. For Laos and Indonesia, the collection should be rated "good," there being, for example, some 20 volumes of items from Indonesia. The Philippine collection is strong and contains several items of special interest, including one volume of stamps from the period of Spanish domination, one volume from the Aguinaldo revolutionary period with documentation, and one volume of local and national seals from the late nineteenth century. A significantly smaller number of items from French Indochina are also to be found. For the region, there is a good collection of literature on post markings.

For further information on the collection, researchers may confer with Lowell S. Newman, Museum Technician (202/357-1796). The unit's specialized reference library contains extensive sets of catalogs, handbooks, journals, and other literature related to philately.

DEPARTMENT OF NATIONAL HISTORY

(202) 357-2825

Division of Numismatics
(202) 357-1798

The Numismatics Division maintains a relatively small but interesting collection of coins and related items from Southeast Asia. Included are some early forms of money, or more properly, mediums of exchange; e.g., porcelain tokens. This representative collection also includes various examples of paper money. The collection is quite strong for the Philippines and includes items impossible to find elsewhere, such as certified proofs for Philippine currency from the Bureau of Engraving.

Division of Naval History
Philip K. Lundeberg, Director
(202) 357-2249

This division has only a few items related to Southeast Asia. Included are two cannons used by Dewey at the battle of Manila Bay, 1898.

Division of Military History
Craddick Goins, Curator
(202) 357-1883

The Military History Division maintains a small but interesting cris collection from Malaya.

DEPARTMENT OF HISTORY OF TECHNOLOGY

John T. Schlebecker, Chairman
(202) 357-2095

Division of Textiles
Rita J. Adrosko, Curator
(202) 357-1889

This division has a substantial collection of Indonesian batik and a large number of baskets and fiber products from the Philippines. The batik collection was assembled to illustrate technique as opposed to representing the finest examples of the art. There are about 40 specimens plus two series showing the step-by-step process of making traditional tjanting batika.

The nucleus of the collection was purchased from the Netherlands East Indies Commission at the close of the Panama-Pacific International Exposition, which was held in San Francisco in 1915. The 22 specimens of Javanese batik work on cotton and silk and a series of 14 pieces illustrating the batik process had been exhibited in the official government pavilion of the Netherlands and its colonies at the exposition. Division records indicate that the batiks were made by prisoners in penal institutions in Java.

Some of the specimens in this group are traditional forms of native dress, but more than half are items made expressly for European trade. A booklet from the Netherlands exhibit says that to help support the art of "true" batik (drawing with wax using a tjanting as opposed to printing with wax using blocks), the making of batik articles for export to Europe was tried. The booklet also tells of the difficulties the European supervisors had in trying to get the Javanese women to work within a rigid symmetry imposed by European ideas of design. Among the export items are a glove sachet, a reticule, table and piano runners, men's ties, book covers, a handkerchief, and a tea cosy. Six of the batika for European trade were done on silk.

The native garments include two shirt cloths of particular interest. One is in a pattern called "Tambal," which can be translated as "beggar's blanket." This pattern is similar in appearance to simple American pieced quilts made of squares and triangles. The design comes from a Javanese legend, which tells of a prince who could fly when he wore a magical patchwork garment. The "Tambal" pattern was traditionally used only for special garments worn by court officials. The second sarong is interesting because it has an unusual, individualistic design showing large sailing ships and many sea creatures. The red and green color combination also sets it apart from the rest of the group.

Another accession includes four batiks made in the 1920s at Sie King Goan, Solosch Batikkug, Solo, Java. Three of these show figures representing characters from Wayang, the traditional drama of early Java. These figures look like Javanese shadow puppets. Among other specimens in the collection, a dark blue and brown dodot stands out both for the quality of the batik work and the fineness of the cotton. A photograph on page 69 of *The Art of Batik in Java,* by Tassilo Adam (The Needle and Bobbin Club, New York, 1935), shows the Chancellor of Jokjakarta wearing a dodot identical to this one.

Finally, there is an unusual multi-colored batik of skirt-cloth size (41½″ × 97½″) done like a decorative panel. It has a house in the center and, below that, two figures, perhaps a farm couple. The rest of the batik is covered with dozens of animals and birds—rabbits, camels, elephants, chickens, cranes, and others—among palm trees and flowers. In addition to the Division of Textiles batiks, there are more than two dozen in the collections of the Department of Anthropology in the Museum of Natural History (entry C6).

Of equal interest is the collection of basketry from the Philippines. This collection, consisting of several hundred items, is the result of acquisitions during the early 1900s from a variety of sources including: the Bureau of Education in Manila (1912); "Fibers from the Growing Plants to the Finished Product," Philippine Exhibit Board (1916); and a private collection received in 1915.

A sampling of items in this collection includes: sewing basket, coiled work basket, nest of octagonal baskets, nest of midrib baskets, coiled serving tray, plaited work basket with lid, abaca basket, button basket, and waste basket. There are also a sizable number of items illustrating the process used to construct various items; e.g., items illustrating steps in the weaving of coiled baskets, the weaving of decoration for baskets, and the making of hexagonal baskets.

In addition, the division collections include about 50 examples of embroidery on pina cloth (nineteenth- or twentieth-century origin), and fibers, mats, sarongs, and hats, among other items.

Division of Photographic History
Eugene Ostroff, Curator
(202) 357-2059

The division has a few exotic scenes from nineteenth-century Southeast Asia. Of particular interest is a daguerreotype of the king and queen of Siam presented to the president of the United States circa 1850.

EISENHOWER INSTITUTE FOR HISTORICAL RESEARCH

Forrest D. Pogue, Historian
(202) 357-2183

This institute conducts scholarly studies into the meaning of war, its effect on civilization, and the role of the armed forces.

Note: The Dibner Library (Mary Rosenfeld, Librarian, 202/357-1568) is a rare book collection of approximately 13,000 items. There are no substantial Southeast Asia items included in the collection. There may be a few scattered items of secondary value in the natural history field. The library is open from 8:45 A.M. to 5:15 P.M., Monday–Friday. An appointment is required for visiting the library.

4. No comprehensive guide to the museum is available at this time. A project for computerization of an index to the collection, which could be a boon to those interested in this facility as a source for scholarly research materials, is being considered.

C6 National Museum of Natural History (NMNH) (Smithsonian Institution)

1. a. *10th Street and Constitution Avenue, N.W.*
    Washington, D.C. 20560
    (202) 357-2664

   b. Public exhibits:
    10:00 A.M.–5:30 P.M. every day except Christmas Day
    Departmental offices and research facilities:
    8:45 A.M.–5:15 P.M. Monday–Friday

c. Exhibit areas are open to the public. Appointments are recommended for visiting offices and research facilities.

d. Exhibits may be photographed, but clearance is needed for publication. Color transparencies and prints of many exhibition objects are for sale in the museum gift shop. Photoreproduction services are also available through the departmental offices.

e. Richard S. Fiske, Director

2.   A national and international center for the natural sciences, the National Museum of Natural History contains more than 60 million objects in its research collections and maintains one of the finest natural-history reference collections available to qualified researchers. The scientific staff conducts basic research on man and his artifacts, plants, fossils, organisms, rocks, minerals, and materials from outer space. The museum staff participates in joint educational programs with universities by teaching courses, training graduate students, and conducting science seminars. A Scientific Event Alert Network (SEAN) notifies scientists throughout the world of geo-physical, biological, astronomical, and anthropological events such as volcanic eruptions.

Fortunately, most of the subdivisions within the museum have fairly good estimates of their Southeast Asia related holdings. Most Southeast Asia items are on the computerized collections file, which greatly increases the scholar's chances for locating items of specific interest. Although objects concerning Europe and America dominate the collection, Southeast Asia holdings are significant. These materials are discussed below under the appropriate departments responsible for their custody and study.

3.   DEPARTMENT OF ANTHROPOLOGY

Douglas H. Ubelaker, Chairman
(202) 357-2363

Division of Archaeology
William Trousdale, Curator, Far Eastern Archaeology
(202) 357-2671

This division has a small collection of archaeological items from several Southeast Asian countries. The collection includes a wide variety of items. Researchers should consult the division where staff experts in the field can answer specific questions. The collection contains approximately 600 items from Southeast Asia, broken down as follows: Cambodia, 377; Java, 110; Laos, 82; Thailand, 11; and the Philippines, 1.

A card catalog in the processing lab lists archaeological items serially, and gives a description of the items as well as date of accession, origin, and donor.

Division of Ethnology
Paul Taylor, Curator
(202) 357-2363

The Southeast Asia ethnological collection is sizable, consisting of approximately 17,000 items. The collection consists of clothing and jewelry, tools and utensils, toys, household objects and furnishings, books, musical instruments, textiles, religious objects, baskets and boxes, and a representative collection of weapons from Java and the Philippines, mostly nineteenth century. Items are cataloged by culture, country, and additional provenance levels, such as state, region, and village.

The country breakdown for these items is as follows: Burma, 2489; Cambodia, 47; Indonesia, 3104; Laos, 247; Malaysia, 1697; Philippines, 7105; Singapore, 80; Thailand, 1783; Vietnam, 319; and French Indochina, 15.

Notable within this sizable collection are several small collections of Thai diplomatic gifts. Among these are 37 pieces given in 1857 by the Royal Siamese government to President Franklin Pierce, a collection given to the United States in 1877 by the King of Siam, and items donated by the Royal Siamese Commission for the Louisiana Purchase Exposition.

Several card catalogs and inventory lists are maintained in the department's processing laboratory (George E. Phebus, supervisor, 202/357-2483) which may be consulted by visiting scholars. Researchers should also contact Vince Wilcox (202/357-1394), collection manager and head of the ADP for the Anthropology Department, who can be of immense help to those seeking information on this collection.

Anthropology Branch Library
Barbara Veloz, Librarian
(202) 357-1819

The library is open to the public for on-site use from 1:00 P.M.– 5:00 P.M., Monday–Friday. The specialized collection consists of some 55,000 volumes and 1,200 periodicals, of which the Southeast Asian portion consists of some 250 volumes on antiquities, archaeology, anthropology, and description and travel. The country breakdown is as follows: Burma, 20; Cambodia, 10; Indonesia, 42; Laos, 8; Malaysia, 40; Philippines, 60; Singapore, 2; Thailand, 40; Vietnam and Indochina, 28.

The collection is served by two card catalogs. Interlibrary loan and photoduplication facilities are available.

For a description of the Anthropology Department's photographic and manuscript collections relating to Southeast Asia, see entry B8, National Anthropological Archives.

DEPARTMENT OF MINERAL SCIENCES

Daniel E. Appleman, Chairman
(202) 357-2632

Division of Mineralogy
Paul E. Desautels, Curator
(202) 357-2226

This division has a strong collection of gems from Southeast Asia, especially rubies from Burma. The division also has volcanic samples from Indonesia, on which the staff has been conducting research. In 1980 and 1981 the staff conducted research on volcanology in Southeast Asia, including the 1968 eruption of Mount Mayon.

DEPARTMENT OF VERTEBRATE ZOOLOGY

George R. Zug, Chairman
(202) 357-2740

An outstanding collection of 30,000 to 35,000 birds and mammals from Southeast Asia, with particularly strong holdings for Vietnam, the Philippines, Thailand, Malaysia, and Indonesia can be found here. The Vietnam materials were collected prewar and also during the conflict by Naval medical research teams. In addition to a huge collection of mammals from the Philippines, there are some 5,000 specimens of its birds.

Of particular note is the W. L. Abbott collection of mammals from the East Indies (Indonesia), which includes a large number of orangutang specimens, making the NMNH's collection of this primate the largest in the world.

The museum is still receiving materials through the Island Naval Research Unit, which operates in the Southeast Asia region.

The following other departments may also contain items of interest: Department of Botany (Dieter C. Wasshausen, Chairman, 202/357-2534); Department of Entomology (Wayne N. Mathis, Chairman, 202/357-2078); Department of Invertebrate Zoology (Clyde S. E. Roper, Chairman, 202/357-2030); Department of Paleobiology (Martin A. Buzas, Chairman, 202/357-2211).

4. Until 1979, inventories of the museum's collection had been performed piecemeal, partially by manual means and partially by using the museum's automatic data processing (ADP) facilities. But now an accelerated ADP program has begun with the objective of establishing computerized records of the museum's full collection. By the end of fiscal year 1981, several million specimen and lot records had been programmed into the computer.

C7 National Rifle Association (NRA) Firearms Museum

1. a. *1600 Rhode Island Avenue, N.W.*
   Washington, D.C. 20036
   (202) 828-6000

   b. 10:00 A.M.–4:00 P.M., every day except Christmas, New Year's, Thanksgiving, and Easter days

   c. Open to the public.

   d. Permission is required for photographing items in the collection.

   e. Dan R. Abbey, Curator

2–4. The museum has an extensive firearms collection with a few items related to Southeast Asia, including: a Krag rifle; a unique Philippine constabulary pistol—manufactured by Colt Company—having a handle scaled to the Philippine hand; several handmade rifles from the Vietnam conflict; a Soviet rifle from the Vietnam conflict; and a Soviet rifle captured in North Vietnam. Those interested in weaponry will find the NRA's collection of considerable interest.

C8 Navy Memorial Museum (Naval Historical Center)

1. a. *Building 76*
   Washington Navy Yard
   Washington, D.C. 20374
   (202) 433-2651

   b. 9:00 A.M.–4:00 P.M.   Monday–Friday
   10:00 A.M.–5:00 P.M.   weekends and holidays except Thanksgiving, Christmas, and New Year's days

c. Open to the public.

d. Visitors may take pictures with the permission of the museum office.

e. Commander T. A. Damon, Director

2–3.   This organization is the Navy's central historical museum. It has over 30,000 square feet of indoor display area plus an outdoor park of almost equal size. The museum's displays depict the Navy's wartime operations, weapons, and leaders, as well as the service's peacetime contributions in such fields as aeronautics, diplomacy, electronics, exploration, humanitarian service, marine engineering, medicine, navigation, oceanography, and space flight. The museum's centerpiece is a fighting top from the frigate *Constitution*. More than 5,000 other artifacts are displayed, including models of notable warships, memorabilia from the men who served in them, and naval art. The outdoor display contains many large naval artifacts.

    This collection contains approximately 550 items from the Vietnam conflict, including materials used by the Navy, the North Vietnamese, and the Viet Cong. A partial listing of such items includes: a Viet Cong harbor mine, homemade rifles and pistols, a 75-mm tank gun, Viet Cong uniforms, land mines, a Viet Cong decoration, propaganda items, Viet Cong gas mask helmets, and survival kits. The collection is made up of in-country items and materials taken from U.S. Naval ships and stricken from the record.

4.   Copies of the *Navy Memorial Museum* brochure and *The Navy Memorial Museum's Guide to Willard Park* are available without charge on request. Researchers may consult with the Director, Commander T. A. Damon and with Dr. Oscar Fitzgerald, Associate Director of the Museum, who can assist researchers interested in Southeast Asian Studies. This collection holds real potential for serious researchers as well as being of great interest to the general public.

C9 Textile Museum

1.   a. *2320 S Street, N.W.*
       Washington, D.C 20008
       (202) 667-0441

    b. 10:00 A.M.–5:00 P.M. Tuesday–Saturday
      Noon–4:00 P.M. Sunday

    c. Open to the public. Items in the permanent collection, which are not on public display, may be viewed by researchers on an appointment basis.

    d. Some black-and-white photographs of items in the collection are available for purchase. The museum also maintains a large file of black-and-white negatives (as well as some color transparencies), covering much of the museum's collection. Visitors wishing to photograph items in the collection should make arrangements with the curator in advance.

    e. Patricia Fiske, Acting Director

2.   The Textile Museum has over 10,000 textiles and 1,000 rugs from all over the world. Among these are 235 weavings and batiks representing Southeast Asia. The pieces from Indonesia are especially strong in number and represent many of the country's different islands and areas. The following is a breakdown of the number of textiles by country: Cambodia, 1; Indonesia,

196; Laos, 5; Philippines, 12; Thailand, 19; and Vietnam, 2. There are an additional 30 textiles from the Minangkabau area of Indonesia on indefinite loan.

3.   The substantial number of Indonesian textiles represents many of the country's islands and areas including Bali, Sumatra, Java, and Kalimantan. Different types of textiles are also well represented, including warp and weft ikats, supplementary warp and weft, printed cotton, beaded and embroidered pieces, batiks on cotton and silk, batik with gold brads, beaten bark cloth, and—of special note— eight pieces of *geringsing* or double ikat from Bali.

4.   For individual items in the collection, researchers should request to see in the library the author's card catalog, which is arranged by country and subdivided by region or village. Dr. Mattiebelle Gittinger is the museum's research associate for the Asian collection. In 1979, Dr. Gittinger prepared a very extensive exhibit of Indonesian textiles, which displayed pieces from the museum's holdings as well as many pieces borrowed from several Dutch museums. This exhibition is well documented, along with historical and cultural information in the Textile Museum's publication, *Splendid Symbols: Textiles and Tradition in Indonesia,* by Mattiebelle Gittinger (1979). An annual journal and a quarterly newsletter are distributed to the museum's associate membership.

The museum also sponsors a number of visiting special exhibits, workshops on such topics as textile analysis and repair, lectures, tours to other textile museums and collections, and major conferences, such as the International Conference on Oriental Carpets (1980). The Arthur D. Jenkins Library of the Textile Museum is described in entry A38.

D Collections of Music and Other Sound Recordings

Collections of Music and Other Sound Recordings Entry Format (D)

1.   General Information
   a. *address; telephone numbers*
   b. hours of service
   c. conditions of access
   d. name/title of director and key staff members

2.   Size of Holdings Pertaining to Southeast Asia

3.   Description of Holdings Pertaining to Southeast Asia

4.   Facilities for Study and Use
   a. availability of audio equipment
   b. reservation requirements
   c. fees charged
   d. reproduction services

5.   Bibliographic Aids Facilitating the Use of Collection

Introductory Note

In Washington, the sound-recording collection related to Southeast Asia is limited. However, some valuable items will be found in the National Archives and Record Service (entry D5), particularly major-network news items and special recordings from the Vietnam War period. Traditional Southeast Asian music and folk music from the region is in short supply, although a representative collection of current recordings is held by the American University Record Score Collection (entry D1).

D1 American University Record Score Collection

1.   a. *Room 218*
         Kreeger Building
         American University
         Massachusetts and Nebraska avenues, N.W.
         Washington, D.C. 20016
         (202) 686-2165

b. 9:00 A.M.– 7:30 P.M.   Monday–Friday
9:00 A.M.–noon   Saturday

c. Open to the public.

d. James R. Heintze, Head Librarian

2–3.   The Record-Score Collection, containing over 7,000 recordings that feature music from all parts of the world, includes some 30 recordings of Southeast Asian music. The collection is representative and includes music from all countries of the region, with the possible exception of Laos. Southeast Asian music is included in: the Folkways Records series of ethnomusicology, recordings in the Barenreiter Unesco Collection, and Desto Records (sponsored by World Federation of United Nations Association).

While the size of this collection may not seem impressive, it must be noted that there are few large collections to be found in the area. Furthermore, of great importance is the fact that this collection is easily accessible and under the supervision of a knowledgeable staff.

4a–d.   Listening equipment is available without charge. The collection has the capacity to reproduce recordings. Persons desiring to have copies of materials must make arrangements with the staff in advance.

5.   The collection is served by a card catalog.

Division of Performing Arts (Smithsonian Institution) See entry C2

D2 Folklife Program (Smithsonian Institution)—Music and Recorded Sound Collection

1.   a. *2600 L'Enfant Plaza*
Washington, D.C. 20560
(202) 287-3424

b. 9:00 A.M.–5:00 P.M.   Monday–Friday

c. Open to the public. Appointments required.

d. Ralph Rinzler, Director
Richard Derbyshire, Archivist

2–3.   The on-going program of folkloric exhibitions and special activities presented by the Smithsonian's Folklife Program have included both American and international participants. Many of these activities have been captured on tape particularly since 1967, when the program began its series of Folklife Festivals. As a result, within the total collection of over 10,000 hours of recorded performances (including cassettes and open-reel tapes) are examples of Vietnamese folk music, 1979; and Hmong, Khmer, Lao, and Vietnamese folk music from the 1980 festival.

In addition, Folklife Program staff have been involved in preparing an oral history archive of immigrants relating their experiences. The bulk of this material was collected between 1976 and 1977, and contains a limited amount of material gathered from Indochinese refugees.

4.   a. Audio equipment is available for use at the archive.

b. Reservations are required.

c. No fees are charged for use of the archival materials or the equipment.

d. Standard Smithsonian Institution reproduction procedures and fees apply. An information sheet describing these regulations is available on request.

5.   No published or unpublished finding aids presently exist. An inventory of the holdings and a set of program books and schedules are available and will assist scholars in their search for possible resources in the collection.

Note: See also entries C2 and F9.

D3 Library of Congress—American Folklife Center—Archive of Folk Culture

1.   a. *Jefferson Building, Room G-152*
10 First Street, S.E.
Washington, D.C. 20540
(202) 287-5510

      b. 8:30 A.M.–5:00 P.M.   Monday–Friday

      c. The Reading Room is open to the public during the above hours. Make arrangements in advance to use listening equipment.

      d. Joseph C. Hickerson, Head
Gerald E. Parsons, Reference Librarian

2–3.   The archive was originally part of the LC's Music Division and was to be the national repository for documentary manuscripts and sound recordings of American folk music. Although the majority of materials in the archives deal with the U.S., there is a growing collection of traditional music and lore from all parts of the world. The Archive of Folk Culture ended its affiliation with the Music Division in 1978 to become a part of the American Folklife Center established in 1976. The archive maintains and administers all LC acquisitions, reference- and reader-service activities in the broad fields of folklore and ethnomusicology. Commercial recordings of folklore and ethnomusicology are under the control of LC's Motion Picture, Broadcasting, and Recorded Sound Division.

Archive holdings consist of approximately 30,000 recordings (cylinder, disc, wire, and tape) containing some 300,000 items of American and foreign folk song, folk music, folk tale, oral history, and other types of folklore. There are, in addition, over 225,000 sheets of manuscript material. The reading room contains books, periodicals, magazines, and newsletters of interest to ethnomusicologists and folklorists.

There is relatively little Southeast Asia material in the archive. There are, however, a number of items worth mentioning: 120 cylinders of folk music, mostly Burmese and Indonesian, from the Erich von Hornbostel collection; 1 8-inch reel of tape, including the Hanoi delegation at the 1900 World's Fair in Paris; 3 7-inch reels of national music of Laos; a collection of songs of the Vietnamese war, recorded in 1967 at the home of General Edwin Lansdale in Saigon; 6 10-inch "DT" Tapes with 160 songs by United States military personnel relating to the Vietnam war, collected between 1962 and 1972 by General Edwin Lansdale in Thailand. Vietnam, and in the United States; and 3 7-inch reels of Malayan folk music from Radio Malay 1960.

4. a. Listening equipment is available without charge.

b. An appointment is required for using listening facilities and is advisable for lengthy reference services.

c. The collection may be used without charge.

d. Duplication and photocopying of materials may be arranged through the reference staff.

5.   Collections are accessible through an alphabetical card index and a shelflist. Most Southeast Asian materials can be located via subject headings in the card index. There are four additional indexes: a numeric file, an alphabetical title index, an alphabetical index of information, and a geographic index, which may be helpful in locating items in the collection.

Also see the following publications: *Music, Books on Music, and Sound Recordings,* its predecessor, *Library of Congress Catalog: Music and Phonorecords,* and the outdated 3-volume *Checklist of Recorded Songs in the English Language in the Archive of American Folk Song to July 1940.* The archive also distributes free its brochure, "The Archive of Folk Song and a Guide to the Collection of Recorded Folk Music and Folklore in the Library of Congress."

D4 Library of Congress—Motion Picture Broadcasting and Recorded Sound Division

1. a. *Madison Building, Room LM-113*
    Independence Avenue, S.E., between 1st and 2nd Streets
    Mail: 10 First Street, S.E.
    Washington, D.C. 20540
    (202) 287-5509

b. 8:30 A.M.–4:30 P.M.   Monday–Friday

c. The Recorded Sound Office is open to the public. Make arrangements in advance to use listening equipment.

d. James Smart, Reference Librarian

2–3.   In 1978, the Recorded Sound Office was separated from the Music Division and was merged with the newly created Motion Picture Broadcasting, and Recorded Sound Division. Music lovers will be pleased with the new and spacious quarters in the James Madison Building.

The Recorded Sound Section is responsible for the acquisition, custody, and servicing of all LC's sound recordings, including commercial recordings, interviews and speeches, and recorded radio programs. For a description of the division's film and television collection see entry F12.

The Recorded Sound Section holds approximately 1.5 million recordings, commercial and unpublished. Unfortunately, 80 percent of these recordings are uncataloged. For those that are, none are geographically indexed. To locate an item, one must know the manufacturer's name and catalog number. Staff members can be very helpful in locating materials.

It is not possible to estimate the number of recordings dealing with Southeast Asia in the Section. There is a small uncataloged collection of 78-r.p.m. recordings from Southeast Asian countries. The catalog revealed another 100 items related to Southeast Asia, the majority of which are network broadcasts, U.S. government recordings, and products of private institutions dealing mostly with Vietnam.

The collection includes a variety of non-musical recordings, including materials produced by: Office of War Information, Voice of America, National Press Club, the major radio news networks, the United Nations, and the U.S. House of Representatives. The entire NBC radio archive of 175,000 recordings of radio programs and events broadcast from 1933 to 1970 is now in the collection.

4. a. Listening equipment is available without charge.

    b. Appointments should be made well in advance of coming to the section for serious and extended work.

    c–d. Duplication is permitted as long as no restrictions apply to the items in question. There are charges for duplication.

5. The section's reading room has a card catalog for sound recordings. The reference office just off the reading room has a card index of uncataloged recordings that researchers may also use. A catalog for long playing recordings is down the hall in the more spacious Music Division.

    See also the following publications: *Music, Books on Music and Sound Recordings,* and its predecessor, *Music and Phonorecords,* and the U.S. Copyright Office work, *Catalog of Copyright Entries: Sound Recordings.* The section also distributes several mimeoed brochures without charge.

Library of Congress—Music Division See entry A27

Marine Corps Historical Center—Oral History Program See entry B6

Martin Luther King, Jr., Memorial Library See entry A28

Maryland University Library See entry A29

D5 National Archives and Record Service (NARS)—Motion Pictures and Sound Recordings Branch (Audiovisual Archives Division)

1. a. *8th Street and Pennsylvania Avenue, N.W.*
    Washington, D.C. 20408
    (202) 523-3267

    b. 8:45 A.M.–5:00 P.M. Monday–Friday

c. Open to researchers with a National Archives identification card obtainable from the Central Reference Division, Room 200-B. First-time users are recommended to consult the reference staff before beginning any work.

d. William T. Murphy, Chief

2. The branch has the custody of approximately 100,000 discs, reels of magnetic tape, cartridges, and cassettes. These spoken-word recordings are received primarily from United States government agencies and from private, commercial, and foreign sources. Although much of the material in this branch relates to the United States, the collection contains some Southeast Asia related items although the quantity cannot be accurately determined. This entry deals only with sound recordings. For a discussion of the motion picture holdings of the branch see entry F16.

3. The audio materials in the collection are organized into the record groups (RG) established by the National Archives. For an explanation of the concept of record groups see entry B7. Southeast Asian audio materials are to be found in the following record groups:

RG 200: National Archives Gift Collection. This record group contains the radio news broadcasts of National Public Radio (NPR) and Washington radio station, WTOP, with numerous short segments dealing with the Vietnam conflict.

RG 262: Records of the Foreign Broadcast Intelligence Service (FIS). This is a large collection of over 35,000 recordings of foreign broadcasts in English and other languages by German and Japanese radio during World War II. Within this collection are a number of recordings of Tokyo Rose broadcasts to United States forces in the South Pacific.

RG 306: Records of the United States Information Agency. Some items of interest to Southeast Asianists are: a small collection of military marches of Vietnam, the national anthem of South Vietnam, President Richard Nixon's speech on Cambodia, April 30, 1970; and a recording of the opening session of the Manila Summit Conference, October 24, 1966, with opening remarks by President Ferdinand Marcos and Nguyen Thieu.

RG 330: Records of the Office of Secretary of Defense. Included are recordings of press conferences, briefings, question and answer sessions, and remarks by former secretarys of defense Laird, Schlesinger, and Rumsfeld. Many of these items contain material on or are entirely devoted to the Vietnam conflict.

4. a. Audio equipment is available for use in the research room.
b. Audio equipment and recordings are to be used only in the research room and may be reserved in advance. Requests for same-day service may require some waiting.
c. No fees are charged for the use of the facilities.
d. Staff assistance for a fee is available for duplicating material not encumbered by copyright or other restrictions. Researchers may also make audio copies using their own equipment, provided the material is in the public domain, or prior permission has been secured.

5. Researchers may wish to consult the following publications: *Sound Recordings in the Audiovisual Archives Division of the National Archives* (1972), by Mayfield S. Bray and Leslie C. Waffen; *Audiovisual Records in the National Archives Relating to World War II* (1974), by Mayfield S. Bray and William T. Murphy; and the audiovisual record, *The Crucial Decade:*

Voices of the Post War Era, 1945–1954 (1976). Researchers may also find it useful to consult the *Guide to the National Archives of the United States* (1974). Card catalogs and indexes are available to researchers and provide reasonably good coverage of the materials. Archivists are available for consultation.

D6 National Public Radio—Audio Library (NPR)

1. a. *2025 M Street, N.W.*
    Washington, D.C. 20036
    (202) 785-5540

    b. 9:00 A.M.–5:00 P.M.   Monday–Friday

    c. Open to the public.

    d. Susan Bau, Librarian

2–3. News broadcasts and special programs produced by National Public Radio (NPR) are taperecorded and stored in the library. A variety of Southeast Asia related news items are contained in this collection, the holdings of which cover the period from 1974 to the present. Earlier tapes have been transferred to the National Archives and Records Service (entry D5).

4. Although audio equipment is available, priority is given to the staff, which, as a practical matter, makes nonstaff use impossible. Copies of tapes may be purchased for noncommercial use.

5. A catalog and other finding aids are maintained, however, a geographic search of these materials would be difficult and time consuming. The staff recommends that requests be submitted in advance, in writing or by telephone, enabling personnel familiar with the collection to perform a preliminary search.

Senate Historical Office See entry K32

D7 Vietnam Imports

1. a. *922 West Broad Street*
    Falls Church, Virginia 22046
    (703) 534-9441

    b. 10:00 A.M.–8:00 P.M.   Monday–Friday

    c. Open to serve the public.

    d. Hoc Khoa Tran, Manager

2–3. A commercial establishment, Vietnam Imports has a large stock of Vietnamese, Thai, Lao, and Cambodian records and tapes available for purchase.

Voice of America (International Communication Agency) See entries K21 and Q28

E Map Collections

Map Collections Entry Format (E)

1.   General Information
   a. *address; telephone numbers*
   b. hours of service
   c. conditions of access
   d. reproduction services
   e. name/title of director and heads of relevant divisions

2.   Size of Holdings Pertaining to Southeast Asia

3.   Description of Holdings Pertaining to Southeast Asia

4.   Bibliographic Aids (inventories, calendars, etc.) Facilitating Use of Collection

Introductory Note

The map collections in Washington are few but valuable. Copies of U.S. government produced maps and maps of foreign areas obtained by the federal government on an exchange basis are often deposited in the National Archives and Records Service collection (entry E5), the U.S. Geological Survey (entry E3), or the Library of Congress (entry E4). The LC also augments the U.S. government holdings with valuable retrospective holdings obtained from gifts and purchases. The Defense Mapping Agency (entry E1) is the government agency specifically charged with preparing maps of foreign areas, including Southeast Asia. Unfortunately, the most current maps from this agency are classified. For quick reference, the National Geographic Society collection (entry E6) is useful, but the Library of Congress with its new and gigantic facility for maps should be your first stop.

Many of the above agencies sell copies of their maps, but researchers may also want to contact the Southeast Asian embassies (see Section L) for specific country maps, or visit the Map Store, 1636 I Street, N.W., Washington, D.C. 20036 (202/628-2608).

Air Force History Office See entry B1

Army Center of Military History See entry B3

Census Bureau (Commerce Department) See entry K8

Central Intelligence Agency See entry K6

E1 Defense Mapping Agency Hydrographic/Topographic Center (DMAHTC)

1. a. *6500 Brookes Lane, N.W.*
   Washington, D.C. 20315
   (202) 227-2700

   b. 7:30 A.M.–4:00 P.M.   Monday–Friday

   c. The center is not open to the public. Researchers may obtain special permission for limited access to the collection. For further information contact the Public Affairs Office (J. D. Miller, 202/227-2006).

   d. The Defense Mapping Agency (DMA) Office of Distribution Services, Customer Services, and Sales Management Division is responsible for providing cost and ordering information on DMA-produced topographic maps and aeronautical charts available for public sale. Their telephone number is 202/227-2816. The Chart Issue Room, 6101 MacArthur Boulevard, N.W., Washington, D.C. 20315, stocks a variety of nautical charts for public sale. This facility is open from 6:30 A.M. to 2:30 P.M., Monday–Friday. For additional information call 202/227-3048.

   e. Captain Wallace C. Palmer, USN, Director

2–3. The mapping, charting, and geodesy functions of the Defense Mapping Agency are principally conducted by its two major components. The Aerospace Center (DMAAC) (St. Louis, Missouri) produces aeronautical charts. The Hydrographic/Topographic Center produces nautical and topographical maps and charts. DMAAC-produced aeronautical charts available for public sale are distributed by the National Ocean Survey's Distribution Division, Riverdale, Maryland 20840 (301/436-6990).
   The center's data facilities contain approximately 700,000 maps and some 300,000 books, periodicals, and documents on cartography, geodesy, and geography. Materials in the map collection are for the most part classified or for limited distribution. It is difficult to determine the extent of Southeast Asia holdings; however, they are estimated to be significant. Unclassified maps produced by DMA are distributed to several repositories, which include the Library of Congress, Geography and Map Division; the George Washington University Library; the University of Maryland Library; and, on an exchange basis, the National Geographic Society.

4. The DMA does not publish an inventory of its maps, charts, and related products. Requests for nonpublic sale items must be submitted in writing to the Defense Mapping Agency, Office of Distribution Services, Attention: DOL, Product Release Officer, 6500 Brookes Lane, Washington, D.C.

20315. A copy of the *DMA Price List of Maps and Charts for Public Sale* is available free of charge from: Defense Mapping Agency, Office of Distribution Services, Attention: Customer Service and Sales Management Division, 6500 Brookes Lane, Washington, D.C. 20315.

E2 Earth Satellite Corporation

1. a. *7222 47th Street*
    Bethesda, Maryland 20815
    (301) 652-7130

    b. 8:00 A.M.–4:30 P.M. Monday–Friday

    c. Open to scholars.

    d. Copies of maps and imagery may be obtained for a fee.

    e. J. Robert Porter, President

2–3. The Earth Satellite Corporation is a private, commercial consulting firm, which provides various mapping services and natural resources inventories based upon remote sensing. Its inventory of Southeast Asia materials is fair in size and includes approximately 48 imageries covering most of Indonesia, 3 imageries of Burma, 6 of central Thailand, and 1 each of Kedah state in West Malaysia, Brunei, and Manila.

4. The corporation does not publish a list of its holdings for public use. Requests for project reports should be made directly to the appropriate client or funding agency. The staff may assist scholars interested in locating imageries or maps of specific regions or countries.

Folger Shakespeare Library See entry A15

E3 Geological Survey Library (Interior Department)—Map Collection

1. a. *12201 Sunrise Valley Drive, Fourth Floor*
    Reston, Virginia 22092
    (703) 860-6671 (Reference)

    b. 7:45 A.M.–4:15 P.M. Monday–Friday

    c. Open to the public. Shuttle service from the Interior Department building in Washington is available daily.

    e. Barbara Chappell, Head of Reference

2. The library's map collection consists of approximately 290,000 sheet maps, including approximately 1,800 maps on Southeast Asia. The drawer count for each country or region is given below. The number of maps per drawer is estimated at fifty.

Burma	2
Indochina	2
Vietnam	1
Laos	1

Cambodia	2
Indonesia	5
Malaysia	5
Malay Archipelago	2
Sabah/Sarawak	5
Borneo	2
Philippines	5
Singapore	1

3. The collection consists largely of geologic and topographic maps, organized by geographic area, subject, scale, and date (1850–present). Coverage includes general topographic, geologic, and geophysical features, mineral resources (including petroleum and mining maps), soils, water, and natural vegetation.

4. The library utilizes the on-line computerized cataloging system operated by OCLC (Online Computer Library Center). No published catalog or inventory for the map collection is available. However, a bibliographic record of thematic maps published by the U.S. Geological Survey (USGS) is provided in the catalogs *Publications of the Geological Survey, 1879–1961* and *Publications of the Geological Survey, 1962–1970*. These are available from the USGS Distribution Center, 1200 South Eads Street, Arlington, Virginia 22202. Current USGS maps are listed in *New Publications of the Geological Survey* (monthly) which is available from the USGS National Center in Reston, Virginia 22092.

Note: See also entries A17, A22, and K20.

George Washington University Library See entry A18

E4 Library of Congress—Geography and Map Division

1. a. *Madison Building*
First Street and Independence Avenue, S.E.
Washington, D.C. 20540
(202) 287-6277

  b. 8:30 A.M.–5:00 P.M. Monday–Friday
8:30 A.M.–12:30 P.M. Saturday

  c. Open to the public. Limited interlibrary loan service.

  d. Photoduplicaton facilities available.

  e. John A. Wolter, Chief

2–3. The division has the largest and most comprehensive cartographic collection in the world, consisting of 3.6 million maps, 42,000 atlases, more than 250 globes, and over 8,000 reference books. Virtually every type of map is included in this collection—topical, topographic, geologic, soil, mineral— as well as nautical and aeronautical charts. The collection covers all countries of the world. In spite of the large volume of materials in the division, one does not have that cramped feeling as is the case with so many of the other divisions located in the older facilities. The Madison Building is spacious and well appointed.

At a minimum, the Southeast Asia map collection in the division is comparable in size to the holdings for other non-Western regions of the world. In comparison to other map collections of the region, it is quite large—a geographer's candy store. The collection consists of at least 250 atlases, over 1,400 cataloged maps—of which some 300 are set maps containing up to 200 items in a set—and almost 10,000 uncataloged maps. The following is a breakdown by country (and geographic region) of the above:

Country/area	Cataloged maps	Set maps	Atlases	Number of drawers*
Burma	45	21	4	5
Cambodia	49	4	4	5
Laos	45	7	2	3
Vietnam	141	30	8	15
Indochina	65	50	19	25
Indonesia	480	30	125	65
Malaya/Malaysia	226	30	22	18**
Philippines	255	62	50	83
Singapore	17	8	6	–
Thailand	90	35	20	14
SEA general	100		18	10

*Uncataloged maps, 40 per drawer.
**Uncataloged maps of Singapore are included in the Malaysia collection. Several maps of Brunei are also in this collection.

In addition to the above materials, there is a smaller number of uncataloged maps published by Southeast Asian countries. A count of these materials revealed the following: Indonesia, 2 drawers; Philippines, 6 drawers; and Thailand, 3 drawers. There is an additional collection of approximately 150 titles related to Southeast Asia—many of which are Southeast Asian government publications—listed in the *Bibliography of Cartography*.

4.   No single comprehensive catalog of the division's holdings exists. There are, however, several card catalogs that provide access to part of the collection. For those uncataloged items, the reference personnel are very helpful. Card indexes for maps, atlases, and reference materials are located in the reading room.

Scholars may wish to consult *A List of Geographical Atlases in the Library of Congress with bibliographic notes,* by Philip Lee Phillips (1920), and 4 supplementary volumes (1974) compiled by Clara Egil LeGear. Also see the *Bibliography of Cartography,* (Boston: G. K. Hall and Co., 1973), a comprehensive, analytical index to the literature of cartography that provides author, title, and subject access to books and journal articles relating to maps, mapmakers, and the history of cartography. In 1968, a computer-assisted cataloging system was initiated for current accessions of single-sheet maps. The division also distributed the brochure, "Geography and Map Division," as well as several more extensive introductory publications.

Marine Corps Historical Center See entry B6

Martin Luther King, Jr., Memorial Library (District of Columbia Public Library) See entry A28

Maryland University Libraries See entry A29

National Aeronautics and Space Administration–Audio Visual Services See entry K25

E5 National Archives and Records Service (NARS)—Center for Cartographic and Architectural Archives

1. a. *8th Street and Pennsylvania Avenue, N.W.*
    Washington, D.C. 20408
    (202) 523-3062

    b. 8:45 A.M.–5:00 P.M.   Monday–Friday

    c. Open to researchers with a National Archives research card, obtainable from the Central Reference Division, Room 200-B.

    d. Photoreproduction services are available for a fee.

    e. William Cunliffe, Director

2. The National Archives's cartographic holdings in this center exceed 1.6 million maps and 2.25 million serial photographs and constitute one of the world's largest cartographic collections. Maps of Southeast Asian countries and the region as a whole are scattered throughout the collection. No numerical estimate is possible. Some of the significant holdings pertaining to the region are described below under the record group (RG) numbers into which the holdings are organized.

3. Southeast Asian cartographic materials include diverse basic maps, nautical charts, aeronautical charts, military maps, and various topical maps; e.g., economic resources, production and consumption, transportation and communications systems, commerce and trade routes, and demographic charts. Some of these maps and other graphic records are in manuscript form. Much of the cartographic material on Southeast Asia belongs to the World War II period and was generated by the U.S. defense and security agencies.
    RG 18: Records of the Army Air Force. The Aeronautical Chart Service was responsible for the cartographic activities of the Army Air Forces. Among the chart series produced were the World Long Range, World Planning, World Weather, Approach Charts of Strategic Areas, and large-scale Target Charts.
    The cartographic records of the group contain an undetermined number of maps and charts of Southeast Asia in small territorial segments, and the waters surrounding the region, e.g., the Andaman Sea, the Java Sea, the Philippine Sea, the South China Sea, and the Straits of Malacca.
    RG 37: Records of the Hydrographic Office. Included in this record group are U.S. Navy surveys of the Western Pacific. There are also some items from U.S. consular officials on various cities in the Netherlands East Indies.
    RG 38: Records of the Office of the Chief of Naval Operations. "Maps of the World" published in 1929, showing naval bases, stations, and other installations of the British Empire, Japan, the United States, France, and

Italy are included here, along with a number of general maps on Asia, 1894–1919.

RG 59: General Records of the Department of State. This is a relatively large and important collection of cartographic materials, consisting of miscellaneous maps showing the location of United States diplomatic and consular posts from 1844 to 1951; maps enclosed in confidential and diplomatic inspection reports, showing American and foreign consulates, embassies, and significant commercial and industrial establishments; maps and graphs showing natural resources and economic activities in various foreign countries (1943–1949); and maps and charts of foreign countries maintained by the Office of the Geographer of the State Department.

The following are some examples of materials found in the Foreign Service inspection reports: Dutch East Indies, showing coasting routes at Makassar, 1915; Indo-China, Cambodia, Tonkin, and Cochin-China, 1915; Indo-China, Saigon, 1915; Malay Peninsula, 1911; 2 maps of Batavia, Java, 1913 and 1921; 2 maps of Medan, Sumatra, 1930 and 1935; 2 maps of Penang Straits Settlement, 1921 and 1935; Rangoon and suburbs, 1935; Singapore, 1935; and several maps of Surabaya, Java, 1913, 1921, and 1935.

RG 77: Records of the Office of the Chief Engineer. This is a large and important group. Researchers should first consult the very useful Index of Maps at the Army Map Service Library. The U.S. Army Map Service (AMS) contains about 12,000 topographic maps on East Asan countries. There are at least 500 maps dealing with Southeast Asia, most of these from the World War II period. The scale varies from 1:500,000 to 1:25,000. Also included is a topographical model of North Vietnam.

For Malaya there are rail and road maps, area maps of the various states including Johore, Kelantan, Pahang, Singapore, and Trengganu; maps showing the Georgetown, Koto Bharu, and Singapore areas, and some city plans including Butterworth, Ipoh, Kuala Lumpur, and Port Sweetenham.

There is a large group of topographical maps covering Indo-China broken down into small segments. Maps of Cholon, Hanoi, Haiphong, Phnom Penh, Saigon, Vinh, and other cities are included.

A smaller number of topographical maps of Thailand and Burma are to be found, along with plans for Chiangma, Phuket, and other Thai cities.

Maps of the Philippines are extensive, covering all the major islands. Some of these maps are scaled at 1:50,000 showing considerable detail.

Maps of the Dutch East Indies include maps of Java, Sumatra, Timor, the Molukka Islands, North Borneo (Sabah), and Sarawak. Some road and rail maps are included.

Some of the more unusual items in this record group are: a "Sketch of Saigon-Cap. St. Jaques Road (1907)," map of East Indies Islands (Malaysia and Melanesia), showing communication and transportation routes; and a Philippine map of the operations against Manila, August 13, 1898.

Within this record group is a subgroup titled "Fortifications Map File," which includes maps of the Philippines and plans of fortifications and military equipment (1845–1942). The War Department Map Collection contains a large number of maps on the Philippines pertaining to the Philippine pacification program. There are also some topographical maps of the Philippines.

RG 83: Records of the Bureau of Agricultural Economics (BAE). Entry 24 contains the following material on Southeast Asia: a 1917 "dot" map of Java showing crop production on the island and a 1917 "dot" map of the Philippines showing crop and livestock production. See Special List 28,

Cartographic Records of the Burea of Agricultural Economics for infor- mation on this record group.

RG 95: Records of the Forest Service. This record group contains maps showing the distribution of forests by the type of tree for all parts of the world.

RG 120: Records of the American Expeditionary Forces, World War I (1917–1923). This record group contains some topographical maps of South- east Asia.

RG 127: Records of the U.S. Marine Corps. Several general maps on Southeast Asia and Indo-China can be found here.

RG 165: Records of the War Department General and Special Staffs. Cartographic records of the group include maps of World War II theaters of operations. Much of this material has been transferred to RG 277. In- cluded are railway maps of Burma as well as topographic models of Burma, the Philippines, Okinawa, and other locations in the Pacific Theater of Operations.

RG 226: Records of the Offices of Strategic Services. This is an important record group for the Southeast Asianist. The group contains in excess of 100 regional items, some of which are real gems. These maps are generally thematic in nature, depicting information that relates to transportation systems, utilities, population distribution, land utilization, and industrial activities. There is an incomplete, but excellent, index that is available to the researcher. While there are items for all countries in the region, the largest holdings are for the Philippines and Indo-China. Some of the maps to be found in this group are: railway routes in India and Burma (1942); navigable waterways of Burma (1942); Thai and Indo-China territorial changes, 1869–1907 (1944); French Indo-China, Phon Penh, water supply system (1945); Thailand plans of the British-American Tobacco Company (1944); Philippine Islands, Transportation Facilities of Palawan (1944); and Brunei, City Plan, Town of Brunei (1945).

RG 242: National Archives Collection of Foreign Records Seized, 1941—. This record group includes several Japanese maps of the region and the Pacific. Some descriptive material accompanies certain items.

RG 324: Records of the Office of Geography. The Office of Geography provides research and other staff services on foreign geographic nomen- clature for the interdepartmental Board of Geographic Names and the Secretary of the Interior. Included in the records of the office are gazetteers from the Board of Geographic Names and the Central Intelligence Agency on Burma, Cambodia, Indonesia (including Malaya, North Borneo, and Sarawak), Indochina, and the Philippines. Gazetteers give the name, lat- itude, and longitude of cities, towns, and villages. There seems to be an extensive amount of data for Indonesia even taking into consideration the inclusion of Malaya, North Borneo, and Sarawak.

RG 332: Records of U.S. Theaters of War, World War II. This record group includes maps of Southeast Asia showing military targets and bases, including maps of rail lines, highways, and port facilities.

RG 341: Records of the Headquarters, United States Air Force. This record group may contain aeronautical charts of Southeast Asia.

RG 395: Records of U.S. Army Overseas Operations and Commands 1898–1942. Included are over 2,200 maps—from both tactical and direc- tional units—relating chiefly to the Spanish–American War and the Phil- ippine Pacification (1898–1902).

The following record groups may also be of interest to the Southeast Asia scholar:

RG 32: Records of the United States Shipping Board; RG 46: Records of the United States Senate; RG 94: Records of the Adjutant General's Office; RG 114: Records of the Soil Conservation Service; RG 169: Records of the Foreign Economic Administration; RG 253: Records of the Petroleum Administration for War; RG 331: Records of the Allied Operational and Occupation Headquarters, World War II; and RG 456: Records of the Defense Mapping Agency.

In addition to the finding aids maintained by this center, researchers may wish to consult the *Guide to Cartographic Records in the National Archives* (1971), by Charlotte M. Ashby et al., and the United States Hydrographic Office's *Manuscript Charts in the National Archives, 1838–1908* (1978), by William J. Keynan.

E6 National Geographic Society—Cartographic Division Map Library

1. a. *Membership Center Building*
    11555 Darnestown Road
    Gaithersburg, Maryland 20760
    (301) 857-7000, extension 1401

    b. 7:30 A.M.–4:00 P.M.   Monday–Friday

    c. Open to the public for on-site use only. Maps from this collection may also be made available to scholars through the National Geographic Society Library (see entry A31).

    d. Photoduplication facilities are available.

    e. Margery Barkdull, Map Librarian

2–3.   This excellent worldwide collection is estimated to contain some 100,000 maps, mostly of recent origin. The cartographic materials include topographic, administrative, subject, and highway maps, as well as lunar maps, nautical and aeronautical charts, and city plans. The library is the depository of all maps produced by the National Geographic Society. Library holdings also include extensive acquisitions from various foreign national mapping agencies. A good selection of atlases, reference books, and gazetteers are also available. Southeast Asian items include: Burma, 5; Indonesia, 15; Malaysia, 7; Philippines, 46; Singapore, 2; Thailand, 8; and Vietnam, 13.

4.   A card catalog arranged by geographical region and country provides access to the collection. Maps published by the society may be purchased at the Explorers Hall sales desk located at 1145 17th Street, N.W., Washington, D.C. 20036 (202/857-7589).

Naval Historical Center (Navy Department)—Operational Archives Branch See entry B9

E7 World Bank Cartographic Information Center

1.   a. *1919 K Street, N.W.*
     Washington, D.C. 20433
     (202) 676-0229

     b. 8:30 A.M.–4:30 P.M.   Monday–Friday

     c. Open to the public for on-site use only. Appointment required.

     d. Reproduction facilities are available.

     e. Christine Windheuser, Librarian

2–4.   This small reference collection of some 10,000 items contains approximately 800 basic general maps and topographic sheets on the countries of Southeast Asia. There is no catalog or inventory available for this collection. It may be noted that most items in this collection are also available at the Geography and Map Division of the Library of Congress (see entry E4).

F Film Collections (Still Photographs and Motion Pictures)

Film Collections Entry Format (F)

1.   General Information
    a. *address; telephone numbers*
    b. hours of service
    c. conditions of access
    d. name/title of director and key staff members

2.   Size of Holdings Pertaining to Southeast Asia

3.   Description of Holdings Pertaining to Southeast Asia

4.   Facilities for Study and Use
    a. availability of audiovisual equipment
    b. reservation requirements
    c. fees charged
    d. reproduction services

5.   Bibliographic Aids Facilitating Use of Collection

Introductory Note

The motion picture and still photographic collections in Washington contain some remarkable items. Prints and photographs in the Library of Congress (entry F13) include some superb nineteenth- and early twentieth-century views of people and places in Southeast Asia. From these photos a fascinating picture of the colonial era in the region emerges. Of particular interest is the collection of some 900 stereos, which depict the Philippines in the late 1800s. Likewise, the National Archives Still Picture Branch (entry F17) contains thousands of fascinating scenes of life in Southeast Asia.

Washington also holds tremendous photo resources covering the Vietnam conflict. The combined collections of the Air Force Still Photographic Depository (entry F2), the Army Audiovisual Center (entry F4), the Marine Corps Still Photographic Archive (entry F14), and the Naval Historical Center (Photographic Section) (entry F19) provide a virtually complete photo history of the Vietnam conflict and U.S. participation in it. This combined resource is unsurpassed. In addition, readers should note that a tremendous collection of World War II photos is maintained by these same facilities.

The amount of film footage on Southeast Asia in the Washington area is staggering. As an example, the National Archives, Motion Picture, Sound and Video Branch (entry F16) has, on video tape, all Vietnam related news items of the three major television networks.

In addition to the above, several embassies—Indonesia (entry F5), Malaysia (entry F6), Singapore (entry F7) and Thailand (entry F8)—maintain small collections of films depicting life in those countries. Other organizations, such as the World Bank (entry F22), maintain photo or film collections that focus on various facets of life in Southeast Asia.

For more detail on cinematography, the reader may wish to consult this series' volume by Bonnie Gail Rowan, *Scholars' Guide to Washington, D.C. Film and Video Collections* (Washington, D.C.: Smithsonian Institution Press, 1980).

F1 Agency for International Development (AID)—Photo Collection

1. a. *AID Office of Public Affairs*
State Department Building
320 21st Street, N.W., Room 4890
Washington, D.C. 20523
(202) 632-4330

    b. 9:30 A.M.–11:30 A.M., 1:30 P.M.–3:30 P.M.   Monday–Friday

    c. Open to researchers. Appointment required.

    d. Edward Caplan, Chief of Publications

2–3. The AID photograph collection contains approximately 20,000 photographs (black and white) and a large collection of color slides covering such AID foreign-aid projects as the construction of dams, hospitals, and schools, and documenting the living conditions and various scenes of the populations and habitats of the U.S. aid recipients. The Southeast Asian portion of this collection is fair, covering mostly the Philippines, Indonesia, and Thailand. A numerical estimate is not possible.

4. A fee is charged for reproducing photos and duplicating slides. Requests for prints must be made in person. Loans are for two weeks. No originals are lent.

F2 Air Force Still Photographic Depository

1. a. *1212 South Fern Street*
Arlington, Virginia 22202
(202) 695-1147

    b. 7:30 A.M.–4:00 P.M.   Monday–Friday

    c. Visitors are encouraged to telephone ahead to insure that appropriate personnel and the required materials are available.

2. This collection of still photographs consists of approximately 400,000 items. Some 60,000 still pictures pertain to East Asia (including Southeast Asia), with about 30,000 of these being from Vietnam and the Vietnam conflict.

A substantial number of stills from World War II will also be of interest to Southeast Asianists.

An approximate breakdown of the collection is as follows: Vietnam, 106 color and 144 black-and-white albums; and Thailand, 71 color and 20 black-and-white albums. For the World War II period, there are 67 albums for the Burma-India Theater, 24 for the Philippines, 7 for the Netherlands East Indies, 19 for New Guinea, 1 for the Malay Peninsula, and 2 for Indochina. These photographs are primarily in black and white.

A sampling of headings to be found include: airplanes, banking, civil affairs, maintenance, medical, prisons, psychological warfare, Viet Cong, and wrecks.

4.   Copies of unclassified photography are made available to the public for a nominal charge to cover the cost of services and reproduction.

5.   The depository maintains a visual-print file arranged by subject and geographic area. These prints are kept in albums (referred to in point 2) on open shelves. Each photo has its own identification number plus a brief caption citing the background as well as the date and location of the picture taken. The depository also has a valuable cross-indexing system. An information sheet is available on request.

It should be noted that by early 1982 this collection will be moved to the U.S. Naval Station where the Navy Motion Media Depository is now located. No additional information is available at this time. See entry F20.

American Film Institute (AFI) See entry M7

F3 American Red Cross Photograph Collection

1.   a. *Office of Communications Resources—Photographic Services*
431 18th St., N.W.
Washington, D.C. 20006
(202) 857-3428

b. 8:30 A.M.–4:45 P.M.   Monday–Friday

c. Open to the public. Appointment recommended.

d. Phillip A. Gibson, Chief, Photographic Services

2–3.   The total collection consists of more than 20,000 black-and-white photographs and some 1,000 color transparencies. Coverage includes nursing and relief activities of the Red Cross and the humanitarian efforts in the aftermath of natural calamities, disasters, and warfare. Most of the photographs deal with the period since 1950.

4.   Photoduplication services are available.

5.   Southeast Asian related prints are arranged chronologically, by country, in an International Services File.

F4 Army Audiovisual Center (Army Department)

1. a. *The Pentagon, Room 5A486*
   Washington, D.C. 20310
   (202) 687-2806 (Reference Library)

   b. 10:00 A.M.–4:00 P.M. Monday–Friday

   c. Access to the Pentagon is restricted, although the photograph collection is open to the public. Researchers should call in advance.

   d. Vickie Destefano, Reference Librarian

2. The collection contains more than one million prints in both black and white and color. Over 20,000 of these still photographs are on Vietnam and cover virtually all phases of army involvement in the conflict. An additional 5,000-plus photos cover World War II activities in the Philippines, New Guinea, and the China-Burma-India Theater.

3. The collection spans a period from the 1940s to the present. Subjects covered include army officers, troops, equipment, defense installations, U.S. military-assistance activities in Vietnam, U.S.–Vietnam military ceremonies, and U.S. military operations and activities in Vietnam and the Pacific (World War II).

4. Commercial photoreproduction services and the current fee schedule are described in a free information leaflet, which is available on request.

5. Separate card indexes, arranged geographically, are maintained for both the black-and-white and color prints.

F5 Embassy of the Republic of Indonesia

1. a. *2020 Massachusetts Avenue, N.W.*
   Washington, D.C. 20036
   (202) 293-1745

   b. 9:00 A.M.–5:00 P.M. Monday–Friday

   c. Open to the public.

   d. T. M. Soelaiman, Educational and Cultural Attaché

2–4. The Indonesian Embassy has a small collection (6 titles) of films. The collection includes documentaries—produced by oil companies, the National Geographic Society, and a Japanese television station—on the geography and culture of Indonesia. Subjects include the Ramayana, batik, and Bali.

   Films may be borrowed in person or by mail. Reservations should be made one week in advance. A projector is available for restricted use. For television rights and purchase of copies, contact the embassy.

5. A list of the films is available on request.

F6 Embassy of Malaysia

1. a. *2401 Massachusetts Avenue, N.W.*
    Washington, D.C. 20008
    (202) 234-7600

    b. 9:30 A.M.–1:00 P.M., 2:00 P.M.–5:00 P.M.   Monday–Friday

    c. Open to the public.

    d. Gopalan Narayanan Nair, First Secretary (Information)

2–4.   The Malaysian Embassy has a collection of 30 films mostly on Malaysia and Southeast Asia, which include short documentaries covering such topics as geography, agriculture, history, arts and crafts of Malaysia, and political development. Several films feature dance and dance drama from Malaysia and other Southeast Asian countries. Other films deal with weaving, kites, silver, batik, and the Jenka Project.

   Films may be borrowed by mail and in person. Reservations should be made at least two months in advance, and in writing. A 16-mm projector is available for use at the embassy, but the staff prefers to lend the films. For information on television rights and purchase of copies, contact the embassy.

   The embassy also has a small collection of old black-and-white photographs.

5.   A descriptive list of holdings is available by mail on request.

F7 Embassy of Singapore

1. a. *1824 R Street, N.W.*
    Washington, D.C. 20009
    (202) 667-7555

    b. 9:00 A.M.–5:00 P.M.   Monday–Friday

    c. Open to the public.

    d. Peter Chan, Counselor

2–4.   The Singapore Embassy has approximately 12 recent films, most of which are 20 to 30 minutes in length. Subjects covered include Singapore history and geography, festivals, housing, and satellite communication.

   Reservations can be made by phone, and films may be borrowed via mail or in person. A projector is available for very limited use. For information on television rights and purchase of copies, contact the embassy.

5.   A list of titles is available by mail.

F8 Embassy of Thailand

1. a. *2300 Kalorama Road, N.W.*
    Washington, D.C. 20008
    (202) 667-1446

b. 10:00 A.M.–5:00 P.M.   Monday–Friday

c. Open to the public.

d. Pawa Watanasupt, Public Relations Attaché

2–4.   The Embassy has a small collection of 10 films that show the geography and culture of Thailand. There is one 90-minute film in Thai, *Investiture of the Crown Prince*. Also featured in the shorter films are museums, life of a Buddhist monk, silk and sculpture.

    Reservations should be made at least one month in advance. Films may be borrowed by mail or in person. A projector is available for very limited use. For television rights and purchase of copies, contact the embassy.

5.   A descriptive list of the films is available by mail.

F9 Folklife Program (Smithsonian Institution)—Film and Still Photographs Collection

1.   a. *2600 L'Enfant Plaza*
Washington, D.C. 20560
(202) 287-3424

b. 9:00 A.M.–5:00 P.M.   Monday–Friday

c. Open to the public. Appointments required.

d. Ralph Rinzler, Director
Richard Derbyshire, Archivist

2–3.   The Festivals of American Folklife, sponsored by the Smithsonian Institution's Folklife Program, have included a number of participants from overseas, including several Southeast Asian groups in the 1980 festival. Since 1967, but particularly since 1974, the various exhibitions of the Folklife festivals and other special programs and shows presented by this program have been recorded on film. The collection of these materials now exceeds 3,000 black-and-white contact print sheets (of up to 36 exposures each), 35,000 color transparencies, and 144,000 feet of motion-picture film. These materials include visual examples of Southeast Asian folk dancing and Buddhist religious ceremonies.

4.   a. Viewing facilities are available.

b. Reservations are required.

c. No fees are charged for use of the archival materials of the equipment.

d. Standard Smithsonian Institution reproduction procedures and fees apply. An information flyer describing these regulations is available on request.

5.   An unpublished catalog of the film collection is available at the archive facility. No finding aids exist for the other materials; however, an inventory of the holdings and a set of program books and schedules are available and will assist scholars in their search for possible resources in the collection.

F10 Food and Agriculture Organization (FAO)—Liaison Office for North America (United Nations)—Photographic Collection

1. a. *1776 F Street, N.W.*
    Suite 101
    Washington, D.C. 20437
    (202) 376-2306

    b. 8:30 A.M.–4:00 P.M.   Monday–Friday

    c. Open to the public. Appointment required.

    d. Jay J. Levy, Information Officer

2. The collection consists of nearly 6,000 black-and-white prints, of which several hundred relate to Indonesia, the Philippines, and Thailand.

3. The collection covers FAO and other UN development activities in the fields of land and water use, animal and plant production, rural welfare, nutrition, fisheries, forestry, wildlife and more, on a worldwide basis. The coverage of general agricultural, cultural, and environmental subjects is substantial. Photos date from the 1950s to the present.

4. A limited number of prints will be supplied to researchers without charge.

5. The photo collection is arranged by country or major development activity or both, but is not indexed beyond 1970. The holdings are drawn from the extensive collection (100,000 black-and-white prints and 10,000 color slides) maintained at FAO headquarters in Rome. See the *FAO Photo Library Catalogue* (Rome, 1972) and the *FAO Color Transparencies Catalogue* (Rome, 1979) for further information on content, arrangement, and ordering instructions.

F11 International Labor Office (International Labor Organization)— Washington Branch Office Photograph Collection

1. a. *1750 New York Avenue, N.W.*
    Room 330
    Washington, D.C. 20006
    (202) 376-2315

    b. 8:30 A.M.–5:00 P.M.   Monday–Friday

    c. Open to the public.

    d. Patricia S. Hord, Librarian

2. The collection consists of some 2,000 black-and-white prints. A few hundred are on Southeast Asia.

3. The collection is worldwide in scope and includes a variety of photographs of workers and working conditions in Southeast Asia. The topical arrangement of the holdings covers such subjects as agriculture cooperatives, child workers, construction, employment, environment, health, housing, International Labor Organization (ILO) conferences and projects, labor con-

ditions, living conditions, management development, petroleum, planta-
tions, pollution, productivity, small-scale industries, technical cooperation,
village scenes, vocational training, welfare facilities, women workers, and
youth. General Southeast Asia scenes plus items from the Philippines,
Malaysia, Indonesia, Thailand, Singapore, and Vietnam are included in the
collection. The time period runs from the early 1900s to the present, but
most items fall into the post-1950 period.

4.   Prints can be made available to researchers without charge.

5.   The prints maintained at the Washington office have been drawn from the
larger photo library at the ILO headquarters in Geneva. The *ILO Photo
Library Catalogue* (Geneva, 1973), which is available from the Washington
office, describes the content and arrangement (by subject and geographic
area) of the collection. Instructions are included for obtaining photos from
Geneva.

F12   Library of Congress—Motion Picture, Broadcasting, and Recorded Sound Division

1.   a. *Madison Building, Room LM 338*
   101 Independence Avenue, S.E.
   Washington, D.C. 20540
   (202) 287-5840

   b. 8:30 A.M.–4:30 P.M.   Monday–Friday

   c. Open to the public.

   d. Paul Spehr, Acting Chief

2.   This division is responsible for the acquisition, cataloging, preserving, and
servicing of the motion picture and television collections, including items
on film, videotape, and videodisc. The division is also responsible for LC's
holdings of sound recordings. For a description of sound recordings see
entry D4.
    The film and television collections contain over 75,000 titles, with several
thousand titles being added each year. The collection also includes approximately 300,000 stills.

3.   The actual size of the Southeast Asia collection is undetermined, although
it is doubtful that more than several hundred items on the area are included.
One can locate a number of items by checking appropriate country headings
in the card catalog. However, many films can be located only by title.
    The most interesting Southeast Asia material is the collection of some
20 films on the Vietnam conflict, most of which were produced by the South
Vietnamese government. Some of the titles in this collection are: *A Night-
mare Ten Years Long* (1964); *As Saigon Slept* (1966?); *Communist Massacre
in Hue* (1969); and *A Message from Vietnam* (1964). This small collection
is accessible through a file folder that may be seen by asking a reference
person.
    There are a few films for Burma, Indonesia, and Singapore as well as an
NBC series of three films: *Thailand: the New Front* (1966); *Laos: the Forgotten War* (1966); and *Indonesia: the Troubled Victory* (1967).

There is also a very large Japanese film collection of some 1,400 items produced in Japan primarily during the 1930s and 1940s. This collection includes a number of short documentaries that deal with such subjects as Japanese military activities in Southeast Asia.

4.   a. Film and television collections are not available for projection, rental, or loan. Limited viewing facilities are available for 35 mm, 16 mm, and videotape viewing.

    b. Advance appointments are required for the use of viewing facilities.

    c. There is no charge for use of research facilities.

    d. Some materials may be reproduced subject to copyright or donor restrictions.

5.   The division reading room has a collection of 1,500 books and approximately 20 periodicals. Vertical files are arranged by subject and title. Also available are descriptions, including synopses, pressbooks, and scripts, for films and television programs registered for copyright in the United States since 1912.

    The following finding aids are available in the Motion Picture, Broadcasting, and Recorded Sound Division office:

Directors File: Arranged alphabetically by name of director, entries contain the titles of films by the directors in the LC collection.
Nitrate Shelflist: Films are arranged by title, company, and date.
Shelflist: Contains an entry, by title, for each motion picture in the LC collection (safety films only).
Silent Film Files: Films are arranged by title, company, and date.
Special Collections Card Catalog. Arranged by collection, with an entry for every motion picture in a specific collection.

Scholars may wish to consult the Library of Congress, Copyright Office *Catalog of Copyright Entries: Motion Pictures* and *Library of Congress Catalog—Audiovisual Materials*. Another useful publication is entitled *Motion Pictures from the Library of Congress Paper Print Collection: 1894–1912*, by Kemp R. Niver (Berkeley: University of California Press, 1967). The division distributes a printed guide, *Film and Television*, containing basic information on the division.

F13 Library of Congress—Prints and Photographs Division

1.   a. *Madison Building, Third Floor*
    101 Independence Avenue, S.E.
    (202) 287-6394

    b. 8:30 A.M.–4:30 P.M.   Monday–Friday

    c. Open to the public.

    d. Oliver Jensen, Chief

2.   This division is responsible for LC's collection of more than 10 million photographs, negatives, prints, posters, and other pictorial materials. The division's general collection of 9 million photographs and negatives is one

of the finest general historical collections in the world. The collection is international in scope, though most materials relate to the United States.

Still photographs are arranged by lot rather than by individual piece. One may therefore locate not a specific item, but rather a group of photos related to an area of interest. Lots are accessible through the division's card catalog, which is arranged by subject, photographer or creator, and collector, and through other reference indexes, inventories, and the staff.

3.   The Southeast Asia materials, while moderate in volume are fascinating in their diversity. There are, at a minimum, 100 lots of Southeast Asia materials. Some examples are as follows:

Burma: Card no./lot 2581—a varied collection of ethnological and archaeological photos in Annam, Tonkin, Cambodia, Laos, Cochin China, and Bali, 5 albums, 1920–1925; No. 10980—the career of Dr. Gordon Stifler Seagrave, the "Burma Surgeon," 1939–1963, 311 photos; No. 7071—the Stilwell Road 1945, 29 photos.

Cambodia: No. 2841—collection of anthropological photos, 1925–1935; No. 5789—Collection of maps, plans, and photos used to illustrate the *Ancient Khmer Empire*, by Lawrence Briggs.

Indochina: No. 6287—"Operation Mercure," a military engagement near Thu Binh in Tonkin, 1952, 10 photos.

Indonesia: No. 6647—opium factory in Batavia, 1928, 8 photos; No. 9033—collection taken by Indonesia Press Photo Service, showing Indonesia's struggle for independence, 201 photos.

Malaya: No. 8116—picture survey of Malayan rivers, 1943, 300 photos; No. 6664—waterfront and other views in or near Penang, 1880, 73 photos.

Philippines: No. 2952—aspects of the Philippine Islands in 1890–1910?, 100 photos; No. 8637—William Howard Taft and his party in Hawaii, Japan, and the Philippines, taken by Burr McIntosh in 1905, 54 photos.

Thailand: No. 6091—aerial views of Siam collected by Brigadier General William (Billy) Mitchell, n.d., 24 photos; No. 8960—Siamese people, views, and events, 1894–1898, 200 photos.

The division also has a stereo file that contains approximately 900 stereoscopic photos of Southeast Asia. There is a modest collection of 120 stereoscopic scenes of Burma, and some 30 showing various parts of New Guinea. The remainder of these items, approximately 750, are from the Philippine Islands, produced in the late 1890s and in 1900. This collection depicts many facets of Philippine life at the turn of the century.

4.   d. Most materials may be reproduced subject to copyright laws.

5.   There is no comprehensive catalog of still pictures. The only published reference is LC's *Guide to the Special Collections of Prints and Photographs in the Library of Congress* (1955) compiled by Paul Vanderbilt. The best finding aids are the several card catalogs. There are separate card catalogs for fine prints, historical prints, posters, and master photographs. The *Look* (magazine) Collection has its own index. Also see the Prints and Photographs Division's *Viewpoints, a Selection from the Pictorial Collections of the Library of Congress* (1975).

F14 Marine Corps Still Photographic Archives

1. a. *Marine Corps Historical Center*
    Building 58
    Washington Navy Yard
    9th and M streets, S.E.
    Washington, D.C. 20374
    (202) 433-3364

    b. 10:00 A.M.–4:00 P.M.   Monday–Friday

    c. Visitors are encouraged to telephone ahead to insure that appropriate personnel and the required records are available.

    d. Sergeant W. K. Judge, Head, Still Photographic Archives

2. The Marine Corps Still Photographic Archives currently contains over 550,000 negatives and transparencies depicting Marine Corps history, personnel, and mission from December 1941 through the present. The archives do not contain classified or restricted material, and all records are considered to be in the public domain. Publication rights are not required. Reproduction services are limited to those documents in the official file.

3. Photographic coverage of the Marine Corps during World War II represents about half of the photo collection. Combat photographs include all major battles in the Pacific. Most photos are in black and white. The Vietnam War era collection begins with coverage of Corps helicopter operations in 1963. Documentation of Corps activities is comprehensive. Coverage of many company and platoon size actions are available. Documentation includes equipment, weapons, construction, aviation, and other topics. Combat photos of the major offensive actions include Hue City, Khe Sanh, Con Tien, Dong Ha, and the "Rockpile." The majority of photos in this collection is in color.

4. The archives personnel do not reproduce materials. All photo work is done at a Marine Corps photo lab, but requests for photoduplication can be processed through the archives. Reproduction is limited to three copies for each item, and a fee is charged for this service.

5. The Still Photographic Archives maintains a photo reference library that is open to the public. Items are identified on index cards, filed by major subject. Each card contains a sample print, information caption, and the negative number. Also available is a cross-index of names identifying the records of over 32,000 individuals on index cards that are filed alphabetically.

F15 Martin Luther King Memorial Library—Audiovisual Division

1. a. *901 G Street, N.W.*
    Room 226
    Washington, D.C. 20001
    (202) 727-1265

    b. 9:00 A.M.–9:00 P.M.   Monday–Thursday
    9:00 A.M.–5:30 P.M.   Friday–Saturday

c. Open to the public. All library patrons are eligible to borrow films for an overnight period during weekdays.

d. Diane Henry, Division Chief

2–3. The entire collection of the division comprises over 3,000 film titles, some 700 filmstrips, and numerous slides covering a wide range of subjects. This growing collection includes some 10 films on Vietnam, including *Part of the Family, Holy War,* and *Sad Song of Yellow Skin.*

4. a. Equipment for viewing is available.

b. Borrowers are encouraged to reserve films as far in advance as possible but at least three days before pickup.

c. No fees are charged.

d. No reproduction services are available.

5. *DC Public Library Media Catalog* (1979) lists all the films in the collection.

F16 National Archives and Record Service (NARS)—Audiovisual Archives Division—Motion Picture, Sound, and Video Branch

1. a. *8th Street and Pennsylvania Avenue, N.W.*
Washington, D.C. 20408
(202) 523-3267

b. 8:45 A.M.–5:00 P.M.   Monday–Friday

c. Open to all serious researchers with a National Archives identification card, obtainable from the Central Reference Division, Room 200-B. First-time visitors are advised to consult with a reference specialist before beginning work.

d. William T. Murphy, Chief of the Branch

2. The Motion Picture, Sound and Video Branch has approximately 120,000 reels of motion-picture films including an undetermined number of items related to Southeast Asia. Sound recording collections under the jurisdiction of this branch are discussed in entry D5.

Materials in the film depository are organized in record groups as is the case with other divisions and branches. For an explanation of the concept and record groups, see entry B7. The following record groups contain materials of interest to Southeast Asia specialists:

RG 18: Records of the Army Air Force. This record group contains approximately 6,000 reels of motion pictures, most of which deal with the World War II period. There is some unedited film of bombing missions in Indochina, including some footage of the bombing of Hanoi and Haiphong (1943).

RG 59: General Records of the Department of State (1911–1965). Approximately 200 reels of film made by the department, related agencies, other government departments, and private companies can be found in this group. Included is a fair amount of footage of television shows, speeches, interviews, and discussions featuring secretaries and assistant secretaries of state, including Dean Acheson, Christian Herter, Dean Rusk, George Ball, and W. Averell Harriman, 1950–1965. Vietnam related material should be well represented in these films.

RG 107: Records of the Office of the Secretary of War (1941–1945). Contains 191 reels of film from the Bureau of Public Relations, including two films of the Philippine Congress in 1946, one of which shows General MacArthur addressing the opening session.

RG 111: Records of the Office of the Chief Signal Officer (1905–1954). This large collection of almost 16,000 reels provides documentary coverage of all aspects of World War II, including the conduct of the war in all theaters, mobilization and training, entertainment for the troops, and post-war problems in Asia. Included are motion pictures made by the Navy Department, Red Cross, and newsreel organizations. There are approximately 200 films of the Philippine Islands covering various topics. Much of the footage is from the island of Luzon.

There is also a small number of films on Indochina, including one film on French refugees fleeing to China (1945), a 1944 film, "Spotlight on Indochina," three films of the Netherlands East Indies, and one film from Singapore, "The Enemy Japan."

RG 200: National Archives Gift Collection (1896–1969). Within this very large gift collection of more than 13,000 items, there are approximately 1,000 films that deal with one or more Southeast Asian countries. The record group contains a very large collection of the Universal News for the period 1929–1967, excluding 1942–1943. There is a very good card index accompanying the collection, which houses approximately 150 films that deal with Burma, Indonesia, Malaya, Singapore, and Thailand. Included is a 1957 film of the Merdeka celebration in Malaya, and a 1945 film of the Japanese surrender in Burma. There are also some 200 films on the Philippines in the Universal collection. Many of these films cover the World War II period and focus on the armed forces and the government after independence.

The record group also includes films made by Fox, MGM, Movietone, News of the Day, Paramount, and other film companies. Scattered throughout this part of the collection are approximately 400 films on Indochina and Vietnam. About 75 films deal with Indochina, focusing mostly on the war during the period 1947–1955. The remaining 300-plus films, mostly MGM and Movietone, deal with the Vietnam conflict, with some films of the television show, "Face the Nation," included. Topics covered include senators Edward M. Kennedy and Joseph D. Tyding's visit to Saigon, the United Nations Security Council Meeting on Vietnam, Vice President Humphrey's visit to the second front in Vietnam, the Ho Chi Minh trail, and numerous battle reports.

The remaining countries in the region are covered in varying degree; e.g., Laos, Malaya/Malaysia, Singapore, and Thailand have approximately a dozen entries each. Films on the Philippines number in excess of 100. In addition to the above, a few government films, such as the International Cooperation Administration's *Report to the American People on Technical Cooperation (in Thailand)*, are included.

RG 208: Records of the Office of War Information (1941–1945). About 700 primarily documentary films covering various phases and aspects of World War II. A few scattered items on Southeast Asian countries are included.

RG 242: National Archives Collection of Foreign Records Seized (1941—). Most of this material deals with World War II. A few items related to Southeast Asia are included; for example, a 1941 Nippon News film of

Japanese officials' visit to Thailand, a 1942 Japanese film showing the invasion of Malaya and Borneo, and a 1942 film showing Japanese war activities in Singapore, Indonesia, and Malaya. Also included is the Japanese made film, *The Victory Story of the Orient* (1942), which runs 2 hours and 11 minutes.

RG 286: Records of the Agency for International Development. Included is the International Cooperation Administration's report-to-the-American-people series. Several of these films focus on Southeast Asia, and some films are on United States military assistance programs to the Southeast Asia Treaty Organization (SEATO).

RG 306: Records of the United States Information Agency. This collection contains a few items of interest to Southeast Asianists; for instance, the USIA's *Journey to the Pacific*—an agency documentary on the Indes war, 1945–1949—and *Asian Journey* (1961).

RG 330: Records of the Office of Secretary of Defense. A large collection of news footage on Vietnam broadcast by the three major networks, ABC, NBC, and CBS, for the period 1966–1976. For each program (news broadcast), items dealing with Vietnam are listed in the 10-volume program summaries (log books), which are available on level 20-E.

RG 342: Records of the United States Air Force Commands, Activities, and Organizations. Within this record group are approximately 150 films of Bien Hoa Air Base in South Vietnam. The films cover various activities at the base, off-loading of personnel, construction, parades, and combat action. This record group will rapidly increase in size, and significance to Southeast Asianists as more Vietnam related footage is turned over to the archives by the Air Force.

4. a. Audiovisual equipment is available for viewing of materials.

    b. Advance reservation of audiovisual equipment is advisable. Requests for same-day service may require a long wait.

    c. No fees are charged for the use of the facilities.

    d. Reproduction of audiovisual materials is available at a cost and requires prior scheduling. For those materials under copyright, or other restrictions, prior written permission is required. Researchers may use their own equipment to reproduce materials at no cost.

5. Researchers may wish to consult *Motion Pictures in the Audiovisual Archives Division of the National Archives* (1972), by Mayfield S. Bray and William T. Murphy, and *Audiovisual Records in the National Archives Relating to World War II* (1974), by the same authors. The more general *Guide to the National Archives of the United States* (1974), may also be useful. The branch maintains several card catalogs that provide fairly complete coverage of materials. As the traffic in this branch seems to be moderate, archivists are easily accessible.

F17 National Archives and Record Service (NARS)—Still Picture Branch (Audiovisual Archives Division)

1. a. *8th Street and Pennsylvania Avenue, N.W.*
    Washington, D.C. 20408
    (202) 523-3236

b. 8:45 A.M.–5:00 P.M.   Monday–Friday

c. Open to scholars with a National Archives identification card obtainable from the Central Reference Division, Room 200-B.

d. Joseph Thomas, Chief

2.   The Still Picture Branch has a collection in excess of 5 million items, including black-and-white original and copy photographs, glass and film negatives, prints, color transparencies and negatives, stenographs, posters, artwork, and photographs of art-work dating from the seventeenth century. The holdings include the archival photograph files of over 140 U.S. federal agencies and several gift collections. Although the bulk of the material relates to the United States, Southeast Asia is fairly well represented in the collection.

3.   The following record groups contain material relating to Southeast Asia. Other record groups, not mentioned below, may contain items of interest.

RG 18: Records of the Army Air Force (1901–1964). Various types of World War II pictures of Burma, the Molucca Islands, and the Philippines may be found in this record group.

RG 27: Records of the Weather Bureau. Included are photographs of the bureau's projects and facilities, as well as shots of natural disasters, cloud formations, and freakish atmospheric conditions, 1871–1945. A number of photos are from the Philippines.

RG 59: General Records of the Department of State (1774–1955). This group is made up of photographs received by the department from United States consular and diplomatic representatives. Covering a variety of subjects, the photos are of buildings, bridges, farming, commerce, communications, industry, living conditions, trade, and transport. A fair number of pictures from Southeast Asia may be found here. One particular item of interest is the photographic record of Richard Nixon's trip to the Far East in 1953, when he was vice president. Three boxes of photos from Burma and Indonesia are included.

RG 77: Records of the Office of the Chief of Engineers. Included are pictures of buildings, fortifications, coastal defenses, and equipment at camps, posts, and stations in the Philippines, 1850–1941. A second group of photographs consists of scenes in the Philippine Islands, including Manila, 1918–1919.

RG 94: Records of the Adjutant General's Office, 1780s–1917. Miscellaneous photographs relating to the Spanish-American War and the Philippine Insurrection, 1898–1900, are to be found in this group.

RG 111: Records of the Office of the Chief Signal Officer. Contains illustrations of the Spanish-American War and the Philippine Insurrection. Also of interest are the newspaper clippings of Allied and Axis troops, 1941–1945, some of which relate to Southeast Asia.

RG 151: Records of the Bureau of Foreign and Domestic Commerce. Photographs in this group depict functions of the bureau and were taken in more than 80 countries. The photos show people, institutions, ways of life, transportation facilities, agriculture, and industrial commodities, 1899–1939. The collection houses a few pictures of Siam, a large number of photos dealing with the Philippines, and an interesting group of several hundred items on the Netherlands East Indies.

RG 165: Records of the War Department General and Special Staffs.

RG 165 includes three boxes of prints of the Philippine Insurrection, 1899–1903, along with an album from 1900 of prints of nature, buildings, and military activities in the Philippines.

RG 200: National Archives Gift Collection. Philippine Insurrection photographs of troops and activities in the islands and of General Amilio Aguinaldo are here.

RG 208: Records of the Office of War Information. This record group contains a number of Southeast Asia related photos scattered throughout the files. There are few country specific headings; for example, pictures of some Southeast Asian leaders may be found in the Prints of the Delegates of the United Nations Conference on International Organization.

RG 239: Records of the American Commission for the Protection and Salvage of Artistic and Historical Monuments in War Areas. Aerial photographs of cities in Burma, 1943–1946, are included.

RG 268: Records of the Philippine War Damage Commission. RG 268 contains 1,100 before-and-after-reconstruction photographs of schools, waterworks, hospitals, government buildings, tenement houses, the Philippine University, and the School of Art and Trade, and other buildings damaged by war or typhoons, 1945–1951.

RG 306: Records of the United States Information Agency. The photographic file of the Paris Bureau of the *New York Times,* 1900–1950, houses photographs covering a broad range of subject matter, including worldwide coverage of sports, festivities, industries, institutions, and fashions. Included is an interesting collection of some 500 photos of Siam, the royal family, Thai officials in Berlin and the U.S., and numerous other subjects. Some captions are in French. One folder of approximately fifty photos of Singapore, including some shots of British installations and the mock battle staged in preparation of the defense of Singapore, is included.

Approximately 300 photos of Indonesia, including shots of all facets of Indonesian life and the Malay states, are included. An additional 100 photos, mostly of Manila during the war years, is also of interest, as is a collection of approximately 500 photos from Indochina, covering all facets of life. Many of these photos are of Hanoi and Saigon.

RG 350: Records of the Bureau of Insular Affairs. This RG covers the period 1898–1955 with over 14,000 items. Included are photographs of Philippine agricultural products and methods, native tribes, customs, crafts, industries, modes of transportation and development of railroads, educational facilities, public roads and buildings, native and American military organizations, American and Philippine officials, political bodies, historic events, and the islands and selected cities, 1898–1935.

RG 391: Records of United States Regular Army Mobil Units, 1821–1942. Included are some photographs of the Philippines for the period 1896–1906.

RG 407: Records of the Adjutant General's Office, 1917—. Included are non mapping aerial photographs of areas in the Philippine Islands during World War II and charts used to instruct in defense against chemical warfare, 1942.

4.   A variety of audiovisual equipment is available without charge for use in the research room. Reproduction facilities are available for materials not restricted by copyright or other restrictions. Researchers may use their own equipment for duplication or enlargement of materials.

5.   Researchers may wish to consult *Still Pictures in the Audiovisual Archives Division of the National Archives* (1972), by Mayfield S. Bray. Several other card indexes, preliminary inventories, and folders are also available for various record groups; however, none of the above sources is exhaustive. Therefore, archivists in the branch should be consulted without hesitation.

F18 National Human Studies Film Center (NHSFC)—(Smithsonian Institution)

1.   a. *955 L'Enfant Plaza, S.W.*
       Washington, D.C. 20560
       (202) 287-3428

       b. 9:00 A.M.–5:00 P.M.   Monday–Friday

       c. Open to the public, but prior appointment is recommended.

       d. E. Richard Sorenson, Director

2–3.   The NHSFC (Center for the Study of Man) seeks to take greater advantage of the potential for visual and aural records as a means of furthering human understanding. The center deals with such topics as the nature of the human condition, including all aspects of the human heritage, such as behavioral development, philosophy, ethics, cultural history, aesthetics, the visual arts, and the behavioral and human sciences. Currently, the NHSFC is collaborating with leaders and scholars in several Third World nations on film documentaton of their threatened cultural heritage. Facilities for preservation and retrieval of the visual data obtained are being developed in response to interest and invitations received by the center. NHSFC is currently exploring the possibility of such a program with the Philippines.

    The center's growing collection now exceeds 2 million feet of film. In its efforts to build up a documentary collection of aspects of life throughout the world, the NHSFC has been experimenting with various kinds of support to film-makers and scholars interested in producing films as permanent scholarly resources. This effort includes: providing consulting services, film-making expertise, or equipment; supplying film stock, processing facilities, logistic support, training, assembly, and annotation services; helping with grant applications; and supplying preservation service and facilities for analysis. In providing such assistance, the NHSFC maintains a flexible policy aimed at filling project gaps with resources not otherwise available.

4.   Viewing equipment is available in the center without charge.

5.   A computer index is planned. The center is described in E. Richard Sorenson, "To Further Phenomenological Inquiry: The National Anthropological Film Center," *Current Anthropology*, vol. 16, no. 2, June 1975, pp. 267–69.

National Museum of Natural History (Smithsonian Institution)
National Anthropological Archives—Photograph Collection See
entry B8

F19 Naval Historical Center (Navy Department)—Curator Branch—Photographic Section

1. a. *Washington Navy Yard, Building 76*
   9th and M Streets, S.E.
   Washington, D.C. 20374
   (202) 433-2765

   b. 9:00 A.M.–4:00 P.M.   Monday–Friday

   c. Although not mandatory, appointments should be made in advance of visits.

   d. Charles Haberlein, Jr., Head of the Photographic Section

2. The Naval Historical Center's Photographic Section has been the Navy's primary repository for pictorial materials of historical interest. Its files are the most comprehensive available source of illustrations of the nation's naval heritage, particularly for the period prior to World War II. The collection has individual references for well over 200,000 photographs, paintings, prints and documents, with annual growth averaging some 5,000 new items. The collection has many unique items as much of the material comes from private collections. Extensive cross-referencing for most of the collection permits thorough, rapid research on a broad range of naval and maritime subjects.

3. The collection includes several thousand items from Southeast Asia. Several hundred photos are from the Philippines, covering the early 1900s and showing a variety of scenes. Also to be found are 600 to 700 photos from Vietnam, showing military operations, installations, and scenes from Vietnamese cities and villages. The other countries of the region are less well represented, though there are some interesting items from Indonesia in the 1920s. Although this collection is not overwhelming in size, the fact that it is cross-referenced and served by a knowledgeable staff, makes it potentially one of the most valuable stops in your search for Southeast Asia photo items in the Washington area.

4. The Photographic Section does not lend file prints. However, reproductions of most unrestricted views can be purchased from either the Naval Photographic Center or the National Archives. Researchers may also copy unrestricted views in the collections, using their own equipment. Rush orders are available through the Navy Department's Office of Information, (202/697-6752).

5. A printed description of the Photographic Section is available free of charge.

F20 Navy Motion Media Depository

1. a. *Naval District Washington, Building 168*
   U.S. Naval Station
   Washington, D.C. 20374
   (202) 433-2168 (Still Pictures)
   (202) 433-2115 (Motion Pictures)
   (202) 433-2175 (Production Control Office)

    b. 7:30 A.M.–3:30 P.M.   Monday–Friday

    c. Open to the public. Researchers are requested to call in advance for an appointment.

    d. Jack Carter, Chief, Still Picture Depository
    Edith James, Chief, Motion Picture Depository

2.   The photo collection consists of approximately 750,000 black-and-white and color prints, including some 3,000 photos from Southeast Asia: Vietnam 2,000, Thailand 300, Philippines 200 (Subic Bay 250, additional), and Indonesia 100. Virtually all of the collection is unclassified. The depository also holds negatives for most of the photos in the Naval Historical Center's photo collection (see entry F19).

    The film collection consists of some 110 million feet of stock motion picture and videotape and the record copy of approximately 26,000 edited motion picture productions, totaling 45 million feet. Major subjects covered include: weapons systems, military hardware, and operational, training, and recreational activities of the Navy dating from 1958. Unedited footage of interest to Southeast Asianists includes: River patrol Vietnam, gunship support, and combat footage of copter strike. Also included is footage of the A-37 Squadron at Bien Hoa. Edited films of interest include *Strike from the Sea—The Navy Off Vietnam.*

3.   The Naval Motion Media Depository collections are designed to provide photographic and film documentation for current and recent naval activities. Most of the holdings date from the 1960s to the present. This is in contrast to the Naval Historical Center's Photographic Section (see entry F19), which collects pictorial materials of historical interest. It should be noted that the stock film collection was scheduled to be moved to Norton Air Force Base in California in late 1981.

4.   For extensive searches of the holdings or other research service requirements, the Film Depository Division charges an hourly fee.

    Copies of some of the photographic materials are available for purchase on premises. Additional materials can be ordered through:

    Chief of Information
    Department of the Navy (01–22)
    Room 2d340, Pentagon
    Washington, D.C. 20350
    (202) 697-0866

5.   Indexes are maintained for both the still picture and motion picture collections. For the still pictures, 3″ × 3″ prints are arranged in an electronically operated file drawer by subject (including geographic descriptors) and class of ship and aircraft. A similarly organized and mechanized card file is maintained for the film collection.

F21 United Nations Information Centre—Film Collection

1.   a. *2101 L Street, N.W.*
    Washington, D.C. 20037
    (202) 296-5370

b. 9:00 A.M.–1:00 P.M.   Monday–Friday

c. The center makes the U.N. films available on loan to individuals and organizations for a period of one week.

d. Jeanne Dixon, Film Librarian

2–3.   This collection consists of some 700 films. Titles of interest include:
Indonesia: *Amongst the Island Flowers; A Place to Live;* and *Tale of Three Children.* Laos: *Laos Airlift.* Malaysia: *Brighter Dawn; A Call from Malaysia;* and *A Mandate to Assist.* Philippines: *And the Gates Shall Not Be Shut; Joselito;* and *Rebirth of a City.* Singapore: *Beyond Family Planning* and *Singapore, My Singapore.* Thailand: *Building a Ferro-cement Fishing Boat; Children of the World: Thailand;* and *Copains d'Ailleurs,* no 1. Vietnam: *Beyond the Ruins; Most Precious Property;* and *Out of Darkness.*

4.   Reservations for films should be made one week in advance of the date the film is required. No fees are charged for the use of films. All U.N. films are available for purchase.

5.   A free catalog of the center's film collection, *Films Available for Distribution* (1980), is updated periodically. *Films of the United Nations Family* (1980–81), which is a comprehensive catalog of all films made by the different U.N. agencies, has a geographic and subject index. It is also available free at the center.

F22 World Bank Photo Library

1.   a. *801 19th Street, N.W.*
Washington, D.C. 20433
(202) 676-1638

b. 9:00 A.M.–5:00 P.M.   Monday–Friday

c. Open to the public by appointment only.

d. Robert C. Newton, Photo Librarian

2–5.   The photo library contains over 45,000 35-mm color slides and 12,000 black-and-white prints that cover some 70 developing countries of the world. The collection has been developed from the photographs taken in conjunction with World Bank overseas projects. Major subject areas are agriculture, industry, social services, and transportation. The collection is substantial for Indonesia, Malaysia, and the Philippines. Singapore and Thailand are less well represented. Photographs may be freely reproduced and used for nonadvertising purposes, but must be properly acknowledged.
A World Bank photo library catalog lists the countries, categories, and photo-type (color slides or black-and-white print) available, and is free on request. The library also maintains a card catalog, organized by country, and is preparing a subject catalog, which it hopes to computerize in the future.

G Data Banks

Data Banks Entry Format (G)

1. General Information
   a. *address; telephone numbers*
   b. hours of service
   c. conditions of access (including fees charged for information retrieval)
   d. name/title of director and key staff members

2. Description of Data Files (hard data and bibliographic references) Pertaining to Southeast Asia

3. Bibliographic Aids Facilitating Use of Storage Media

Introductory Note

A large number of Washington area libraries, government agencies, academic institutions, and research organizations maintain their own series of subscriptions to a wide variety of data banks that can be accessed throughout the U.S. and, in many cases, throughout the world. The listing included here is primarily of those database systems that are developed or prepared in Washington and contain significant resource material of potential interest to Southeast Asia specialists. Due to the nature of the medium, it is not surprising that the vast majority of the collections listed below is of scientific or economic data.

G1 Agency for International Development (AID)—Office of Development Information and Utilization (DIU)

1. a. *Room 509 Pomponio Plaza (SA-14)*
      1735 North Lynn Street
      Arlington, Virginia 22209
      (703) 235-9207

   b. 8:45 A.M.–5:30 P.M.   Monday–Friday

   c. The DIU's data bases are primarily maintained for the use of AID project designers, field project managers, and contract researchers. Private researchers may, however, have access to the system on the basis of prior appointment.

d. Lida Allen, Director

2.   The DIU's computerized storage and retrieval system contains several data components. The Development Information system consists of project-specific information on more than 2,000 AID funded or supported projects. This data includes the project number, title, a summary of the project, some financial information, project designs, feasibility studies, evaluation documents, and task-force reports.

The Research and Development Report system contains over 9,000 titles from AID supported research. Subject and country searches may be run on the computer for the Research and Development Reports. Copies may be ordered in paper or microfiche from the AID R&D Report Distribution Center, P.O. Box 353, Norfolk, Virginia 23501.

The Economic and Social Data system maintains combined economic and social data from IBRD, IMF, USDA, and AID sources for virtually all countries, covering, in most cases, a 20-year period.

The Economic and Social Data System provides data analysis services for researchers, analysts, economists, and project designers in developing areas of specific concern.

In addition, the DIU contract or other working arrangements are maintained with the USDA, Bureau of the Census, Department of Commerce, and organizations such as Volunteers in Technical Assistance (see entry N39) to allow rapid access to additional specialized information of priority interest to AID.

3.   In 1982 DIU was preparing a *Ready Data Book* for each AID country and region. It should provide, on a regular basis, selected economic and social data in policy and sectorial areas of priority interest.

G2 Agency for International Development (AID)—Program Information Analysis

1.   a. *Room 3842 New State*
320 21st St. N.W.
Washington, D.C. 20523
(703) 235-9167

b. 8:45 A.M.–5:30 P.M.   Monday–Friday

c. This data bank is primarily for the use of AID personnel. Private scholars should call in advance for possible access to the data bank.

d. Anna K. Lee, Chief

2.   The Program Information Analysis maintains a comprehensive data bank of all bilateral and multilateral assistance programs abroad from the United States and international organizations. The data includes economic and military assistance from the U.S., assistance from the Export-Import Bank, PL-480 aid data from the Commodity Credit Corporation, and records of assistance provided by international organizations.

3.   This data is also available in printed form as the AID annually updated publication. *U.S. Overseas Loans and Grants and Assistance from International Organizations: Obligations and Loan Authorization,* July 1945—. Copies of a discontinued periodical, *Operations Report,* which contains extensive data on U.S. economic assistance programs in Southeast Asia, are available for reference use in the division.

G3 Agriculture Department—Data Services Center

1.   a. *500 12th Street, S.W.*
Washington, D.C. 20250
(202) 447-7577

b. 8:30 A.M.–5:00 P.M.   Monday–Friday

c. The data base is maintained primarily for internal use. Researchers should make special arrangement before visiting the center.

d. Larry Otto, Chief, International Economic Systems Branch

2.   The center's data files contain indexes of world agricultural production from 1950 to the present, compiled by the United States Department of Agriculture; USDA–generated data on international grain crop acreage and yields; international trade data compiled by the United Nations (1969–present); trade and production data (1961–1974) compiled by the U.S. Agency for International Development.
      In addition the Data Systems Division (Eldon Hildebrandt, Director, 202/447-5255) of the department's Foreign Agricultural Service maintains USDA-generated machine-readable data on foreign agricultural production, supply, and distribution for several Southeast Asian countries from 1960 to present; as well as extensive U.S. Census Bureau data on U.S. trade with Southeast Asian states.

G4 Commerce Department Data Bases

1.   a. *14th Street and Constitution Avenue, N.W.*
Washington, D.C. 20230
(202) 377-2000

b. 8:30 A.M.–5:00 P.M.   Monday–Friday

c. Most data is accessible to the public; some services are free.

d. Key personnel are listed with the appropriate units below.

2.   No single facility stores all of the machine-readable data generated within the department. Data files containing Southeast Asian materials are located in several bureaus.

BUREAU OF THE CENSUS: The Population Division's Demographic Data Retrieval System (DDRS) contains unevaluated demographic data, consisting primarily of census reports, demographic surveys, and government publications containing vital statistics for all developing countries. The data base also contains the results of selected demographic data analyzed by demographers in the Census Bureau. Some U.N. data not generally found in published sources is also included. The data base is on microfilm. Data tables from the sources mentioned above are microfilmed and coded according to a cross classification of data variables, date of information, and country name. The basic demographic topics selected for the data base include population composition and characteristics; population dynamics, including fertility, mortality, migration, marriage, and divorce; population projections; educational attainment and school enrollment; and labor-force characteristics. Service from the DDRS is free of charge unless a large amount of photocopying is required. Researchers may contact Martha A. Barger (301/763-2834) for further information on DDRS data.

The bureau's Foreign Trade Division can make available magnetic tapes containing statistics of the United States trade with Southeast Asian countries. The division's Trade Information Branch (301/763-5140) can provide order forms and further details.

BUREAU OF ECONOMIC ANALYSIS: The bureau's Data Retrieval and Analysis Branch (202/523-0652), within the International Investment Division, compiles data on U.S. private investments abroad. Computer tapes of some of the crude data collected by the division are available on a commercial basis. In addition, the bureau's Balance of Payment Division (202/523-0621) has tapes containing data on the balance of payments between the U.S. and Southeast Asian countries.

BUREAU OF EXPORT DEVELOPMENT (International Trade Administration): The bureau's Trade Information Services Division (202/377-4532) compiles the *Foreign Traders Index,* containing data on non–U.S. foreign business firms and products in various areas of the world, including the ASEAN states.

NATIONAL BUREAU OF STANDARDS (NBS): The bureau's Standard Information Service (SIS) (301/921-2587) maintains a reference collection of engineering and related standards, which include standards and specifications of the major foreign and international standardizing bodies. By means of a computer-produced key-word-in-context index, SIS has generated a publication of special interest for overseas users—the *Index of International Standards,* available from the Government Printing Office or the National Technical Information Service.

NATIONAL OCEANIC AND ATMOSPHERIC ADMINISTRATION (NOAA): The Environmental Data and Information Service (EDIS) (202/634-7236) has files of environmental data in a system of data bases known as Environmental Data Index (ENDEX). These data bases can be searched by geographic area, type of data, institution holding the data, and projects. EDIS provides users with rapid computerized referral to available environmental data files, published literature, and on-going research projects in the atmospheric sciences, marine and coastal studies, and a wide range of other subjects. A *Guide to NOAA's Computerized Information Retrieval Services* (1979) is available free on request from the EDIS Publications and Media Staff (202/634-7305).

Note: See also entry K8.

G5 Defense Technical Information Center (DTIC) (Defense Department)

1. a. *Cameron Station*
   Alexandria, Virginia 22314
   (202) 274-7633, -6434

   b. 7:30 A.M.–8:00 P.M.   Monday–Friday

   c. The center provides support to those organizations registered to use its services from among Defense Department components, research and development agencies within the U.S. government, and their associated contractors, subcontractors, and grantees with current government contracts, as well as potential contractors approved by the military services. DTIC serves the general public only indirectly, where unclassified/unlimited documents are concerned, through a special arrangement with the National Technical Information Service (NTIS). See entry Q19. DTIC provides NTIS with copies of research and development reports that are sponsored, co-sponsored, or generated by the Department of Defense. Additionally, reports that were formerly classified or limited are also furnished as soon as they are approved for public release. NTIS announces these reports through its *Government Reports Announcements and Indexes*. DTIC responds to inquiries from individual researchers seeking information on the availability of technical reports that are not in the public domain.

   d. Hubert E. Sauter, Administrator

2. DTIC is the clearinghouse for the Defense Department's collections of research and development reports in virtually all fields of science and technology, including behavioral and social sciences. There are four major data banks resident at DTIC: R&D Program Planning Data Bank (R&DPP)—a repository of research and program-planning documentation at the project and task levels; R&T Work Unit Information System (WUIS)—a collection of technically oriented summaries describing research and technology projects currently in progress at the work-unit level; Technical Report Data Bank (TR)—a collection of descriptive summaries for formally documented scientific and technical results of Department of Defense sponsored research, development, test, and evaluation; and Independent Research and Development Data Bank (IR&D)—a data bank of summaries describing the technical programs being performed by Department of Defense contractors as part of their independent research and development programs. The strength of the collection is in the physical sciences, technology, and engineering as they relate to national defense and military matters. Considerable social-science research of military interest (international affairs including Southeast Asia, human engineering, and group dynamics, for instance) are also included.

3. An unclassified *DTIC Digest* is distributed to registered users announcing plans, changes in service, new DTIC publications, and other developments in the scientific and technical information field. On request, DTIC will provide a registration kit with an explanation of the various forms required to request services, as well as other informational materials concerning programs, products, and services offered by the center to U.S. government organizations and their contractors.

G6 Educational Resources Information Center (ERIC)

1. a. *National Institute of Education (U.S. Department of Education)*
      ERIC Administrative Offices
      1200 19th Street, N.W.
      Washington, D.C. 20208
      (202) 254-5500

   b. 8:00 A.M.–4:30 P.M.   Monday–Friday

   c. Open to the public. Fee schedules vary for different services. ERIC data bases may be accessed from many university libraries, state departments of education, educational information centers, research centers, and commercial organizations. The ERIC Processing and Reference Facility is located at 4833 Rugby Avenue, Bethesda, Maryland 20014 (301/656-9723).

   d. Charles Hoover, Acting Head

2. ERIC is a national information system supported and operated by the National Institute of Education (NIE), providing ready access to descriptions of exemplary programs, research and development efforts, and related information that can be used in developing more effective educational programs.

   There are 16 clearinghouses in the nationwide ERIC network. Each specializes in a different, multidisciplinary educational area. Each searches out pertinent documents, current research findings, project and technical reports, speeches and unpublished manuscripts, books, and professional journal articles. These materials are screened according to ERIC selection criteria, abstracted, and indexed. All of this information is put into the ERIC computer data base and announced in the ERIC reference publications. Through these sources, any person interested in education has easy access to reports of innovative programs, conference proceedings, bibliographies, outstanding professional papers, curriculum-related materials, and reports of the most significant efforts in educational research and development regardless of where they first appeared.

3. Useful bibliographic aids include: *A Bibliography of Publications about the Educational Resources Information Center; How to Use ERIC; Directory of ERIC Microfiche Collections; Directory of ERIC Search Services;* and *ERIC Information Analysis Products.*

Note: Also see entry K12.

Health and Human Services Department—Division of Research Grants—Research Documentation Section—CRISP Data Bank See entry K18

Housing and Urban Development Department (HUD)—Foreign Information Retrieval System (FIRS) See entry K19

G7 International Bank for Reconstruction and Development (World Bank)—Data System

1. a. *1818 H Street, N.W.*
    Washington, D.C. 20433
    (202) 477-1234

    b. 9:00 A.M.–5:00 P.M.   Monday–Friday

    c. The World Bank maintains a variety of data systems for internal use. Copies of magnetic tapes are exchanged with U.S. government agencies and other international organizations, and are available to private users (universities, research centers, individual scholars) upon request, at little or no charge.

    d. Ramesh Chander, Statistical Adviser
    (202) 676-1822

2–3.   The World Bank's Economic Analysis and Projections Department transfers a broad spectrum of statistical data into machine readable format. The Systems and Methods Division (Jean-Paul Dailly, Chief, 202/676-9083) is responsible for tape management, while the following sectional divisions develop and maintain the data sets and may provide information about contents and utilization capabilities to scholars. National accounts, balance-of-payments estimates, social indicators, trade (prepared by the United Nations), and industrial development data are updated by the Economic and Social Data Division (Sang Eun Lee, Chief, 202/676-1901). Capital markets data are prepared by the International Trade and Capital Flows Division (Peter Miovic, Chief, 202/334-8395). Commodities and commodity-price data are assembled and maintained by the Commodities and Export Projections Division (Enzo Grilli, Chief, 202/334-8419). Data on public borrowing and external indebtedness by country is prepared by the External Debt Division (Nicholas Hope, Chief, 202/676-0049). Country modeling is handled by the Comparative Analysis and Projections Division (John Shilling, Chief, 202/667-1862).

   The statistics and other information are published in the following bank publications: *Borrowing in International Capital Markets* (quarterly); *Commodity Trade and Price Trends* (annual); *Economic and Social Indicators* (quarterly); *The World Bank Atlas* (annual); *World Bank Country Studies* (occasional); *World Bank Staff Working Papers* (occasional); *The World Bank Annual Report;* and the *World Development Report* and its annex, *World Development Indicators.*

International Communication Agency (ICA)—Documents Index System (DIS) See entry K21

G8 International Monetary Fund (IMF)—Data Fund Division

1. a. *700 19th Street, N.W.*
    Washington, D.C. 20431
    (202) 477-3207

    b. 9:00 A.M.–5:00 P.M.   Monday–Friday

c. The IMF programs data from 4 of its statistical publications into machine-readable form. Copies of magnetic tapes are made available on a commercial subscription basis. Each subscription consists of 12 monthly tapes, the corresponding IMF book publication—which serves as a guide to the contents of the tape—and documentation and instructions on how to use the data and programs contained on the tape.

d. Robert L. Kline, Chief, Data Fund Division

2–3. *International Finance Statistics* tape subscriptions contain approximately 17,000 time series, including series appearing in the IMF's published *International Finance Statistics* country pages and world tables, exchange rate series, and international liquidity series for all countries, and 19 major series on countries' relationships with the IMF. Annual entries begin in 1948, with quarterly and monthly entries at later dates.

Direction of Trade tape subscriptions contain approximately 4,000 time series reported in the IMF's published *Direction of Trade* country pages. Data include sources of imports and destination of exports for some 150 countries. Annual entries began in 1948, and quarterly entries in 1969. All series are expressed in millions of U.S. dollars.

Balance of Payments Statistics (BOPS) tape subscriptions consist of approximately 43,000 time series of balance-of-payments data corresponding to those published in the IMF's Balance of Payments Statistics Yearbook; aggregates from these series are published in the *BOPS* monthly issues. These series cover the time span from 1967 (and in many cases from 1965) to date for about 120 countries and are expressed in Special Drawing Rights (SDRs). The U.S. dollar/SDR rate, as well as the national currency/SDR rates for each country, are also included in the *BOPS* subscription tape.

Government Finance Statistics tape subscriptions contain approximately 6,000 annual time series of data reported in the IMF's published *Government Finance Statistics Yearbook*. Included are data on revenues, expenditures, grants, lending, financing, debts, and social-security funds.

G9 National Aeronautics and Space Administration (NASA)—National Space Science Data Center

1. a. *Goddard Space Flight Center*
    Building 26
    Greenbelt, Maryland 20771
    (301) 344-7354

    b. 8:00 A.M.–4:30 P.M. Monday–Friday

    c. Open to researchers by appointment. There is normally no charge for outside researchers to use the data bases at the center.

    d. James I Vette, Director

2. The National Space Science Data Center maintains bibliographic information, substantive reports, technical data, and other materials on space programs of the United States and certain foreign countries including Indonesia. Information concerning Indonesian satellite launchings may be found in two files: Automated Internal Management file, and the Committee for Space Resources (COSPAR) reports file.

3.   *Data and Distribution Services,* a basic guide to the center, is available on request.

G10 National Archives and Records Service (NARS)—Machine Readable Archives Division

1.   a. *711 14th Street, N.W.*
Washington, D.C. 20408
(202) 724-1080

      b. 8:45 A.M.–5:15 P.M. Monday–Friday

      c. Open to the public. Substantial fees are charged for documentation and computer processing. The reproduction service for files in the division's holdings is presently limited to copying from card to card, tape to card, card to tape, tape to tape, tape to printout, extracts of specific information, and electrostatic copying of documentation. A fee schedule is available on request. See also entry (B7).

      d. Charles M. Dollar, Director

2.   Originated in 1969, the Machine Readable Archives Division maintains magnetic tape records of archival value as received from various U.S. government agencies. These records may have been created for specific projects or may be part of a continuing data collection. The division's Record Groups (RGs) that may contain Southeast Asia related materials are listed below:

      RG 77: Records of the Office of the Chief of Engineers—domestic and international transportation of U.S. foreign trade. Contains records of 44,502 commodity shipments in U.S. foreign trade during 1970 by world areas, states, custom districts, and production and market areas. The survey from which the data in the file were obtained was sponsored jointly by the Department of Transportation and the U.S. Army Corps of Engineers and was conducted by the Census Bureau.

      RG 90: Record of the Public Health Service–World Health Organization—international collaborative study of medical care utilization (1968–69). This study grew out of meetings held under World Health Organization auspices in 1963–64. Records may contain some scattered materials on Southeast Asia.

      RG 166: Records of the Foreign Agricultural Service—U.S. agricultural imports and exports trade history. U.S. agricultural imports and exports statistics are derived from the foreign trade statistics program conducted by the Bureau of the Census. The period covered is from January 1967 to June 1974.

3.   *A Catalog of Machine Readable Records in the National Archives of the United States* is available without charge.

G11 *New York Times* Information Bank—Washington Office

1.   a. *1111 19th Street, North*
Arlington, Virginia 22209
(703) 243-7220

      b. 9:00 A.M.–5:00 P.M. Monday–Friday

c. Open to the public. Researchers may utilize, for a fee, the retail service of the Information Bank.

d. Sharon Taylor, Regional Manager
Paul Taylor, Marketing Representative

2. The *New York Times* Information Bank contains more than 2 million abstracts of news stories, editorials, and other significant items published in the *New York Times* since 1959 and some 55 national and international periodicals. The bank may be searched by a variety of indicators: geographical location, subject, and name. Abstracts vary in length from 3 to 50 lines. The bank is accessible through selected university libraries and research institutions.

3. An information flyer describing the bank, its services, and its sources is available free on request.

State Department—Foreign Affairs Information Management Center See entry K34

G12 United Nations Environment Program (UNEP)—International Referral System (INFOTERRA)

1. a. This system operates out of the offices of the
    U.S. Environmental Protection Agency—U.S. International Environmental Referral Center (USIERC)
    401 M Street, S.W. (PM 211A)
    Washington, D.C. 20460
    (202) 755-1836

    b. 8:00 A.M.–4:30 P.M.   Monday–Friday

    c. Open to the public. The services provided by INFOTERRA are free.

    d. Carol Alexander, Director

2. In 1972 the Stockholm Conference on the Human Environment set up an International Referral System to direct the flow of environmental information from those who have it to those who need it. The over-all purpose of INFOTERRA is to insure that—in making important decisions in relation to the environment—governments and others will have access to the latest scientific and technical data and expertise. INFOTERRA neither stores information nor answers substantive questions; its task is simply to enable the potential user of environmental information to locate the most appropriate source of information required. This it does by employing a network of government-designated national focal points (NFPs), which feed into the INFOTERRA international directory potential sources of environmental information and assist users in their own country to identify the sources to which they need to refer.

    Over 7,000 sources of environmental information have been classified into approximately 1,000 computer-coded subject areas from which the required list of contact sources can be provided to the inquirer. In 1975 USIERC was named as the U.S. national focal point. NFPs have been functioning in Indonesia, Malaysia, the Philippines, Thailand, and Vietnam.

When a question is directed to a focal point, that NFP codes the question and carries out a manual or computer search of the international directory for the relevant sources of information. NFPs not having local access to a computer may also forward the question to the system's central data bank in Geneva, Switzerland. Once a computer search has identified the information sources, the user may contact the sources directly for substantive information. NFPs have enabled each cooperating nation to develop self-reliance for its information needs and to promote global cooperation for improving the flow of information on the environment.

3.   Several brochures describing the INFOTERRA data base and the UNEP are available from USIERC.

ORGANIZATIONS

H Research Centers

Research Centers Entry Format (H)

1. *Address; Telephone Numbers*

2. Name and Title of Chief Official

3. Programs and Research Activities Pertaining to Southeast Asia

4. Libraries and Research Facilities

5. Publications

Introductory Note

Some of the nation's most prestigious research institutions make Washington their home, and a number of these organizations are active in Southeast Asia related research. The Brookings Institution (entry H9), the American Enterprise Institute for Public Policy Research (entry H2), the Carnegie Endowment for International Peace (entry H11), and the Center for Naval Analysis (entry H16) are among the best known, but they are far from alone in this city where private consultants and nonprofit institutions vie for government contracts for political, military, legal, economic, and technical research.

The scholar should approach the information contained in this and subsequent sections with the awareness that, in both the private and public sectors in Washington, programs and personnel can change very rapidly. A Southeast Asia related program may disappear from the roster of activities of one organization or agency only to reappear with another one at a later date. Personnel may be brought into an organization for a specific research contract and leave at the project's conclusion, changing the entire character of the organization's program.

It is also important to note that Washington, D.C., boasts a wide variety of consulting firms that may, from time to time, become involved in Southeast Asia related activities. These firms appear in Section N (Cultural Exchange and Technical Assistance Organizations) of this *Guide*. Private research firms and consultancy groups—those either specializing in Southeast Asia related work or producing studies and reports that are available to outside scholars—have been included in this section (H) and in Section N. Scholars wishing to locate other Washington-based consultancy firms with Southeast Asia operations not included here should contact the Commerce

Department (entry K8), which monitors contracts obtained by U.S. firms, and examine the lists prepared by various government agencies, particularly the State Department (entry K34), the Agency for International Development (entry K1), and the Defense Department (entry K11) of contracts awarded by the federal government for work on or in Southeast Asia.

Included here as well are a number of information offices which promote the points of view of particular interest groups, both foreign and domestic, which have taken positions on Southeast Asia issues. Often this information can provide insights into the diversity of viewpoints on particular questions, but researchers should bear in mind, when evaluating this material, the advocacy roles played by these organizations.

The growing interest in Southeast Asia has made it difficult to keep up with the continuing proliferation of organizations devoting part or all of their energies to Southeast Asia related research and information activities. This is particularly true for Indochina related organizations.

H1 Advanced International Studies Institute (AISI)

1. *East-West Towers*
   4330 East-West Highway
   Washington, D.C. 20014
   (202) 951-0818

2. Mose L. Harvey, Director and Senior Analyst

3. AISI was established in 1968 as a nonprofit research and educational organization in association with the University of Miami at Coral Gables, Florida. AISI conducts research and brings out publications on international affairs and U.S. foreign policy, with a primary focus on the Soviet Union. The institute also sponsors various workshops, conferences, and seminars dealing with international affairs. AISI's interest in Southeast Asia is limited, though some studies on Vietnam were produced in the early 1970s. Future interest in Southeast Asia would be dictated by the Soviet Union's goals and strategy in that region. Researchers may contact Morris Rothenberg (Senior Analyst) for information concerning the institute's research activities relevant to Southeast Asia.

4. The institute maintains a small reference collection. Researchers may use the collection by special arrangement.

5. Publications include occasional papers and monographs in international affairs; *Research Notes* (monthly); *Soviet World Outlook* (monthly); and special reports that provide time-sensitive responses to newly arising critical issues or developments affecting U.S. international interests and objectives.

H2 American Enterprise Institute for Public Policy Research (AEI)

1. *1150 17th Street, N.W.*
   Washington, D.C. 20036
   (202) 862-5800

2. William J. Baroody, Jr., President
   Robert J. Pranger, Director of International Programs

3.   The AEI, established in 1943, is an independent, nonprofit, nonpartisan, research and educational organization that studies public policy issues, both national and foreign. Through its continuing series of Public Policy Forums, the institute features scholarly discussions on major public policy problems of current interest. Proceedings of the forums are available in cassettes and films. The forum programs are also broadcast across the country. In addition, the AEI sponsors conferences on issues of vital public interest. The institute offers an associates' program and a small number of fellowships to visiting scholars for research.

4.   The institute's small reference library (Evelyn Caldwell, 202/862-5831) of some 15,000 volumes is open to the public by appointment only.

5.   AEI publications of interest include: Dale R. Tahtinen, *Arms in the Indian Ocean: Interests and Challenge* (1977); Robert Scalapino, *Asia and the Major Powers: Implications for the International Order* (1972); Sheldon W. Simon, *Asian Neutralism and U.S. Policy* (1975); Allan W. Cameron, *Indochina: Prospects after "The End"* (1976); Wolfgang Kasper, *Malaysia: A Study in Successful Economic Development* (1974); Yuan-Li Wu, *Strategic Significance of Singapore: A Study in Balance of Power* (1972); Claude A. Buss, *The United States and the Philippines: Background for Policy* (1977); Morton A. Kaplan, et al, *Vietnam Settlement: Why 1973, Not 1969?* (1973); Pat M.Holt, *The War Powers Resolution: The Role of Congress in U.S. Armed Intervention* (1978); Howard R. Penniman, *Vietnam's Electoral Roadblock,* (1973); and Lucian W. Phe, *Redefining American Policy in Southeast Asia* (1982). The institute also publishes several periodicals: *The AEI Economist* (monthly); *Public Opinion* (bimonthly); *AEI Foreign Policy and Defense Review* (bimonthly); and *Memoranda* (quarterly). A catalog of *New Publications* (1981) and an information booklet, *Public Policy Forums,* are available on request.

H3 American Foreign Policy Institute (AFPI)

1.   *499 South Capitol Street, S.W., Suite 500*
Washington, D.C. 20003
(202) 484-1569

2.   Robert C. Richardson III, Executive Director

3.   The American Foreign Policy Institute (AFPI) is a private research organization associated with the American Security Council, which is headquartered in Boston, Virginia. AFPI sponsors occasional conferences and symposia and brings together the expertise of a number of research associates to analyze critical foreign policy issues. Southeast Asia–American national security has been the focus of several recent studies by the institute.

5.   The institute publishes occasional monographs and distributes the publications of its associated organizations which contain articles on Southeast Asia: *International Security Review* (quarterly of the Center for International Security Studies of the American Security Council Educational Foundation), *Washington Report* (newsletter of the American Security Council), and *Situation Report* (a quarterly newsletter of the Security and Intelligence Fund).

American Society of International Law See entry M16

H4 American University—Foreign Area Studies (FAS)

1. *5010 Wisconsin Avenue, N.W.*
   Washington, D.C. 20016
   (202) 686-2769

2. William Evans-Smith, Director

3. FAS produces, under contract with the U.S. Department of the Army, a series of over 100 handbooks ("Country Studies") on the social, economic, political and national security of foreign countries. The 30-member staff includes 18 foreign-area research specialists. Volumes have been produced for all of the countries of Southeast Asia.

4. The FAS library of some 7,000 volumes of reference books and periodicals is accessible to private researchers by previous appointment.

5. A listing of Country Studies is available on request. Copies of the Country Studies may be purchased from any of the 28 sales outlets of the U.S. Government Printing Office (Q11) throughout the country.

Army Center of Military History See entry B3

H5 Asia Foundation—Washington Office

1. *2301 E Street, N.W.*
   Washington, D.C. 20037
   (202) 223-5268

2. Allen C. Choate, Representative

3. Headquartered in San Francisco (550 Kearny Street, San Francisco, California 94108, 415/982-4640), the Asia Foundation is a publicly supported, nonprofit, philanthropic organization. The foundation utilizes a small grant approach to respond to Asian-initiated efforts to further economic, social, and cultural growth in their own societies. It also encourages understanding among the peoples of Asia and between Asians and Americans. The foundation assists in the following areas: education, public administration, law, economics, management, community development, communications, family planning, food, nutrition, and health-care delivery. Through its Books for Asia project, the foundation distributes each year hundreds of thousands of donated books and specialized journals to individuals and institutions, ranging from graduate research facilities to rural mobile libraries. The foundation maintains resident representatives in Indonesia, Malaysia, the Philippines, and Thailand.

5. Publications include *The Asia Foundation News; Asian Student Orientation Handbook* (bimonthly); the *Presidents Review and Annual Report;* and occasional papers on developmental and social changes in Asian countries.

H6 Aspen Institute for Humanistic Studies

1. *2010 Massachusetts Avenue, N.W.*
    Washington, D.C. 20036
    (202) 466-6410

2. Stephen P. Strickland, Vice President

3. The New York–based Aspen Institute for Humanistic Studies (717 Fifth Avenue, New York, N.Y. 10022, 212/759-1053) is an independent, international, nonpartisan, and nonprofit organization that considers contemporary issues in terms of their impact on individuals, communities, and society as a whole. International affairs cover a range of concerns from arms control to concepts of basic human needs and fulfillment and the impact of the interrelationship between industrialized and developing nations. The institute's activities have included seminars on Asian thought, but there has been no specific Southeast Asia seminar to date.

5. Inquiries concerning Aspen's publications may be addressed to the institute's Publication Office, P.O. Box 150, Queenstown, Maryland 21658.

H7 The Atlantic Council of the United States

1. *1616 H Street, N.W.*
    Washington, D.C. 20006
    (202) 347-9353

2. Kenneth Rush, Chairman

3. The Atlantic Council of the United States is a bipartisan, nonprofit organization working to encourage and strengthen political, military, economic, and social ties and institutions among the nations of Western Europe, North America, Japan, Australia, and New Zealand. The council also serves as the Washington office of the Atlantic Institute for International Affairs, headquartered in Paris. Operating usually through working groups of 30 to 40 members drawn from government, business, labor, the media, and the academic community, the council considers a wide range of issues and problems facing the industrialized democracies, their relations with the developing nations, and their relations with the communist states. Questions related to the Pacific Basin and Southeast Asia have occasionally been treated by one of the council's working groups. Six recent examples are the council's policy papers on: "The Common Security Interests of Japan, the United States and NATO;" "The Credibility of the NATO Deterrent: Bringing the NATO Deterrent up to Date;" "US Energy Policy and US Foreign Policy in the 1980s;" "US–Japan Energy Relationships in the 1980s;" "Securing the Seas: Soviet Naval Challenge and Western Alliance Options;" and "Some Unfinished Business of the Tokyo Round Trade Negotiation: A New Safeguard Code."

    A new project, which will continue through 1983, concerns the long-term interests of the industrialized democracies and the People's Republic of China.

4. The council maintains a specialized working library of over 1,500 volumes, 150 periodicals, and U.S. government and international documents. These

materials are available for scholars and practitioners in international relations.

5.   The council's publications in the security series include: *The United States and the Developing Countries* (1977) and *The Common Security Interests of Japan, the U.S. and NATO* (1981), the latter covering in part, general security questions in Asia. The council also publishes a monthly newsletter, *The Atlantic Community News,* and the *Atlantic Community Quarterly.*

H8 Battelle Memorial Institute—Washington Operations

1.   *2030 M Street, N.W.*
Washington, D.C. 20036
(202) 785-8400

2.   George B. Johnson, Vice President and Director

3.   An independent nonprofit research organization with headquarters in Columbus, Ohio (614/424-4533), the Battelle Memorial Institute seeks to achieve the advancement and utilization of science through technological innovation and educational activities. Research in the metropolitan area includes population studies. Since 1977 Battelle has become involved in demographic research and technical assistance operations through its Human Affairs Research Centers' Population and Development Policy Program (Michael Micklin, director). The program focuses on several social and economic issues related to the determinants of fertility, the changing status and roles of women, consequences of family size for personal and family welfare, population impact analysis, and bottlenecks to effective population- and family-planning programs.

    In 1980 the Human Affairs Research Centers' International Development Study Center (IDSC), with Leonard H. Robinson, Jr., as director, was established in the Washington office and now encompasses the work of the Population and Development Policy Program and budding programs in International Health, Food and Agriculture Policy, and Refugees. The IDSC has no definitive programs involving the countries of Southeast Asia at this time; however, based upon staff expertise, these countries are likely areas for future work.

4.   The IDSC is developing a library that contains staff reports, working papers, policy papers, and reference books in the field of population studies. The collection may be consulted by prior arrangement.

5.   Several brochures and newsletters, including one describing the IDSC's Population and Development Policy Program, are available upon request.

H9 Brookings Institution

1.   *1775 Massachusetts Avenue, N.W.*
Washington, D.C. 20036
(202) 797-6000

2.   Bruce K. MacLaury, President

3.   The Brookings Institution is a private, nonprofit organization devoted to research, education, and publication in economics, government, foreign

policy, and the social sciences generally. Its activities are carried out through three research programs—Economic Studies, Governmental Studies, and Foreign Policy Studies—an advanced study program, a Social Science Computer Center, and a publication program. To identify issues for study, the institution conducts continual reviews of its fields of interest. Subjects are selected for study on the basis of their significance and timeliness among other criteria. Several studies dealing with Southeast Asia have been completed by institution personnel.

Brookings's educational activities include fellowships and guest scholar appointments awarded to faculty members, graduate students, and others whose research is related to the purposes of the institution. The Brookings Social Science Computer Center provides computing services for Brookings and other nonprofit organizations engaged in social science research.

4. Brookings maintains a specialized library of books and periodicals designed to meet the needs of its research programs. Its current holdings include 60,000 volumes, 500 periodical titles, vertical files of pamphlets and government documents, and a selective United Nations collection. An on-line bibliographic data base facilitates research activities in the institution. Use of the library is restricted to resident staff members and guests.

5. Brookings has an extensive publications program. Titles of interest include *The Irony of Vietnam* (1979), *Nuclear Arms in the Third World: U. S. Policy Dilemma* (1979), *Technology for Developing Nations: New Directions for U.S. Technical Assistance* (1972), and *Economic Interaction in the Pacific Basin* (1980). Brookings's annual report, program description, and publications list are available on request.

H10 Business Council for International Understanding (BCIU) Institute

1. *c/o The American University*
    3301 New Mexico Avenue, N.W., Suite 244
    Washington, D.C. 20016
    (202) 686-2771

2. Gary E. Lloyd, Director

3. The BCIU Institute of the American University conducts programs (including lectures, films, and discussions conducted by area specialists) that prepare managers and their families to function effectively in any area, country, or community in the world. BCIU has presented programs for 105 countries, including Burma, Indonesia, Malaysia, the Philippines, Singapore, and Thailand.

5. The institute publishes an annual report and occasional papers, such as *Moving Your Household Overseas*. Publications are available for sale through the institute's office.

H11 Carnegie Endowment for International Peace—Washington Office

1. *11 Dupont Circle, N.W.*
    Washington, D.C. 20036
    (202) 797-6400

2.   Thomas L. Hughes, President

3.   An operating (not a grant-making) foundation, the Carnegie Endowment for International Peace conducts programs of research, discussion, and publication in international affairs and U.S. foreign policy. Program areas change periodically; in recent years they have included: national security and arms control; executive-congressional relations in foreign policy; U.S.– Soviet relations; South Africa; the Middle East; South and Southeast Asia; the Horn of Africa; and international economic issues. The endowment also has an office in New York City at 30 Rockefeller Plaza, New York, N.Y. 10112 (212/572-8200).

5.   The Endowment is the publisher of the quarterly *Foreign Policy*. A list of publications and a report, *Carnegie Endowment for International Peace in the 1970's*, are available free on request. Of particular interest to Southeast Asianists are the studies by Raul Manglapus, *Japan in Southeast Asia* (1976), and by Selig S. Harrison, *China, Oil, and Asia* (1977).

H12   Center for Applied Linguistics

1.   *3520 Prospect Street, N.W.*
     Washington, D.C. 20007
     (202) 298-9292

2.   G. Richard Tucker, Director
     Dora Johnson, Director, Communications and Publications

3.   The Center for Applied Linguistics (CAL) is a private, nonprofit organization involved in the study of language and the application of linguistics to educational, cultural, and social concerns. Through in-depth research, the development of teaching and scholarly materials, technical assistance programs, and active participation in language policy formulation, CAL has become the leading resource organization of its kind, with programs serving the education and linguistic professions and the general public.

   As an autonomous program of the Modern Language Association, CAL was established in 1959 with three objectives: to improve the teaching of English as a second or foreign language; to improve the teaching of uncommonly taught languages; and to incorporate the findings of the language sciences into the American education process. In 1964 CAL was incorporated as an independent organization.

   CAL engaged in a wide range of activities including: information collection and analysis, publications, conferences, and liaison between institutions, organizations, foundations, and government agencies and ministries. Based in Washington, D.C., CAL occasionally utilizes offices in other locations for special purposes such as language training. CAL has offices in Thailand, California, and Florida to provide language training for refugees.

5.   CAL publications include a number of items of interest to Southeast Asianists. A volume on *Southeast Asia and the Pacific* is currently available as part of the center's series, "Survey of Materials for the Study of the Uncommonly Taught Languages." The center has an extensive collection of educational volumes available in its "Indochinese Refugee Education" se-

ries, including: *English–Vietnamese Phrasebook; Vietnamese–English Phrasebook; Colloquium on the Vietnamese Language; From the Dragon's Cloud* (Vietnamese Folk Tales); *English–Khmer Phrasebook; Engish–Lao Phrasebook;* and additional volumes on health care, legal status, job opportunities, and a variety of other topics.

The center also publishes the information pamphlet *Center for Applied Linguistics* and *Catalog 1981, Center for Applied Linguistics* (with updated price list).

H13 Center for Defense Information

1. *303 Capitol Gallery West*
    600 Maryland Avenue, S.W.
    Washington, D.C. 20024
    (202) 484-9490

2. Gene R. LaRocque, Director

3. The center is a nonprofit, nonpartisan, public-interest organization that provides objective information and analysis of U.S. national-defense issues. In June 1980, Admiral LaRocque, the center's director, testified before the House Appropriations Subcommittee on Foreign Operations, on the East Timor issue. The center also prepared a background paper on Timor. Stephen Goose is the senior research analyst for Asian affairs.

4. The center's library houses a growing specialized collection of congressional documents and analyses essential to the work of its research staff. The collection is available to researchers for on-site use.

5. In addition to occasional papers, monographs, and analyses, the center publishes a monthly newsletter, *The Defense Monitor,* which occasionally contains material on Southeast Asia. See for example *Soviet Geopolitical Momentum, Myth or Menace* (vol. 9, no. 1, January 1980), which contains a section on Vietnam and Indonesia.

H14 Center for International Policy

1. *120 Maryland Avenue, N.E.*
    Washington, D.C. 20002
    (202) 544-4666

2. Donald L. Ranard, Director
    William Goodfellow, Deputy Director

3. The Center for International Policy is a nonprofit, education and research organization concerned with U.S. foreign policy towards the Third World and the resultant impact on human rights and needs. Southeast Asian activities are entirely related to the center's Indochina Project, which seeks ways to develop a better understanding of the countries of Indochina and their relations with the United States. Indochina Project staff members are: Linda Gibson Hiebert, Murray Hiebert, and Gareth Porter (202/546-8181). The project publishes *Indochina Issues,* a series.

5.   Center publications include the booklet *A Guide for Helping Indochinese Refugees in the United States,* and (ten times a year), *Indochina Issues.* Titles in this series include: *A New Look at America's Refugee Policy* (September 1980); *ASEAN's Vietnam Problem: Confrontation or Dialog?* (August 1980); *Kampuchea's UN Seat: Cutting the Pol Pot Connection* (July 1980); *Indochina in Crisis: Dilemma for U.S. Policy: A Conference Report* (June 1980); *Vietnam's Soviet Alliance: A Challenge to U.S. Policy* (May 1980); *Kampuchea: Breaking the Cycle* (April 1980); *Famine in Kampuchea: Politics of a Tragedy* (December 1979); *Vietnam's Embargoed Economy: In the U.S. Interest?* (August 1979); *Laos: The Widening Indochina Conflict* (June 1979); and *The Chinese Invasion of Vietnam: Changing Alliances* (March 1979).

H15 Center for National Security Studies (CNSS)

1.   *122 Maryland Avenue, N.E.*
Washington, D.C. 20002
(202) 544-5380

2.   Morton Halperin, Director

3.   The Center for National Security Studies, affiliated with the Fund for Peace and the American Civil Liberties Union (ACLU), promotes its stated objective, "to reduce government secrecy, to limit the surveillance or manipulation of lawful political activity and to protect the rights of Americans to write and speak on issues affecting the national security" through litigation on behalf of victims of intelligence-agency abuses and through litigation for release of documents under the Freedom of Information Act. The Center monitors legislation affecting the intelligence agencies and government secrecy. Center personnel testify before congressional committees, appear on radio and TV, and speak before groups around the country. The staff also writes and publishes books, reports, articles, and pamphlets on national security and civil liberties questions. U.S. intelligence activities in Southeast Asia, while not a central concern, are monitored.

4.   The library is a small facility containing some 500 books and reports plus journals, newsletters, congressional hearings, and CIA documents obtained under the Freedom of Information Act. The library is open to researchers by appointment. Copying services are available at cost.

5.   The CNSS issues a number of publications including a monthly newsletter, *First Principles,* several books and reports on various aspects of the security establishment, and two items of particular value for scholars seeking classified government documents: *Using the Freedom of Information Act: A Step by Step Guide* (1979) and *The 1980 Edition of Litigation Under the Federal Freedom of Information Act and Privacy Act* (5th ed.), edited by Christine M. Marwick. Also useful is the report *From Official Files: Abstracts of Documents on National Security and Civil Liberties Available from the Center for National Security Study Library* (CNSS Report No. 102–3), which catalogs a diverse set of documents that include CIA memos on whether the secret war in Laos is legal, CIA documents on the antiwar movement in this country, a CIA memo on assassination plots against South Vietnamese leaders, and a number of NSC memos of related interest.

H16 Center for Naval Analysis (CNA)

1. *200 North Beauregard Street*
   Alexandria, Virginia 22311
   (703) 998-3500

2. David B. Kassing, President

3. An affiliate of the University of Rochester (Rochester, New York 14627), the Center for Naval Analysis is a nonprofit organization that conducts operations research, systems analysis, and economic studies for the U.S. Navy and other government agencies. The research staff in the Program, Plans and Policy Division of the Institute of Naval Studies monitors and conducts research on Soviet naval developments and diplomacy in the Indian Ocean. Technical studies have also been done on Vietnam, e.g., *Market Time: Countering Sea-Borne Infiltration on South Vietnam* (1966). For further information call Richard Remnek (703/998-3674), who has done several studies on naval security in the Indian Ocean region. Most of the work done by the division is classified. For access to classified materials, address inquiries to the Office of the Chief of Naval Operations, Systems Analysis Division, Navy Department, Washington, D.C. 20350.

4. The center's library contains some 9,000 bound volumes and over 500 periodical subscriptions in the fields of political and social science, economics, weapons research, and development and other related areas. A security clearance and special permission from the Management Information Office are required. The same restrictions apply to the center's computer facilities.

5. Unclassified CNA materials are listed in the periodically updated *Index of Selected Publications* (1980), which is available at no cost, as is the CNA's *Annual Report*.

H17 Center for Strategic and International Studies (CSIS) (Georgetown University)

1. *1800 K Street, N.W.*
   Washington, D.C. 20006
   (202) 887-0200

2. David M. Abshire, Chairman
   Michael A. Samuels, Executive Director for Third World Studies

3. The Center for Strategic and International Studies of Georgetown University is a nonprofit, nonpartisan research institution founded in 1962 to foster scholarship and public awareness of emerging international issues on a broad interdisciplinary basis. In 1978 the center initiated the Pacific Basin Project (Robert Downen, director). While the primary focus of the project has been Northeast Asia, the ASEAN states of Southeast Asia are also of interest to project staff. In 1981 and 1982, the project has moved into a new phase: studying the emerging Pacific-basin economic-community concept. A congressional study group has been formed and will include—in addition to five congressmen—academics, businessmen, and journalists,

who will periodically discuss the pros and cons of the formation of such a community, the possibility of U.S. involvement, and related questions. The project produces publications, holds conferences, seminars, and briefings. There are four permanent staff members and a number of part-time staff. The center has initiated a new program of studies on the Third World, but so far no specific program has been adopted on Southeast Asia.

5.   The center has an extensive publications program. In addition to the *Washington Quarterly*, the center publishes numerous reports and monographs. Some titles of interest include: *Population and Politics in the Philippines* (1978); *Seminar on World Food Supply, Health, and Nutrition* (1977); and *World Food: A Three Dimensional View of Production* (1977). Publication lists and the annual report are available on request.

H18 Committee for Economic Development (CED)

1.   *1700 K Street, N.W.*
      Washington, D.C. 20006
      (202) 296-5860

2.   Robert C. Holland, President

3.   The Committee for Economic Development is a nonprofit, business-related, research and educational organization composed of approximately 200 trustees, who are, for the most part, board chairmen or presidents of major corporations or universities, with offices in New York and Washington, D.C. A small contingent of the research staff works out of the Washington office, assisting in the preparation of CED policy statements and recommendations on public policy and international economic issues. Research in international economics has not dwelt directly with Southeast Asia, but a special project on economic relations between industrialized and less-developed countries, directed by Isaiah Frank (202/785-6261), professor of economics at the School of Advanced International Studies (see entry J9), has implications for the experience of some Southeast Asian countries, and particularly the ASEAN states.

5.   Recent publications include the results of the above-mentioned study, *Foreign Enterprise in Developing Countries,* by Isaiah Frank (1980), and a CED policy statement based on this study, *Transnational Corporations in Developing Countries* (1980). Other recent CED publications on international affairs include *International Economic Consequences of High-Priced Energy* (1975); *Toward a New International Economic System: A Joint Japanese–American View* (1974); *The Japanese Economy in International Perspective* (1975); and *How the United States and Japan See Each Other's Economy: An Exchange of Views Between the American and Japanese Committees for Economic Development* (1974).

H19 Environmental Fund

1.   *1302 18th Street, N.W.*
      Washington, D.C. 20036
      (202) 293-2548

2.   Garrett Hardin, Executive Officer

3.   An operating foundation primarily concerned with the effect of continued population growth on the environment, the Environmental Fund conducts forums and programs of research on the relationship of population growth to such problems as resource depletion, pollution, and other social problems. The fund's main objective is to create, around the world, an awareness of the urgent need to stabilize the size of world population.

4.   The Environmental Fund's small reference library contains some secondary materials, U.N. reports, magazines, and newspaper clippings on Indonesian population problems.

5.   Fund publications include an irregular newsletter, *The Other Side,* which has featured articles on Indonesia and Singapore, and an annual *World Population Chart,* which is broken down by region and country.

H20 Foreign Policy Institute (FPI) (The Johns Hopkins University— School of Advanced International Studies) (SAIS)

1.   *1740 Massachusetts Avenue, N.W.*
Washington, D.C. 20036
(202) 785-6800

2.   Lucius D. Battle, Chairman

3.   A successor organization to the SAIS Washington Center of Foreign Policy Research, the Foreign Policy Institute was established in July 1980 to conduct research on current issues such as international security, energy, and economic policies, and to serve as a resource for policy makers, journalists, and others interested in foreign affairs. The institute continues to sponsor discussions, seminars, and meetings on current trends and issues on a variety of specialized subjects. The institute's current Asia–Pacific Forum focuses, in part, on Southeast Asian issues. The institute has a special program for a limited number of scholars and government officials from foreign nations to participate, as fellows, in the activities of the institute and to pursue their own research and study projects.

5.   The FPI publishes *SAIS Review* (quarterly). This student-edited journal featured two articles of interest to Southeast Asianists in the winter 1981 issue: "The Decline of U.S. Diplomacy in Southeast Asia," by Gareth Porter, and "The Second Transition in Asia: America in Asia Under Carter," by Kim Woodard. The FPI has also introduced a new monograph series which focuses on critical foreign-policy issues. The first monograph, *A Socialist France and Western Security,* by Drs. Michael M. Harrison and Simon Serfaty, appeared in October 1981.

H21 The Fund for Investigative Journalism

1.   *1346 Connecticut Avenue, N.W.*
Washington, D.C. 20036
(202) 462-1844

2.   Howard Bray, Executive Director

3.   The Fund for Investigative Journalism was incorporated in 1969 for the purpose of increasing public knowledge about the concealed, obscure, or complex aspects of matters significantly affecting the public. Towards that end, the fund makes grants to writers, enabling them to probe abuses of authority or the malfunctioning of institutions and systems that harm the public. The fund has made more than 450 grants to writers since 1969. Seymour Hersh, for his work entitled *Cover Up* (New York: Random House, 1972), which dealt with the My Lai massacre, received support from the fund.

H22 General Research Corporation (GRC)

1.   *7655 Old Springhouse Road*
McLean, Virginia 22101
(703) 893-5900

2.   John L. Allen, President

3.   The General Research Corporation, a subsidiary of Flow General, Inc., is a private research organization that studies domestic and foreign policy issues. Much of the GRC research is produced on contract for the Defense Department. The corporation has taken a research interest in military, political, and economic questions related to Southeast Asia and also sponsors both open and closed meetings and seminars on topics of interest to Southeast Asia specialists.

4.   The library facilities of GRC are divided into two sections: a reading room of unclassified materials (28,000 books and 500 periodical subscriptions) and a documents section containing some 30,000 classified and unclassified documents, which are continually being weeded. Most of the documents found here are also to be found at the Defense Technical Information Center (entry G5) and should be used there. Duplicates of index cards for holdings are sent to the Army Library (entry A6). Researchers interested in the reading-room materials should contact librarian Patricia Wolf.

5.   Eugene J. Suto, Director of Security and Documentation, can answer questions about the documents collection and GRC publications.

H23 Heritage Foundation

1.   *513 C Street, N.E.*
Washington, D.C. 20002
(202) 546-4400

2.   Edwin J. Feulner, President

3.   The Heritage Foundation is a nonprofit research organization that analyzes and disseminates information on a variety of public policy issues both domestic and foreign. The foundation sponsors a continuing series of congressional briefings, lectures, symposia, and conferences to facilitate the exchange of ideas on public-policy issues. The foundation's research interest in Southeast Asia has been recently focused on human rights in Vietnam. William Scully is the Asia analyst for the foundation.

Through its Resource Bank Program, the foundation works to keep academics and organizations across the country in constant touch with Washington. Over 1,000 scholars and 300 organizations are linked to the bank. Another Resource Bank activity, the International Visitors Center, gives foreign dignitaries a unique opportunity to observe and contribute to the Washington policy-making scene. For further information contact Willa Ann Johnson, Director, Resource Bank.

4.   The foundation's small reference library of secondary materials and periodicals is primarily for the use of the staff.

5.   Southeast Asia related publications include one *Backgrounder* report (No. 118) entitled *Indochina: Five Years of Communist Rule* (April 1980). The foundation's journal, *Policy Review*, has also featured articles on Southeast Asia. A publication list and an annual report are available free on request.

H24 Institute for International Law (Georgetown University Law Center)

1.   *600 New Jersey Avenue, N.W.*
Washington, D.C. 20001
(202) 624-8330

2.   Don Wallace, Director

3.   Georgetown University Law Center's Institute for International Law is an academic center serving law students, lawyers, officials, and the business community of the U.S., Europe, and developing countries. The institute offers a combination of research and practical training that focuses on the legal aspects of international trade and investment. The institute sponsors an annual three-week orientation on the U.S. legal system for foreign lawyers about to begin graduate law studies in the United States. The institute also organizes conferences and colloquia and awards limited fellowships to foreign students and officials.

The institute's Investment Negotiation Center (INC) was established in 1974. It provides research and training services for officials from developing countries, enabling them to negotiate more effectively with foreign direct investors and contractors. The INC is cosponsored by the Parker School of Foreign and Comparative Law of Columbia University. In addition to conducting seminars in Washington, D.C., and abroad, the INC also serves as consultant to international organizations.

Since 1973, a substantial number of Southeast Asians have participated in the center's investment and procurement seminars in this country. The number of participants by country is as follows: Indonesia, 28; the Philippines, 27; Malaysia, 14; and Thailand, 7. In addition, investment and procurement seminars have been conducted in Indonesia and Thailand. The institute also has sponsored, for a number of years, an orientation course for foreign persons who come to the U.S. to undertake the study of law. There have been approximately 10 individuals from Thailand who have participated in this course.

5.   *Law and Policy in International Business*, the quarterly international law journal of the Law Center analyzes legal aspects of transnational trade and investment. The institute's publications include: *Career Opportunities in*

International Law and *A Lawyer's Guide to International Business Transactions* (in 2 parts). A list of recent publications and several brochures on the institute and the INC are available on request. The INC periodically publishes a newsletter, *Foreign Exchange.*

H25 Institute for Policy Studies (IPS)

1.   *1901 Q Street, N.W.*
      Washington, D.C. 20009
      (202) 234-9382

2.   Robert Borosage, Director

3.   The Institute for Policy Studies is an independent, nonprofit center for "research, education, and social invention. IPS sponsors critical examination of the assumptions and policies that define American posture on domestic and international issues, and offers alternative strategies and visions." The institute focuses on domestic policy, national security, international economics, and human rights. Although the institute does not have a Southeast Asia program per se, various aspects of U.S. policy for that region, the topic of human rights, and political, economic, and social changes have been studied by IPS staff fellows.

      The institute's staff consists primarily of resident fellows. In addition, project directors and research associates are affiliated with the organization on a temporary, contractual basis. Positions as research assistants and volunteer interns are also available.

5.   IPS publishes approximately 20 books, issue papers, and reports each year. The Militarism and Disarmament Project has published a *Report on East Asia* (1979) that includes Indonesia and the Philippines and should be of interest to Southeast Asianists. A complete publications list is available on request.

H26 International Center for Research on Women (ICRW)

1.   *1010 16th Street, N.W.*
      Washington, D.C. 20036
      (202)293-3154

2.   Mayra Buvinic, Director

3.   The International Center for Research on Women is a nonprofit institution contributing to the formulation and implementation of development policy that considers the differences economic modernization has on men and women in poverty. Toward this end, the ICRW emphasizes applied, policy-relevant research on the social and economic situation of women at the national, local, and household levels, and gives technical assistance in the design and evaulation of strategies and projects that incorporate women in the development process.

      The ICRW has specialized in issues related to women's employment, their income-generating productivity, and their roles as component of women's roles. Implementation has taken four programmatic approaches: policy-relevant research, program and project technical assistance, information dissemination, and educational activities.

With respect to Southeast Asia, ICRW is currently (1982) active in Indonesia and Thailand, providing USAID missions with technical assistance and backup research in the areas of income and employment for women.

ICRW maintains an international network of contacts that include national research institutes, women's organizations, researchers, and practitioners. The center also has on file the vitae of more than 100 consultants who are experts on women and development. The center also organizes informal seminars and workshops.

4. ICRW maintains a collection of some 1,000 reports and studies, some of which are unpublished, on women and development from an international group of social scientists and development practitioners. The library is open to scholars.

5. A list of publications is available on request.

H27 International Economic Policy Association (IEPA)

1. *1625 Eye Street, N.W., Suite 908*
   Washington, D.C. 20006
   (202) 331-1974

2. Timothy W. Stanley, President

3. The International Economic Policy Association is a nonprofit research organization engaged in fostering a consistent international economic policy and in promoting and disseminating information on international economics. The association analyzes U.S. and foreign government policies affecting international trade, aid, investments, finance, taxation, and related international monetary developments. The IEPA has specialized in U.S. balance of payments, foreign investment, and raw-materials problems. In 1981, IEPA completed a basic study of the developing countries of the Pacific Basin, which includes the five ASEAN states. Dr. Samuel Rosenblat was the study director.

   An IEPA affiliate, the Center for Multinational Studies, conducts research on the effects that multinational corporations have upon the U.S. and world economy. Another associated IEPA organization, the International Economic Studies Institute (IESI), has specialized in raw materials, technology transfer, and the interaction between international economics and security. Both affiliates are located at the IEPA address.

5. IEPA publications include a monograph series and research reports on U.S. foreign economic policy issues. The Center for Multinational Studies publishes an *Occasional Paper Series,* while the IESI publishes a *Contemporary Issue Series* and *Conference Papers.* A list of IEPA publications is available on request.

H28 International Food Policy Research Institute (IFPRI)

1. *1776 Massachusetts Avenue, N.W.*
   Washington, D.C. 20036
   (202) 862-5600

2. John W. Mellor, Director

3.　　A nonprofit research and educational institution, the IFPRI's purpose is to analyze the world food situation, especially as it affects developing countries, and conduct research on major policies to increase the availability of food in those countries. The primary target audience of IFPRI is that of the policy makers. Research results are distributed to those involved in making food-policy decisions at national and international levels. IFPRI relies on data collected by the Food and Agriculture Organization (FAO), the World Bank, and regional and national organizations dealing with food and related issues. IFPRI sponsors seminars and workshops in collaboration with other organizations. IFPRI has observer status in UN organizations with food policies.

　　Research programs of the institute include analysis of trends in the production, exchange, and consumption of food in developing countries; policies that affect agricultural production in developing countries; programs and policies to improve distribution of available foodstuffs, with special attention to populations with inadequate diet; and policies that will increase the ability of developing countries to make effective use of international trade. The institute currently has a project underway that focuses on rice policies in Southeast Asia. This project is being undertaken in conjunction with the International Fertilizer Development Center in Muscle Shoals, Alabama; and the International Rice Research Institute in Manila. Mark Rosegrant is a good source of information for this project. Eventually, the project will issue papers on the rice industry in each of the Southeast Asian countries.

4.　　The institute's small, specialized library contains representative collections in general food policy, agricultural economics and statistics, development economics, and specialized periodicals. Country-level field data from some developing countries is also available at the library, which is open to private researchers for on-site use. Interlibrary loan facilities are available.

5.　　Publications include: *Developed-Country Agricultural Policies and Developing-Country Supplies: The Case of Wheat* (1980); *Investment and Input Requirements for Accelerating Food Production in Low-Income Countries by 1990* (1979); *Food Security for Developing Countries* (1980); and *Economic Analysis of Irrigation Development in Malaysia* (working paper) (1981). The IFPRI annual report and publications list are available on request.

H29　International Institute for Environment and Development (IIED)— Washington Office

1.　　*1319 F Street, N.W., Suite 800*
　　Washington, D.C. 20004
　　(202) 462-0900

2.　　David Runnalle, Director

3.　　IIED is a nonprofit, private foundation headquartered in London (27 Mortimer Street, London WIN 8DE, telephone: 01-580 7656-7). Currently its concerns include the issues of future energy and food supply, the development of sufficient shelter and clean water for mankind, and environmental consequences of major aid programs, especially in the Third World countries. The institute runs an environmental information unit, called "Earthscan," for the press and maintains close working contact with many nongovernmental organizations operating in similar fields around the world. In 1981 and 1982, IIED had two projects in Southeast Asia: in the Philippines, a solar-energy project in conjunction with several private solar-research groups; and in Malaysia, a study of the legal and institutional aspects of the country for the National Parks Service. Publications reviewing these operations will be available at a later date.

4. The Washington Office library contains a collection of specialized United Nation's conference documents relating to environmental issues. The collection is open to scholars on the basis of prior appointment.

5. IIED publications include: Anil Agarwal, *Drugs and the Third World* (1977); *International Directory of Environment Film Sources* (1977); Arjun Makhigani, *Energy Policy for the Rural Third World* (1976); R. P. Misra (ed.), *Habitat Asia: Issues and Responses,* 3 vols. (1979); and Stuart Donelson et al., *Aid for Human Settlements in the Third World: A Summary of the Activities of the Multilateral Agencies* (1979). An IIED annual report and a list of publications is available on request.

H30 National Association of Manufacturers (NAM)—International Economic Affairs Department

1. *1776 F Street, N.W.*
   Washington, D.C. 20006
   (202) 626-3700

2. Lawrence A. Fox, Vice President

3. The International Economic Affairs Department conducts research on international trade, investment, and finance for NAM member companies. The department also organizes and directs trade missions overseas, although there have been none organized to Southeast Asia as of this writing.

5. Publications include an annual review and perspective, *International Economic Issues;* a monthly newsletter, *International Economic Report;* and special research reports, such as *LDC External Debt: Facts, Figures, Perspectives* and *Indicators of International Economic Performance.* A list of publications is available on request.

H31 National Planning Association (NPA)

1. *1606 New Hampshire Avenue, N.W.*
   Washington, D.C. 20009
   (202) 265-7685

2. Neil J. McMullen, Executive Director
   Theodore Geiger, Director of International Studies

3. The National Planning Association is a nonprofit association of businessmen, trade unionists, and a few professionals that meets periodically throughout the year to discuss medium-term economic-policy issues. To arrange these meetings and to provide more detailed background information on particular issues, there is a small permanent staff in Washington. The staff also undertakes approved economic research, which is sometimes funded by outside sources. Research projects are conducted under the

direction of committees composed of leaders from business, labor, agriculture, and education. Many of these projects are relevant to Southeast Asia.

5.   NPA prepares, under contract for the U.S. Agency for International Development, the quarterly *Development Digest,* which has carried articles on Southeast Asia. The *New International Realities* is an in-house magazine published three times a year. A list of NPA publications is available on request.

H32 Overseas Development Council (ODC)

1.   *1717 Massachusetts Avenue, N.W.*
Washington, D.C. 20036
(202) 234-8701

2.   John W. Sewell, President

3.   ODC is an independent, nonprofit research center concerned with increasing American understanding of the economic and social problems confronting developing countries. The council stresses the importance of these countries to the U.S. in an increasingly interdependent world, and pursues its objectives through research, conferences, publications, and liaison with mass-membership organizations interested in U.S. relations with the developing world.
       Prominent emphasis in the council's current work programs includes: analysis of the implications of the increasing interdependence of economic growth or stagnation in the industrialized and developing countries; assessment of the costs and benefits for all countries of the major proposals for a new international economic order (North–South dialogue); identification of improved ways to achieve Third World population and health goals, including analysis of how development can affect health and fertility; continued study of alternative development strategies; and refinement of a new tool for measuring development achievement. Most council studies are done from a global, rather than a regional, perspective.

4.   ODC has a small research library primarily for the use of the staff.

5.   ODC has an extensive publications program of monographic studies, occasional papers, and communiqués. Recent publications include: Martin M. McLaughlin, *The United States and the World Development Agenda 1979* (1979); William R. Cline, *Policy Alternatives for a New International Economic Order: An Economic Analysis* (1979); Morris David Morris, *Measuring the Condition of the World's Poor: The Physical Quality of Life Index* (1979); and Jairam Ramesh and Charles Weiss, *Mobilizing Technology for World Development* (1979). The ODC annual report and a catalog of publications is available free.

H33 Population Reference Bureau, Inc. (PRB)

1.   *1337 Connecticut Avenue, N.W.*
Washington, D.C. 20036
(202) 785-4664

2.   Robert Worrell, President

3.   The Population Reference Bureau is a nonprofit, educational organization that compiles and disseminates information on national and international population issues. The PRB relies principally on United Nations data for Southeast Asian statistics, but includes information supplied by a network of consultants. Public reference services are provided.

4.   A 15,000-volume research library is open to serious researchers 8:30 A.M.–4:30 P.M. weekdays.

5.   The bureau publishes the *Population Bulletin,* bimonthly, providing in-depth analysis of population trends and policies; *The World Population Data Sheet,* with current data on a variety of demographic variables; *Intercom,* the International Population News Magazine; *Interchange,* a quarterly newsletter for teachers, accompanied by learning materials for students; *Population Trends and Public Policy,* occasional reports on policy implications of population trends and events; and special publications such as the *Population Handbook,* a guide to demographic terms and concepts, the *World's Women Data Sheet,* and the *World's Children Data Sheet.* The bureau's annual report and publication list are available on request.

H34 Rand Corporation—Washington Office

1.   *2100 M Street, N.W.*
     Washington, D.C. 20037
     (202) 296-5000

2.   Paul T. Hill, Director, Washington Operations

3.   The Rand Corporation is a private, nonprofit research organization head-quartered in Santa Monica, California. It analyzes domestic and international issues affecting U.S. public welfare and national security, and its National Security Research Divisions have produced numerous reports and studies on Southeast Asian politics, economic conditions, social developments, defense strategies, and U.S. security interests. The Washington staff, which varies in size, has some 50 researchers at the time of this writing.

4.   The Rand Washington office library contains several thousand volumes, mostly in the social sciences. Although the facility is restricted to Rand personnel, unclassified materials may be borrowed on interlibrary loan.

5.   Most of Rand's strategic research is produced under contract for U.S. government agencies and is security classified. Unclassified publications are disseminated to some 350 U.S. libraries on a subscription basis. In the Washington area, these repositories include the Library of Congress, the George Washington University Library and the Army Library at the Pentagon.
     Rand prepares selected and annotated bibliographies of their own publications for over 40 subject areas and geographic regions. The September 1981 issue of *A Bibliography of Selected Rand Publications: Asia* contained citations to numerous book reports and memoranda. These bibliographies are available free from the Washington office. The publications cited are available either from Rand's head office (1700 Main Street, Santa Monica, California 90406) or from commercial publishers, as specified. Rand publications of interest to Southeast Asianists in 1980 include two books, *Asian Security in the 80's: Problems and Policies for a Time of Transition* (1980)

and *The Fall of South Vietnam: Statements by Vietnamese Military and Civilian Leaders* (1980); and the following reports: *Indonesia 1979: the Record of Three Decades* (January 1980); *Indonesia in the Pacific Community* (January 1980); and *Three Approaches to Computer Processing Data on Family Planning in Malaysia* (July 1980).

H35 Resources for the Future (RFF)

1. *1755 Massachusetts Avenue, N.W.*
   Washington, D.C. 20036
   (202) 328-5000

2. Emery N. Castle, President

3. RFF is a nonprofit corporation whose purpose is to advance research and education of domestic and international policy issues relating to natural resources, environmental quality, population, and energy. A majority of its programs are carried out by resident staff, but a few are supported through grants to universities and other nonprofit organizations. RFF's research and other work are supported by grants and contracts from foundations, government, and private industry. Most of its studies are in the social sciences and are broadly concerned with the relationships of people to the natural environment. RFF's Southeast Asia related research is carried on in the developing world by its Center for Energy Policy Research and the Renewable Resources Division. The center currently has a short term project in Indonesia analyzing rural electrification. A final report is expected by January 1983. In 1980 the Renewable Resource Division conducted a three-country study (India, Columbia, Indonesia), which focused on problems of the environment and nuclear power; energy transition; migration and urbanization; application and development of managerial skills and technological know-how; long-term planning; and long-run social, institutional, and political factors. RFF's Wednesday Seminar series include such themes as "Energy Aspects of Poverty in Developing Countries" and "Material Requirements and Economic Growth."

5. The results of RFF research are disseminated primarily through books and monographs published and distributed by The Johns Hopkins University Press. Relevant publications include: *Household Energy and the Poor in the Third World* (1979); *Economic Equality and Fertility in Developing Countries* (1979); *Rural Women at Work: Strategies for Development in South Asia* (1978); and *Energy Strategies for Developing Nations* (1981). RFF's annual report and a publication list are available free on request.

State Department–Office of the Historian See entry K34

H36 United Nations Information Centre

1. *2101 L Street, N.W., Suite 209*
   Washington, D.C. 20037
   (202) 296-5370

2. Marcial Tamayo, Director
   Patricia O'Callaghan, Information Officer

3.　　The U.N. Information Centre is the Washington branch of the U.N. Office of Public Information. The center engages in a range of reference services and utilizes all forms of public media (publications, press, radio, television, films, and exhibition activities) to disseminate information about the work and activities of the United Nations and its various specialized agencies. The center maintains ties with the press, information media, educational institutions, and governmental and private organizations.

4.　　The center's library is described in entry A40; its photo and film collection, in entry F21.

H37 Woodrow Wilson International Center for Scholars (WWICS)

1.　　*Smithsonian Institution Building*
1000 Jefferson Drive, S.W.
Washington, D.C. 20560
(202) 357-2429

2.　　James H. Billington, Director

3.　　The Woodrow Wilson International Center for Scholars was created by the United States Congress in 1968 as the nation's official living memorial to its twenty-eighth president. As a national institution with international interests, the center seeks to encourage the creative use of the unique human, archival, and institutional resources in the nation's capital for studies illuminating our understanding of the past and present.

　　　Through its residential fellowship program of advanced research, the WWICS seeks to commemorate both the scholarly depth and the public concerns of Woodrow Wilson. The center welcomes outstanding project proposals representing a wide diversity of scholarly interests and approaches from individuals throughout the world. It has no permanent or tenured fellows. Its fellowships are awarded, for periods ranging from four months to one year or more, in one broadly defined program and five more focused programs of research. The broadly defined program—History, Culture, and Society—enables the center to attract superior projects, from the entire range of scholarship in the humanities and social sciences, that promise to make major contributions to our understanding of the human condition or that attempt broad synthesis involving different fields or different cultures. The five designated programs are the Kennan Institute for Advanced Russian Studies, the Latin American Program, the International Security Studies Program, the East Asia Program, and the Program in American Society and Politics. The WWICS also operates a Guest Scholar Program for the short-term use of the center's facilities by a small number of visiting scholars and specialists.

　　　In 1982 The East Asia Program (Ronald A. Morse, Secretary, 202/357-1937) has intensified the coverage of Southeast Asia. In 1982 and 1983 fellowships were granted to Syed Hussein Alatas and Lin Ken Wong, both from the National University of Singapore, for the following projects, respectively: "Reflections on Corruption in Asian Society" and "Straits of Malacca in History."

　　　Between 1973 and 1981, center fellows and guest scholars, with Southeast Asian specialities, (and their projects) have included: Peter Braestrup, "Interpretation of the Crisis of Tet, 1968, by the American Press and Television"; John Cobb, "The Western Experience of Time and Divinity in Light of Buddhist Thought;" Ikuhito Hata, "Origins of the Korean and Vietnam wars;" Gerald C. Hickey, "Historical Study of the Development of Leadership among the Highland Ethnic Minorities of South Vietnam;" Muhammad Shamsul Huq, "Alternative Patterns of Growth in Developing Countries, with Special Attention to South and Southeast Asia;" Benedict Kerkvliet, "Peasant Unrest and Huk Rebellion in the Philippines, 1930's–1950's;" Lawrence Lichty, "A Comprehensive History and Analysis of the Television Coverage of the Indochina War, 1965–1976;" Ronald Nairn, "World Food and Fiber Situation and Its Relationship to U.S. Economic and Foreign Policy;" Neil Sheehan, "John Paul Vann and the American Experience in Vietnam;" and Kamol Somvichian, "The Impact of Buddhism and Islam on Politics in Thailand and Indonesia."

The center's activities include frequent colloquia, evening seminars, and other discussions designed to foster intellectual community among the participants. Since 1976 the WWICS has organized major meetings on the following Southeast Asian topics: "The Process of Ethnicity: A Focus on the People of the Vietnamese Central Highlands;" "The Tet Offensive and the Escalation of the Vietnam Wars, 1965–1968;" and "The Vietnam War on TV." In 1982 and 1983, the East Asia Program held a year-long series of seminars examining the relationship between Asian energy developments and broader regional security issues. Among other matters, the seminars focused on how the United States and other Western Hemisphere countries (including Canada and Mexico) could contribute to the energy security of East and Southeast Asia as a geopolitical entity (Indonesia, Japan, Malaysia, China, the Philippines, Singapore, South Korea, Taiwan, and Thailand). The scheduled events are announced in the monthly *Calendar of Events*.

4.   The Wilson Center has a working library containing 16,000 volumes of basic reference works, bibliographies, and essential monographs in the social sciences and humanities, with an emphasis on the areas covered by the center's programs. The library maintains a small reference collection for Southeast and East Aia. It subscribes to and maintains the back files of about 300 scholarly journals and periodicals. As part of a National Presidential Memorial, the WWICS library has special access to the collections of the Library of Congress and other government libraries. The librarian is Zdeněk V. David (202/357-2567).

5.   The *Wilson Quarterly* (circulation 105,000) carries occasional articles on Southeast Asia. The Spring 1981 issue, for example, included three articles on Indonesia and a bibliographic essay. The WWICS also sponsors the preparation and publication of *Scholars' Guides to Washington, D.C.* Available from the Smithsonian Institution Press (P.O. Box 1579, Washington, D.C. 20013), the *Guides* survey the collections, institutions, and organizations pertinent to the study of particular geographic areas, such as Africa, Central and Eastern Europe, East Asia, Latin America and the Caribbean, the Middle East, Russia/Soviet Union, South Asia, and other world regions. A separate *Guide* covers film and video collections in the Washington, D.C., area. The center's programs (Kennan Institute, Latin American, International Security Studies, and East Asia) publish *Occasional/Working Papers*, which are distributed free of charge to interested parties upon request. Lists are available from the Publications Office or individual program offices. The *Annual Report* and an occasional bulletin, the *Newsletter*, are sent to former fellows and other friends of the Wilson Center.

H38 World Peace Through Law Center (WPTLC)

1. *1000 Connecticut Avenue, N.W., Suite 800*
   Washington, D.C. 20036
   (202) 466-5428

2. Charles S. Rhyne, President

3. Dedicated to the replacement of force by law in international affairs, the World Peace Through Law Center is a world-wide organization of judges, lawyers, law professors, and law students representing 151 nations, including the ASEAN states of Southeast Asia and Burma. A nonprofit and nonpolitical organization, the center draws its members from its constituent professional associations: World Association of Judges, World Association of Lawyers, World Association of Law Professors, and World Association of Law Students. WPTLC maintains separate specialized sections for dealing with issues such as human rights and international legal education.

   The center sponsors World Law Day, and biennial World Law Conferences, featuring demonstration trials on such themes as human rights and law of the sea, at different locations throughout the world. Within the vast spectrum of law, the council's widespread concern includes investment disputes, human rights, refugee rights, and many other international issues. The center has consultative status as a nongovernmental organization with the United Nations, and through its computer list of over 150,000 judges, lawyers, law professors, and law students from 151 nations, WPTLC reaches the legal profession of the world.

5. WPTLC's extensive publications include: *The Law and Woman; Model Code of Conduct for Transnational Corporations; International Legal Protection for Human Rights: The Handbook for World Law Day, August 21, 1977; Peace with Justice under World Rules of Law; Law and Judicial Systems of Nations;* and *World Legal Directory.* The center also publishes a monthly newsletter, *The World Jurist,* and *World Law Review,* which contains the proceedings of the biennial conferences. A list of the center's publications and *A Report on the Activities of the World Peace Through Law Center* is available on request.

H39 Worldwatch Institute

1. *1776 Massachusetts Avenue, N.W., Suite 701*
   Washington, D.C. 20036
   (202) 452-1999

2. Lester Brown, President

3. The Worldwatch Institute is a nonprofit research organization that studies, from a global perspective, issues of population, energy, food, environment, and the changing roles of women. Though its studies are not specifically focused on Southeast Asia, most deal with problems germane to the region.

5. Research is published in the *Worldwatch Papers* series, which appears eight to ten times a year and in a book series. A subscription service is available.

J Academic Programs and Departments

Academic Programs and Departments Entry Format (J)

1. *Address; Telephone Numbers*

2. Name and Title of Chief Official

3. Degrees and Subjects Offered; Program Activities Related to Southeast Asia

4. Libraries and Research Facilities

Introductory Note

The academic institutions of the Washington metropolitan area offer undergraduate and graduate students many options for designing a degree course of study with emphasis on Southeast Asia. Through the Washington Consortium, undergraduate and graduate students can enroll in courses at several institutions and receive credit from their home universities. Prospective students should inquire at the university with which they intend to be primarily associated. It is also possible to obtain advanced degrees in several disciplines including political science, history, anthropology, linguistics, and others, with a Southeast Asia concentration. Prospective students should contact the appropriate department head for specifics.

Of the several institutions in the Washington, D.C., area that offer Southeast Asian courses, only one, the American University (entry J1), offers a fully developed area-studies program. This small but vigorous program operates through the Center for Asian Studies, School of International Service. Because of its location in the nation's capital, this program constitutes one of the most exciting opportunities for the study of Southeast Asia in the entire country.

Most of the academic programs listed here sponsor special public lectures, symposia, and other events during the year. Scholars wishing to attend these activities should contact the school or department concerned. Calendars of up-coming events are often available without charge.

J1 American University (AU)

1. *Massachusetts and Nebraska avenues, N.W.*
    Washington, D.C. 20016
    (202) 686-2000

2. Richard Berendzen, President

3. The American University, established in 1893, is an independent Methodist related university. Originally founded as a graduate school of history and public affairs, it currently provides a wide range of undergraduate and graduate programs in almost every academic discipline in its five colleges and schools. Current enrollment includes foreign students from 117 countries. The Office of International Programs (202/686-2077) is responsible for all international programs offered by the university, ascertains the needs and problems of the international students, and maintains the International Student Center.

    In the Washington metropolitan area, the American University has the greatest number of course offerings in Southeast Asian studies. The Department of History (James A. Malloy, Chairman, 202/686-2401), which offers several undergraduate and graduate programs, includes one course that deals, in part, with Vietnam. The Department of Language and Foreign Studies (Bruno F. Steinbruckner, Chairman, 202/686-2280) offers two years of both Thai and Indonesian language training.

    The School of International Service (SIS) (William C. Olson, Dean) offers a number of undergraduate and graduate programs, including international affairs, international relations, and language and area studies. The school's Center for Asian Studies (Llewellyn D. Howell, Director) coordinates Asian studies throughout the university and administers SIS Asia programs at the undergraduate, masters, and doctoral levels. The Center for Asian Studies also sponsors occasional seminars on Southeast Asia related topics. These programs are usually held in the SIS lounge.

    SIS course offerings in the Southeast Asia field include: Civilization of Asia (6 credits), Contemporary Southeast Asia, Selected Topics in Regional International Systems, Interdisciplinary Seminar (selected foreign areas), and International Relations of Southeast Asia (graduate and undergraduate), and Seminar on Southeast Asia Domestic Politics and Foreign Policy (graduate). SIS currently has three Southeast Asia specialists on the teaching faculty.

4. The American University Library is described in Entry A4.

American University—Foreign Area Studies (FAS) See entry H4

J2 Catholic University of America

1. *620 Michigan Avenue, N.E.*
    Washington, D.C. 20017
    (202) 635-5000

2. William J. Byron, President

3.   The Catholic University of America, founded in 1887, is the national university of the Catholic Church in the United States. The university offers undergraduate and graduate programs in numerous disciplines. The Department of Politics (Claes Ryn, Chairman, 202/635-5128) currently gives a course on the International Politics of Southeast Asia. Anthropology (Phyliss Chock, Chairman, 202/635-5080) offers two area courses: Mainland Southeast Asia, and Island Southeast Asia. The campus has a significant number of international students. Information and other assistance for international students may be obtained from the Office of International Studies (202/635-5630).

4.   University library facilities are described in entry A8.

J3 University of the District of Columbia (UDC)

1.   *4200 Connecticut Avenue, N.W.*
     Washington, D. C. 20008
     (202) 282-7300

2.   Lisle C. Carter, President

3.   Created in 1977 through the merger of D.C. Teacher's College, Federal City College, and Washington Technical Institute, UDC serves as the only public land-grant university in the District of Columbia. Courses are taught in its recently consolidated colleges at three locations: Georgia Avenue–Harvard Street campus, Mount Vernon Square campus, and Van Ness campus. The university offers no courses or programs in Southeast Asian studies. An introductory course in Asian civilization, given by the Department of History (Ali Bakri, Chairman, 202/727-2534) deals selectively with Southeast Asian themes. Krishna Mathur in the Department of Political Science (202/727-2292) may offer, from time to time, a South and Southeast Asia related course. The university accepts a limited number of students who are citizens of other countries. Selection of international students for admission is competitive and is based on grade point average or equivalent.

4.   UDC's Library and Media Services (202/727-2500) contains a combined collection of some 400,000 items. The library's Southeast Asia related holdings are a minor resource. The library is open to the public.

Foreign Service Institute (State Department) See entry K34

J4 George Mason University (GMU)

1.   *4400 University Drive*
     Fairfax, Virginia 22030
     (703) 323-2000

2.   George W. Johnson, President

3.   Founded in 1957, George Mason University gained independent university status in 1972. An independent, state institution, GMU offers more than

40 undergraduate and 19 graduate programs. In addition to a two-semester course, Survey of East Asian civilization, taught in the Department of History (Joseph L. Harah, Chairman, 703/323-2242) and a course on Religions of the Orient, listed by the Department of Philosophy and Religion (Debra Bergoffen, Chairman 703/323-2252), the Department of Public Affairs (Robert P. Clark, Chairman, 703/323-2272) offers an interdisciplinary program of study in International Studies leading to BA and MA degrees, and currently lists one course, "Third World Development in the New International Economic Order," of interest to Southeast Asianists. For further information on the program, contact Nguyen Hung (703/323-2065). George Gangloff in the Admissions Office (703/323-2108) provides information and counseling to the international students on the campus.

4.   The university's Fenwick Library (John G. Veenstra, library director, 703/323-2391) is open to the public for on-site use from 7:30 A.M. to 11:00 P.M., Monday through Thursday; 7:30 A.M. to 5:00 P.M., Friday; 9:00 A.M. to 7:00 P.M., Saturday; and 11:00 A.M. to 9:00 P.M., Sunday, when classes are in session. Interlibrary loan and photoduplication services are available. The library contains some 180,000 volumes, 230,000 microfilm units, and 2,660 current periodical subscriptions. Southeast Asia related materials in the collection consist of some 250 monographs and reference works. The library follows the LC classification schedule.

J5 George Washington University

1.   *2121 Eye Street, N.W.*
       Washington, D.C. 20052
       (202) 676-6000

2.   Lloyd Hartman Elliott, President

3.   Established in 1821, the George Washington University is a private nonsectarian institution, which now offers undergraduate, graduate, and professional programs in its 12 schools and divisions. As a service to the university's large international population, the university maintains an International Student Advising Office (202/676-6860), which serves as a consultation, information, and resource center for the foreign students on campus. The following Southeast Asia related courses are currently available at the university:

       The School of Public and International Affairs (B.M. Sapin, Dean, 202/676-6420), an interdisciplinary, policy-oriented school that emphasizes both domestic and foreign governmental policy, offers a graduate program in international affairs, which allows geographic concentration on Southeast Asia. Also within the framework of a doctoral program in International Relations, which is directed by a committee whose members are drawn from the Economics, Political Science, and History Departments, a limited concentration on Southeast Asia is possible. The Department of Religion (H.E. Yeide, Chairman, 202/676-6325) teaches a course on religions of the East.

       The Department of Political Science (B. Reich, Chairman, 202/676-6290) offers courses on government and politics of South and Southeast Asia, Southeast Asia in world politics, and international politics of the Far East (including Vietnam). The Department of Economics (Charles Stuart, Jr., Chairman, 202/676-6150) gives courses on economic development and a seminar on rural and regional development projects, which may be of interest to Southeast Asianists.

4. The George Washington University Library is described in entry A18.

J6 Georgetown University

1. *37th and O Streets, N.W.*
   Washington, D.C. 20057
   (202) 625-0100

2. R. J. Henle, President

3. Established in 1789, Georgetown is the oldest Catholic university in the United States. Composed of four graduate and professional schools and five undergraduate colleges, the university presents a wide variety of academic programs, both at the undergraduate and the graduate levels. The university attracts a good number of foreign students, to whom information and counseling is provided through the International Student Center (Eric Hyeberg, Foreign Student Advisor, 202/625-4386).

   The university does not offer any special program of studies on Southeast Asia. Southeast Asia related courses taught in different schools or departments include: a course on Southeast Asian history in the Department of History (Ennett Curran, chairman, 202/625-4007); courses on Asian governments and politics in the Department of Government (Karl Cerney, chairman 202/625-4941); a course on Asian international relations offered by the School of Foreign Service (Peter Krogh, dean, 202/625-4216); a course on Buddhist religious tradition, in the Department of Theology, (William McFadden, chairman, 202/625-4311); and two courses, "Economics of Pacific Asia" and the "New International Economic Order," offered by the Department of Economics (Bradley Billings, chairman, 202/625-4121).

4. Georgetown University Library is described in Entry A19.

J7 Howard University

1. *2400 6th Street, N.W.*
   Washington, D.C. 20059
   (202)636-6100

2. James E. Cheek, President

3. Jointly supported by congressional appropriations and private funds, Howard University was established in 1867. Through its 17 schools and colleges, the university offers undergraduate and graduate instruction in a wide variety of fields and disciplines. The university has a large enrollment of foreign students, who may contact the International Students Services (Barry Bem, director, 202/636-7517) for information and advising.

   At present, there are no graduate or undergraduate courses offered on Southeast Asia.

4. The University library facilities including the Bernard B. Fall Collection are discussed in entry A21.

J8 University of Maryland

1. *College Park, Maryland 20742*
    (301) 454-0100

2. John S. Toll, President

3. A landgrant institution established in 1859, the University of Maryland administers a number of undergraduate and graduate programs through its five campuses. The university is a member of the South–East Consortium for International Development, whose purpose is to respond to the economic and social needs of peoples in less developed countries. The campus attracts a large number of foreign students. The Office of International Education Services (301/454-3043) provides information and consulting services to the international students on campus. Although currently no specific courses are offered on Southeast Asia, selected area-related topics are covered in several courses in the departments of Government, History, Music, and Economics.

4. The university library is described in entry A29.

National Defense University (Defense Department)—Southeast Asia Studies See entry K11

J9 School of Advanced International Studies (SAIS) (The Johns Hopkins University)

1. *1740 Massachusetts Avenue, N.W.*
    Washington, D.C. 20036
    (202) 785-6200

2. George R. Packard, Dean

3. The School of Advanced International Studies is a graduate division of the Johns Hopkins University. SAIS offers a two-year course of study leading to a Master of Arts degree. SAIS also offers a degree of Master in International Public Policy and has a small Ph.D. program. In addition to general courses in comparative politics and modernization, international economics, and international relations, two courses on Southeast Asia ("History of Southeast Asia" and "Survey of the Mixed Economies of the Southeast Asia States") are given. Students can arrange reading courses with faculty where regular courses do not adequately cover special needs. The school sponsors numerous public and private lectures and symposia in which visiting scholars, SAIS faculty members, and members of the local diplomatic and foreign policy community participate.

4. The SAIS library is described in entry A35.

Note: See also entry H20.

K United States Government Agencies

United States Government Agencies Entry Format (K)*

1. General Information
    a. *address; telephone numbers*
    b. conditions of access
    c. name/title of director and heads of relevant divisions

2. Functions, Programs, and Research Activities (including in-house research, contract programs, research grants, employment of outside consultants, and international exchange programs)

3. Libraries and Reference Facilities

4. Publications and Records (including unpublished materials, indexes, and vertical files, among other data)

    *In the case of large, structurally complex agencies, each relevant division or bureau is described separately in accordance with the above entry format.

Introductory Note

The agencies and departments of the United States government may prove to be among the richest resources in Washington for information on contemporary Southeast Asia. Most government personnel are very willing, within the constraints imposed by their work schedules and security regulations, to discuss research projects with visiting scholars.

Southeast Asia area specialists will also find significant research material in government reports and internal documents. In attempting to gain access to those written records that are not directly obtainable from the relevant government agency or openly available at the National Archives and Records Service (see entry B7), researchers will wish to familiarize themselves with Freedom of Information Act processes.

The Freedom of Information Act (Public Law 89–487 of 1966, as amended by Public Law 93–502 of 1974) provides that any citizen has the right of access to, and can obtain copies of, any document, file, or other record in the possession of any federal agency or department, with specified exceptions (including certain personnel records and classified documents whose classification can be justified as essential to national security). Most government agencies have a Freedom of Information office or officer available to process requests for internal agency documents. When contacting these offices (in writing or via telephone), researchers should cite the Freedom of Information Act and should make their requests as detailed and specific as possible. Researchers are not required to explain or justify their requests.

Denials of requests may be appealed to the director of the agency. Such appeals are often successful, and rejected appeals may be challenged through court litigation. By law, agencies have 10 working days in which to respond to an initial Freedom of Information Act request and 20 days in which to respond to an appeal. Researchers should note that agencies are permitted to charge rather substantial fees for documents searches and photoreproduction of released documents. Information on such fees should be requested when filing an initial Freedom of Information Act request. In most cases, researchers are permitted to examine released records in person at the agency.

Several organizations in Washington can assist researchers in using the Freedom of Information Act processes. They include the Freedom of Information Clearinghouse, P.O. Box 19367 (2000 P Street, N.W., Suite 700), Washington, D.C. 20036 (202/785-3704), which is a project of Ralph Nader's Center for the Study of Responsive Law; the Campaign for Political Rights, 201 Massachusetts Avenue, N.E., Washington, D.C. 20002 (202/547-4705); and the Project on National Security and Civil Liberties, 122 Maryland Avenue, N.E., Washington, D.C. 20002 (202/544-5380), an organization sponsored by the American Civil Liberties Union and the Center for National Security Studies (see entry H15). Both organizations distribute free guides to Freedom of Information Act processes. Another useful guide can be found in the October 1975 issue of the American Historical Association's Newsletter (see entry M10). One particularly useful source of information on declassified government documents is Carrollton Press (see entry Q6).

Researchers should be aware that bureaucratically inspired reorganizations are frequent; indeed, various agencies within the national intelligence community regularly reorganize their internal structures in order to disguise their functional activities and confuse foreign observers. As preparation for this *Guide* began, the Department of Health, Education and Welfare was being transformed into two separate agencies, the Education Department (entry K12) and the Health and Human Services Department (entry K18); the Energy Department (entry K13) was continuing to shift offices between its headquarters in the Forrestal Building and several dispersed office locations. As this volume nears completion, the fate of Energy and Education seems problematic. Elections also often lead to major administrative disruptions within the federal bureaucracy. As a result, many of the names and telephone numbers listed in the entries below are subject to change and must be considered somewhat transitory.

Researchers would be well advised to obtain the latest telephone numbers for various offices by consulting the most current edition of each government department's telephone directory. Some are up-dated on a quarterly basis. Most are available for purchase from the Government Printing Office (entry Q11). If all else fails, contact the Federal Information Center (202/755-8660) for assistance.

K1 Agency for International Development (AID) (International Development Cooperation Agency)

1. a. *320 21st Street, N.W.*
   Washington, D.C. 20523
   (202) 632-9620

b. Open to the public with prior appointment.

c. M. Peter McPherson, Administrator

2.   The Agency for International Development administers most of the U.S. government's foreign economic-assistance programs, which are designed to help the people of certain less developed countries cultivate their human and economic resources, increase productive capacities, and improve the quality of human life as well as to promote economic and political stability in friendly countries. As of October 1, 1979, AID was no longer part of the State Department but was shifted to the newly created International Development Cooperation Agency (IDCA), whose director is now the principal international development adviser to the president and the secretary of state.

AID programs provide two kinds of economic assistance: development assistance and security-supporting assistance. The agency implements its economic-assistance programs by means of concessional loans, technical cooperation, and development grants—including specific grant authorities for U.S. research and educational institutions. The agency, in cooperation with the Department of Agriculture, also implements Public Law 480 (The Agricultural Trade Development and Assistance Act of 1954, popularly known as the "Food for Peace Program," as amended). AID focuses its development-assistance programs in the following sectors: food, nutrition, and rural development; population, planning and health; education and human-resources development; technical assistance; energy; research reconstruction; and selected development problems. The agency is also concerned with several specific programs, including the international disaster-assistance program. Most AID programs in Southeast Asia concentrate on development assistance and food for peace.

The vast bulk of AID research is produced under contract and research grants to educational institutions and research centers. Southeast Asian specialists are also periodically engaged as consultants. It is also AID policy to encourage the collaboration of research bodies in the developing countries in its work. Southeast Asian research institutions are involve with several AID programs.

The agency's retired files and unpublished reports are in the custody of the National Archives and Records Service (entry B7). Both the AID Records Management staff (202/632-8518) and the originating agency offices maintain indexes to retired documents. For access to AID's classified materials, researchers may contact Arnold H. Dadian, Freedom of Information officer (202/632-1850).

3.   For AID library and reference facilities, see entries A2, F1, and G2.

4.   A selected list of materials of interest to Southeast Asianists is given below. Bibliographic control of AID publications has, until recently, been difficult since the great majority do not appear in the *Monthly Catalog of U.S. Government Publications*. Also, the *Catalog of Selected AID Publications* (1974), as the title indicates, is not comprehensive; it is also out of date. *AID Memory Documents*, a restricted comprehensive quarterly catalog of AID–generated documents, was published for only a short period: 1972–1974.

The series of AID newsletters, pamphlets, and brochures produced for popular use include: *Agenda*, a monthly devoted to international development; *Front Lines*, a weekly newsletter; *A.I.D. Forum*, a monthly exchange of views about AID and development; *A.I.D. News,* frequently used for brief announcements; *World Development Letter,* a biweekly report of facts, trends, and opinion in international development; *AID's Challenge,* a pamphlet explaining the agency's purpose; *AID's Work in Nutrition,* one of several informative and educational pamphlets; and *AID in the Third World,* a series of fliers on different aspects of AID programs in the less-developed countries.

More substantial publications include: *U.S. Overseas Loans and Grants and Assistance from International Organizations, Obligations and Loan Authorizations,* July 1, 1945–September 30, 1979, which includes all countries receiving any type of loan or grant (economic, military, and others) since July 1945; *AID–Financed University Contracts and Grants Active during the Period October 1, 1978 through September 30, 1979; Current Technical Service Contracts and Grants Active during the Period October 1, 1978 through September 30, 1979; A.I.D. Research and Development Abstracts,* a quarterly abstract of materials from AID–funded projects financed through contracts or grants; *Directory of Development Resources* (1979), a list of on-call technical support services, information clearinghouses, field research facilities, newsletters, data banks and training currently available to less developed countries; *Research Literature for Development,* in 2 volumes (1976–1977), covering the period 1962–1976; and *Asia Economic Growth Trends* (1977), a summary of basic data, including rate of population growth, density, urbanization, labor forces in agriculture, agricultural land, gross national product per capita, and power per capita.

The agency also publishes Project Impact Evaluations (PIEs). Some recent PIEs for our area are: *The Potable Water Project in Rural Thailand,* (PIE No. 3, May 1980); *Rural Roads in Thailand,* (PIE No. 13, December 1980); and *The Philippines: Rural Electrification,* (PIE No. 15, December 1980). Other AID documents of interest to Southeast Asianists are: *The Study Program for Feeder Roads Management,* 1 and 2 (for Indonesia); *Fertility and Mortality Changes in Thailand, 1950–1975, Philippine Municipal Fisheries: A Review of Research, Technology and Socioeconomics;* and *The "Nutribun" Connection: The Role of an Anthropologist in the Planning of a Philippine Nutrition Project.*

For information concerning AID publications, contact the Press and Publications Division (Edward Caplan, chief, 202/632-4330).

BUREAU FOR ASIA (ASIA)

Eugene S. Staples, Acting Assistant Administrator
(202) 632-9223

OFFICE OF BURMA, PHILIPPINES AND THAILAND AFFAIRS
Dennis Chandler, Director
(202) 632-9084
William McKinney, Desk Officer, Burma
(202) 632-9086
Carl Penndorf, Desk Officer, Philippines
(202) 632-8526
Edward Ploch, Desk Officer, Thailand
(202) 632-9086

OFFICE OF INDONESIA AND SOUTH PACIFIC AFFAIRS
William R. Ford, Director
(202) 632-9842
Jonathan Sperling, Desk Officer, Indonesia
(202) 632-9843
Louis H. Kuhn, Desk Officer, South Pacific/ASEAN
(202) 632-9843

One of the four geographic bureaus, the Bureau for Asia is the principal AID office with responsibility for the planning, formulation, and management of U.S. economic development and supporting assistance programs in Southeast Asia. The bureau maintains liaison with other AID offices, the Department of State, other U.S. bilateral and multilateral agencies, and officials of recipient countries; and represents AID at country consortia and consultative group meetings. AID's overseas field missions and offices in Southeast Asia report to this bureau.

The country directors and desk officers have expertise on the AID programs in the countries under their charge and should be a first point of contact within the agency. Other subunits of the bureau that may provide researchers with valuable information are: Office of Development Planning (Robert Halligan, 202/632-9044), which reviews and approves research proposals from within the agency and from outside researchers; Office of Project Development (Bruce Blackman, East Asia Division chief, 703/235-8582), which designs and implements bureau programs and monitors performance; and the Office of Technical Resources (Thomas M. Arndt, director, 703/235-8880), which is responsible for social and human resources, population, health and nutrition, agriculture and rural development, and scientific, technical and environmental problems.

BUREAU FOR SCIENCE AND TECHNOLOGY
Nyle C. Brady, Assistant Administrator
(202) 632-1827

This bureau administers the agency's International Training Program (703/235-1853) and provides professional leadership and technical support for agency activities through the unit offices of: Agriculture (703/235-8945), Nutrition (703/235-9779), Education (703/235-9015), Health (703/235-8929), Urban Development (703/235-8902), Rural Development and Development Administration (703/235-8918), Science and Technology (703/235-9046), Population (703/235-8117), Engineering (703/235-9827), and Energy (703/235-9090), all of which are located in the Rosslyn Plaza Building, 1601 Kent Street, Arlington, Virginia 22209. Each office administers AID contract research projects in its field of specialization. Usually within each office, persons with expertise in Southeast Asian matters are available. The bureau's Office of Development Information Utilization (703/235-9207), a memory bank for AID missions and project designers, administers its Development Information Center (see entry A2).

BUREAU FOR PRIVATE ENTERPRISE (PRE)
Elise DuPont, Assistant Administrator
(202) 632-8298

A newly established bureau, the PRE is attempting to increase the role of the private sector in the development process of Third World countries.

The bureau has identified ten "target countries," including Indonesia and Thailand, and is applying specific strategies in these nation-states to stimulate capital investment, technology transfer, and manpower development. The bureau looks at the private sector economy in terms of the climate for investment and seeks to identify specific investment opportunities. For more detailed information, contact David Levintow, program policy officer, 202/632-8634.

BUREAU FOR FOOD FOR PEACE AND VOLUNTARY ASSISTANCE
Julia-Chang Bloch
(703) 235-1800

OFFICE OF PRIVATE AND VOLUNTARY COOPERATION
Thomas Fox, Director
(703) 235-1623

This office works to enlarge the role of volunteerism in the development process; maintains liaison with the American Council on Foreign Aid, the Advisory Committee on Overseas Cooperative Development, and with the community of voluntary agencies in general—for example, CARE, Asia Foundation, International Voluntary Services—and provides staff support to the Advisory Committee on Voluntary Foreign Aid. Steve Bergen (703/235-8420) deals with Asia–related matters.

OFFICE OF FOOD FOR PEACE
1735 North Lynn Street
Arlington, Virginia 22209
Robert C. Chase, Coordinator
(703) 235-9238

In cooperation with the Department of Agriculture, this office administers U.S. food aid programs in Southeast Asia under Public Law 480 (Agricultural Trade Development and Assistance Act of 1954, as amended). Currently, programs are in operation for Indonesia, the Philippines, and Cambodia. Paul Mulligan (703/235-9238) and Bob Sears (703/235-9084) handle Title 1 and 2 programs, respectively, for Southeast Asia.

OFFICE OF UNITED STATES FOREIGN DISASTER ASSISTANCE
Martin Harrell, Director
(202) 632-8924

This office serves as the national coordinating center to provide both public and private international emergency relief or technical assistance for foreign disasters that result from earthquakes, droughts, famines, epidemics, floods, storms, civil strife, power shortages, and accidents. In addition to emergency responses to disasters, programs in disaster preparedness, prediction, and prevention are also supported. The office publishes an annual report entitled *Foreign Disaster Relief.*

BUREAU FOR PROGRAM AND POLICY COORDINATION (PPC)
John R. Bolton, Assistant Administrator
(202) 632-0482

This bureau is responsible for AID program policy formulation, planning, coordination, resources allocation, and evaluation activities, as well as the program-management information systems that support them. The bureau develops economic-assistance policies, provides guidance on long-range program planning, economic analysis, sector-assistance strategies, and project analysis and design. The bureau reviews and monitors all country program strategies and project proposals and selectively reviews project papers from other AID bureaus.

The bureau also provides statistical services to the agency. The Economic and Social Data Service, located at 1735 North Lynn Street, Arlington, Virginia 22209 (703/235-9170), maintains a computerized Economic and Social Data Bank (ESDB) that contains country information and some microdata components of household surveys. The data bases are accessible to the public. The Program Data Services Division (703/235-9167) located at the same address in Virginia compiles *U.S. Overseas Loans and Grants.* The bureau also compiles *Selected Economic Data for the Less Developed Countries, Food and Total Agricultural Production in Less Developed Countries,* and *Economic Growth Trends.*

OFFICE OF WOMEN IN DEVELOPMENT (WID)
Paula Goodard, Acting Coordinator
(202) 632-3992

The WID conducts—from both a regional and a comparative perspective— research and contract grants on the role of women in the development process in less-developed nations that include those of Southeast Asia.

The office has a resource center that distributes some 100 publications, including current WID reports, conference proceedings, research papers, and project reports from AID as well as from other institutions. These publications cover a variety of topics involving rural women and the development process: agriculture and food production, appropriate technology, employment and income-generating activities, formal and nonformal education, and the status of women in specific developing countries. Limited copies are available to those working in the area of women in development. *An Annotated Bibliography of Available Materials* may be obtained free from the resource center.

Some of the WID reports of interest include: *International Conference on Women and Food* (1978), background papers and proceedings of a WID– sponsored conference held at the University of Arizona on the role of women in meeting basic food and water needs in developing countries; and *Progress Towards an A.I.D. Data Base on Women in Development* (1977), a study of the establishment of data bases on women in AID–recipient countries. Other useful publications prepared by the Office are: *International Directory of Women's Development Organizations* (1977) and *Women in Development.*

OFFICE OF PUBLIC AFFAIRS
Herb Harmon, Director
(202) 632-9170
Arnold H. Dadian, Freedom of Information Officer
(202) 632-1850
Rhea Johnson, Privacy Act Coordinator
(202) 632-9614

This office insures that information about AID policies, objectives, and operations is disseminated fully and freely to the Congress and to the public.

The office also responds to public inquiries and to requests for information filed under the Freedom of Information Act and the Privacy Act.

K2 Agriculture Department (USDA)

1. a. *Independence Avenue between 12th and 14th streets, S.W.*
    Washington, D.C. 20250
    (202) 447-2791

    b. Open to the public; appointments are recommended.

2. The Department of Agriculture, in addition to its numerous domestic services and programs, also develops and expands markets abroad for agricultural products and "assumes global responsibilities for food and agricultural technical assistance." Most research is done within the department.

3. For the department's libraries and reference facilities see entries A30 and G3.

4. Numerous USDA publications, on a wide variety of subjects for farmers, suburbanites, homemakers, and consumers, are available free from the Office of Governmental and Public Affairs (202/447-4894). Some useful USDA publications include: *World Fertilizer Review and Prospects* (1976); *The World Food Situation and Prospects* (1974); *World Population Growth: Analysis and New Projections of the United Nations* (1977); *Foreign and Domestic Prospects for the U.S. Fast Food Franchise Industry* (1976); *An Analysis of the UNCTAD Integrated Programs for Commodities* (1978); *Development and Spread of High-Yielding Varieties of Wheat and Rice in the Less Developed Nations* (1974); *World Economic Conditions in Relation to Agricultural Trade* (twice a year); *Foreign Agricultural Trade of the United States* (monthly); and the annual Report of the *Secretary of Agriculture,* which also summarizes the condition of agriculture in the U.S. and in the world during the year. For bibliographic reference to USDA publications, consult the *List of Available Publications of the United States Department of Agriculture* (1979) and *Fact Book of U.S. Agriculture* (1979). Additional publications are noted with descriptions of the following concerned units.
    The department's principal Freedom of Information Act contact is Hal R. Taylor, deputy director of information, Office of Governmental and Public Affairs (202/447-7903). For information concerning retired or inactive files stored in the Federal Record Center in Suitland, Maryland, contact Roxanne R. Williams, chief, Information Systems and Planning Division (administration) (202/447-2118). Most records and documents of the department are open to the public.

INTERNATIONAL AFFAIRS AND COMMODITY PROGRAMS
Sealey Lodwick, Under Secretary
(202) 447-3111

Most international activities of the department are carried on by this unit. The responsibilities of the International Affairs and Commodity Programs cover several broad areas including the following:

FOREIGN AGRICULTURAL SERVICE (FAS)
Richard Smith, Administrator
(202) 447-3935

The FAS is an export promotion and service agency for U.S. agriculture. FAS also provides staff support for the department's participation in international organizations, international conferences and meetings to consider policy and operating programs that deal with agriculture, trade in agricultural products, over-all economic problems, and technical and scientific activities related to agriculture.

Foreign Market Development
Jimmy D. Minyard, Assistant Administrator
(202) 447-4761

This section works to maintain and expand export sales by cooperating with domestic, nonprofit trade associations, with agriculture departments of the fifty U.S. state governments, and with others on jointly financed market-development projects abroad; by appraising overseas marketing opportunities and communicating them to the U.S. agricultural trade; and by encouraging and cooperating with state and regional groups involved in export promotion.

Currently, there is an agriculture trade office in Singapore working to promote U.S. exports to the region. American associations concerned with exports of soybeans, feed grain, and wheat are active participants in the region.

International Trade Policy (ITC)
Rolland E. Anderson, Jr., Assistant Administrator
(202) 447-6887

This section attempts to improve access to foreign markets for U.S. farm products by sending representatives to foreign governments and by participating in formal negotiations. ITC also acts as the department's liaison with the General Agreement on Tariffs and Trade (GATT), Food and Agricultural Organization (FAO), and other international organizations to reduce international trade barriers, increase world trade in agricultural products, and further trade policies advantageous to U.S. agriculture. Inquiries concerning Southeast Asia may be addressed to the Developing Asia and Africa Group, Larry Blum, group leader (202/382-9057), of the Asia, Africa and Eastern Europe Division (202/382-1289).

International Agricultural Statistics (IAS)
Richard J. Cannon, Assistant Administrator
(202) 447-7233

Formerly known as Commodity Programs, International Agricultural Statistics conducts analyses of foreign commodities with reference to production, trade, marketing, prices, consumption, and other factors affecting U.S. exports and imports. Divisions within IAS are: Reports and Projects, Lloyd Fleck, director (202/382-1035); Trade and Economic Information, Dewain Ray, director (202/382-1294); Export Sales Reporting, Richard Finkbeiner, director (202/447-5651); Foreign Production Estimates, Gerald A. Bange, director (202/382-8888); and Data Systems, Eldon C. Hildebrant, director (202/447-5255).

The commodity divisions formerly under Commodity Programs (see above) now function as autonomous units within the Foreign Agricultural Service. They are as follows;

Dairy, Livestock and Poultry Division
Bryan Wadsworth, Director
(202) 447-8031

Grain and Feed Division
Donald J. Novotny, Director
(202) 447-6219

Horticultural and Tropical Products Division
Gilbert Sindelar, Director
(202) 447-5330

Oilseeds and Products Division
Philip Mackie, Director
(202) 447-7037

Tobacco, Cotton and Seeds Division
Glenn R. Samson, Director
(202) 382-5635

Researchers interested in a particular commodity should contact the appropriate division for information.

Foreign Agricultural Affairs
Larry F. Thomasson, Assistant Administrator
(202) 447-6138

The department's global reporting and analysis network, covering world agricultural production, trade, competition, and policy situations affecting U.S. agriculture, is operated by this section. The service is made possible through the agricultural attachés and officers stationed at 65 key posts, covering more than 100 countries, and through specialists who make surveys abroad. In addition to reporting and analysis, attachés engage in "agricultural diplomacy" to assure markets for U.S. agricultural products in the country of assignment and to eliminate trade barriers. Currently, USDA attachés are stationed in Bangkok, Djakarta, Kuala Lumpur, and Singapore. Cline Warren (202/447-7053) is the area officer for Southeast Asia. Unclassified attaché reports may be obtained from the Records and Communications Office (202/447-6135). An informative pamphlet on *The Agricultural Attache* is available on request.

Office of the General Sales Manager (OGSM)
Alan T. Tracy, General Sales Manager and Associate Administrator
(202) 447-5173

This office works to improve the department's ability to develop export policy and assist in orderly export marketing of agricultural commodities in ample supply in the U.S. In addition to its numerous responsibilities concerning commercial exports, the OGSM also administers Public Law 480 (Agricultural Trade Development and Assistance Act of 1954, as amended) which seeks to "use the abundant agricultural productivity of the United States to combat hunger and malnutrition and to encourage economic development in developing countries."

PL 480, also known as the Food for Peace Program, includes concessional sales (Title I); donation and disaster relief (Title II); and food for development and barter (Title III). Title III aims at assisting developing countries in their efforts to increase the availability of food for the poor, and at improving the quality of life for the poor by permitting the funds accumulated from the local sale of PL 480 Title I commodities to be applied against the repayment obligations of these countries to the U.S. Currently

PL 480 programs are operative in Indonesia, Title I and II; the Philippines, Title II, which focuses on the child health problem; and Thailand, Title I and II, the latter being a large operation, through the World Food Program, for refugee relief for Kampuchea.

An annual review of department export activities carried out under the PL 480 program is to be found in the Secretary of Agriculture's annual report to the Congress, entitled *Food for Peace.* Another annual report, *Title I Public Law 480,* prepared by the Foreign Agricultural Service, shows statistical information about total quantity and value of export under PL 480 by country and commodity from the beginning of the program to the date of the publication. The OGSM also collects information from private exporters of agricultural commodities on their export sales and related transactions and publishes a weekly compilation, *U.S. Export Sales.*

Foreign Agricultural Service publications related to Southeast Asia include: *Foreign Agriculture,* a weekly, containing summary reports on world agriculture and its impact on U.S. farmers; *Foreign Agriculture Circulars* (irregular) available only to U.S. residents, provides statistical information on such items as canned deciduous fruits, coffee, and cocoa; *World Agricultural Production and Trade, Statistical Report,* a monthly, also restricted to U.S. residents, contains statistical data and comments; *Weekly Roundup of Food Production and Trade,* a news release summarizing global agricultural developments; and the miscellaneous publication, *Special Reports,* covers such topics as *The Palm Oil Industry in West-Malaysia* (1976). For information concerning FAS publications, contact FAS Information service staff (202/447-7937).

OFFICE OF INTERNATIONAL COOPERATION AND DEVELOPMENT (OICD)
Joan Wallace, Administrator
(202) 447-3157

The USDA is the largest single source of agricultural expertise in the world. The OICD coordinates, plans, and directs the department's efforts in: international development and technical cooperation in food and agriculture, and overseas international-organizational affairs and scientific-exchange programs for the department. OICD assists other U.S. international organizations in utilizing the scientific and institutional resources of American agriculture in carrying out development-assistance programs. An information brochure, *Sharing Agricultural Knowledge with Other Nations,* outlines the activities of this agency.

International Organization Affairs
Martin Kriesberg, Deputy Administrator
(202) 447-4493

This unit is responsible for liaison between the department and international organizations dealing with agricultural development; e.g., Food and Agriculture Organization (FAO), the World Bank (IBRD), and the U.N. World Food Council. Together with the Foreign Agricultural Service, the division also helps in liaison work with the United Nations Conference on Trade and Development.

Interagency and Congressional Affairs Division
George Waldman, Assistant Administrator
(202) 447-4143

This unit is responsible for coordinating agricultural development activities with other U.S. departments and agencies; e.g., the Department of State and AID.

International Training Division
Robert I. Ayling, Deputy Administrator
(202) 447-4711

The division conducts a series of technical short courses and coordinates academic programs in a wide range of agricultural, nutritional, management, and rural development skills for foreign participants in the U.S. and overseas. The following is a breakdown of Southeast Asian participants for 1980: Indonesia, 34; Philippines, 99; Malaysia, 14; Burma, 21; and Thailand, 27. Most of these training programs are funded by AID or the World Bank. For further information, contact Dr. Ralph Otto, head of the Participant Services Unit (202/447-5835) of the division.

Technical Assistance Division
William S. Hoffnagle, Deputy Administrator
(202) 235-2285

This division provides technical-assistance personnel to various agricultural-development projects funded by other U.S. agencies, particularly AID. A. J. Dyer (202/235-2290) is the leader of the division's Asia Program. The division has recently prepared a paper on maize and seed-oil production in Burma and has completed a long-term professional-resources development project, which utilized two technical-assistance staff persons. Since 1981, the division has had a resident assignee in Malaysia to work on a two-year plant-quarantine project for the ASEAN states. Technical assistance has had a community-development project in Thailand and has a short-term (TDY) remote-sensing assignee to assist in the field of agricultural planning. In the Philippines, the division worked on the Bicol River Basin Program, and more recently, has had a short-term assignee working in the field of irrigation. Useful, annual project data and information on the division's program are provided in a booklet entitled *Summary of USDA International Technical Assistance Activities.*

Scientific and Technical Exchange Division
Roger E. Neetz, Deputy Administrator
(202) 447-4445

This division coordinates all of the department's overseas, agricultural scientific- and technical-exchange activities. Currently there are no activities in Southeast Asia; however, the division is negotiating with Indonesia and the Philippines for future exchange plans. This division is also open to contact with American agriculturalists having an interest in Southeast Asia. For further information, contact Maria Morgan, International Affairs Officer.

Development Project Management Center
Morris J. Solomon, Deputy Administrator
(202) 447-5804

This AID–funded unit helps developing countries to improve project management capabilities by providing training, materials, and technical assistance. In 1979 and 1980, the center assisted the Indonesian government in a decentralization project to improve the capabilities of local government officials. At present the center is awaiting approval of a proposal for a management information system for the Thai government. Contact Dr. Merlyn Kettering, International Training Adviser, for further information.

Reports and Technical Inquiries Group
Patricia Wetmore, Technical Information Officer
(202) 447-2893

Another AID–funded unit, this group provides agricultural information needed for the design and implementation of AID's agricultural programs overseas. Its small reference collection of monographs, OICD reports and studies, and vertical country files may be reviewed by researchers with prior appointments.

AGRICULTURAL STABILIZATION AND CONSERVATION SERVICE (ASCS)
Everett Rant, Administrator
(202) 447-3467

ASCS provides accounting, budget, personnel, and other administrative and management support for the Office of General Sales Manager in administering the department's Commodity Credit Corporation (CCC), export credit sales, and Public Law 480 (Food for Peace) programs.

COMMODITY CREDIT CORPORATION (CCC)
Edward Hews, Chairman
(202) 447-7583

With a huge borrowing authority, CCC finances the farm programs and handles domestic and export surplus commodity disposal, foreign assistance, storage activities, and related programs and operations of the department utilizing ASCS personnel.

OFFICE OF ECONOMICS
William G. Lesher, Assistant Secretary
(202) 447-4164

WORLD AGRICULTURAL OUTLOOK BOARD (WAOB)
Terry Barr, Chairman
(202) 447-6030

Created in 1977 when an era of stable world food prices and supplies gave way to extreme price fluctuations and food shortages, the board coordinates USDA analysis of the agricultural situation in the United States and throughout the world. The board is also responsible for leadership of USDA interagency committees on each of the major commodities. In cooperation with the Department of Commerce, the board maintains a Joint Agricultural Weather Facility, which monitors global weather patterns in order to aid experts in interpreting the probable impact of weather on crop production. Publications of the office include the monthly *World Crop Production, Agricultural Supply and Demand Estimate,* and the *Weekly Weather and Crop Bulletin.*

ECONOMICS RESEARCH SERVICES
John Lee, Acting Administrator
(202) 447-8104

This service analyzes and collects domestic and international agriculture-related information, and conducts economic and other social-science research related to food and agriculture, nationally and internationally. The results of these activities are made available to users through research and statistical reports and through outlook and situation reports on major commodities and areas.

International Economic Division
Kelley White, Director
(202) 447-8710

Within this division, the Asia Branch (Carmen O. Nohre, Chief, 202/447-8860) conducts research on Southeast Asian agricultural and economic conditions, market developments, monetary and trade conditions, and governmental policies affecting the export of U.S. farm products. Whereas the Foreign Agricultural Service (FAS) is primarily commodity oriented, this division focuses on countries. Southeast Asia personnel in this branch are: John Dyck, Thailand; Albert Evans, Malaysia, Singapore, and Indonesia; William Hall, the Philippines, Laos, Cambodia, and Vietnam; and Richard Nehring, Burma.

Agricultural History Branch (National Economic Division)
Wayne D. Rasmussen, Chief
(202) 447-8183

Primarily a reference center of key USDA documents and U.S. agricultural history and related materials, the Agricultural History Branch also contains a small amount of materials on U.S. bilateral relations with Southeast Asia. The American Agricultural Economics Documentation Center (Cynthia Kenyon, director, 202/447-4383) of the branch, although concentrating on American and Canadian agricultural literature and documentation, also contains some materials pertaining to our region. The center's on-line retrieval facilities include USDA's AGRICOLA. The center also has access to the bibliographic data files of the American Agricultural Economics Association. Both the Agricultural History Branch and the Documentation Center are open to the public from 8:30 A.M. to 4:30 P.M., Monday through Friday.

The Economics Research Service prepares a number of useful publications that may be obtained from the Publication Division (202/447-7255). Some of the Southeast Asia related publications include: Martin Kriesberg, *International Organizations and Agricultural Development* (1977), a report describing major international organizations having programs to help low-income countries improve their agricultural and rural sectors; *Report Assessing Global Food Production and Needs*, an annual report to the U.S. Congress; *Asia Agricultural Situation*, an annual review and outlook for agricultural production and trade and the economic situation of Asiatic countries, including the countries of Southeast Asia; and *World Agricultural Situation*, published three times a year, that contains summaries of comparative prices, agricultural developments, and international trade agreements.

K3 Air Force Department

1.   a. *Pentagon*
       Washington, D.C. 20310
       (202) 697-7376

     b. Access to the Pentagon is limited to persons with a security clearance or by invitation.

2.   Most research on Southeast Asia is performed in-house.

Office of Public Affairs
Richard E. Abel, Director
(202) 697-6061

The Security Review Branch of this office (Richard D. Hoover, chief, 202/697-3222) reviews all research involving classified materials. The staff can assist researchers in locating needed materials and in obtaining limited clearance

3.   The Office of Air Force History Library is described in entry B1.

4.   Publications are described under relevant divisions.

Note: See also entries C1 and F2.

INFORMATION MANAGEMENT AND RESOURCES DIVISION
(DIRECTORATE OF ADMINISTRATION)
James E. Dagwell
(202) 697-3491

Two components of this division—the Air Force Freedom of Information Act Office (Kip Ward, 202/694-3488) and the Air Force Privacy Act Office (Mark Coon, 202/694-3431)—receive all requests for declassification as provided by law. The staff can also be of assistance in identifying and locating materials.

AIR FORCE INTELLIGENCE SERVICE
Schuyler Bissell
(202) 695-5613

REGIONAL ESTIMATES DIVISION
John Bright, Director
(202) 694-5261

The Asia Branch (Paul Spencer, chief) of this division monitors current events in Southeast Asia and collects additional information of interest to the U.S. Air Force.

DEPUTY CHIEF OF STAFF, OPERATIONS, PLANS AND READINESS
Jerome O'Malley
(202) 697-9991

Various analysts in this unit assist in the formulation of U.S. Air Force policies on international political and military issues such as U.S. foreign military sales.

INTERNATIONAL AFFAIRS DIVISION (OFFICE OF THE CHIEF OF STAFF)
Howard E. Lynch
(202) 695-2251

Activities of the division include protocol affairs, disclosure policy and matters related to munitions and exports.

K4 Arms Control and Disarmament Agency (ACDA)

1. a. *State Department Building*
    320 21st Street, N.W.
    Washington, D.C.
    (202) 632-9610

    b. Open to the public, but researchers should arrange for visits in advance.

    c. Eugene Rostow, Director
    Joseph Lehman, Public Affairs Adviser
    (202) 632-0392

2. ACDA's primary function is to advise the president, secretary of state, and Congress on arms-control matters. ACDA has been the primary agency involved in negotiations with the Soviet Union on strategic arms limitation issues. The agency is also concerned with preventing the spread of nuclear weapons and with monitoring the flow of arms throughout the world. Ed Fei (202/632-3246) is the agency's expert on East and Southeast Asia in the Non-Proliferation Bureau. Gordon Bare (202/632-3831) in the Weapons Evaluation and Control Bureau, Arms Transfer Division, monitors arms transfer proposals for Southeast Asia.

    Research opportunities available in the agency are announced in the *Commerce Business Daily* of th U.S. Department of Commerce. For information on unsolicited research proposals, contact Evalyn W. Dexter (703/235-8248) of the Contract Office. Information concerning the agency's recently instituted graduate fellowship program in social sciences may also be obtained from the Contract Office.

3. The Arms Control and Disarmament Agency Library is located in Room 804, 1700 North Lynn Street, Arlington, Virginia 22209. The library is open to qualified researchers, but prior permission should be obtained from the librarian, Diane Ferguson (703/235-9550). The library is open from 9:00 A.M. to 4:45 P.M., Monday through Friday. Its small collection of approximately 5,500 volumes includes unclassified ACDA publications and contract research reports as well as a few selected titles on Third World arms trade, nuclear proliferation, and other related subjects.

4. ACDA publications of interest include: *World Military Expenditures and Arms Transfers, 1968–1977; Arms Control Report to Congress; ACDA External Research Reports;* and *Official Publications of the United States Arms Control and Disarmament Agency.* For further information, contact the Publications Office (202/632-8715). The agency's internal records, including classified research reports, are maintained by the Communications and Services Section (202/632-0931) of the Office of Administration. For access to the agency's classified records through the Freedom of Information Act, scholars should contact Ray Walters (202/632-0760).

K5 Army Department

1. a. *Pentagon*
    Washington, D.C. 20310
    (202) 697-7589

b. Access to the Pentagon is limited to persons with security clearance or by official invitation.

2. Most research on Southeast Asia is handled in-house.

3. The Army library is described in entry A6, and The Army Center of Military History is described in entry B3.

4. Publications are described under relevant divisions.

Note: See also entry F4.

CHIEF OF PUBLIC AFFAIRS
Llyle J. Barker, Jr.
(202) 695-5135

Since public access is restricted to mainly the work areas, records, and documents of the department, researchers should contact the Media Relations Division, Michael A. Vargosko (202/697-8719), for assistance in locating appropriate personnel and offices. The Freedom of Information officer (William J. Donohoe, Chief, 202/697-4172) processes all requests for declassification provided under the law.

RECORDS MANAGEMENT DIVISION (THE ADJUTANT GENERAL)
HQDA (DAAG-AMR)
Alexandria, Virginia 22331
Guy B. Oldaker, Chief
(202) 325-6183

The four components of this division—Access and Release Branch, W. A. Anderson, chief (202/325-6163); Programs Branch, John Hatcher, Chief (202/325-6044); Declassification Operations Branch, Wendell R. Boardman, Chief (301/763-2742); and Privacy and Rule-Making Branch, Richard S. Christian, Chief (202/325-6227)—provide access to U.S. historical records. The division decides on the maintenance and disposition of records, grants clearance and access to materials, determines what has been classified, and assists the National Archives with the processing of documents and records.

DEPUTY CHIEF OF STAFF FOR OPERATIONS AND PLANS
Pentagon Building
William R. Richardson
(202) 695-2904

This office supports foreign affairs research through a contract with Foreign Area Studies of the American University in Washington, D.C. (202/686-2769) (see entry H4) for the preparation of area handbooks including country studies for Burma, Cambodia, Indonesia, Laos, Malaysia, the Philippines, Singapore, Thailand, and Vietnam (North and South). These handbooks are available from the U.S. Government Printing Office (GPO) (Q11), the U.S. Army Publications Center, and the National Technical Information Service (Q19). In 1982, area handbooks were available for 108 countries.

Strategy Plans and Policy Directorate
John W. Seigle, Director
(202) 695-5032

The Southeast Asia Regional Desk (Michael McCormick, 202/697-8001), of the Politico Military Division, prepares memoranda and position papers (some of which are unclassified) that contribute to the formulation of U.S. Army policy strategy and security issues in Southeast Asia.

ASSISTANT CHIEF OF STAFF FOR INTELLIGENCE (ACSI)
Foreign Intelligence Directorate
(202) 695-3033

The Foreign Intelligence Directorate (J. Meikle, 202/695-2931) of the ACSI monitors developments in Southeast Asia and prepares information papers and Army contributions to the national intelligence estimates.

Note: See also Army Center of Military History, entry B3.

K6 Central Intelligence Agency (CIA)

1. a. *Washington, D.C. 20505*
   (703) 351-1100 (Information)
   (703) 351-7676 (Public Affairs)

   b. Open to persons with security clearance

   c. William Casey, Director

2. The CIA funds contract research for technical studies, model-building, the development of methodology, and for general social-science purposes. The agency employs foreign-area specialists as outside consultants. Research and consultant contracts are administered by the Coordinator for Academic Relations and External Analytical Support (James King, 703/351-7848).

   Much of the work undertaken by the CIA is classified, and information concerning the agency may be difficult to obtain unless you know someone within the organization. In general, agency analysts are open to academic contact on topics of mutual interest, though they cannot discuss any classified work. In our area, Southeast Asia, the agency has a number of professionals who are both highly qualified and open to contact with the academic community.

   Two agency subdivisions are of particular interest to Southeast Asianists. Within the Office of Political Analysis and Research, Division of East Asia Pacific, the Southeast Asia Branch (Elizabeth Graves, Chief, 703/351-4591) carries out short-term, current-affairs research on the countries of the region (Australia and New Zealand are currently included, though they are not part of the region). The branch currently has five area specialists. (Names and assignments change frequently, so that it is not useful here to list personnel.)

   The Office of Geographic and Societal Research, Social Science Research Division, also has several Southeast Asia specialists in its Asia branch (703/351-5667). This recently created program emphasizes long-term, somewhat more methodological research.

3. The Central Intelligence Library (703/351-7701) is not accessible to private researchers. However, some materials may be obtained through institutional, interlibrary-loan channels. The library's unclassified book holdings are indexed in the computerized Online Computer Library Center (OCLC) at Columbus, Ohio.

    The CIA's map collection consists of classified and unclassified materials. The latter are, in most cases, duplicated by the map collections of the Library of Congress (entry E4) and the Interior Department's Geological Survey (entry E3).

4. Most unclassified publications of the agency are released through the Document Expediting (DOCEX) Project of the Library of Congress. Since 1972, when the program was initiated, a large number of unclassified agency publications have been distributed on a subscription basis. Most publications pertain to foreign economic and political affairs, and are listed in an annually updated catalog: *National Foreign Assessment Center, CIA Publications Released to the Public through Library of Congress DOCEX* (March 1981). The DOCEX staff also maintains a card index of all CIA publications received since the program's inception.

    Some examples of CIA publications relevant to Southeast Asianists are: *National Basic Intelligence Factbook,* a semi-annual compilation giving outline data on land, water, government, the economy, communications, and defense forces of all nations; *Potential Implications of Trends in World Population, Food Production and Climate* (irregular); *Chiefs of State and Cabinet Members of Foreign Governments* (monthly); *Economic Indicators* (weekly); *International Energy Biweekly Statistical Review; Communist Aid to the Less Developed Countries of the Free World* (annual); *Annotated Bibliography on Transnational and International Terrorism* (1976); and *Arms Flow to LDC's: U.S.–Soviet Comparisons, 1974–1977* (1978). The agency also produces a series of unclassified color maps and atlases on most countries of the world, including the countries of Southeast Asia. These maps are available through the U.S. Government Printing Office sales outlets (Q11).

    For materials unavailable through the DOCEX program and for information concerning access and other research assistance, scholars may contact the Public Affairs Office, Charles E. Wilson, chief (703/351-7676). Requests for release of CIA internal documents, under the provisions of the Freedom of Information Act, are processed by the agency's Information and Privacy Coordinator (John Bacon, 703/351-2770).

K7 Civil Aeronautics Board (CAB)

1. a. *1825 Connecticut Avenue, N.W.*
    Washington, D.C. 20428
    (202) 673-5990

    b. Open to the public.

    c. C. Dan McKinnon, Chairman

2. The CAB promotes and regulates the civil air transport industry within the United States and between the United States and foreign countries in the interests of the foreign and domestic commerce of the U.S., the postal service, and the national defense.

BUREAU OF INTERNATIONAL AVIATION
Daniel M. Kaspar, Director
(202) 673-5417

Air transportation between the U.S. and foreign countries is conducted pursuant to international agreements. The bureau, on behalf of the CAB, advises and assists the Department of State in the negotiations of these agreements, and participates in the formulation of U.S. positions for international civil aviation conferences. Anthony Largey (202/673-5110) is the desk officer for South East Asia and South Pacific.

K8 Commerce Department

1. a. *Main Commerce Building*
   14th Street and Constitution Avenue, N.W.
   Washington, D.C. 20230
   (202) 337-2000 (Information)

   b. Open to the public.

2. The work of a number of Commerce Department offices includes examining the commercial and business climate in—and United States trade possibilities with—Southeast Asian countries. Research is conducted primarily in-house, but some opportunities exist for contract research by private individuals and institutions. The department's main objective is to facilitate trade and promote United States economic development and technological advancement.

3. The main Commerce Department library is described in entry A10. Other, smaller libraries and reference collections are described below with their respective offices.

4. Internal department records are stored in the records management facilities of each major sub-unit of the Commerce Department until they are transferred to the National Archives. Inventories of retired office files are maintained. Ivy Parr (202/377-3630), chief of the Records Management Division, can direct researchers to appropriate records-management officers and provide assistance in obtaining retired documents.

   The head of the Central Reference Records Inspection Facility, Geraldine LeBoo (202/337-4217), is the department's primary Freedom of Information officer. She can direct researchers to the appropriate Freedom of Information officers in other departmental sub-units as required.

   The department compiles a biweekly periodical, *Commerce America,* which is intended to aid exporters by providing information on international trade, economic growth, technological development, and business services. A helpful key business indicator and guide to the department's publications is the weekly *Business Service Checklist.* The *Commerce Publication Catalog and Index* (annual) may also be of use to researchers. The department's Office of Publications (202/377-3721) should be contacted for information on publications and sales. Other relevant publications are described below under the appropriate sub-units.

BUREAU OF THE CENSUS
Federal Office Building
3 Silver Hill and Suitland Roads
Suitland, Maryland 20233
Bruce Chapman, Director
(301) 763-5190

Daily shuttle-bus service—between the Potomac Avenue Metro station and the Bureau of the Census office in Suitland—is available.

The bureau is a general-purpose, statistical agency that collects, tabulates, and publishes a wide variety of statistical data primarily about the people, economy and foreign trade of the United States. The bureau if also involved in a wide variety of international activities, including the collection and analysis of selected demographic and economic data on Southeast Asian countries. The following sub-units of the bureau are concerned with Southeast Asia.

INTERNATIONAL STATISTICAL PROGRAM CENTER (ISPC)
James M. Aanestad, Acting Chief
(301) 763-2832

The ISPC is responsible for collecting and compiling most of the international statistics of the bureau, its primary focus being on population. Other areas of interest include: economic and social subjects, systems analysis, data processing, methodology, and sampling.

The center's accumulated international demographic statistics and information provide planners and researchers with readily available source materials for studies and analyses. It provides the Agency for International Development (AID) with data bases for evaluating programs and determining policies—particularly in the population field—to construct mathematical models that will help developing nations project trends and quantify the results of alternative demographic, economic, education, and health policies.

The ISPC also assists developing countries in improving their statistical capabilities. To this end, the center provides training—in its own classrooms and through correspondence courses—overseas workshops and consultations, and the development of methodological materials. Since 1975 the center, in collaboration with The George Washington University, the United Nations, and the Office of Population (AID), has offered a Master of Science Program in social and economic statistics for visiting foreign statisticians, demographers, economists, and computer specialists. For further details, see the free pamphlet *International Statistical Programs of the Bureau of the Census* and the *Summary Report U.S. Bureau of the Census International Statistical Training* (1974), available at the center. The ISPC's Overseas Consultation, Training and Information Services, which provides the training programs of the center, distributes a free *Training Branch Newsletter* and a syllabus of courses offered.

Some ISPC publications are: *Demographic Reports for Foreign Countries, Country Demographic Profiles, Research Documents,* the *World Mortality Pattern,* and *Current Publications of the ISPC* (irregular series). Also available is a monthly *Acquisition List* compiled by the center's Documentation

Branch. The center is also equipped with an automated microfilm storage and retrieval system, containing a wide range of global demographic and family-planning statistics with concentration on developing countries. Census reports, statistical publications, sample surveys, family-planning program reports, U.N. documents, professional journals, and the center's internal working papers and publications provide the data bases.

INTERNATIONAL DEMOGRAPHIC DATA CENTER (IDDC)
Samuel Baum, Chief
(301) 763-2870

The IDDC collects, compiles, and analyzes data on all developing countries of the world, particularly countries with AID programs since IDDC is funded by the AID's Office of Population. The division's annual publication, *World Population,* contains basic vital statistics of birth, mortality, and growth rates arranged by country. IDDC staff analysts also compile *Country Demographic Profiles* which present detailed data, both adjusted and unadjusted, on individual countries, including urban-rural and age-sex distribution of population, marital status, fertility, family planning, mortality, migration, education, land use, labor force, occupation, and other selected indicators. Thus far, *Demographic Profiles* have been published on Indonesia, Malaysia, and Thailand. Peter Way (301/763-2834), staff analyst for Southeast Asia, monitors the region and maintains notebooks and files of background information for Southeast Asian countries. The staff analyst may be consulted by researchers for additional information and data. The division's Demographic Data Retrieval System (DDRS) is a data bank on microfilm with unevaluated data for all developing countries including some family-planning data on Southeast Asia. Researchers may contact Martha A. Bargar (301/763-2834) for further information on DDRS data. The division also occasionally compiles *Information Research Documents* that focus on methodology and other specialized topics in demographic studies. The Population Division's recent publication, *A Compilation of Age Specific Fertility Rates for Developing Countries* (1980), may be of interest to those engaged in Southeast Asian demographic studies.

Researchers may also benefit by contacting the International Programs Staff (Anthony Turner, chief, 301/763-1121) of the Statistical Methods Division (Charles D. Jones, chief, 301/763-2672); Foreign Demographic Analysis Division (Samuel Baum, acting chief, 301/763-4010); and Foreign Trade Division (Emanuel A. Lipscomb, chief, 301/763-5342). The last-named division publishes a number of technical and statistical reports and classifications on foreign trade—both waterborne and airborne—by commodity, country, and region. Most of these materials are also available on microform and computer tape. For further information, contact Foreign Trade Division Information Branch (301/763-5140).

BUREAU OF ECONOMIC ANALYSIS
Tower Building
1401 K Street, N.W.
Washington, D.C. 20230
George Jaszi, Director
(202) 523-0777 (Information)

The Bureau of Economic Analysis prepares, develops, and interprets the economic accounts of the United States, including balance of payments accounts, which give details on U.S. transactions with foreign countries.

The bureau's monthly *Survey of Current Business* occasionally contains data of interest to Southeast Asianists and is available from the U.S. Government Printing Office, Washington, D.C. 20402. The bureau's information office maintains a small reference room (202/523-0595), which contains a collection of the bureau's periodicals and staff papers.

INTERNATIONAL INVESTMENT DIVISION
George R. Kruer, Chief
(202) 523-0657

This unit monitors U.S. direct investment overseas and analyzes the economic impact of multinational corporations. The division publishes several annual statistical aggregates on foreign investments in the bureau's *Survey of Current Business*. Other publications include *U.S. Direct Investment Abroad (1966–1977)*, containing data—arranged by industry and region—on the value of U.S. overseas investments and the involvements of foreign affiliates in those investments; *Revised Data Series on U.S. Direct Investment Abroad, 1966–1974* (1976), containing data on net capital outflow, reinvestment earnings, balance-of-payment income, and other earnings, fees, and royalties; and *Special Survey of U.S. Multinational Companies, 1970* (1972), detailing the activities of U.S. multinationals and their foreign affiliates from 1966 to 1970. Aggregate data on U.S. private investment in Southeast Asia may be obtained by researchers from the staff, though, for reason of confidentiality, information concerning the investments of individual companies is not accessible. Computer tapes of some of the crude data collected by the division are available at cost from the division's Data Retrieval and Analysis Branch (202/523-0652).

BALANCE OF PAYMENT DIVISION
Christopher L. Bach, Chief
(202) 523-0621

This division prepares statistics and analyses of the quarterly U.S. balance of payments and annual international investment position. This information is published quarterly in the bureau's *Survey of Current Business*.

INTERNATIONAL TRADE ADMINISTRATION (ITA)
(Formerly Industry and Trade Administration)
Main Commerce Building
Lionel H. Olmer, Under Secretary
(202) 377-3808

The ITA's objective is to promote progressive business practices and world trade, strengthen the international trade and investment position of the United States, actively support the vital private economic sector, and assist in adapting to changes within the U.S. economic system. The administration's principal publication is the biweekly *Business Review*, which contains reports on foreign and domestic business conditions and is available from the U.S. Government Printing Office, Washington, D.C. 20402 (Q11).

BUREAU OF EXPORT DEVELOPMENT
Robert H. Nath, Deputy Assistant Secretary
(202) 377-5261

The bureau assists United States business in securing international markets by a variety of means, such as providing counseling and marketing information services, organizing and conducting overseas sales and trade misions, and other promotional activities.

Office of Pacific Basin
Roger Severance, Director
(202) 377-4008

This office is organized into several geographical divisions; Southeast Asia is covered by the ASEAN Division (Susan Blackman, director, 202/377-5341). Each division is further organized into regions under the responsibility of Regional Marketing Managers who collect, compile, and analyze relevant economic data of the countries under their charge. As desk officers, these managers also serve as contacts with the U.S. diplomatic missions abroad and foreign missions in the U.S. LoRee Silloway (202/377-2522) is the regional manager for the countries of our interest.

The office compiles and publishes international marketing information. The annual or semi-annual *Foreign Economic Trends and their Implications for the United States* (FET) are prepared with the assistance of U.S. embassies and consulates abroad. This priced series of approximately 150 reports a year presents current business and economic developments in nearly every country and analyzes the market for United States goods. There are separate FET reports on Burma (80–025), Indonesia (80–124), Malaysia (80–090), the Philippines (80–125), Singapore (80–059), and Thailand (80–083).

Another series of interest is entitled *Overseas Business Reports,* which present basic information for exporters, importers, manufacturers, researchers, and those concerned with international trade and economic conditions. These reports are prepared with information furnished by United States Missions abroad. Reports on Southeast Asia include *World Trade Outlook for the Far East and South Asia* (80–10), *Market Profiles for Asia and Oceania* (79–14), *Marketing in Indonesia* (77–05), *Marketing in Malaysia* (77–02), *Marketing in the Philippines* (79–20), *Marketing in Singapore* (77–35), and *Marketing in Thailand* (79–38). Also of interest will be *A Business Guide to the Association of Southeast Asian Nations* (1981). For information on the above publications contact Yvonne Jenkins, 202/377-2522.

Office of Export Planning and Evaluation
Jonathan C. Menes, Director
(202) 377-5055

Another organ of the bureau for export promotion operation, this office is responsible for the publication of *Country Market Sectoral Surveys,* which pinpoint the best United States export opportunities in a single foreign country, and the *Global Market Surveys,* which provide detailed information on a number of the best foreign markets for the products of a single United States industry or a group of related industries.

Office of Export Marketing Assistance
Richard Garnitz, Director
(202) 377-5131

This office is also responsible for stimulating United States exports and investments abroad. Its *Foreign Market Reports* series contains data on foreign economic conditions by country. A monthly index is available. The office also prepares, on request, *World Traders Data Reports,* describing the history, operation, sale, territories, business connections, and chief executives of individual foreign business firms. The Export Communication Section (C. L. White, 202/377-5783) can provide researchers and other interested persons with information on export development publications.

Office of Trade Information Services
Saul Padwo, Director
(202) 377-1469

Within this recently created office is the Trade Facilities Information and Services Division (formerly under the Office of Export Market Assistance). The division maintains a reference room (Room 1063, 202/377-2997) containing a variety of reports and research papers of the International Bank for Reconstruction and Development (World Bank) (IBRD), including monthly operational summaries of loans under consideration by the IBRD, appraisal reports on bank-funded projects, and World Bank economic and country studies. This facility is open to the public from 8:30 A.M. to 5:00 P.M. weekdays.

In addition, researchers may find it useful to contact the bureau's Office of Export Promotion (John Roose, director, 202/377-4231) and the Office of International Commercial Representation (Betty D. Neuhart, director, 202/377-5777).

BUREAU OF INTERNATIONAL ECONOMIC POLICY AND RESEARCH (BIEPR)
Main Commerce Building
Raymond J. Waldmann, Assistant Secretary
(202) 377-3022

The BIEPR is responsible for coordinating activities involving the research, analysis, and formulation of international economic and commercial programs and policies relating to trade, finance, and investment as well as those of a bilateral, multilateral, or regional nature. The bureau's activities also include: initiating and reviewing research studies on developments affecting U.S. foreign trade and commercial interests abroad; representing the department in international trade and related negotiations; and carrying out the department's interagency policy role in such organizations as the National Security Council and the National Advisory Council on International Monetary and Financial Policies.

Office of International Economic Relations
James R. Johnston, Acting Director
(202) 377-5341

This office is a useful primary contact and referral point for Southeast Asia researchers. The desk officers or country specialists in this office monitor trade and economic trends in the countries under their charge and advise U.S. businesses and government agencies on matters of foreign trade and investments. The ASEAN countries are currently the responsibility of Maureen Smith, director of the Developing Nations Division (202/377-2954).

Office of Planning and Research
Donald Weinig, Director
(202) 377-5638

This office has little direct involvement in South Asia and generally conducts research on international economic-policy issues, sector analysis, export projections, and world-wide trade developments and trends. However, several of its published and unpublished reports contain Southeast Asian regional information.

The *Staff Economic Report* series includes: *U.S. Trade with Developing Economies: The Growing Importance of Manufactured Goods* (1975); *Capital Requirements of the Non-OPEC Developed Countries* (1976); *Selected Basic References on Trade Barriers and International Trade Flows* (1976); and an annotated bibliography, *Survey of Current International Economic Research,* which is updated periodically. Other publications of the unit include: *Trends in U.S. Foreign Trade,* containing data by country and commodity; *International Economic Indicators,* a quarterly that presents a wide variety of comparative economic statistics; the monthly *Current Price Development in the U.S. and Major Foreign Countries,* which provides information on consumer, wholesale world commodity, export, and import prices, and nonfarm wages and currency shifts; and the annual *Market Share Reports* (MSRs), issued in two series (with data for 5 years (1973–1977); the country series—which includes reports on 88 import markets, comparing U.S. performance in 880 manufactured products with those of 8 other principal suppliers—and the commodity series, which includes individual reports on 880 manufactured products, comparing the U.S. export performance in 92 foreign markets with those of 13 other major exporting countries. MSRs on Indonesia, Malaysia, the Philippines, Singapore, Thailand, and Vietnam are available from the National Technical Information Service, Springfield, Virginia 22161 (703/487-4600).

Office of International Finance and Investment
Brant W. Free, Acting Director
(202) 377-4925

The unit monitors and analyzes global activities in the fields of international lending, taxation, transfer of technology, anti-trust matters, expropriations, and other investment disputes. Its publications include the two-volume, priced report, *The Multinational Corporation: Studies on U.S. Foreign Investments (1972–1973).*

Office of International Trade Policy
William H. Cavitt, Acting Director
(202) 377-5327

Primarily concerned with unfair trade practices, this office assists in the development of U.S. positions in international trade negotiations and monitors and analyzes developments relating to foreign tariffs, import quota systems, and international commodity agreements. In the department's biweekly *Commerce America,* the office publishes progress reports concerning multinational trade negotiations.

Office of Trade and Investment Analysis
Alan Lenz, Director
(202) 377-2568

This unit is responsible for monitoring individual foreign investments and analyzing their impact on the U.S. economy. It also conducts in-house and contract research on foreign investment and its ramifications. Summaries of the findings are released in the *Commerce News;* however, because Southeast Asian investment in the U.S. is insignificant, there is little of direct interest to Southeast Asianists here.

Additional Southeast Asia–related information and materials may be available from the United States Commercial Service (Bruce Strong, director, 202/377-3922) of the Bureau of Field Operations, and from the Office of Export Administration (William Skidmore, director, (202/377-4293), which evaluates export licenses for all countries including those of Southeast Asia.

NATIONAL BUREAU OF STANDARDS
Gaithersburg, Maryland 20234
Ernest Ambler, Director
(301) 921-2411

OFFICE OF INTERNATIONAL RELATIONS (OIR)
Dr. Kurt F. J. Heinrich, Chief
(301) 921-2463

This office has been responsible in the past for exchanging information and providing scientific and technological assistance to several Southeast Asian countries. Under an Agency for International Development (AID) grant, the office has sponsored seminars, training courses, surveys, and workshops in the area of metrology and related fields for the ASEAN states and South Vietnam. An information brochure, *National Bureau of Standards at a Glance,* is available free, as are copies of *National Standard Reference Data System Publication List, 1964–1977.*

NATIONAL OCEANIC AND ATMOSPHERIC ADMINISTRATION (NOAA)
15th Street and Constitution Avenue, N.W.
Washington, D.C. 20030
John Byrne, Administrator
(202) 377-3567

The mission of NOAA is to explore, map, and chart the global ocean and its living resources; to manage, use, and conserve those resources; to describe, monitor, and predict conditions in the atmosphere, ocean, sun, and space environment; to issue warnings against impending destructive natural events; to develop beneficial methods of environmental modification, and to assess the consequences of inadvertent environmental modification over several scales of time.

NATIONAL MARINE FISHERIES SERVICE
3300 Whitehaven Street, N.W.
Washington, D.C. 20235
William G. Gordon, Assistant Administrator
(202) 634-7283

Office of International Fisheries Affairs
Carmen Blondin, Director
(202) 634-7514

This office has three divisions dealing with international fisheries affairs: Foreign Fisheries Analysis Division (Milan A. Kravanja, chief, 202/634-7307); International Fisheries Development and Services Division (Prudence Fox, chief, 202/634-7263); and International Organization and Agreements Division (Henry Beasley, chief, 202/634-7257).

The office maintains country and subject files, which contain maps and photographs. On the basis of information primarily available through foreign and U.S. government publications, as well as trade journals, this office prepares extensive data on several aspects of international fisheries; e.g., economics of fishing, trade, marketing, government policies and regulation, the activities of government agencies, and international disputes.

OCEANIC AND ATMOSPHERIC SERVICES
6010 Executive Boulevard
Rockville, Maryland 20852
Richard E. Hallgren, Acting Assistant Administrator
(301) 443-8110

International Affairs Office
Nels Johnson, Director
(301) 443-8635

Researchers may obtain advice from the staff pertaining to NOAA's worldwide technical, climatological, meteorological, oceanographic, and marine resources data-gathering activities.

NATIONAL OCEAN SURVEY
6001 Executive Boulevard
Rockville, Maryland 20852
Herbert R. Lippold, Jr., Director
(301) 443-8204

Aeronautical Charting and Cartography
Walter J. Chappas, Associate Director
(301) 443-8189

A few maps and charts of interest may be found in this unit. A *Catalog of Aeronautical Charts and Related Publications* (1979) is available. Most U.S. government charting and mapping activities are handled by the Defense Mapping Agency (See entry E1).

ENVIRONMENTAL SCIENCE INFORMATION CENTER (ENVIRONMENTAL DATA AND INFORMATION SERVICE)—LIBRARY AND INFORMATION SERVICES DIVISION
6009 Executive Boulevard
Rockville, Maryland 20852
Elizabeth J. Yeates, Chief
(301) 443-8330

NOAA's library collection, which is international in scope, contains extensive literature on atmospheric science, fisheries, marine biology, oceanography, and law of the sea. The collection is dispersed among several library centers throughout the metropolitan area. However, through NOAA's automated library and information system, researchers have access to an integrated processing and retrieval system for all NOAA library resources and information centers. Information on NOAA–supported computer bases is provided in the publication *Computerized Information Retrieval Services*. NOAA's Atmospheric Sciences Library (8060 13th Street, Silver Spring, Maryland, 301/427-7800) maintains selected research reports on microfilm; these are drawn from government agencies and from in-house searches.

From time to time, also the division prepares a *Packaged Literature Search* on particular topics of interest.

NATIONAL TECHNICAL INFORMATION SERVICE (NTIS)
Sills Building
5285 Port Royal Road
Springfield, Virginia 22161
Joseph F. Saponio, Acting Director
(703) 487-4636

The National Technical Information Service aims at simplifying and improving public access to publications of the Department Commerce and to data files and scientific and technical reports sponsored by other federal agencies. The NTIS is the central point in the United States for the public sale of government-funded research and development reports and other analysis prepared by federal agencies, their contractors, or grantees.

Through agreements with more than 300 organizations, NTIS adds about 70,000 new reports a year to its collection, now exceeding one million titles. The agency also coordinates the publishing and technical-inquiry functions of various special-technology groups.

Researchers may easily locate abstracts of interest from among the 680,000 federally sponsored research reports completed and published since 1964 by using the agency's on-line computer-search service (NTISearch, 703/487-4640). Copies of the research reports are sold in paper or microfiche. The NTIS Bibliographic Data File, which includes published and unpublished abstracts, is available on magnetic tape for lease. A *Reference Guide* to the *NTIS Bibliographic Data File* (1978) is available on request.

Current abstracts of new research reports, and other specialized technical information in various catagories of interest, are published in some 33 weekly *Abstract Newsletters.* A comprehensive biweekly journal, *Government Reports Announcements and Index,* is published for libraries, technical information specialists, and those requiring such all-inclusive volumes. A standard order microfiche service (SRIM) automatically provides subscribers with the full texts of research reports selected to satisfy individual requirements. Scholars may also note that over 1,000 *Published Searches* on various topics are available from computer searches already conducted by the NTIS. The *NTIS Search Catalog* provides a subject index to the materials. The staff will perform, for a fee, an on-line custom search for topics requested by individual researchers.

NTIS publications of interest include monthly foreign trade reports, such as the *Foreign Market Reports,* the *Foreign Market Airgrams,* and the Foreign Broadcast Information Service's (Q9) *Daily Reports* (volume V of which includes Southeast Asia). NTIS also distributes various reports, abstracts, and translations of the Joint Publication Research Service (JPRS) (Q14), some of which are listed in the annual *Reference Aid Directory of JPRS Ad Hoc Publications* and in the biweekly *Government Reports Announcement and Index.* For general information about the services and resources of NTIS, researchers may consult *NTIS Information Services* (1979) and *Subject Guide to NTIS Information Collection.* The Information and Sales Center for the NTIS services and publications is located at 425 13th Street N.W., Washington, D.C. (202/724-3509).

OFFICE OF INTERNATIONAL AFFAIRS
Terrance L. Lindemann, Chief
(703) 487-4820

This office, formerly known as the Developing Countries Staff, acting for the U.S. Agency for International Development (AID), has an on-going, expanding program through which U.S. scientific and technological information is made available to the developing countries through local cooperative agencies. The program currently includes Indonesia, the Philippines and Thailand. John Hounsell (703/487-4829) is the desk officer dealing with Southeast Asian countries. The office is responsible for publishing the two AID bulletins: *ACESS to Information for International Development* and *AMTID, Application of Modern Technology to International Development,* both of which contain valuable materials on Southeast Asia. An informative pamphlet, *Technical Information for Development,* describes the program of the office and lists the foreign cooperative agencies.

PATENT AND TRADEMARK OFFICE (PTO)
Crystal Plaza Building 3
2021 Jefferson Davis Highway
Arlington, Virginia 20231
Gerald J. Mossinghoff, Commissioner
(703) 557-3811

The PTO, in addition to its responsibility of examining all U.S. applications for patents, also processes international applications for patents under the provisions of the Patent Cooperation Treaty.

OFFICE OF LEGISLATION AND INTERNATIONAL AFFAIRS
Michael Kirk, Director
(703) 557-3065

OFFICE OF INTERNATIONAL PATENT CLASSIFICATION
Thomas Lomont, Director
(703) 557-0667

The staff of these offices may be consulted for information and publications on patent laws and regulations for Southeast Asian countries.

SCIENTIFIC LIBRARY (PATENT DOCUMENTATION ORGANIZATION)—FOREIGN PATENT BRANCH
Barrington Balthrop, Chief
(703) 557-2970

The library collects materials on international patents and trademarks including those of Southeast Asia. A card catalog and separate inventories of holdings by country are available. The collection may be useful for studies of science and technology in Southeast Asia.

Note: See also entries A9, A10, G4, and Q19.

K9 Congress

1. a. *The Capitol*
    Washington, D.C. 20510
    (202) 224-3121

    b. Senate and House of Representatives galleries and most committee hearings are open to the public.

2. The work of preparing and considering legislation is done largely by committees of both Houses of Congress. There are 15 standing committees in the Senate and 22 in the House of Representatives. Committees and subcommittees, concerned with Southeast Asian affairs are listed below. Staff members of those committees may be consulted by interested scholars for information concerning legislative processes and committee operations.

    Committee hearings are frequently attended by academics and other professional experts who provide oral or written testimony. Proceedings of public hearings are eventually published and are available from the committee conducting the hearing or from the Government Printing Office.

    Although committee schedules are subject to frequent alterations, legislative calendars are available. The Daily Digest section of the *Congressional Record* announces the legislative program for each day and, at the end of the week, gives the program for the following week. The *Washington Post* also publishes the schedules of congressional activities each day.

    The Congressional Research Service (CRS) is the principal research arm of the Congress (see entry K10). CRS works exclusively for the members of Congress. Its analyses and reports are not available to the public unless made available by a member of the Congress to a constituent. Southeast Asia specialists, however, may be willing to confer with researchers for information on congressional activities related to the region.

3. The Library of Congress is discussed in entry A27.

4. Proceedings of the Congress are published in the *Congressional Record,* issued daily when the Congress is in session, and a permanent bound edition of the *Record* is also published. University Microfilms International (Ann Arbor, Michigan) publishes the *Congressional Records* on microfiche, with a monthly index and a *Guide to the Congressional Record*. Each house also publishes a journal at the end of each session for members of Congress— staff and committees. Other publications of interest are: the Senate Foreign Relations Committee's occasional compilation of *Legislation on Foreign Relations*; the House and Senate hearings on *Foreign Aid Authorization* (titles vary); *Foreign Aid Appropriations* (titles vary); *Department of State Appropriations*; and the series of *Required Reports to Congress in the Foreign Affairs Field*. Checklists of Congressional hearings are also available. Bibliographies of congressional publications on foreign affairs and U.S. intelligence activities are available from the U.S. Government Printing Office (Q11).

STANDING COMMITTEES OF THE SENATE

Foreign Relations Committee
Dirksen Senate Office Building (SOB), Room 4229

Charles H. Percy, Chairman
(202) 224-4651

Specializing in matters relating to all U.S. treaties and agreements with foreign countries, this committee deals with Southeast Asia–related issues through several of its subcommittees, such as: East Asian and Pacific Affairs (S. I. Hayakawa, chairman, Dirksen SOB, Room 4229, 202/224-5481); International Economic Policy (Charles McC. Mathias, chairman, Dirksen SOB, Room 4229, 202/224-4192); and Arms Control, Oceans and International Operations and Environment (Larry Pressler, chairman, Dirksen SOB, Room 4229, 202/224-4651).

AGRICULTURE, NUTRITION AND FORESTRY COMMITTEE
Russell SOB, Room 322
Jesse Helms, Chairman
(202) 224-2035

Southeast Asia–related issues are one of the concerns of the subcommittee on Foreign Agricultural Policy (Rudy Boschwitz, chairman, Russell SOB, Room 322, 202/224-2035).

APPROPRIATIONS COMMITTEE
Russell SOB, Room 1235
Mark O. Hatfield, Chairman
(202) 224-3471

This important committee has jurisdiction over funding of all government programs. Of particular interest to the Southeast Asian scholar are the subcommittees on Defense (Jed Stevens, chairman, Dirksen SOB, Room 1239, 202/224-7255), and Foreign Operations (Robert Kasten, chairman, The Capitol, Room S-128, 202/224-7274).

ARMED SERVICES COMMITTEE
Russell SOB, Room 212
John Tower, Chairman
(202) 224-3871

This committee has jurisdiction over matters, including research and development, relating to the national military establishment. Subcommittees include Sea Power and Force Projection (William S. Cohen, chairman, Dirksen SOB, Room 1251, 202/224-2523).

BANKING, HOUSING AND URBAN AFFAIRS COMMITTEE
Dirksen SOB, Room 5300
Jake Garn, Chairman
(202)224-7391

Of special interest are the activities of the Subcommittee on International Finance (John Heinz, Dirksen SOB, Room 5300, 202/224-0891) relating to international economic affairs as they affect U.S. monetary policy, credit, and financial institutions, economic growth, and urban affairs.

FINANCE COMMITTEE
Dirksen SOB, Room 2227
Robert Dole, Chairman
(202) 224-4515

This committee has jurisdiction over revenue and tax matters. The Subcommittee on International Trade (John C. Danforth, chairman, Dirksen SOB, Room 2227, 202/224-4515) is concerned with Southeast Asian affairs in the areas of customs, tariffs, and import quotas.

COMMERCE, SCIENCE AND TRANSPORTATION COMMITTEE
Dirksen SOB, Room 5202
Bob Rockwood, Chairman
(202) 224-5115

This committee is concerned with foreign commerce, science, transportation, communication, and transfer of technology to developing nations.

JUDICIARY COMMITTEE
Dirksen SOB, Room 2226
Strom Thurmond, Chairman
(202) 224-5225

Responsibilities of this committee include refugees, escapees, immigration, naturalization, and espionage.

STANDING COMMITTEES OF THE HOUSE OF REPRESENTATIVES

COMMITTEE ON AGRICULTURE
Longworth House Office Building (HOB), Room 1301
E. de la Garza, Chairman
(202) 225-2171

COMMITTEE ON APPROPRIATIONS
The Capitol, Room 4218
Jamie L. Whitten, Chairman
(202) 225-2771

Subcommittee on Defense
The Capitol, Room 4144
Joseph P. Addabbo, Chairman
(202) 225-2847

Subcommittee on Foreign Operations
The Capitol, Room 4308
Clarence D. Long, Chairman
(202) 225-2041

COMMITTEE ON ARMED SERVICES
Rayburn HOB, Room 2120
Melvin Price, Chairman
(202) 225-4151

COMMITTEE ON BANKING, FINANCE, AND URBAN AFFAIRS
Rayburn HOB, Room 2129
Fernand St. Germain, Chairman
(202) 225-4247

Subcommittee on International Development, Institutions and Finance
HOB Annex 1, Room 604
Jerry Patterson, Chairman
(202) 225-2495

Subcommittee on International Trade, Investment, and Monetary Policy
HOB Annex 2, Room H-2179
Stephen L. Neal, Chairman
(202) 225-1271

COMMITTEE ON THE BUDGET
HOB Annex 1 Room A-214
James R. Jones, Chairman
(202) 225-7200

Task Force on National Security and Veterans
Longworth HOB, Room 1111
Jim Mattox, Chairman
(202) 225-2231

COMMITTEE ON FOREIGN AFFAIRS
Rayburn HOB, Room 2170
Clement J. Zablocki, Chairman
(202) 225-5021

Subcommittee on Asian and Pacific Affairs
HOB Annex 1, Room A-704
Steven Solarz, Chairman
(202) 225-3044

Subcommittee on International Economic Policy and Trade
HOB Annex 1, Room A-707
Jonathan B. Bingham, Chairman
(202) 225-3246

Subcommittee on International Organizations
HOB Annex 1, Room A-703
Don Bonker, Chairman
(202) 225-5318

Subcommittee on International Operations
Rayburn HOB, Room B-358
Dante B. Fascell, Chairman
(202) 225-3424

Subcommittee on International Security and Scientific Affairs
Rayburn HOB, Room B-301B
Clement J. Zablocki, Chairman
(202) 225-8926

COMMITTEE ON ENERGY AND COMMERCE
Rayburn HOB, Room 2125
John D. Dingell, Chairman
(202) 225-2927

COMMITTEE ON THE JUDICIARY
Rayburn HOB, Room 2137
Peter W. Rodino, Jr., Chairman
(202) 225-3951

Subcommittee on Immigration, Refugees and International Law
Rayburn HOB, Room 2137
Romano Mazzoli, Chairman
(202) 225-5727

COMMITTEE ON WAYS AND MEANS
Longworth HOB, Room 1102
Dan Rostenkowski, Chairman
(202) 225-3625

Subcommittee on Trade
Cannon HOB, Room 233
Sam Gibbons, Chairman
(202) 225-3943

JOINT COMMITTEES

JOINT ECONOMIC COMMITTEE
Dirksen SOB, Room G-133
Henry Reuss, Chairman
Roger Jepsen, Vice Chairman
(202) 224-5171

This committee is concerned with economic growth, fiscal policy, and international economics

SELECT COMMITTEES

HOUSE PERMANENT SELECT COMMITTEE ON INTELLIGENCE
Capitol, Room H-405
Edward P. Boland, Chairman
(202) 225-4121

HOUSE SELECT COMMITTEE ON NARCOTIC ABUSE AND CONTROL
HOB Annex 2, Room 234
Leo Zeferetti, Chairman
(202) 226-3040

This committee has done some studies of drug traffic in Southeast Asia. However, the future orientation is likely to be toward the domestic side.

SENATE SELECT COMMITTEE ON INTELLIGENCE
Dirksen SOB, Room G 308
Barry Goldwater, Chairman
(202) 224-1700

K10 Congressional Research Service (CRS)

1.   a. *Library of Congress*
     James Madison Memorial Building
     First Street and Independence Avenue, S.E.
     Washington, D.C. 20540
     (202) 287-5775

     b. Not open to the public.

     c. Gilbert Gude, Director

2.   The Congressional Research Service works exclusively for the Congress, conducting research, analyzing legislation, and providing information at the request of members, committees, and their staffs. Southeast Asian-area specialists Marjorie Niehause (202/287-7684) and Larry Niksch (202/287-7680) in the Foreign Affairs and National Defense Division prepare studies, reports, compilations, digests, and background briefings on Southeast Asian issues of concern to the Congress.

3.   See Library of Congress (entry A27).

4.   Although CRS studies are not for general distribution, if you know of a specific title of interest, you may be able to obtain it directly from the Foreign Affairs and National Defense Division if sufficient copies are available, or researchers may obtain CRS materials from the office of a member or from a committee of the Congress. Also, from time to time CRS studies are read into the *Congressional Record* or published in congressional committee reports. CRS *Issue Briefs,* distributed only to members of Congress, review major policy topics, summarize the pertinent legislative history, and provide reference lists for further reading. In addition, the *Congressional Research Service Review,* the *UPDATE from CRS,* and the cumulative *Subject Catalog of CRS Reports in Print* (1980) are all exclusive publications for the members of Congress. Researchers may note that the CRS indexes current periodical articles on public-policy issues, including foreign affairs by country, from some 3,000 U.S. and foreign journals and magazines. The "Bibliographic Citation" file is accessible to researchers in machine-readable format through the LC's SCORPIO automated data base.

K11 Defense Department (DOD)

1.   a. *The Pentagon*
     Washington, D.C. 20301
     (202) 545-6700 (Information)
     (202) 697-5737 (Public Affairs)

     b. Closed to those without security clearance or an appointment arranged in advance.

2.   Some external research is supported on a contract basis by the Department of Defense and its Departments of the Air Force, the Army, and the Navy (see entries K3, K5, and K29, respectively). DOD divisions with activities relating to Southeast Asia are described following point 4, below; however, most such activities are of an operational and classified nature.

3. See Army Library (entry A6) and Navy Department Library (entry A34).

4. A good review of DOD activities is provided in the *Annual Defense Department Report* to the Congress on the military budget. Publications of DOD components are described below within the appropriate sub-unit.

    The Defense Documentation Center (entry G5) is the repository of all research reports produced under DOD contracts. Unclassified reports received at the center are made available to the National Technical Information Service (entry Q19). The latter lists them in its own indexes and makes them available to the public.

    DOD components control their own records until the records are retired to the custody of the National Archives. DOD's Documents Division (202/ 695-5363), under the Office of the Joint Chiefs of Staff, can assist researchers with the various record-control facilities in the department. This division's sub-units consist of: Information Release and Safeguards Branch (Janet Lakang, 202/697-9660); Records and Information Retrieval Branch (Herman C. Crocker, 202/697-9127); and Records and Information Management Branch (Sterling S. Smith, 202/695-2693).

    The Directorate for Freedom of Information and Security Review (Charles W. Hinkle, director, 202/697-4325), in the Office of the Assistant Secretary for Defense (Public Affairs), processes all requests under the Freedom of Information Act for the records of the Office of the Secretary of Defense and the Joint Chiefs of Staff. The directorate's Freedom of Information Specialist Robert I. Farrif (202/697-7171) can refer researchers to other appropriate departmental branch offices dealing with Freedom of Information inquiries.

OFFICE OF THE SECRETARY OF DEFENSE

PUBLIC AFFAIRS OFFICE
Henry E. Catto, Jr., Assistant Secretary
(202) 697-9312

Office of Public Correspondence
Philip Farris, Staff Assistant
(202) 697-5737

The sensitive nature of DOD operations inhibits precise description of its activities. The Public Affairs Office is therefore a useful starting point for scholars interested in locating divisions and personnel best able to give assistance.

HISTORICAL STAFF
Alfred Goldberg, Historian
(202) 697-4216

The Historical Staff conducts and prepares historical studies of the department. It maintains a reference file of unclassified materials of departmental publications as well as documents and press clippings related to the structural evolution of the department and the military services. The two-volume history of United States prisoners of war in Southeast Asia is scheduled for completion in 1983.

OFFICE OF THE ASSISTANT SECRETARY OF DEFENSE FOR IN-
TERNATIONAL SECURITY AFFAIRS (ISA)
Richard L. Armitage, Deputy Assistant Secretary for East Asia and Pacific
Affairs
(202) 697-2307

Donald Jones, Director, East Asia and Pacific Region
(202) 695-4175

Thomas Bromphy, Desk Officer, Vietnam, Laos, and Cambodia
(202) 695-4175

Mahlon Henderson, Desk Officer, Malaysia, Singapore, Philippines, and
Thailand
(202) 695-4175

James Riordan, Desk Officer, Indonesia
(202) 697-7757

The ISA develops and coordinates DOD policies and procedures in the
fields of international political affairs, and military and foreign economic
affairs. This responsibility encompasses general problems of international
security, arms control, disarmament questions, military-assistance program
administration, military sales to foreign governments, policy guidance for
U.S. missions, representatives to international organizations, conferences,
and for negotiations and monitoring of agreements with foreign governments with respect to equipment, facilities, operating rights, and status of
forces.

ISA external research programs focus on identifying and analyzing alternative defense policies for dealing with emerging international problems
relevant to the security of the United States. ISA research is performed by
federal contract research centers, other nonprofit analytical centers, commercial research firms, and university-based study centers. Research proposals are accepted from these and other research organizations if they
meet ISA requirements. ISA does not provide any recurring research publications. Unclassified research studies may be purchased from the National
Technical Information Service (see entry Q19).

DEFENSE INTELLIGENCE AGENCY (DIA)
James A. Williams, Director
(202) 695-7353

Edward A. Burkhalter, Jr., Deputy Director for Foreign Intelligence
(202) 697-5128

Charles Desaulniers, Defense Intelligence Officer for East Asia and Pacific
(202) 695-0257

Harold W. Maynard, Assistant Defense Intelligence Officer for East Asia
and Pacific (including Southeast Asia)
(202) 695-0416

In addition to the Defense Intelligence Officer who deals with policy questions at a high level, the agency also has a team of country analysts who
deal with current intelligence and receive reports from the defense attachés
of the three services stationed in U.S. embassies abroad. Analysts in the

South Asia/Pacific Branch of the Eastern Division (202/695-1606) may be willing to talk with serious scholars as time and circumstances permit. Personnel in this branch are as follows: Don Berlin (202/697-6039), Indonesia, Malaysia, Philippines, and Singapore; Dennis Dalpino (202/697-6039), Laos and Cambodia; Joe Kinder 202/697-6039), Vietnam; David Nefzger (202/697-6039), Indonesia, Malaysia, the Philippines, and Singapore; and Dick Rice (202/697-6039), Thailand.

The DIA Reference Library (202/692-5311) is closed to outside researchers. The library does entertain written requests for information on special topics. Limited interlibrary loan and photoduplication facilities are available. Neither the facilities nor the materials generated by the DIA's Defense Intelligence School (202/433-4250) are accessible to private scholars.

Most of the documents and records assembled in the office of the Assistant Vice Director for Attachés and Training (202/694-5657)—which manages the defense attaché program, including selection, training, and evaluation of personnel—are restricted.

NATIONAL SECURITY AGENCY (NSA)
Fort George G. Mead
Maryland 20755
(301) 688-6524
(301) 688-6964 (Freedom of Information)

NSA is perhaps the most secretive U.S. intelligence agency. It conducts highly technical, communications intelligence gathering activities throughout the world. Its organizational structure remains classified.

DEFENSE SECURITY ASSISTANCE AGENCY
James H. Ahmann, Director
(202) 695-3291

This agency administers U.S. military assistance programs in foreign countries. Betty Marini (202/697-7080) is the chief of the East Asia/Latin America Division. The agency issues an annual unclassified *Foreign Military Sales and Military Assistance Facts* containing tabular data on U.S. military assistance programs and arms sales abroad by country and by year for the last ten years, as well as cumulative data, in some instances, from 1950. This publication may be obtained from the agency's Data Management Division (Richard Lally, 202/697-3574).

JOINT CHIEFS OF STAFF
Policy Directorate
Thomas J. Begley, Director
(202) 695-5618

FAR EAST/SOUTH ASIA DIVISION
Raymond Deitch, Chief
(202) 697-8830

The Southeast Asia Branch, Lee Elwell (202/695-3289), prepares classified policy papers and estimates, relating to U. S. security interests, security assistance, and military relations in Southeast Asia, for the Joint Chiefs of Staff.

HISTORICAL DIVISION
Robert J. Watson
(202) 697-3088

This division prepares histories and special background studies, most of which are classified. Some declassified documents from the 1940s are available to researchers in the Modern Military Branch of the National Archives.

DEFENSE ADVANCED RESEARCH PROJECTS AGENCY (DARPA)
1400 Wilson Boulevard
Arlington, Virginia 22209
Robert S. Cooper, Director
(703) 694-3077

A separately organized research and development agency in the Defense Department, the DARPA supplements the research program of the three military services. Its assigned research responsibilities include strategic technology, tactical technology, nuclear monitoring, materials sciences, information-processing techniques, and cybernetics technology. Within the Systems Sciences Division (Craig I. Fields, assistant director, 202/694-1303), foreign and national security-affairs research is carried out at both the basic and exploratory research levels. Specfic areas of emphasis include the development of prototype systems for defining and measuring U.S. national interests abroad; development of quantitative methods for assessing and forecasting strategic threats; and development and application of advanced analytic and computerized approaches to strategic planning and forecasting in short-, medium-, and long-run time frames.

A large majority of the research conducted in these areas is unclassified, and the results are published in professional literature. Inquiries concerning research proposals should be addressed to the director fo the DARPA. The National Technical Information Service furnishes the public with those reports of the agency that are available for general release. An informative Advanced Research Projects Agency, is available on request.

NATIONAL DEFENSE UNIVERSITY (NDU)
Fort Lesley J. McNair
4th and F Streets, S.W.
Washington, D.C. 20319
John S. Pustay, President
(202) 693-1076

NATIONAL WAR COLLEGE (NWC)
Lee E. Surut, Commandant
(202) 693-8318

INDUSTRIAL COLLEGE OF THE ARMED FORCES (ICAF)
Ronald E. Narmi, Commandant
(202) 693-8305

Established in 1976, the NDU consists of two senior-service constituent institutions: the NWC and the ICAF, both located at Fort McNair. The NDU's mission is to insure excellence in professional military education in the essential elements of national security, to prepare selected personnel of the Department of Defense, the Department of State, and other government agencies to exercise senior policy, command, and staff functions, to plan national strategy, and to manage resources of national security.

A graduate-level school in the field of politico-military affairs, the NWC enrolls 160 selected senior military and civilian officers for a 10-month, full-time program of study that focuses specifically on national security policy, formulation, and implementation. The curriculum is broadly divided into a Core Program taken by all students and an Elective Studies Program. Within the latter category, a seminar on Southeast Asia is occasionally offered. International studies, together with domestic studies and national security studies, constitute the three academic departments of NWC. The NWC faculty and guest lecturers are drawn from the services and from the civilian sectors including the State Department, AID, ICA, the CIA, and the professional academic community. An information brochure, *The National War College,* is available on request.

In addition to the resident courses taught at the NWC, the university conducts a defense-strategy seminar, a reserve-components national-security seminar, and a correspondence course. The ICAF, which enrolls 218 selected students annually from any of the defense and civilian branches of the government, concentrates its curriculum on the management of resources for national security.

The NDU Library (202/693-8437) consists of 50,000 monographs and 750 journal subscriptions. The principal focus of the collection is divided among the areas of history, economics, government, international relations, and security studies. The library is open from 8:00 A.M. to 4:30 P.M., Monday through Friday. The library is open to the public; however, an appointment is required. Interlibrary loan and photoduplication facilities are available.

Note: See also entries E1, G5, K3, K5 and K29.

K12 Education Department

1.   a. *400 Maryland Avenue, S.W.*
     Washington, D.C. 20202
     (202) 245-3192

     b. Open to the public.

2.   The Education Department was inaugurated on May 4, 1980. Currently the department administers some 162 programs from the departments of Health, Education and Welfare (of which it constituted a division before the reorganization), Defense, Justice, Housing and Urban Development, Labor, and the National Science Foundation. Responsibilities of the department include insuring equal educational opportunity for all; promoting improvement in the quality of education through research, evaluation, and management; and accounting for federal educational programs.

     Most research is conducted in-house, but outside consultant and contract research is occasionally available. The department also participates in several international exchange programs noted below.

3.   For the National Institute of Education Library see entry A32.

4.   The department's publications are described below within the appropriate units. Other publications include: *Daily Education News*; *Opportunities*

Abroad for Teachers; *Inventory of Federal Programs Involving Education Activities Concerned with Improving International Understanding and Cooperation*; and *Asian Studies in American Secondary Education.*

OFFICE OF INTERNATIONAL EDUCATION
7th and D Streets, S.W.
Washington, D.C. 20202
Kenneth Whitehead, Acting Director
(202) 245-9692

The Office of International Education is responsible for expanding the international and global dimensions of the United States education system and for promoting awareness of other cultures. Its activities include training, curriculum development, research, exchange, and a wide range of services in the field of international education.

A clearinghouse, within the office, responds to inquiries about student-exchange programs, regular academic-year-abroad programs, general educational tours for teachers and students, overseas employment, and programs of financial assistance to foreign students. Some useful publications available from the clearinghouse include: *International Education Programs and Services* (1980); *Study and Teaching Abroad* (1980); *International Teacher Exchange* (1975); and *Selected U.S. Office of Education Publications to Further International Education* (1977).

Also within the Office of International Education is the Dissemination Specialist responsible for coordinating an information network for the advancement of international education among the states, local-education agencies, and institutions of higher education and international organizations.

DIVISION OF ADVANCED TRAINING AND RESEARCH
Richard Thompson, Director
(202) 245-2356

The division administers domestic and overseas programs in foreign language and area studies as authorized by Title VI of the National Defense Education Act of 1958 (NDEA), as amended, and the National Defense Education Act of 1961 (Fulbright-Hays). For statistical information on these programs, see the annual *Fact Book* of the Bureau of Higher and Continuing Education.

Centers and Fellowship Branch
Joseph Belmonte, Chief
(202) 245-2356

This branch provides grants to higher-education institutions and consortia for the establishment of multidisciplinary international studies programs, and foreign-language and area-studies centers at the undergraduate and graduate levels. Currently, there are four Southeast Asian Studies Centers: Cornell University (Stanley J. O'Connor, 607/256-2378); University of Hawaii (Albert Moscotti, 808/948-8439); University of Michigan (Aram Yangoyan, 313/764-0352); and University of Wisconsin (Daniel Doeppers, 608/263-1755). For further information call the Centers Program Specialist (202/245-9588).

The branch also provides grants to higher-education institutions, organizations, and individuals to support surveys and studies to determine the need for increased or improved instruction in modern foreign languages and area and international studies. Interested persons may wish to obtain the publication *Foreign Language Area and Other International Studies, A Bibliography of Research and Instructional Materials.*

Comparative Education Branch
Seymour Rosen, Acting Chief
(202) 245-7401

This branch conducts research and compiles studies on the educational systems of other countries. Southeast Asia–related materials include: *Selected Bibliography on Education in Southeast Asia* (1963); *Educational Data: Burma* (1965); and *Overseas Chinese Education in Indonesia* (1965). Also available is a list of comparative-eduation publications. The branch also provides U.S. educational institutions, agencies, organizations, and individuals with consultative and technical assistance on education systems abroad. Staff reference files, containing reports and documents of U.S. embassies, international organizations, education ministries, and universities in Southeast Asian countries, may be used by researchers.

Research Branch
Julia Petrov, Chief
(202) 245-2794

The Fellowships and Overseas Projects Section (John Paul, 202/245-2356) administers several programs, including the Foreign Language and Area Studies Fellowship Program for graduate students (202/245-9808), the Doctoral Dissertation Research Abroad Program (202/245-2761), providing assistance for graduate students to engage in full-time dissertation research abroad in modern foreign languages and area studies; and the Faculty Research Abroad Program (202/245-2794), designed to assist higher education institutions in strengthening their international studies program.

DIVISION OF INTERNATIONAL SERVICE AND IMPROVEMENT
Ms. Pat K. McIntire, Acting Director
(202) 245-9700

Within this division there are two branches of particular interest to Southeast Asianists.

International Studies Branch
Ralph Hines, Acting Chief
(202) 245-2794

The Group Projects Abroad Program provides grants to U.S. educational institutions or nonprofit educational organizations for training, research, advanced foreign-language training, curriculum development, and instructional materials acquisition in international and intercultural studies. Participants may include college and university faculty members, experienced elementary and secondary school teachers, curriculum supervisors, and administrators, and selected higher-education students specializing in foreign-language and area studies.

A second program of interest is Undergraduate International Studies, which provides grants to institutions of higher education, or consortia, to develop international or global studies programs at the undergraduate level. These programs are of two years' duration and are nonrenewable.

Also within the branch is the Foreign Curriculum Consultant Program, which brings experts from other countries to the U.S. for an academic year to assist American educational institutions in planning and developing their curricula in foreign languages and area studies. State departments of education, large school systems, smaller four-year colleges with teacher-education programs, and groups of community colleges are given priority in securing consultants' services.

Teacher Exchange Branch
Ms. Pat K. McIntire, Chief
(202) 245-9700

Within this branch are two programs of interest, "Seminars Abroad" and "Teacher Exchange." The seminars program provides opportunities for teachers at the elementary, secondary, and college level to participate in a variety of short-term seminars (usually six-to-eight weeks) abroad on a selection of topics. Opportunities for Southeast Asianists do exist. Program deadline for application is November 1.

The Teacher Exchange Program provides opportunities for elementary and secondary school teachers and, in some cases, college instructors and assistant professors, to teach outside the United States. Various arrangements are made by the U.S. government with other countries to provide for a direct exchange of teachers. Currently, most exchanges are with West European countries. However, opportunities for Southeast Asianists may exist in the future.

NATIONAL INSTITUTE OF EDUCATION (NIE)
1200 19th Street, N.W.
Washington, D.C. 20208
Edward Curran, Director
(202) 254-5740

Researchers will be interested in the Educational Resource Information Center (ERIC), with computerized data bases (see entry G6). This system contains bibliographic information on international education (including that of Southeast Asia) and related subjects. Two publications of interest are: *Directory of ERIC Collections in the Washington, D.C. Area,* and *Survey of ERIC Data Base Search Services.*

Note: See also entries A32 and G6.

K13 Energy Department (DOE)

1.   a. *Forrestal Building*
1000 Independence Avenue, S.W.
Washington, D.C. 20545
(202) 252-5565

b. Open to the public. Appointment recommended. Some DOE files and documents are classified. Inquiries should be directed to the Freedom of Information and Privacy Activities Division (Milton Jordan, 202/252-6020).

2. The Department of Energy was established in 1977 to provide the framework for a comprehensive and balanced national energy plan through the coordination and administration of the energy functions of the federal government. DOE's responsibilities include research, development, and demonstration of energy technology; energy conservation; a nuclear weapons program; regulation of energy production and use; and a central energy data collection and analysis program. Many of the activities of the department are international in dimension. Research is both in-house and by outside contract. Contract research on Southeast Asia is limited.

3. The Energy Department Library is a major repository of energy-related information and consists of three separate facilities. The largest of these is the Germantown library (Germantown, Maryland 20545, Denise B. Diggin, Chief, 301/353-2855), which consists of approximately 85,000 cataloged and 20,000 uncataloged volumes. Also included are some 2,000 items of the International Atomic Energy Agency publications; 2,500 current, professional journal subscriptions; approximately 650,000 uncataloged technical reports; and a large collection of congressional reports and documents. Primary focus of the collection is on energy resources and management; economic, environmental, and social effects of energy; and water resources. Southeast Asia material is limited. Interlibrary loan and photoduplication facilities are available. See entry A13.

4. Some publications of interest include: *Guide for the Submission of Unsolicited Proposals* (1980); *The DOE Program Guide for Universities and other Research Groups* (1980); *Energy Abstracts for Policy Analysis*, a monthly, containing worldwide abstracts of journal articles and books on energy analysis; *Annual Report to Congress*, with statistical charts and tables on Southeast Asia; *Energy Meetings*, a listing of conferences, symposia, workshops, congresses and other formal meetings pertaining to DOE's programmatic interests; and the *First Annual Report on Nuclear Non-Proliferation* (1979). Most of these publications are available free in the Office of Public Information Administration (Forrestal Building, Room GA-343, 202/252-6827). Below are described those departmental subdivisions of potential interest to Southeast Asianists.

INTERNATIONAL AFFAIRS (IA)
1000 Independence Avenue, S.W.
Washington, D.C. 20585
Henry Thomas, Assistant Secretary
(202) 252-5800

Charged with formulating U.S. international energy policy, this office is responsible for developing, managing, and directing programs and activities that support U.S. energy and foreign policy. The office assesses world price and supply trends, as well as technological developments, and it studies the effects of international actions on U.S. energy supplies. IA also coordinates cooperative international energy programs and maintains relationships with foreign governments and international organizations. This office prepares the periodically updated unclassified report, *International Bilateral and Multilateral Arrangements in Energy Technology*.

INTERNATIONAL OIL, GAS AND COAL PROGRAMS
Denis O'Brian, Acting Deputy Assistant Secretary
(202) 252-5918

This division monitors world energy markets and trade.

Office of Consumer and Producer Nations
Al Hegburg, Director
(202) 252-6777

This office analyzes worldwide oil production, including that of OPEC (a member of which is Indonesia), and seeks to determine the effect oil and other energy resource production and pricing have on consuming nations. Tom Cutler monitors Southeast Asia within this office.

INTERNATIONAL NUCLEAR AND TECHNICAL PROGRAMS
Holsey Handyside, Deputy Assistant Secretary
(202) 252-5921

Within this division are two offices which oversee a number of nuclear and technical assistance programs.

Office of International R and D Cooperation
Jack Vanderryn, Director
(202) 252-6140

This office is involved around the world in various research, development, and demonstration projects related to energy technology. In 1982 there were no projects related to the countries of Southeast Asia.

Office of International Nuclear Non-Proliferation Policy
Harold D. Bengelsdorf, Director
(202) 252-6175

This office is in charge of the development and implementation of DOE's nuclear energy policy and maintains data on the nuclear technology of various foreign countries. The office also assists in negotiations for bilateral and multilateral cooperative nuclear agreements and is concerned with nuclear proliferation. The staff includes engineers, physicists, and other technical experts.

OFFICE OF MARKET ANALYSIS
Guy Caruso, Director
(202) 252-5893

Researchers may wish to obtain a copy of *The Role of Foreign Governments in the Energy Industries* (October 1977), which is available from this office.

K14 Environmental Protection Agency (EPA)

1.   a. *401 M Street, S.W.*
      Washington, D.C. 20460
      (202) 755-0707

     b. Open to the public. Appointments are recommended.

     c. Anne M. Gorsuch, Administrator

2.	The EPA supports both in-house and contract research and participates in cooperative environmental research on an international level. Most of these programs and projects are coordinated through a single office.

INTERNATIONAL ACTIVITIES OFFICE
Richard Funkhouser, Director
(202) 755-2780

The international activities of EPA are designed to encourage worldwide cooperation in studying and overcoming long-range environmental problems. In pursuing this goal, the EPA maintains contacts with scientists and policy makers from other countries and international organizations.

BILATERAL PROGRAMS DIVISION
Thomas J. LePine, Chief
(202) 755-0523

Bilateral activities include exchanging environmental information and supplying U.S. experts for training and support of environmental research programs abroad. Currently, there are no EPA projects in Southeast Asia, and none are likely until the current budgetary problems are resolved. EPA does maintain informal contact with some of the countries in our region and has supplied technical assistance, through AID, to Indonesia for an environmental survey, and to Thailand for studying problems associated with the use of pesticides. Jane Lovelace, International Program officer (202/755-2780), is the point of contact for Southeast Asianists.

An EPA publication, *Scientific Activities Overseas Programs* (1979), provides a cumulative listing of projects funded from the excess foreign currency program. EPA international activities are briefly summarized in a series of pamphlets, such as *EPA and the World Health Organization,* and *EPA and the United Nations Environmental Program.* A folder, *International Activities of the United States Environmental Protection Agency,* may be obtained free from Janet Fisher, International Visitor coordinator in the Office of International Activities (202/755-9321).

3.	The EPA Headquarters Library (Sami Klein, librarian, 202/755-0308) contains over 7,000 monographs, 180,000 documents and reports and 1,000 periodical subscriptions. The collection is predominantly technical in nature, focusing on pollution and ecology, and is open to the public for on-site use from 8:00 A.M. to 5:00 P.M., Monday through Friday. Reference tools include card catalogs and the quarterly *EPA Reports Bibliography,* available at the National Technical Information Service (see entry Q19). There is also a *Guide to EPA Libraries* available free.

EPA's International Environment Referral Center (Carol Alexander, director, 202/755-1836) has a collection of miscellaneous foreign environmental documents acquired during the years 1972 to 1976 through bilateral information-exchange programs. The collection may be examined by outside researchers. A country index is available. The center also maintains an international directory of environmental information for some 70 participating countries of the U.S. Environmental Program—International Referral System. (See entry G12.)

4.	A monthly publication on EPA overseas activities, *Summaries of Foreign Government Environment Reports,* is distributed by the National Technical

Information Service. Other publications of interest include: *Air Pollution Translations Bibliography with Abstracts*; the annual *Environmental Protection Research Catalog*, which lists all projects funded by the EPA; and the monthly *Air Pollution Abstracts*, which catalogs all journal articles and technical reports on the subject of air pollution.

K15 Export-Import Bank of the United States (Eximbank)

1.   a. *811 Vermont Avenue, N.W.*
Washington, D.C. 20571
(202) 566-8990 (Public Affairs)
(202) 566-2117 (Information)

b. Open to the public. Internal records are restricted.

c. William H. Draper, President

2.   The Eximbank is an independent agency of the U.S. government, providing loans, guarantees, and insurance to facilitate the financing of U.S. exports. The bank's staff, working with both the State and Commerce Departments, assesses the ability of foreign buyers to pay for U.S. imports. Individual country loan records are confidential, though staff officers will discuss general questions with researchers.

DIRECT CREDIT AND FINANCIAL GUARANTEES
Charles Houston, Vice President, Asia Division
(202) 566-8885

International economists and loan officers maintain confidential-loan project files and prepare country and regional studies on economic conditions and the credit worthiness of Asian countries. The loan officers for Southeast Asia are: Kenneth Wickett (202/566-8223), Indonesia and Malaysia; Raymond Ellis (202/566-8956), Singapore and Thailand; Barbara O'Boyle (202/566-8097), Burma; and Terrance Hulihan (202/566-4632), the Philippines. For country studies, contact the following economists: Howard Turk (202/566-8009), Indonesia, Malaysia, Singapore, and Thailand; Alice Mayo (202/566-8966), Burma; and Russell Price (202/566-8915), the Philippines.

POLICY ANALYSIS DIVISION
James Cruse, Vice President
(202) 566-8861

The division prepares studies on international economic developments and their impact on the EXIMBANK and its programs. Research fields include methodologies for economic analysis and review of bank programs, export financing activities in the U.S. and abroad, worldwide trends in individual industries and commodities, international and domestic capital-market developments, and fluctuations in interest rates, prices, and other economic indicators. Most of these studies are restricted.

3.   The EXIMBANK Library (Theodora McGill, librarian, 202/566-8320) is open to the public from 7:30 A.M. to 5:30 P.M., Monday through Friday. Interlibrary loan services are available. There are no photoduplication fa-

cilities. The library's small, but specialized, holdings of approximately 15,000 books and 950 periodical subscriptions concentrate on international banking, finance, commerce, trade, and developmental economics. Southeast Asian materials consist of Central Bank statistical reports from Thailand, Philippine Central Bank reports, and economic statistics from Indonesia. A periodical list is available upon request. A card catalog arranged alphabetically by country provides access to the collection.

4.   An annual, priced publication, *Report to Congress,* lists credits, guarantees, and insurance authorized for each country in the previous year. Other publications include: *Export-Import Bank of the United States,* which describes its history, operations, and programs; *Eximbank Record,* a monthly newsletter; *Eximbank-Export Financing for: American Exporters, Overseas Buyers, Banks* (1978), and *Businessman's Guide to the Cooperative Financing Facility* (1978).

Most of the bank's internal records, research reports, and loan project files are restricted. Researchers may request access under the provisions of the Freedom of Information Act (202/566-8864). Most internal records are under the custody of the Records and Central Files Manager (Helene H. Wall, 202/585-8815) in the Administration Office. The EXIMBANK is currently reproducing its records from 1937 to 1967 in microform, with the originals being transferred to the custody of the National Archives. It is also developing an automated indexing system for its active loan project records.

K16 Federal Reserve System

1.   a. *20th Street and Constitution Avenue, N.W.*
       Washington, D.C. 20551

     b. Open to the public. Appointments are recommended.

     c. Paul A. Volcker, Chairman

2.   The Federal Reserve System serves as the central bank of the United States. The foreign related activities of interest to Southeast Asianists fall within the responsibilities of the Division of International Finance.

INTERNATIONAL FINANCE DIVISION
Edwin M. Truman, Director
(202) 452-3614

This division monitors U.S. balance of payments, movements in exchange rates and transactions in foreign-exchange markets, capital flows between the U.S. and foreign financial centers, and other economic and financial developments abroad that may have an impact on U.S. monetary policy. In addition, this division assists the Federal Reserve in its advisory and consultative role within the U.S. government in discussions of international financial matters; in directing U.S. participation in various international financial and monetary organizations; and in maintaining informational contacts with the central banks of other countries. The division also collects and analyzes information and data relating to the activities of U.S. banks abroad and foreign banks in the U.S.

Within the division, basic research and analysis is conducted by staff economists who are organized into several functional sections listed below.

INTERNATIONAL DEVELOPMENT SECTION
David Dod, Chief
(202) 452-3784

This section focuses on the economic and financial problems and policies of the developing countries. Southeast Asia is covered by Bob Emry (202/452-2372).

INTERNATIONAL BANKING SECTION
Henry Terrell, Chief
(202) 452-3768

U.S. INTERNATIONAL TRANSACTIONS SECTION
Peter Clark
(202) 452-3728

This section follows international trade and capital movements and their influences on the United States economy.

FINANCIAL MARKETS SECTION
Ralph Smith, Chief
(202) 452-3312

Financial Markets Section analyzes the behavior of international capital centers and exchange markets.

WORLD PAYMENTS AND ECONOMIC ACTIVITY SECTION
Raymond Lubitz, Chief
(202) 452-3533

Examines economic trends and policies of the major industrial nations.

INTERNATIONAL TRADE AND FINANCIAL STUDIES SECTION
Guy Stevens, Chief
(202) 452-4708

The section prepares long-range theoretical research studies on international economic problems.

QUANTITATIVE STUDIES SECTION
Peter Hooper, Chief
(202) 452-3775

Develops and maintains econometric models on U.S.–foreign economic interdependence.

INTERNATIONAL INFORMATION CENTER
Cynthia Sutton, Supervisor
(202) 452-3411

The center may be especially useful to researchers. Although a large portion of its collection is classifed, including 45 drawers of documents and approximately one-half of its 35 drawer collection of telegrams; the remaining telegrams plus an additional 5 shelves of documents are unclassified. The holdings contain the research reports, briefing papers and internal papers produced by the division of International Finance along with microfiche copies of documents from other U.S. government agencies, the IMF, the IBRD, and other international organizations. Access to the center is restricted, and scholars must make special arrangements in advance.

3. The Research Library of the Board of Governors (Ann Roane Clary, chief librarian, 202/452-3398) is open to the public from 9:00 A.M. to 5:00 P.M. on Thursdays, and is open to scholars by special arrangement. Interlibrary loan and limited photocopying facilities are available. The collection consists of some 90,000 monographic volumes and 2,300 current periodical subscriptions. The subject strengths in the collection are in the areas of banking, monetary policy, and economic conditions in the United States and abroad. Researchers may note that the library's holdings contain a good number of foreign monetary and banking laws, publications of the foreign central banks, and official statistical releases of more than 100 foreign countries. A biweekly *Research Library Recent Acquisitions* and a computer-generated printout of the library's periodicals are available.

4. *Federal Reserve Board Publications* lists all major publications and staff studies of the Federal Reserve System. *Federal Reserve System Purposes and Functions* (1979) is a handbook presenting a concise account of the responsibilities and operating techniques of the system in the areas of monetary policy, banking and financial regulations, and international finance. Statistical releases and staff studies are published from time to time in the monthly *Federal Reserve Bulletin*. The system's annual report provides useful summaries of its activities.

All requests for access to classified records and documents should be directed to Rose Arnold (202/452-3684), the system's Freedom of Information Officer.

K17 General Accounting Office (GAO)

1. a. *441 G Street, N.W.*
    Washington, D.C. 20548
    (202) 275-2872

    b. Open to the public, previous appointment recommended.

    c. Milton Socolar, Comptroller General

2. An independent agency in the legislative branch of the government, the GAO assists the Congress and its committees and members in carrying out legislative and supervisory responsibilities. Most GAO research is conduced in-house; however, consulting opportunities are also available.

    INTERNATIONAL DIVISION
    Frank C. Conahan, Director
    (202) 275-5518

    This division has produced a significant number of research reports on Southeast Asia. Several groups in this division evaluate the effectiveness of U.S. foreign aid and military-assistance programs; study the impact of U.S. policy on U.S. trade and international financial status; and review all bilateral and multilateral programs and agreements in order to determine whether the intended objectives and purposes as laid down in those programs and agreements have been realized. Evaluation reports on Southeast Asia include: *Review of U.S. Security Consultation and Joint Defense Planning with East Asia and West Pacific Allies* (1981) and *Management of Security Assistance Programs Overseas—Needs To Be Improved* (1978). While some of these reports are classified, most are unclassified and can be obtained on request. For further information, contact Samuel Bowlin (Development Assistance Group, 202/275-5790); Joe T. Kelly (Security and International Relations Group, 202/275-5857); and Allan Mendelowitz (Trade and Finance Group, 202/275-5889).

3.   The General Accounting Office Library (Phyllis Christensen, director, 202/275-3691), including its two constituents, the Technical Library (202/275-5030) and the Law Library (202/275-2585), is open to the public for on-site use from 8:00 A.M. to 4:45 P.M., Monday through Friday. Interlibrary loan and photoduplication facilities are available. The collection consists primarily of materials in the areas of program evaluation, policy analysis, energy, accounting, law, and civilian and military regulatory materials. The library maintains current and retrospective files of most GAO special reports and annual reports. Southeast Asia materials are limited.

4.   GAO's principal publication is its annual *Report to the Congress,* which includes comments on the financial administration of U.S. programs for developing countries. Also available free is a semiannual *Publication List,* which contains information about other special country reports and program target evaluations.

      GAO's Freedom of Information Officer is Nola Casieri (202/275-6172). For information concerning retired and inactive files, contact Shirley Allen (202/275-6213) in the Records Management Branch. Microfilm copies of some of the documents transferred to the National Archives may be available in the library.

K18 Health and Human Services Department

1.   a. *200 Independence Avenue, S.W.*
      Washington, D.C. 20201
      (202) 245-1850

      b. Open to the public.

2.   The Department of Health and Human Services, renamed from the Department of Health, Education and Welfare, works to protect and advance the health of the American people and provides essential human services to improve the American quality of life. Some department activities are, however, international in scope. Currently the department administers more than 300 programs. Research is conducted in-house and by outside consultants.

3.   The National Library of Medicine is described is entry A33.

4.   Selected publications are noted under the concerned units. Additional information is available in the annually updated *Publications Catalog of the*

U.S. Department of Health, Education and Welfare. Most of the documents and records are open to the public. The department's Privacy Act officer is Hugh O'Neill (202/472-7453). Russell M. Roberts is the Freedom of Information officer (202/472-7453).

PUBLIC HEALTH SERVICE
Edward N. Brandt, Assistant Secretary for Health
(202) 245-7694

The Public Health Service is charged by law to promote and assure the highest level of health attainable for every individual and family in America. The Public Health Service is also responsible for developing cooperation in health projects with other nations.

OFFICE OF INTERNATIONAL HEALTH (IH)
John N. Bryant, Deputy Assistant Secretary
(202) 443-1774

This office is the focal point for the over-all coordination and support of the international health activities of the Public Health Service. IH is concerned with health conditions in foreign countries and the evaluation of national and international efforts directed towards improving these conditions.

Program and Policy Analysis Division
Linda Bogel, Acting Director
(202) 443-4550

In cooperation with the Agency for International Development, this division prepares a series of intermittent, priced monographs, entitled *Syncrises: the Dynamics of Health,* on the interactions of health and socio-economic development in various countries. Thus far, *Syncrises* have been published on the Philippines (1972) and Thailand (1974). These publications are available from the NTIS (see entry Q19).

Bilateral Program Division
Linda Bogel, Acting Director
(202) 443-1774

This division is responsible for all U.S. bilateral programs for our region. Linda Bogel is the point of contact for the division's Southeast Asia activities. The annual *Report on the Health, Population and Nutrition Activities of the Agency for International Development,* prepared by the Office of International Health, is available without charge.

NATIONAL CENTER FOR HEALTH STATISTICS
3700 East-West Highway
Hyattsville, Maryland 20782
Dorothy P. Rice, Director
(301) 436-7016

The center collects and disseminates data on health in the U.S. and also fosters research, consultations, and training programs in international health.

Office of International Statistics
Dr. Alvan O. Zarate, Assistant Director
(301) 436-7039

Useful publications from this office include: *Current Listing and Topical Index to the Vital and Health Statistics Series, 1962–1973,* and the annual *Catalog of Publications of the National Center for Health Statistics.* Both are available free.

ALCOHOL, DRUG ABUSE, AND MENTAL HEALTH ADMINISTRATION (ADAMHA)
5600 Fisher's Lane
Rockville, Maryland 20857
William Mayer, Administrator
(301)443-4797

Through its three institutes, the National Institute of Alcohol Abuse and Alcoholism (301/443-3885), the National Institute of Drug Abuse (301/443-6480), and the National Institute of Mental Health (301/443-3673), the administration spearheads the federal effort to prevent and treat problems related to alcohol, drug abuse, and mental and emotional illness. Through its international activities office, the ADAMHA carries on extensive health-related social and behavioral science research programs in many foreign countries.

International Activities Office
Berkeley Hathorne, Director
(301) 443-2600

The International Activities Office maintains contract-research project files and can provide assistance to researchers seeking access to pertinent sources of information. For information on ADAMHA–funded research projects, see the annual *Alcohol, Drug Abuse, Mental Health Research Grant Awards.* It may also be noted that each of the three component institutes of the administration mentioned above has its own information clearinghouse equipped with automated bibliographic data files. Courtesy services are provided to serious researchers in these clearinghouses: National Clearinghouse for Mental Health Information (301/443-4517); National Clearinghouse for Drug Abuse Information (301/443-6500); National Clearinghouse for Alcohol Information (301/468-2600).

NATIONAL INSTITUTES OF HEALTH (NIH)
9000 Rockville Pike
Bethesda, Maryland 20205
Thomas Malone, Acting Director
(301) 496-4461

A leading biomedical research facility in the world, the NIH also encourages international contacts and exchange of scientific knowledge.

FOGARTY INTERNATIONAL CENTER
Mark S. Beaubien, Acting Director
(301) 496-1415

Established in 1968, the center coordinates the agency's participation in international biomedical and behavioral research. The center's International Research and Awards Branch (Betty Graham, 301/496-6688) administers a competitive postdoctoral fellowships program. Currently the program is limited to the Philippines and Thailand. The International Coordination Liaison Branch (Philip Schambra, 301/486-5903) has published a number of studies of health in individual foreign countries. To date, no such studies have been done for Southeast Asia.

Following is a selected list of publications produced by the center: *Annual Report of International Activities,* which contains a description of various international programs and a list of research grants and contracts to foreign institutions and fellowships to foreign scientists; *National Institute of Health; International Awards for Biomedical Research and Research Training* (annual), which includes information on international conferences funded by NIH; and *National Institute of Health: Statistical Reference Book of International Activities,* with summaries of activities, research grants, and contracts.

Research Grants Division
Carl D. Douglass, Director
(301) 496-7211

This division serves as the central research fund granting agency of the department for health related projects. Research proposals from American scholars interested in conducting research abroad in the health sciences are processed by this office. The division's Research Documentation Section (John C. James, 301/496-7795), in addition to publishing the annual *Research Grants Index,* maintains CRISP, a computerized search service, which gives information about the scientific and fiscal aspects of research projects supported by the various research-grants programs of the NIH and other components of the Department of Health and Human Services.

The institute's National Library of Medicine (see entry A33), in cooperation with the Educational Commission for Foreign Medical Graduates, compiles the *Foreign Medical Graduates in the United States,* which includes information on the education of foreign medical graduates abroad, the flow of these graduates to the U.S., and their training and utilization in American medicine. The library's International Program (Mary E. Corning, 301/496-6481) is also responsible for various comparative undertakings in the developing world to improve library and health information services.

HEALTH RESOURCES ADMINISTRATION
3700 East-West Highway
Hyattsville, Maryland 20782
Robert Graham, Acting Administrator
(301) 436-7200

Office of International Affairs
James Mahoney, Acting Director
(301) 436-7179

This office coordinates programs in health, manpower-planning, and health-information assistance. Currently, there are no programs for Southeast Asia, though the office is involved in other Asian countries.

HEALTH SERVICE ADMINISTRATION
5600 Fishers Lane
Rockville, Maryland 20857
John H. Kelso, Acting Administrator
(301) 443-2216

Contact William R. Gemma (301/443-6152) for information on the administration's international activities. There are no programs for Southeast Asia at present.

FOOD AND DRUG ADMINISTRATION
5600 Fishers Lane
Rockville, Maryland 20857
Arthur H. Hayes, Jr., Commissioner
(301) 443-2410

The International Affairs staff (301/443-4400), including John Holton, desk officer for Asia and Western Pacific (301/443-4480) and Barbara H. Van Schoick, PL480 research coordinator (301/443-4480), may be contacted about activities related to Southeast Asia. Also contact Robert W. Week (202/426-8998) international studies assistant to the director of the Bureau of Food.

SOCIAL SECURITY ADMINISTRATION
Office of Research and Statistics
1875 Connecticut Avenue, N.W.
Washington, D.C. 20009
John J. Carroll, Director
(202) 673-5620

The Social Security Administration operates the world's largest social insurance program. The administration acquires, through its Comparative International Studies staff (Elizabeth Singleton, 202/673-5714), comparative data from other countries concerning unemployment insurance, health-care systems, workmen's compensation, and other similar programs. The staff also prepares analytical studies on selected aspects of social security systems in individual foreign countries. A forthcoming publication on international studies by the Social Security Administration will list these country studies.

A comprehensive review of social security programs in some 130 nations is reported in a biennial publication entitled *Social Security Programs throughout the World*. It is supplemented by monthly items in the *Social Security Bulletin* and in occasional research notes. The administration has also published *The Role of Social Security in Economic Development*, a special report of a 1967 seminar sponsored by the administration, and the *Role of Social Security in Developing Countries* (1963, reprint 1967), a study prepared by the Social Security Administration for the Agency for International Development.

A reference room, open to the public, is maintained by the Comparative Studies staff (Ilene Zeitzer, 202/673-5713) and contains a good collection of books, periodicals, and country files.

K19 Housing and Urban Development Department (HUD)

1. a. *451 7th Street, S.W.*
    Washington, D.C. 20410
    (202) 755-5111

    b. Open to the public.

2. In addition to its domestic responsibilities for programs concerned with housing needs, fair-housing opportunities, and urban development, the department is also involved in cooperating with many foreign countries and international organizations.

OFFICE OF INTERNATIONAL AFFAIRS (OIA)
Theodore R. Britton, Jr., Assistant to the Secretary for International Affairs
(202) 755-7058

The OIA assists in the formulation of HUD policy relating to bilateral and multilateral agreements and projects in housing and urban affairs. The office also manages the visitors' program of the department. Although technical research programs, support for research, and educational activities have been scaled down, the staff can provide documentation in response to written requests as well as assist in planning, procedures, and project evaluations.

The OIA recruits technical advisors to serve AID and other U.S. government agencies overseas. A pamphlet, *HUD International Programs and Activities* is available without cost.

An automated foreign information retrieval system (FIRS) of bibliographic reference, on the subjects of housing and urban affairs, is maintained in the OIA. Indexed by subject, country and author, the system may be searched without fee. Susan Judd, information specialist (202/755-5770) can assist researchers with questions.

3. The HUD library is located in Room 8141 (Elsa Freeman, director, 202/755-6370) and is open to the public Monday through Friday from 8:30 A.M. to 5:15 P.M. Interlibrary loan and photoduplication services are available. The library contains nearly 500,000 items including some 2,000 periodical titles. Principal focus of the collection is on American housing, urban planning and development, and related socioeconomic issues. Southeast Asia–related materials are not a major resource. Library holdings are published in the 19-volume *Dictionary Catalog of the United States Department of Housing and Urban Development Library and Information Division* (Boston: G.K. Hall, 1972). A first supplement appeared in 1974. In addition, researchers may consult the bimonthly *Housing and Planning Reference,* which indexes current literature on housing and planning, and the semimonthly *HUD Library Recent Acquisitions.* The library also prepares a reference guide entitled *Bibliography on Housing, Building and Planning for Use of Overseas Missions of the United States Agency for International Development.*

4. The Office of International Affairs publishes *HUD International Country Reports,* a series of reports on housing and related subjects in developing countries. This series is designed to assist in the orientation of AID personnel and American businesses interested in foreign investments, but there are no reports on Southeast Asian countries as of this writing. Other publications include the quarterly *HUD International Review,* the *HUD International Newsletter*; and *International Information Sources.*

HUD's Freedom of Information officer is Velma I. Chandler (202/755-6420).

K20 Interior Department

1. a. *18th and C Streets, N.W.*
   Washington, D.C. 20240
   (202) 343-3171 (Information)

2. The principal responsibility of the Interior Department is the administration of nationally owned public lands and natural resources. However, several agencies within the department also conduct in-house research, gather data about—and promote—information and visitor exchanges with countries in Southeast Asia. Outside scholars are used as consultants occasionally.

3. The Interior Department's Natural Resources Library (Philip Haymond, director, 202/343-5815) is open to the public for on-site use from 7:45 A.M. to 5:00 P.M., Monday through Friday. Interlibrary loan and photoduplication services are available. Holdings consist of over 1,000,000 bound volumes, 21,000 serial titles, 250,000 microfiche, and 8,100 reels of microfilm. There are some 500 items relating to Southeast Asia. A dictionary catalog and the published *Dictionary Catalog of the Departmental Library* provides access to the collection. (See entry A22.)

TERRITORIAL AND INTERNATIONAL AFFAIRS
Pedro Sanjuan, Assistant Secretary
(202) 343-4736

This office is not involved with programs or activities that are Southeast Asia-related, per se, but researchers will find it very useful to contact International Program Officer Robert Sturgill (202/343-3101) about past and current department programs and activities that do relate to Southeast Asia.

BUREAU OF MINES
2401 E Street N.W.
Washington, D.C. 20241
Robert C. Horton, Director
(202) 634-1300

FOREIGN DATA BRANCH
Donald S. Colby, Chief
202/634-8970

Within this branch is the Far East and Southeast Asia Office (Edmond Chin, 202/634-1274), which gathers data and carries out research on minerals development within the countries of the East and Southeast Asia regions. Country files are maintained in the office and may be used by researchers. Staff members are available for consultation.

Staff members prepare testimony for congressional hearings, conduct fact-finding missions to Southeast Asia, and write chapters for several Interior Department publications including the three-volume annual *Minerals Yearbook*. Individual chapters of this publication are released as preprints through the *Information Circulars* series. Individual preprints are available on the mineral industries of Burma, Indonesia, Malaysia, the Philippines, and Thailand. The countries of Brunei, Laos, Singapore, and Vietnam are covered in a preprint entitled *The Mineral Industry of Other Areas of the Far East and South Asia.* Two additional publications of interest are *Mineral Perspectives—Far East and South Asia,* which gives a concise summary and a map of the mineral industries for the countries of Southeast Asia, and *Mineral Commodity Summaries 1981,* which contains comparative data for mineral commodities.

U.S. GEOLOGICAL SURVEY (USGS)
National Center
12201 Sunrise Valley Drive
Reston, Virginia 22092
Dallas L. Peck, Director
(703) 860-6118

The USGS—under the auspices of AID, international organizations, and sometimes a foreign government—plays a significant role in foreign assistance programs, including training of foreign geologists and hydrologists in their own countries and in the U.S., the development of geological and hydrological services within a particular country, and other special projects. USGS staff members seek to collaborate with their foreign counterparts in obtaining information needed to prepare comprehensive geological and resource maps of the developing nations.

GEOLOGIC DIVISION
Robert M. Hamilton, Chief Geologist
(703) 860-6531

International Geology Office
John A. Reinemund, Chief
(703) 860-6418

There are a significant number of Southeast Asia-related programs and activities for which this office is responsible. Currently, there are programs in Indonesia, Malaysia, Thailand, and the Philippines.

In Indonesia the office currently has a four-year program that includes: a geologic-hazard assessment project, part of which is a volcanologic study; an earthquake monitoring study; coal basin analysis; geochemical analysis and laboratory design; and a study of the environmental setting of Kalimantan as it relates to the Indonesian government's transmigration project. In all, there are sixteen different projects in Indonesia that span the geosciences. A small permanent staff was augmented by nineteen temporary employees in 1982, and plans are underway to add thirty more.

There are two programs in progress in Malaysia. Under a bilateral arrangement with the Malaysian government, consultation services are being rendered for the development of a computer data system for the national oil company. The second project is concerned with the development of conservation measures and the establishment of laws to govern off-shore drilling for petroleum.

In Thailand the International Geology Office has been involved in a potash development study, the development of a computer data base for a mineral exploration guide, and studies for the economic exploitation of oil shale and lignite resources. The office has completed an economic feasibility study of the potential for geothermal development. Future projects may include studies on tin and uranium development.

The program of longest duration has been in the Philippines where extensive research on chromite deposits has been undertaken. In addition to the above, the IGO has played a major advisory role to the UN Economic and Social Commission for Asia and the Pacific (ESCAP) headquartered in Bangkok, Thailand. IGO has provided one nonreimbursable staff person for several years and plans to continue this service.

Besides John A. Reinemund, chief of IGO, as a good contact person, Maurice J. Terman (202/860-6555) of the Near Eastern and Asian Geology Branch will also take inquiries from researchers.

NATIONAL MAPPING DIVISION
Rupert B. Southard, Chief
(703) 860-6231

International Activities Office
Clifton J. Fry, Chief
(703) 860-6241

This office provides training support to foreign-government personnel who are responsible for publishing geologic maps and cartographic charts. The office also assists foreign visitors. In 1982, there was a small program involving Philippines government personnel, and there is a possibility of a program for the Thai government. Charles Morrison, program manager (703/860-6244) and Olga Marinenko (703/860-6441), can assist researchers with specific details about training programs.

PUBLICATIONS DIVISION
Gary W. North, Chief
(703) 860-7181

USGA publications on foreign assistance include: *Bibliography of Reports Resulting From U.S. Geological Survey Participation in the United States Technical Assistance Program, 1940–1967* (1968); *Bibliography of Reports Resulting from U.S. Geological Survey Technical Cooperation with other Countries, 1967–1974* (1975); *U.S. Geological Survey International Activities* (annual); *Historical Review of the International Water Resources Program of the U.S. Geological Survey, 1940–1970* (1976); *Worldwide Directory of National Earth-Science Agencies*; and *New Publications of the Geological Survey* (monthly). USGS publications may be obtained from the Distribution Branch, Geological Survey, 1200 South Eads Street, Arlington, Virginia 22202 (703/557-2751).

WATER RESOURCE DIVISION
Philip Cohen, Chief Hydrologist
(703) 860-6548

International Hydrology
Della Laura, Chief
(703) 860-6548

International Hydrology currently has one staff person in Indonesia working on a ground-water assessment project, which is part of the larger environmental study being conducted in Kalimantan by the International Geology office. In the past, International Hydrology has had personnel working in the Philippines.

LAND AND WATER RESOURCES
Garrey Carruthers, Assistant Secretary
(202) 343-2191

BUREAU OF RECLAMATION
18th and C Streets, N.W.
Washington, D.C. 20240
Robert N. Broadbent, Commissioner
(202) 343-4157

Foreign Activities
Marveen Sullivan, Staff Director
(202) 343-5236

Under a bilateral agreement concluded in early 1975 between the Bureau
of Reclamation and the Malaysian government's Ministry of Agriculture
and Rural Development, a six-person staff has been working in Malaysia
on studies and design for the Gombak dam. The Malaysian government
has requested the bureau to supervise construction of the facility.

NATIONAL PARK SERVICE
18th and C Streets, N.W.
Washington, D.C. 20240
Russell E. Dickenson, Director
(202) 343-4621

INTERNATIONAL PARK AFFAIRS DIVISION
Robert Milne, Chief
(202) 523-5260

The Park Service's activities in Southeast Asia are usually funded by other
U.S., international, or foreign government agencies and are primarily consultative. Currently, International Park Affairs is overseeing an AID–funded
project, under which the University of Arizona is preparing an environmental profile of Burma. This study is to be completed in late 1982; for
additional details, scholars may contact Bruce Powell (202/523-5260). International Park Affairs also maintains a useful reference library (David
Reynolds, 202/523-0151), which contains information pertaining to our region. Scholars are welcome to make on-site use of reference materials.

U.S. FISH AND WILDLIFE SERVICE
18th and C Streets, N.W.
Washington, D.C. 20240
Robert A. Jantzen, Director
(202) 343-4717

International Affairs Office
Lawrence N. Mason, Acting Chief
(202) 343-5188

The service currently has an AID–funded ($600,000, annually) project in
the Philippines to reduce the economic impact of ventehrate pests on agricultural production. The project requires one or two persons onsite and
will run through 1982. The Fish and Wildlife Service also has a program
to train people in fish-hatchery management. Under this program, person-

nel attend, in the U.S., a one-year course, which concentrates on fresh-water fisheries for species native to a particular country. Thus far, personnel from the Philippines have participated in this program.

Note: See also entries A17, A22, and E3.

K21 International Communication Agency (ICA)*

1.   a. *1750 Pennsylvania Avenue*
Washington, D. C. 20547
(202) 724-9103 (Information)

b. Open to the public. Advance appointment is recommended.

c. Charles Z. Wick, Director

2.   As a result of a 1977 reorganization, the International Communication Agency was established in April 1978, consolidating the United States In-formation Agency and the Bureau of Educational and Cultural Affairs of the State Department. The ICA has the responsibility of disseminating information about the U.S. abroad and leading educational and cultural exchange programs between the U.S. and other countries. Research is conducted in-house and on a contract basis, primarily on topics of inter-national public opinion and media-affairs.

3.   The ICA library is discussed in entry A23.

4.   ICA's legislative mandate prohibits dissemination within the United States of materials produced for distribution overseas. The agency publishes, in 16 languages, 14 magazines, most of which are printed at overseas Regional Service Centers and major posts. The magazines consist mainly of reprints from the best of American periodicals. Also pamphlets, leaflets, printed exhibits, and posters are distributed in more than 100 countries including all of Southeast Asia except Indochina. The principal publications of interest from the Washington, D.C., headquarters are: *Horizons USA,* a bimonthly in English; *Dialogue,* a scholarly quarterly in English; and *Economic Im-pact,* another English language quarterly. All ICA publications are free.

An agency automated data index system (DIS) (Katherine Shimabukuro, 202/523-4362) lists all agency documents generated since 1973, when the system went into operation; earlier materials are also being added to the system gradually. These documents, some of which are classified, deal with a variety of subjects, including message communications, internal memo-randa, country assessments, and research studies. DIS can be searched by date, subject, or geographic area. There is available an annual, computer-generated list of documents, declassified by the agency. Freedom of In-formation requests are handled by the Access to Information officer (Charles Jones, 202/724-9089) attached to the Office of Public Liaison.

*As of September 1982, the ICA reverted to its former name, United States Information Agency.

OFFICE OF EAST ASIA AND PACIFIC AFFAIRS
Clifton D. Forster, Director
(202) 724-9174

This office provides broad managerial oversight of the posts and programs in Southeast Asia, and relays area and post needs and perspectives to the core management and to functional officers of the agency. Country affairs officers are accessible to researchers and should have itinerary and background information on foreign visitors to the U.S. and should be knowledgeable about the ICA programs in the countries of their specialization. Patrick Hodai (202/724-9062) is the officer for the Philippines, Indonesia, Singapore, Malaysia, and Thailand. Edward Findlay (202/724-9145) is the officer for Burma and the Indochina States, Cambodia, Laos, and Vietnam.

ASSOCIATE DIRECTORATE FOR PROGRAMS (PGM)
John Hughes, Associate Director
(202) 724-9343

OFFICE OF RESEARCH
Gerald Hursh-Cesar, Acting Director
(202) 724-9545

The Media Reaction staff (202/724-9057) and East Asia and Pacific Research staff (Gordon Tubbs, chief, 202/724-9051) of this office evaluate ICA programs, survey public opinion, and analyze changes in the political power structure of Southeast Asian states. The information is used by ICA in assessing issues, and by the White House, the State Department, and other agencies of the government, as well. Unlike the agency's program materials, this research is accessible to scholars and others at forty depository libraries in universities and other institutions throughout the country.

The Office of Research is also responsible for the ICA Library (see entry A23) and the ICA Archive (202/724-9125), which is maintained in Room 532. The archive holds an extensive collection of historical records (such as congressional documents, agency records, and biographical registers, among others), dating from 1933 to the present, related to the ICA, USIA, and their predecessor agencies. Minutes of interagency meetings, cultural-exchange grant records, and other documents may also be found here. In addition, the archive contains a comprehensive collection of publications by ICA and its predecessor agencies. This collection is unique in that ICA is forbidden to distribute these materials in the U.S. Through ICA's documents index system (DIS) (see point 4 above) the archivist can provide access to declassified agency documents especially for the period since DIS was established in 1973.

WASHINGTON FOREIGN PRESS CENTER
National Press Building, Room 225
529 14th Street, N.W.,
Washington, D.C. 20547
Ernest Latham, Managing Director
(202) 724-1640

The Foreign Press Center provides facilities and press services to foreign journalists working in Washington, D.C.

OFFICE OF PROGRAM COORDINATION AND DEVELOPMENT
Edward Schulick, Director
(202) 724-1900

This office analyzes field-program-support requests, develops and maintains program materials, coordinates the acquisition and production of agency media products, and recruits speakers for ICA posts overseas.

Acquisition and production of a variety of media products for use by agency posts abroad are the responsibility of the media offices; e.g., Press and Publication Service (Allan B. Croghan, chief, Far East and Pacific Branch, 202/724-9680) and Television and Film Service (Claude B. Groce, director, 202/376-7806).

VOICE OF AMERICA (VOA) (Associate Directorate for Broadcasting)
330 Independence Avenue, N.W.
Washington, D.C. 20201
Neal T. Donnelly, Chief, East Asia and Pacific Division
John C. Thompson, Deputy Chief
(202) 755-4840

The VOA is the global radio network of the International Communication Agency. VOA seeks to promote understanding abroad for the U.S.—its people, culture, and policies. The VOA broadcasts 3 hours a day, each, in Indonesian and Vietnamese; 1.5 hours daily in Khmer; 1 hour daily in Burmese and Lao; and 30 minutes daily in Thai. The VOA has a full English–language schedule for the Southeast Asia region. Correspondence bureaus are located in Singapore and Bangkok.

The daily *Current Report* provides program titles, newscast subject matter, and sources of information of VOA broadcasts. Some annual VOA broadcast schedules for each geographic area are available. The News Division (Joseph Buday, deputy chief, 202/755-5781) and Current Affairs Division (George Halsey, chief, 202/755-3690) monitor current events in Southeast Asia. Further information on VOA programs may be obtained from the Public Liaison Office (Diana Conklin, chief, 202/755-4744).

ASSOCIATE DIRECTORATE FOR EDUCATIONAL AND CULTURAL AFFAIRS (ECA)
Ronald Trowbridge, Acting Associate Director
(202) 724-9032

OFFICE OF CULTURE CENTERS AND RESOURCES
Richard Moore, Director
(202) 632-6700

This office provides policy direction, program support, professional guidance, and materials to ICA libraries, cultural centers, and binational centers overseas. It also promotes the teaching of English and distributes American books in English and translations abroad. In addition to cultural centers in Burma, Indonesia, the Philippines, Malaysia, Singapore, and Thailand, four binational centers (three in Indonesia and one in Bangkok) operate on a cooperative basis in which the agency provides a director and—in rare instances—limited financial assistance, with the remainder of the operation being run locally. Funds are generated from fees for the English–language courses offered at these centers.

OFFICE OF INTERNATIONAL VISITORS
G. Michael Eisenstadt, Director
(202) 724-9984

This office arranges travel plans for international visitors, and coordinates international information, educational, and cultural exchange programs conducted by other departments and agencies of the U.S. government. E. Patrick Dillon, chief, East Asia Branch (202/724-9612), may be consulted about Southeast Asia–related activities conducted by the office.

OFFICE OF PRIVATE SECTOR PROGRAMS
Robert R. Reilley, Director
(202) 632-6716

This office reviews proposals for short-term professional exchanges (non-academic), and maintains liaison with a wide range of private institutions to encourage and support private exchange programs and to foster institutional links across national boundaries.

OFFICE OF ACADEMIC PROGRAMS
Stephen A. McKnight, Director
(202) 724-9941

This office is responsible for organizing and assisting academic exchanges between the U.S. and other countries (including the Fulbright program), facilitating the establishment and maintenance of close ties between the American academic community and those abroad, encouraging and supporting American studies at foreign universities and other institutions of higher learning, and providing staff support to the presidentially appointed Board of Foreign Scholarship, which supervises the academic-exchange programs. The East Asia Programs Branch (Louise Crane, chief, 202/724-9830) is responsible for Southeast Asian academic-exchange programs and for supporting specialized institutions in the area. Currently, Fulbright programs are available for Indonesia, the Philippines, and Singapore. The East-West Center liaison officer (Carol Owens, 202/724-9333), of the Office of Academic Programs, serves a coordinating function with the Center for Cultural and Technical Interchange between East and West in Hawaii. This autonomous institution of learning for Americans and for the people of Asia and the Pacific promotes better understanding through cooperative programs of research, study, and training.

Note: See also entries A23 and Q28.

K22 International Trade Commission (ITC) (formerly, U.S. Tariff Commission)

1.   a. *701 E Street, N.W.*
      Washington, D.C. 20436
      (202) 523-0173

     b. Open to the public.

2.   The U.S. International Trade Commission monitors the effect of imports on U.S. domestic agriculture and industry. The ITC advises the president and Congress on tariff and trade matters, assists in drafting trade legislation, comments on proposals from other government agencies, and conducts research in tariffs, international trade, and commercial policy.

OFFICE OF INDUSTRY
Norris Lynch, Director
(202) 523-0146

Agriculture Division
Ed Furlow, Chief
(202) 724-0068

Tom Greer (202/724-0004), Commodity Industry Analyst, monitors the sugar industry in the Philippines and Thailand. All reports are commodity specific as opposed to being country or regionally specific. The *Quarterly Report on East-West Trade* contains trade data for Vietnam.

EXECUTIVE LIAISON AND SPECIAL ADVISOR
William T. Hart, Chief
(202) 523-0232

This office monitors the Generalized System of Preferences (GSP), which allows the U.S. to extend duty-free treatment for certain articles to be imported to the U.S. from qualified, underdeveloped countries. The ASEAN states and Burma are covered by the GSP.

3.   The International Trade Commission Library (Dorothy J. Berkowitz, chief, Library Division, 202/523-0013) is open to the public from 8:45 A.M. to 5:15 P.M., Monday through Friday. Interlibrary loan and photoduplication facilities are available. The collection consists of approximately 77,000 volumes and 1,200 current serial subscriptions. The primary focus of the collection is on the areas of international tariff and custom regulations, foreign trade serials, statistical yearbooks, and economics and finance. The library also maintains vertical files of pamphlets and newspaper clippings on some countries of Southeast Asia. Bibliographic tools include a dictionary card catalog and the *Selected Current Acquisitions List*. (See entry A25.)

4.   ITC publications include its annual report and the *Operation of the Trade Agreement Program* (annual), which contains data on U.S.–Southeast Asian trade and changes in Southeast Asian foreign-investment policies. Copies are available from the Office of the Secretary (202/523-0161).

K23 Justice Department

1.   a. *Constitution Avenue and 10th Street, N.W.*
      Washington, D.C. 20530
      (202) 633-2000

      b. Most departmental agencies discussed are open to the public; however, some, such as the FBI, are closed. Researchers should contact each office for their policies on accessibility.

2.   See individual descriptions that follow point 4.

3.   The Justice Department Library (Terry Appenzellar, library director, 202/633-2133) is open to the public from 9:00 A.M. to 5:30 P.M., Monday through Friday. It contains approximately 150,000 volumes of legal, as well as general, reference works. The collection is accessible by special permission. Interlibrary loan is available.

4.   Questions related to the department's restricted internal records are answered by the Freedom of Information officer Patricia Neely (202/633-3452).

CRIMINAL DIVISION
D. Lowell Jensen, Assistant Attorney General
(202) 633-2601

With the exception of the duly accredited diplomats and commercial representatives, all foreign agents and representatives of foreign political parties in the United States are required to register with the division's Foreign Agent's Registration Unit (Joseph E. Clarkson, chief, 202/724-7109) and provide it with a detailed description of their activities and sources of support. Such individuals are also required to file a copy of any material they disseminate in the U.S. These records are accessible to researchers at the Public Office (Federal Triangle Building, 315 9th Street, N.W., Washington, D.C. 20530, 202/724-2332). The *Annual Report of the Attorney General* provides a list of foreign agents registered with this unit.

INTERNATIONAL AFFAIRS OFFICE
Michael A. Abell, Director
(202) 724-7600

This office formulates and executes transnational, criminal-justice enforcement policies, including international extradition proceedings and political asylum.

FEDERAL BUREAU OF INVESTIGATION (FBI)
J. Edgar Hoover Building
Pennsylvania Avenue between 9th and 10th Streets, N.W.
Washington, D.C. 20535
(202) 324-3000

The FBI has a wide range of responsibilities in the criminal, civil, and security fields, including espionage, sabotage, and other domestic security matters. Although internal records are classified, information on past, official FBI investigations may be made available through Freedom of Information procedures. Requests should be sent to the director of the FBI. The Public Affairs Office (202/324-3691) can provide basic information and assistance.

IMMIGRATION AND NATURALIZATION SERVICE (INS)
425 Eye Street, N.W.
Washington, D.C. 20536
Alan Nelson, Commissioner
(202) 633-1900

The INS is responsible for administering the immigration and naturalization laws relating to the admission, exclusion, deportation, and naturalization of aliens.

INFORMATION SERVICES DIVISION
Irvin Klavan, Assistant Commissioner
(202) 633-2989

The Statistical Analysis Branch (Stephen Schroffel, chief, 202/633-3059) collects statistical data that pertains to immigration, naturalization, non-immigrants, passenger travel, annual alien address reports, and service actions relating to aliens. These statistical records are maintained by the entering alien's country of origin, sex, age, and occupation. Tables compiled from these data bases are contained in the *Annual Report: Immigration and Naturalization Service*, which is the principal publication of the INS.
Statistical data maintained by the branch is available to the public. Private researchers may also obtain access to the small reference collection of historical literature and statistical data. The INS Freedom of Information officer is Marye Gannett (202/633-3278).

DRUG ENFORCEMENT ADMINISTRATION (DEA)
1405 Eye Street, N.W.
Washington, D.C. 20537
Francis M. Mullen, Administrator
(202) 633-1249

The Far East Division (John A. O'Neill, acting director, 202/633-1194) of the Office of Enforcement receives information on narcotics production and trafficking from the DEA field agents in Southeast Asia. The DEA is also involved in training and other special overseas programs that may include providing funding assistance to foreign countries purchasing drug-detection equipment. DEA's quarterly magazine, *Drug Enforcement*, features articles relating to international activities. Most DEA files are classified. DEA's Freedom of Information Division chief is Russ Aruslan (202/633-1396).

K24 Labor Department

1. a. *200 Constitution Avenue, N.W.*
   Washington, D.C. 20210
   (202) 523-8165

   b. Open to the public.

2. Southeast Asia–related activities of the Labor Department are described below.
   Research is conducted both in-house and by contract. Requests for proposals are announced in the *Commerce Business Daily* published by the Department of Commerce. Some internal records of the department are classified and available only through the Freedom of Information Act processes. Sofia Petters (202/523-8188) is the department's Freedom of Information officer.

3. The Labor Department Library (Andre C. Whisenton, library director, 202/523-6988), open from 8:15 A.M. to 4:45 P.M., Monday through Friday, is accessible to the public for reference use only. Limited interlibrary loan and photoduplication facilities are available. This library of approximately 535,000 volumes and 3,200 current periodical subscriptions is one of the

most extensive collections in the fields of labor and economics, and includes a considerable collection of foreign labor-union materials. The collection also contains foreign official documents and publications of the International Labor Organization (ILO). Southeast Asia–related materials in the collection consist of some 500 monographs, government serials, and periodicals.

In addition to the two dictionary card catalogs for pre- and post-1975 acquisitions, a 38-volume U.S. *Department of Labor Library Catalog*, published by G. K. Hall in 1975, provides access to the collection. The library also has a list of *Periodicals Currently Received by the U.S. Department of Labor Library* (1980). Also useful is the biweekly, *Labor Literature*, which announces new acquisitions to the library.

4.   Departmental publications are described with the appropriate issuing agency below.

BUREAU OF INTERNATIONAL LABOR AFFAIRS
Robert W. Searby, Deputy Under Secretary
(202) 523-6043

The bureau assists in formulating international economic and trade policies that affect American workers and helps represent the U.S. in multilateral and bilateral trade negotiations with such international bodies as the General Agreement on Tariffs and Trade (GATT), and various other U.N. organizations. The bureau also helps administer the U.S. labor attaché program at U.S. embassies abroad, carries out overseas technical-assistance projects, and arranges trade-union exchanges and other programs for foreign visitors to the U.S.

OFFICE OF FOREIGN LABOR AFFAIRS
Gerald P. Holmes, Director
(202) 523-7571

This office monitors labor and employment trends in foreign countries and administers the foreign labor attaché program. At present, full-time labor attachés are posted in Djakarta (for Indonesia, Malaysia, and Singapore) and Manila. For access to labor attaché reports and other dispatches, consult the Far East and Pacific Area Advisor (Glenn Halm, 202/523-7623). The Foreign Publications Group (Joan Leslie, 202/5236377) of this office compiles *Country Labor Profiles* on selected foreign countries. Currently, profiles are available for Indonesia, Malaysia, the Philippines, Singapore, and Thailand without charge.

OFFICE OF INTERNATIONAL ORGANIZATION AND TECHNICAL ASSISTANCE
Tadd Linsenmayer, Director
(202) 523-6251

This office currently administers two technical cooperation activities in Southeast Asia. As a follow-up to an earlier four-year project, the U.S. Department of Labor, in 1981, completed a short-term technical-assistance program for Thailand's Department of Labor to improve that country's workman compensation system. This project was funded by AID, and may be extended.

A second program has been in effect for eighteen months with the government of Indonesia. The project focuses on manpower-employment issues. For additional information on these projects, contact Reggie Moore, assistant director for Development Cooperation (202/523-9905).

OFFICE OF INTERNATIONAL ECONOMIC POLICY AND PROGRAMS
Gloria G. Pratt, Director
(202) 523-6171

This office helps the Labor Department participate in U.S. interagency teams that negotiate bilateral and multilateral agreements. Currently the office is involved in the negotiations with the ASEAN states on extending the multifiber agreement. Bilateral textile and apparel agreements were negotiated in 1982 (for Singapore) and 1982 (for the Philippines and Thailand). For further information, contact Irving Kramer, senior commodity trade negotiator (202/523-6227).

OFFICE OF INTERNATIONAL VISITORS PROGRAMS
Ron Smith, Director
(202) 523-6301

This office manages the department's wide-ranging professional, governmental, and trade-union exchange programs, which involve over 1,000 visitors per year, including many from Southeast Asia.

BUREAU OF LABOR STATISTICS (BLS).
441 G Street, N.W.
Washington, D.C. 20212
Janet Norwood, Commissioner
(202) 523-1913

The BLS has responsibility for the department's economic and statistical research, which includes certain international aspects. The BLS has no enforcement or administrative functions, and nearly all of the basic data it collects is supplied by voluntary cooperation. The information collected is issued in monthly press releases, special publications, the *Monthly Labor Review,* and the *Handbook of Labor Statistics,* with international sections.

OFFICE OF PRICES AND LIVING CONDITIONS
W. John Layng, Associate Commissioner
(202) 272-5038

The Division of International Prices (Edward E. Murphy, chief, 202/272-5025) measures and analyzes, by commodity, price trends for U.S. exports.

OFFICE OF FIELD OPERATIONS
Juliet F. Kidney, Assistant Commissioner
(202) 523-1096

The office conducts several technical seminars each year that include participants from Southeast Asian countries.

OFFICE OF PRODUCTIVITY AND TECHNOLOGY
Jerome A. Mark, Assistant Commissioner
(202) 523-9294

Within this office, the Division of Foreign Labor Statistics and Trade (Arthur F. Neef, chief, 202/523-9291) collects data on foreign labor conditions, including wage levels, benefits, and productivity.

Of the several BLS publications pertaining to international labor statistics, the following may be particularly useful to Southeast Asian scholars: *Labor Development Abroad*, a discontinued monthly; *Labor Law and Practice*, an irregular series describing conditions in individual countries including those of Southeast Asia; *Labor Development Abroad*, a quarterly, which contained tables and articles on Southeast Asian countries; *Foreign Labor Digests*, a discontinued irregular, containing country briefs; and *Directory of Labor Organizations* in various countries. Publications in the BLS report series include: *The Forecasting of Manpower Requirements* (1963); *Conducting a Labor Force Survey in Developing Countries* (1964); and *How to Make an Inventory of High-Level and Skilled Manpower in Developing Countries* (1964). The bureau also issues quarterly releases on the *U.S. Department of State Indexes of Living Costs Abroad and Living Quarters Allowances*.

K25 National Aeronautics and Space Administration (NASA)

1. a. *400 Maryland Avenue, S.W.*
    Washington, D.C. 20546
    (202) 755-8364

    b. Open to the public. Advance appointment recommended.

    c. James M. Beggs, Administrator

2. NASA interaction with the countries of Southeast Asia is limited to Thailand and Indonesia. NASA research is conducted both in-house and via outside contract and consultation.

    INTERNATIONAL AFFAIRS DIVISION
    Kenneth Pedersen, Director
    (202) 755-3868

    This division coordinates all foreign activities and international exchanges of the agency. Currently, NASA has a launch-services agreement with the government of Indonesia for the launching of two Palapa-B communications satellites in 1983 and 1984. In addition, Landsat stations operating in Indonesia and Thailand have the capability of acquiring Landsat data on these countries and the surrounding region. For additional information on NASA–Southeast Asia activities, contact Brent Smith, international relations specialist (202/755-3880).

3. NASA headquarter's library (Mary E. Anderson, head librarian, 202/755-2210) is open from 8:00 A.M. to 4:30 P.M., Monday through Friday. Subject to security regulations, the library facilities and collections are accessible to the public for on-site use. Limited interlibrary loan and photoduplication services are available. This reference collection is technical in nature, with primary concentration being on current aerospace developments.

    The library has a comprehensive collection of NASA publications and publications of its predecessor, the National Advisory Committee on Aeronautics (NACA). The library has the five-year retrospective runs of *International Aerospace Abstracts* and other scientific and technical information generated by NASA on microfiche. The RENCON data bases, which have citations and abstracts on subjects from aerospace to technology and development, can be accessed through the library. Primarily restricted to agency use, RENCON can be searched geographically.

NASA's Goddard Space Flight Center Library (Adelaide Del Frate, head librarian, Greenbelt, Maryland 20771, 301/344-6244) is open to the public by appointment from 8:00 A.M. to 4:30 P.M., Monday through Friday. Like the headquarters library, this collection is technical in nature, covering such fields as astronomy, space science, and physics, and containing some 58,000 books and 37,000 journals, including 700 current subscriptions.

NASA's Audio Visual Services (Les Gaver, head, 202/755-8366), open from 8:30 A.M. to 4:30 P.M., Monday through Friday, maintains a photo library of over half a million items, including a selection of Landsat photos organized on a geographical basis. Two brief catalogs, *NASA/1981 Photography Index* and *NASA Films* (1982), are available on request.

4. NASA publications are announced in *NASA Publications* and in its biweekly *Scientific and Technical Aerospace Reports* (STAR). All NASA publications should be ordered from the Superintendent of Documents, U.S. Printing Office, Washington, D.C 20402. Many popular materials are available free from the Public Information Services (Room 6027, 202/755-8341).

Note: See also entry G9.

K26 National Endowment for the Humanities (NEH)

1. a. *806 15th Street, N.W.*
   Washington, D.C. 20506
   (202) 724-0386 (Public Affairs Office)

   b. Open to the public.

   c. William J. Bennett, Chairman

2. The National Endowment for the Humanities makes grants to individuals and groups or institutions such as schools, colleges, universities, museums, public television stations, libraries, public agencies, and private nonprofit groups, to increase understanding of the humanities. The disciplines include, but are not limited to, languages, linguistics, literature, history, jurisprudence, philosophy, archeology, comparative religion, the history of criticism, theory and practice of the arts, and those aspects of the social sciences that have humanistic content and employ humanistic methods. The major divisions of NEH are listed below with brief descriptions of the funding program.

   DIVISION OF RESEARCH GRANTS
   Mail Stop 350
   Harold Cannon, Director
   (202) 724-0226

   This division provides grants for conferences, basic research, the development of research materials (research tools, editing, and translating), expanding collections, and promoting publications.

DIVISION OF FELLOWSHIPS
Mail Stop 101
James Blessing, Director
(202) 724-0238

The Fellowships Division, through several programs, provides stipends for scholars, teachers, and members of nonacademic professions to study areas of the humanities that may be directly related to the work they characteristically perform. Through this division, the endowment awarded 1,400 stipends in 1982 for periods ranging from six weeks to one year.

DIVISION OF EDUCATION PROGRAMS
Mail Stop 202
Richard Ekman, Director
(202) 724-0351

This division provides grants to strengthen institutional educational programs from the university level to elementary schools level.

DIVISION OF PUBLIC PROGRAMS
Mail Stop 400
Stephen L. Rabin, Acting Director
(202) 724-0231

Public Programs Division is intended to foster wider public understanding and use of the humanities. The division supports projects to develop and utilize the resources of museums and historical organizations, the media, and public libraries.

DIVISION OF SPECIAL PROGRAMS
Mail Stop 303
Carole Huxley, Director
(202) 724-0261

This division supports projects that do not fit into any other NEH divisions.

3. The National Endowment for the Humanities Library (Jeannette D. Colitti, librarian, 202/724-0360) is a small reference collection of some 6,000 volumes and 500 current periodical subscriptions in the areas of history, philosophy, education, and the humanities. The collection contains copies of NEH annual reports and all publications resulting from NEH grants. The library is open to the public for reference use only from 9:00 A.M. to 5:30 P.M., Monday through Friday. Interlibrary loan and photoduplication facilities are available.

4. In addition to the *Annual Report for the National Endowment for the Humanities*, the NEH disseminates several free brochures and pamphlets concerning its program announcements and deadlines for grant applications. Two NEH newsletters, *Humanities* and *NEH in the News*, are also available free.

K27 National Science Foundation (NSF)

1. a. *1800 G Street, N.W.*
   Washington, D.C. 20550
   (202) 357-9498

b. Open to the public; prior appointments advisable.

c. John B. Slaughter, Director

2.   The NSF initiates and supports fundamental and applied research in all the scientific disciplines. This support is made through grants, contracts, and other agreements awarded to universities and nonprofit and other organizations. Most research is directed to the resolution of scientific questions concerning fundamental life processes, natural laws and phenomena, fundamental processes influencing man's environment, and the forces effecting people as members of society as well as societal behavior. Additional research is focused on selected social problems.

To NSF, science is an international enterprise. Research with Southeast Asian implications, therefore, could be supported by any one of the following directorates: Directorate for Mathematical and Physical Sciences (Ronald E. Kagarise, acting assistant director, 202/357-9742); Directorate for Astronomical, Atmospheric, Earth and Ocean Sciences (Francis S. Johnson, assistant director, 202/357-9715); Directorate for Engineering (Jack T. Sanderson, assistant director, 202/357-9832); Directorate for Science and Engineering Education (Dr. Walter Gillespie, assistant director, 5225 Wisconsin Avenue, N.W., Washington, D.C. 20550, 202/282-7922); Directorate for Biological, Behavioral and Social Sciences (Eloise E. Clark, assistant director, 202/357-9854); and Directorate for Scientific, Technological and International Affairs (Harvey Averch, assistant director, 202/357-7631). The last two of these directorates may be of more use to Southeast Asianists than the others and are described further below.

DIRECTORATE FOR SCIENTIFIC, TECHNOLOGICAL AND INTERNATIONAL AFFAIRS
Harvey Averch, Assistant Director
(202) 357-7631

DIVISION OF INTERNATIONAL PROGRAMS (INT)
Bodo Bartocha, Director
(202) 357-9552

A division within the Directorate for Scientific, Technological and International Affairs, INT carries out NSF's statutory responsibilities for international scientific activities. Established in the International Geophysical Year (1958), the division supports the U.S. side of about 300 cooperative science projects annually with some 40 countries including the ASEAN states.

Latin America and Pacific Section
J. E. O'Connell, Head
Gordon Hiebert, Program Manager, Indonesia, Malaysia, Singapore, Thailand
Gerald Edwards, Program Manager, the Philippines
(202) 357-9537

This section is responsible for INT's Southeast Asia–related activities, which are part of the United States–East Asia Cooperative Science Program. The goal of this program is to increase the level of cooperation between U.S. and East Asia scientists and engineers in the exchange of scientific information, ideas, skills, and techniques. The intent is to join unique resources and research environments that promise advances in the basic and applied sciences not possible through independent work.

The program provides for various modes of cooperation, including short- and long-term visits, cooperative research, and conferences. The program involves five Southeast Asian countries: Indonesia, the Philippines, Singapore, Malaysia, and Thailand. Complementary proposals are submitted simultaneously by the U.S. scientist to NSF and by his or her Southeast Asian colleague to the appropriate country agency. The program involves five counterpart organizations in the ASEAN states. In Thailand, the National Research Council is the cooperating agency, while in the Philippines it is the National Science Development Board. In Malaysia, NSF works with the Ministry of Science, Technology and Environment, and in Singapore with the Ministry of Science and Technology. The Indonesian counterpart agency is the Ministry of Research and Technology.

For additional information, contact Gordon Hiebert, program manager for Indonesia, Malaysia, Thailand, and Singapore; and Gerald Edwards, Program Manager for the Philippines.

In fiscal year 1980, NSF funded a "USA–Thai Symposium on Under Exploited Economic Plants," New York Botanical Gardens; "Short-Term Visit to Discuss Program for Comparative Research on the Dynamic Analysis of Landslides," Purdue University and University of the Philippines; "Short-Term Visit to Develop Cooperative Research on Material Properties of and Design System for Wood-Based Materials," Oregon State University and University of the Philippines; and "Short-Term Visit to Develop Cooperative Research in Philippine Mycoflora," Natural History Museums (Los Angeles) and University of the Philippines.

Members of the U.S. scientific community wishing to participate in the East Asia programs are invited to inquire by telephone (202/357-9537) or by writing to: U.S. East Asia Cooperative Science Programs, Division of International Programs. The inquiry should include a brief, specific description of the proposed activity. Counterpart scientists in cooperating countries may obtain information from NSF's counterpart agency in that country. For further information on U.S.– Southeast Asia activities, contact Gordon Hiebert (202/357-9537) in the Latin America and Pacific Section. An informative booklet, *Division of International Programs* (1979), provides a succint outline of NSF's international activities. Also see the INT program announcement booklet, *Science in Developing Countries Program* (1980), and the *Program Announcement: United States–East Asia Cooperative Science Programs* (annual).

DIRECTORATE FOR BIOLOGICAL, BEHAVIORAL AND SOCIAL SCIENCES
Eloise E. Clark, Assistant Director
(202) 357-9854

DIVISION OF BEHAVIORAL AND NEURAL SCIENCES
Richar T. Louttit, Director
(202) 357-7564

This division includes neurosciences, psychological sciences, and anthropological and linguistic sciences.

DIVISION OF SOCIAL AND ECONOMIC SCIENCES
Otto N. Larsen, Director
(202) 357-7966

This division includes programs in economics, geography, and political science, as well as programs in social measurement and analysis, including history and philosophy of science, law, and social sciences.

3.   The National Science Foundation Library (Herman Fleming, chief, Reference and Record Management Section, 202/357-7811) is open to the public from 8:30 A.M. to 5:00 P.M., Monday through Friday. Interlibrary loan and photoduplication facilities are available. This small reference collection of approximately 16,000 volumes and 500 periodicals includes general works and recent research developments in the fields of environmental, biological, and social sciences and national and international science policy.

4.   *Publications of the National Science Foundation* (1970) lists all annual reports, publications of the National Science Board, descriptive brochures, and program announcements. Some of the useful publications include: *National Science Foundation Guide to Programs* (1980); *A Comprehensive Approach to the National Science Foundation Support for Human Origins Research* (1979); *National Science Foundation Films* (1978); *Applied Research Summary of Awards* (1980); *Federal Funds for Research and Development* (1979); *National Science Foundation Grants and Awards* (annual); and *National Science Foundation Report* (annual). Both *Mosaic*, the official bimonthly magazine of the NSF, and the *NSF Bulletin* provide news about programs, program deadlines, and meetings. Some of these publications noted above may be obtained gratis from the NSF's Forms and Publications Section (Nancy Zenor, chief, 202/357-7811).

K28 National Security Council (NSC)

1.   a. *Executive Office Building*
17th Street and Pennsylvania Avenue, N.W.
Washington, D.C. 20506
(202) 395-3440

        b. No public access.
William P. Clark, Assistant to the President

2.   The National Security Council advises the president on domestic, foreign, and military policies relating to U.S. national security. NSC staff members are not accessible to private researchers. Academic specialists are occasionally contracted as consultants.

3.   Most NSC internal records are classified and restricted to a small number of authorized government personnel. Brenda Reger (202/395-3116) is the Freedom of Information officer for the NSC. Some declassified NSC policy papers, intelligence directives, and other internal records—together with an updated list of all such materials released—are available at the Modern Military Branch (Military Archives Division) of the National Archives and Records Service (see entry B7).

K29 Navy Department

1.   a. *The Pentagon*
Washington, D.C. 20350
(202) 697-4627

b. Open to those with a security clearance or an official invitation.

2.   Most Southeast Asian research is done in-house.

3.   The Naval Historical Center is described in entries A34, B9, C8, and F19.

4.   Publications are described under relevant divisions.

Note: See also entry F20.

OFFICE OF INFORMATION
Bruce Newell, Chief
(202) 697-7391

The Information Office provides assistance to researchers in locating appropriate offices and personnel.

NAVAL RECORDS MANAGEMENT AND ADMINISTRATION
SERVICES DIVISION
(Office of the Chief of Naval Operations)
Keyman Patton, Chief
(202) 697-2330

The division is responsible for management, disposal, declassification, and access to all records of the department. Some useful contacts are: Freedom of Information and Privacy Act (Gwen Aitkens, 202/697-1459) and Records Disposal (Margaret Daymude, 202/695-1921).

OFFICE OF NAVAL RESEARCH (ONR)
800 North Quincy Street
Arlington, Virginia 22217
Leland S. Collmorgen
(703) 696-4258

The ONR is engaged in a wide variety of naval research, much of which is international in dimension, including branches of the physical, mathematical, biological, and psychological sciences. No index to the research projects or completed reports is available, but the staff will assist in locating materials. Most research is done through external research contracts. Currently there are no on-going research projects related to Southeast Asia, but several cooperative research programs, especially in the field of microbiology (marine plant life, natural antiviral substances, diarrheal diseases, and malarial control), may be under consideration. For further information, contact A. J. Emery (703/696-4056). In addition, researchers should note the following contact numbers: Physical Sciences Division (T. G. Berlincourt, 703/696-4212); Mathematical and Information Sciences Division (J. C. T. Pool, 703/696-4310); Biological Sciences (Ronald Oshlund, 703/696-4051); and Psychological Sciences Division (G. L. Bryan, 703/696-4425).

OFFICE OF NAVAL INTELLIGENCE (ONI)
Sumner Shapior, Director
(202) 695-3944

ONI monitors developments and collects data on global naval activities. However, most of its work is classified. D. Nargele (202/697-0313) of the

Politico Military Affairs Branch is responsible for Southeast Asian matters. An informative book, *Naval Intelligence Command* (1975), and an organizational chart are available free.

DEPUTY CHIEF OF NAVAL OPERATIONS (Plans, Policy and Operations)
Sylvester R. Foley
(202) 695-3707

POLITICO MILITARY POLICY AND CURRENT PLANS DIVISION
Ronald J. Kurth, Director
(202) 695-2453

The division's East Asia/Pacific Branch (Thomas Bender, 703/697-1192) monitors political and military developments in Southeast Asia and prepares policy papers on issues, including arms transfer and security assistance, of special interest to the U.S. Navy. This branch currently has several Southeast Asia specialists.

K30 Overseas Private Investment Corporation (OPIC)

1. a. *Board of Trade Building*
    1129 20th Street, N.W.
    Washington, D.C. 20527
    (202) 653-2920

    b. Open to the public, but prior appointment is recommended.

    c. Craig Nalen, President

2. The Overseas Private Investment Corporation is a U.S. government agency established "to mobilize and facilitate the participation of United States private capital and skills in the economic and social development of less developed friendly countries and areas." OPIC has two principal self-sustaining programs: financing projects sponsored by U.S. investors in less developed countries and insuring these investments against the political risks of expropriation, inconvertibility of local currency, or war, revolution, or insurrection. Preference is given to countries with a per-capita income under $520 a year and to projects sponsored by cooperatives or U.S. small businesses. OPIC has assisted investors in over 80 countries, including the ASEAN states of Southeast Asia. OPIC helps project sponsors design financial plans; it provides information and counseling, and participates in financing project costs.

    For information on business opportunities and the investment climate in Southeast Asia, contact Jane Troy, deputy director for Europe, Middle East, Africa, and Asia (202/653-2960) in the Insurance Department; and Brooks H. Browne, investment officer for Asia (202/653-2882) in the Finance Department.

3. OPIC's small library (Myra Norton, librarian, 202/653-2863) of approximately 5,000 selected volumes of monographs and documents, and 350 current periodicals, focuses on international economics, business and finance, and other related subjects. The library maintains country files of miscellaneous data on some 90 developing nations, including Southeast

Asia. The collection also contains records and documents of OPIC activities in overseas investment disputes and settlements; World Bank country reports and project assessments; publications of U.S. government agencies, including the departments of State, Commerce, Agriculture, and Treasury; and reports from private U.S corporations having interests in Southeast Asia. The library is open to the public by appointment. A card catalog facilitates access to the collection.

4. OPIC publications include an annual report, *A Guide for Executives of Smaller Companies*, *Investment Financing Handbook*, *Investment Insurance Handbook*, and *Topics* (bimonthly newsletter). All publications are available free. For access to confidential internal records, such as claims settlement files and information submitted by U.S. firms operating in Southeast Asia, researchers should contact OPIC's Freedom of Information officer (Robert L. Jordan, 202/653-2800).

K31 Peace Corps

1. a. *806 Connecticut Avenue, N.W.*
    Washington, D.C. 20525
    (202) 254-7970

    b. Open to the public. Appointments are recommended

    c. Loret Miller Ruppe, Director

2. The Peace Corps, which under 1982 reorganization, was separated from ACTION, administers overseas programs and is organized along geographic and functional lines. Programs for Southeast Asia are managed through the North Africa, Near East, Asia and Pacific Regional Office (Jody K. Olsen, director, 202/254-9830). Desk officers Edward Geibl (202/254-8782), Malaysia and Thailand, and Melanie Williams (202/254-8870), the Philippines, provide liason between Washington and field volunteers in Southeast Asia.

3. The ACTION (Peace Corps) library is described in entry A1.

4. Peace Corps publications include: annual reports; the *Bi-Annual Statistical Summary*, giving details of the volunteers and trainees of the corps; *Peace Corps Volunteer*; *Peace Corps Program and Training Journal* (monthly); and *Guidelines for Peace Corps Cross-Cultural Training* (4 volumes, 1970).
    There is no comprehensive bibliography of all Peace Corps publications. For information concerning retired and inactive files, contact the Peace Corps Freedom of Information officer (John Nolan, 202/254-8105).

K32 Senate Historical Office

1. a. *The Capitol, Room S-413*
    Washington, D.C. 20510
    (202) 224-6900

    b. Open to the public on the basis of prior appointment.

    c. Richard A. Baker, Senate Historian

2–4.   A clearinghouse for Senate–related research, this office provides scholars with bibliographic and research assistance in locating and gaining access to the documents and records of the Senate. In 1982, the staff compiled for publication a catalog of senators' papers; also under preparation is a check-list of unpublished hearings. Both compilations contain material of interest to Southeast Asianists. Southeast Asia–related materials may also be found in *The Executive Sessions of the Senate Foreign Relations Committee*, a historical series edited by the Senate Historical Office. Volume 10, covering 1958, is being processed for publication. A newsletter, *Senate History*, contains many useful research notes.

The Senate Historical Office maintains an extensive photo archive of some 20,000 items that provide photographic documentation of Senate activities. An oral history project is also under way for recording the rec-ollections of retired Senate staff members.

K33 Smithsonian Institution

1.   a. *Smithsonian Institution ("Castle") Building*
       1000 Jefferson Drive, S.W.
       Washington, D.C. 20560

(202) 357-1300 (Information)
(202) 357-2020 ("Dial-A-Museum," which provides daily information on new museum exhibits and special events)

b. The main Smithsonian Institution Building and other Smithsonian museums and galleries located throughout the metropolitan Washington area are open to the public. Visitors to the administrative offices should make appointments in advance.

2.   Smithsonian programs relating to Southeast Asia are described following point 4 below. See also entries C2, C3, C5, C6, D2, F9, F18 and H37.

3.   See entries C3, C5, C6, and H37.

4.   See entries B8 and B10 for the Smithsonian's National Anthropological Archives and the Smithsonian Institution Archives, respectively.

5.   The monthly *Smithsonian* magazine is available through membership as a Smithsonian Associate. Also published is the Institution's annual report, *Smithsonian Year*, and a series of *Smithsonian Research Reports*, containing news of current research projects conducted by the Smithsonian staff.

OFFICE OF FELLOWSHIPS AND GRANTS (OFG)
Gretchen Gayle Ellsworth, Director
(202) 287-3271

The OFG administers the Smithsonian predoctoral and postdoctoral fellowship programs, which enable scholars and students to work with Smithsonian staff experts, research collections, and laboratories. Awards range in length from a few weeks up to a year. Disciplines emphasized in these programs that are of interest to Southeast Asia specialists coincide with several of the Smithsonian's traditional interests: archeology, anthropology, art and cultural history, and museum management. A brochure, *Smithsonian Opportunities for Research and Study in History, Art, Science*, is available on request.

While the Fellowship Program and other academic offerings for research visitors are designed to bring scholars to the Smithsonian for the benefit of specialized work with staff researchers, the Smithsonian Special Foreign Currency Program (SFCP) awards research grants to American institutions of higher learning for studies in countries where the U.S. holds excess foreign currencies derived largely from the sale of agricultural commodities under Public Law 480. The authority that the Smithsonian has received from the Congress for the use of excess foreign currencies allows grants to be awarded in the disciplines of archeology, physical and cultural anthropology, ethnology, and linguistics; systematic and environmental biology; astrophysics and earth sciences; and museum programs.

As for Southeast Asia, grants for new projects under SFCP are currently available in Burma. For further information on SFCP, contact the Foreign Currency Program Office (Francine C. Berkowitz, program specialist, 202/287-3271) in the Office of Fellowships and Grants. The SFCP Program Announcement (1981) is available free from OFG.

The following projects were supported in Burma during the period 1981–82 by the Smithsonian Foreign Currency Program: "Theravada Buddhism and Its Subsidiary Cults: A Study of Cosmological Order and Religious Practices in Burma" and "The Jatakas in Burmese Art and Policy."

OFFICE OF INTERNATIONAL ACTIVITIES (OIA)
Kennedy B. Schmertz, Director
(202) 357-2519

The OIA supports Smithsonian programs by advising on foreign affairs affecting Smithsonian museological, cultural, and scientific research programs. It assists in communications with foreign governments and institutions and reviews opportunities for cooperation in international projects important to the Smithsonian professional staff. It also maintains liaison with the Department of State, the International Communication Agency, embassies in Washington, and international organizations, as well as with private institutions concerned with cooperative international programs. This office currently facilitates Smithsonian contacts with Thailand, the Philippines, Singapore, and Indonesia.

SMITHSONIAN RESIDENT ASSOCIATES PROGRAM
Janet Solinger, Director
(202) 357-2696

The Smithsonian offers various categories of membership including Resident Associate, National Associate, and Contributing Member. Public members are entitled to participate in numerous special Smithsonian educational and cultural programs, including occasional lectures on Southeast Asian art, archeology, culture, and natural history. Smithsonian Associates may also take advantage of special, cultural, educational tours of foreign countries, either through the "foreign study tours" program or via the regular "travel program" (202/357-2477). Members receive the monthly *Smithsonian* magazine and the monthly *Associate* newsletter.

K34 State Department

1. a. *2201 C Street, N.W.*
    Washington, D.C. 20520
    (202) 632-6575

    b. Access to the building is restricted. Appointments with department personnel should be made in advance.

2. Described below are the many State Department offices that monitor, research, and prepare policy papers on Southeast Asian affairs. Within the limits of security restrictions and time constraints, personnel are usually willing to talk with researchers. The geographic bureaus and the Bureau of Intelligence and Research engage consultants and contract for outside research on our region.

3. The State Department library is discussed in the libraries section, entry A37.

4. General foreign policy publications issued by the department include: the *Department of State Bulletin*, for sale weekly and including policy statements, texts of treaties, special articles, and selected press releases; *Background Notes*, presenting short, updated country summaries that describe the people, history, government, economy, and foreign relations of each country; *Department of State Newsletter*, a priced monthly containing various articles, biographic descriptions, news, notes, and other information primarily for foreign-service personnel abroad; *Special Reports, Selected Documents,* and *Current Policy*, pamphlets (irregular) containing verbatim and excerpted statements by senior departmental officials; *Gist*, a series of brief reference aids on current international issues; and *Digest of International Law*, which covers all sources of international law, including materials from treaties, executive agreements, legislation, testimony and statements before congressional and international bodies, and diplomatic notes.

    In addition, the department publishes a number of useful directories and pamphlets, including: *Diplomatic List*, a quarterly list of foreign diplomats in Washington; *Employees of Diplomatic Missions*, a quarterly companion to the *Diplomatic List*, giving names and addresses for mission employees; *Foreign Consular Offices in the United States*, an annual listing of offices, their jurisdiction and personnel; the recently classified *Biographic Register* of U.S. foreign service officials; *Key Officers of Foreign Service Posts: Guide for Businessmen*, a quarterly directory prepared to aid Americans with business interests abroad; *Memorandum to U.S. Business Community from Department of State, Subject: Assistance in International Trade* (1975), another directory to assist U.S. businessmen; periodically revised *Lists of Visits of Presidents of the United States to Foreign Countries, Lists of Visits of Foreign Chiefs of State and Heads of Government,* and *United States Chiefs of Mission 1778–1973.*

    Other publications are issued in several series such as: *General Foreign Policy Series; Commercial Policy Series; International Information and Cultural Series; International Organization Series;* and *Treaties and Other International Act Series.* The department also prepares the *Report Required by Section 657 Foreign Assistance Act*, which is submitted to the U.S. Congress and contains a myriad of information on U.S. foreign assistance and other transactions; and the annual *Country Reports on Human Rights,* which is also submitted to the U.S. Congress. Another major publication is the *Foreign Relations of the United States*. *Foreign Policy and the State Department* is a useful but outdated pamphlet on the organization of the department and its overseas posts.

For bibliographic access to the department's publications, scholars may consult: *Major Publications of the Department of State: An Annotated Bibliography* (revised edition, 1977); issues of *Publications of the Department of State*, 1929–1952, 1953–1957, and 1958–1960; *Selected Publications and Audiovisual Materials of the Department of State*; and a *Pocket Guide to Foreign Policy Information Materials and Services of the Department of State*. Other useful reference guides to the department's publications are Frederic O'Hara's *Government Publications Review* (Vol. III, pp. 143–49, 1976) and *U.S. Federal Official Publications* (1978), by J. A. Downey. All publications of the department are also listed in the *Monthly Catalog of U.S. Government Publications*.

For information on specific publications, scholars may contact the Office of Public Communications (Room 4831) of the Bureau of Public Affairs (202/632-8872). Scholars interested in being included on the department's mailing list may contact Dorothy S. Gregory (202/632-9859) of the Publications Distribution unit of the Office of Plans and Opinion Analysis (Bureau of Public Affairs). Additional publications are discussed under the bureau that generates them.

The Department of State's internal classified records—dispatches, telegrams and other communications between Washington and the department's diplomatic posts abroad, inter- and intraoffice memoranda, research studies, and policy papers—are filed with the Foreign Affairs Information and Management Center (202/632-0394) of the Bureau of Administration. When these documents are retired from the department's active files, they are transferred to the Diplomatic Branch (Civil Archives Division) of the National Archives and Records Service (see entry B7). Computerized indexes are maintained for all documents processed by the center since 1973.

Classified documents are usually declassified 25 to 30 years after their origin and often coincide with the latest year for which the department's documentary volume, *Foreign Relations of the United States*, has been published. As of 1982, most documents through 1949 in the National Archives are open to the public. Requests for reviews of the classified records, as provided by the Freedom of Information Act (FOIA) and the Privacy Act may be directed to Sharon B. Kotok, chief of the Information Access Branch (202/632-1267) of the Bureau of Administration. FOIA requests should provide as much identifying information as possible about the document to assist the department in locating it. Include subject matter, time frame, originator of the information, or any other helpful data. Only persons who are U.S. citizens or aliens who are lawfully admitted to the U.S. for permanent residence can request information under the Privacy Act. Under this act, individuals may request access to records that are maintained under the individual's name or some other personally identifiable symbol. Descriptions of record systems from which documents can be retrieved by the individual's name are published in the *Federal Register*.

BUREAU OF EAST ASIA AND PACIFIC AFFAIRS
John H. Holdridge, Assistant Secretary
(202) 632-0826

Frederick Brown, Director, Indonesia, Malaysia, Burma, Singapore
(202) 632-3276
Sylvia Stanfield, Country Officer, Malaysia, Singapore
(202) 632-3276
Allan Jury, Country Officer, Indonesia
(202) 632-3276
Charles B. Smith, Jr., Country Officer, Burma
(202) 632-3276
Frazier Meade, Director, the Philippines
(202) 632-1222
Jeffrey Gallup, Country Officer (Political), the Philippines
(202) 632-1221
Charles Reynolds, Country Officer (Economic), the Philippines
(202) 632-1669
L. Desaix Anderson, Director, Vietnam, Cambodia, Laos
(202) 632-3132
Barbara Harvey, Country Officer, Vietnam, Cambodia, Laos
(202) 632-3132

This bureau supervises and coordinates U.S. diplomatic activities in Southeast Asia as well as East Asia and the Pacific. Staff members prepare policy recommendations, background papers and public-policy statements on Southeast Asia for State Department personnel. The country and functional desk officers listed above are an important source of current information on Southeast Asia and U.S. policy in that region. The officers can make available unclassified documents and provide assistance and information to scholars. The department's *Background Notes* for the countries of Southeast Asia are prepared by this bureau.

BUREAU OF INTELLIGENCE AND RESEARCH (INR)
Hugh Montgomery, Director
(202) 632-0342

The INR coordinates programs of intelligence, research, and analysis for the department and other federal agencies, and produces current intelligence analysis essential to foreign-policy determination and execution. INR's work and publications are discussed in the State Department's *Research in Action* (1968), and *Intelligence and Research in the Department of State* (1973). Publications of the bureau, most of which are classified, include: *External Research Studies*; *Intelligence Brief*; *Intelligence Notes*; *Research Studies*; *INR Daily Summary*; *Communist States and Developing Countries: Aid and Trade*; and *World Strength of the Communist Party Organizations*.

OFFICE OF LONG RANGE ASSESSMENTS AND RESEARCH (INR/LAR)
E. Raymond Platig, Director
(202) 632-1342

Third World Research Group
Daniel Fendrick, Chairman
(202) 632-2758

The INR/LAR maintains liaison with cultural and educational institutions and with other federal agencies on a wide range of matters relating to government contractual and private foreign-affairs research. From time to time, the office invites Southeast Asian experts as consultants or speakers for official conferences, colloquia, roundtable discussions, and ambassadorial briefings. This office also acts as the coordinator and information clearinghouse for all interagency, government-supported research on foreign affairs. The staff does not engage in research but can provide researchers with copies of unclassified departmental in-house and contract research studies and bibliographies.

The office publishes a quarterly and annual inventory of *Government-Supported Research on Foreign Affairs: Current Project Information*, which lists research contracts and grants supported by the various departments and agencies of the executive branch. These projects have to do with the application or advancement of the social-behavioral sciences and humanities as they bear substantively on foreign areas and international relations. Another publication, *A Directory of Government Resources*, describes foreign-affairs research within the federal government.

The Foreign Affairs Research Documentation Center, administered by the Office of External Research, was abolished in 1979. The center's collection of some 15,000 government supported and privately funded research papers on foreign affairs have now been transferred to the Defense Technical Information Center (202/274-6871) (see entry G5) and the National Technical Information Center (703/557-4788). For bibliographic access to the collection, the Documentation Service published two inventories: *Foreign Affairs Research Papers Available* and *Special Papers Available*. Copies of these inventories are available on request from B. W. Morlet (703/235-8079).

Office of Research and Analysis for East Asia and Pacific (INR/EAP)
(202) 632-1338

Southeast Asia Division
Allen Kitchens, Chief
(202) 632-2061

The country analysts in this division are Paula Causey (202/632-1182), Burma, Indonesia, Malaysia, and Singapore; Roberta Chew (202/632-9542), the Philippines; Algis Aviznis (202/632-2277), Cambodia and Vietnam; Allen Kitchens (202/632-2061), Laos; and Paul T. Belmont (202/632-2289), Thailand.

The division is the department's principal research arm for Southeast Asian affairs. It produces numerous research papers, reports, studies, and memoranda covering short- and medium-term policy issues for the Bureau of East Asia and Pacific. Analysts are generally receptive to academic contact.

OFFICE OF ECONOMIC ANALYSIS (INR/ECA)
Emil Ericksen, Director
(202) 632-2186

This office studies global economic issues including U.S.–Southeast Asian economic relations. The Commodity and Developing Country Division (Emily Perreault, chief, 202/632-0453) analyzes the North–South dialogue, trade, and commodities. The Trade Investment and Payments Division (David Konkel, acting chief, 202/632-0090) is concerned with balance-of-payments problems, foreign exchange, debt problems, and investment disputes involving private U.S. companies overseas.

Regional Economic Division
John Danylyk, Chief
(202) 632-9128

This division was recently reorganized to include the Communist Economic Relations Division. The enlarged Regional Economic Division conducts economic research on specific geographic regions including Southeast Asia. Corazon S. Foley (202/632-9264) is responsible for Burma, Indonesia, Malaysia, the Philippines, and Thailand. Percilla Stowe (202/632-9770) is responsible for Cambodia, Laos, and Vietnam.

OFFICE OF THE GEOGRAPHER (INR/RGE)
Lewis M. Alexander, Director
(202) 632-1428

The INR/RGE monitors international affairs involving boundaries, law of the sea, and related topics. The office publishes the following series, intended mainly for government use: *Geographic Bulletin*, an irregular reference booklet on world or specific areas; *Geographic Note*, another irregular bulletin describing significant changes of sovereignty; *Geographical Reports*, which give details on geo-administrative divisions; and *International Boundary Studies*, providing intermittent discussions of border areas.

OFFICE OF POLITICAL-MILITARY ANALYSIS (INR/PMA)
Robert A. Martin, Director
(202) 632-2043

INR/PMA conducts studies, some pertaining to Southeast Asia, on international arms sales, national military production and military capabilities, international security issues, nuclear capabilities, and potential global confrontations. The activities of the former Office of Strategic Affairs have been incorporated into this office.

BUREAU OF CONGRESSIONAL RELATIONS (H)
Powell A. Moore, Assistant Secretary
(202) 632-8744

This bureau is responsible for communication between the members and committees of Congress and the staff, on the one hand, and the various bureaus and offices of the department, on the other. It seeks the views of Congress on major foreign-policy issues, explains U.S. foreign-policy initiatives, and arranges numerous formal and informal meetings, briefings, and appearances before committees. The Congressional Relations Bureau also plays an important role in drafting and monitoring legislation affecting foreign policy and the department. Legislative management officer Will Itoh (202/632-8802) serves as the coordinator for Southeast Asian affairs. There are also separate legislative management officers for human rights (Timothy Towell, 202/632-1246) and refugees (Lee Hunt, 202/632-8732).

BUREAU OF POLITICAL-MILITARY AFFAIRS (PM)
Richard Burt, Director
(202) 632-9022

The PM develops policy guidelines and provides general direction within the department on issues that affect U.S. security policy, military assistance, nuclear policy, and arms control and disarmament matters. In addition, the bureau maintains liaison, on a wide range of political and military matters, with the Defense Department and other federal agencies. Most records and documents of the bureau are classified.

OFFICE OF MUNITIONS CONTROL
William B. Robinson, Director
(202) 235-9755

The Munitions Control Office licenses private U.S. arms exporters.

OFFICE OF REGIONAL SECURITY AFFAIRS
Richard Haass, Director
(202) 632-1862

This office analyzes broad regional problems such as arms buildups, border tensions, and revolutionary activities.

OFFICE OF THEATER MILITARY POLICY
James F. Dobbins, Director
(202) 632-3136

This office is concerned with visits of foreign military personnel to the U.S. and monitors U.S. military aircraft and ship movements in various geographic regions.

OFFICE OF SECURITY ASSISTANCE AND SALES
Dr. Richard Ogden, Director
(202) 632-3882

This office monitors U.S. and other international arms transfers to regions of the world including Southeast Asia. Craig Murphy (202/632-3564) monitors the East Asia Pacific area.

Other offices within the bureau are: Office of Nuclear Policy and Operations (Edward Malloy, director, 202/632-1835); Office of Security Assistance–Special Projects (Robert B. Mantel, director, 202/632-5104); and Office of Strategic Nuclear Policy (Christopher Lehman, director, 202/632-1616).

BUREAU OF HUMAN RIGHTS AND HUMANITARIAN AFFAIRS (HA)
Paula Kuzmich, Public Affairs Advisor
(202) 632-0855
Donald Roberts, Regional Affairs Officer (HA/NEA)
(202) 363-2264
Lawrence L. Arthur, Asylum Officer
(202) 632-2551
Stephen Palmer, Country Reports Director
(202) 632-0855

This small bureau monitors human-rights in Southeast Asian countries as reported by U.S. embassies and other sources, and makes policy recommendations on U.S. economic and military assistance programs to these countries. It also coordinates the compilation of the department's unclassified annual publication, *Country Reports on Human Rights Practices*, which covers those countries in Southeast Asia receiving U.S. military or economic aid.

BUREAU OF INTERNATIONAL ORGANIZATION AFFAIRS (IG)
Nicholas Platt, Acting Assistance Secretary
(202) 632-9600

IG coordinates and develops policy guidance and support for United States participation in the activities of the U.N., its specialized agencies, and other international organizations. The bureau's staff in the various functional offices monitors the activities of Southeast Asian representatives to the U.N. and specialized agencies, and the repercussions of these representatives on U.S. policy positions. Various functional offices of the bureau include: U.N. Political Affairs (Edward Dillery, directory, 202/632-2392); Human Rights Affairs (Warren Hewitt, director, 202/632-0520); Health and Narcotic Programs (Neil Boyer, agency director, 202/632-1044); UNESCO Affairs (David Rowe, agency director, 202/632-8588); International Women's Programs (Julia Jacobson, agency director, 202/632-1120); International Economic Policy (Lee Sanders, director, 202/632-2506); Science and Technology (Thomas G. Gabbert, agency director, 202/632-2752); Office of International Agriculture Development (Ishmael Lara, chief, 202/632-0492); and Office of International Conferences (John W. Kimball, director, 202/632- 0384).

A useful publication is the *U.S. Participation in the U.N.: Report by the President to the Congress* (annual). Researchers may examine the bureau's collection of U.N. documents through its U.N. Documents and Reference Staff (Mary Rita Jones, chief, 202/632-7992).

BUREAU OF OCEANS AND INTERNATIONAL ENVIRONMENTAL AND SCIENTIFIC AFFAIRS (OES)
James L. Malone, Assistant Secretary
(202) 632-1554

OES handles U.S. representation in international organizations and conferences, and assists in formulating U.S. policy in the areas of environment, health, and natural resources, nuclear energy and energy technology, oceans and fisheries, science and technology, and population. Bureau sub-units having Southeast Asia–related activities are: Population Affairs (Richard Benedict, coordinator, 202/632-3472), which monitors demographic trends and population-control programs; Environment, Health, and Natural Resources (Donald King, acting deputy assistant secretary, 202/632-9278), which deals with a broad range of environmental issues, such as natural-resources depletion, land and sea pollution, endangered species, and weather modification; Nuclear Energy and Energy Technology Affairs (James Devine, deputy assistant secretary, 202/632-4360), which is concerned with nuclear nonproliferation and safeguards, export and import control, and technology cooperation; and Oceans and Fisheries Affairs (Theodore Kronmiller, deputy assistant secretary, 202/632-2396), which is concerned with maritime boundaries, marine pollution and resources, and law-of-the-sea issues.

This unit also represents the U.S. in the International Fisheries Commission.

BUREAU OF ECONOMIC AND BUSINESS AFFAIRS (EB)
Robert D. Hormats, Assistant Secretary
(202) 632-0396

EB formulates and implements foreign economic policy, trade promotion, and international business services, and coordinates regional economic policy with other concerned bureaus. The bureau is organized on a functional basis. Many of its offices are concerned with Southeast Asian economics.

INTERNATIONAL FINANCE AND DEVELOPMENT
Elinor G. Constable, Deputy Assistant Secretary
(202) 632-9496

Office of Business Practices
Harvey J. Winter, Director
(202) 632-1486

The Office of Business Practices deals with the legal aspects of technology transfer, copyright laws, and antitrust matters.

Office of Development Finance
Adrian Bafora, Director
(202) 632-9426

The Development Finance Office represents the department in interagency discussions on U.S. loan policies and contributions to international financial institutions and acts as the department's liaison with the World Bank and other international lending institutions.

Office of Monetary Affairs
William B. Milam, Director
(202) 632-1114

In addition to monitoring international monetary affairs, this office has primary responsibility for the department's relations with the International Monetary Fund (IMF) and the U.S. Department of the Treasury.

Office of Investment Affairs
John McCarthy, Director
(202) 632-1128

Responsibilities of this office include investment policy, investment disputes, expropriation cases, and problems involving multinational corporations.

INTERNATIONAL TRADE AND COMMERCIAL AFFAIRS
Denis Labm, Deputy Assistant Secretary
(202) 632-2532

Office of International Trade
Teresita Schaffer, Director
(202) 632-9458

The Office of International Trade drafts commercial treaties and trade agreements for conducting bilateral and multilateral international trade negotiations and reviewing Southeast Asian participation in various international economic forums.

Office of Business and Export Affairs (*formerly* Commercial Affairs)
James Tarrant, Director
(202) 632-0354

In cooperation with the Commerce Department, this unit works to promote
U.S. trade.

INTERNATIONAL RESOURCES AND FOOD POLICY
Michael Calingaert, Deputy Assistant Secretary
(202) 632-1625

Office of International Commodities
Ann L. Holick, Director
(202) 632-7952

This office is involved in the negotiation of international commodities agreements.

Office of Food Policy and Programs
Donald F. Hart, Director
(202) 632-3090

The Food Policy and Programs Office coordinates U.S. food-aid programs
with the U.S. Department of Agriculture.

INTERNATIONAL ENERGY POLICY
E. Allan Wendt, Deputy Assistant Secretary
(202) 632-1498

This unit formulates the department's energy policy and represents the U.S.
in international conferences.

TRANSPORTATION AND TELECOMMUNICATIONS AFFAIRS
Matthew Scocozza Deputy Assistant Secretary
(202) 632-4045

Office of International Communications Policy
Arthur L. Freeman, Director
(202) 632-3405

Primary responsibilities of this unit are in the areas of radio, telephone,
telegraph, satellite and underseas cable communications, and related international agreements and regulations.

Office of Maritime Affairs
Todd Stewart, Director
(202) 632-0704

The Office of Maritime Affairs is involved in questions on maritime trade
and commerce. It monitors international shipping regulations and cargo-
preference laws and endeavors to discourage discrimination against U.S.
commercial shipping.

Office of Aviation
James Ferrer, Director
(202) 632-0316

U.S. bilateral commercial aviation negotiations are conducted through the
Office of Aviation.

BUREAU OF PUBLIC AFFAIRS (PA)
Dean Fischer, Assistant Secretary–Spokesman
(202) 632-6575

Concerned with effective exchange of information and views on U.S. foreign relations between the department and the public, the PA advises other elements of the department on public opinion and arranges continuing public contacts between departmental officials, private citizens, and groups through conferences, briefings, speaking and media engagements, publications, films, and other means.

OFFICE OF OPINION ANALYSIS AND PLANS
Bernard Roshco, Director
(202) 632-0474

This office coordinates public-affairs guidance on foreign policy within the department and with other agencies, reviews and guides public statements, prepares analysis of public opinion, and develops plans for public information.

OFFICE OF PRESS RELATIONS
Allen Ronberg, Deputy Spokesman
(202) 632-2492

The Press Relations Office provides information services concerning foreign policy and the operation of the department to the press and others who are interested.

OFFICE OF THE HISTORIAN
William Z. Slany, Acting Historian
(202) 632-8766
David Mabon, Chief, Asian Division
(202) 632-3518

The specialists for Southeast Asia are historians, Robert J. McMahon (202/ 632-9701) and Edward C. Keefer (202/632-3519). The principal responsibility of this office is to prepare the official record of U.S. diplomacy, a series of volumes entitled *Foreign Relations of the United States* (1861–). In addition, the publications of this office include: *American Foreign Policy— 1950–1955: Basic Documents* (2 vols.), and *American Foreign Policy: Current Documents* (12 annual vols., 1956–1967). The office also publishes a useful reference guide, *Major Publications of the Department of State: An Annotated Bibliography*, as well as occasional historical studies on selected topics in U.S. diplomatic history.

Information concerning retrospective and current record-filing systems of the department and the retrieving of diplomatic records and documents may be obtained from the staff, who are available for consultation and research guidance. The staff maintains close contact with the department's Information Management Center (202/632-0394), the Diplomatic Branch of the National Archives, and the presidential libraries throughout the country.

OFFICE OF PUBLIC COMMUNICATION
Paul E. Auerswald, Director
(202) 632-3656

The office of Public Communication is the principal public information outlet of the department. It publishes and disseminates *Current Policy*, *Background Notes*, and other documents on foreign policy; responds to public inquiries on current international events; and directs individuals to appropriate bureaus and offices for assistance.

OFFICE OF PUBLIC PROGRAMS
Thomas Bleha, Director
(202) 632-1433

This office arranges speaking engagements for department officials; sponsors conferences and special briefings on U.S. foreign policy; and organizes the department's Scholar–Diplomat, Media–Diplomat, and Executive–Diplomat Seminars. Southeast Asian seminars are held approximately once a year. Information pamphlets describing the services provided by this office are available on request.

BUREAU OF ADMINISTRATION (A)
Thomas M. Tracy, Assistant Secretary
(202) 632-1492

The bureau operates the department's automated foreign-affairs data-processing center and the library, provides audio-visual services, and processes records and documents of the department.

FOREIGN AFFAIRS INFORMATION MANAGEMENT CENTER
William Price, Director
(202) 632-0394

The center administers the central file of the department's documents and records until they are transferred to the National Archives. Records received by the center from July 1973 have been computer indexed. Most of the material in the custody of the center is classified, and access may be possible only through the Freedom of Information Act, requests for which may be directed to the Center's Information Access Branch (202/632-1267). The center prepares a *Monthly Highlights Report* of major items selected from incoming State Department message traffic. This is organized by geographic region of the world and subdivided by type of reporting (political, economic, military, sociological, and technological). This publication is classified and for internal use only.

POLICY PLANNING STAFF (S/P)
Paul D. Wolfowitz, Director
(202) 632-2372

The Policy Planning Staff advises the Secretary of State with broad, long-range global policy recommendations and perspectives independent from the viewpoints of the geographic bureaus. The staff includes functional as well as area specialists who are accessible to researchers. Most work, however, is classified, including its publication, *Open Forum*, which deals with foreign policy issues and analysis.

OFFICE OF THE LEGAL ADVISER (L)
East Asia and Pacific Affairs
Terrence Fortune, Assistant Legal Advisor

Gilda Brancato, Attorney Adviser
(202) 632-8900

The legal adviser is the principal adviser to the secretary and the department on all legal matters concerning the department and its overseas posts. Researchers may consult the staff of the East Asia and Pacific Affairs branch for information on Southeast Asian legal matters, including the status of treaties and other international agreements. The following other office branches that deal with various functional issues and are headed by assistant legal advisers often deal with specific Southeast Asian questions and issues: Economic and Business Affairs (John Crook, 202/632-0242); Public Affairs (Ely Maurer, 202/632-2682); Human Rights (Andre Surena, 202/632-3044); Ocean, Environment and Scientific Affairs (David Colson, 202/632-1700); Politico; Military Affairs (Michael J. Matheson, 202/632-7838); Treaty Affairs (Robert Dalton, 202/632-1074); and United Nations Affairs (David H. Small, 202/632-1320).

Publications of the office on international law include: *Digest of United States Practice in International Law*, an annual, containing policy statement of the official U.S. position on all major questions of international law, including human rights and the law of the sea; *Treaties in Force* (TIS), an annual list of all U.S. international agreements in force as of January 1 of each publication year; the annual *United States Treaties and Other International Agreements* (1950—); *Treaties and other International Agreements of the United States of America, 1776–1949*, 15 vols.; and *Whitman's Digest of International Law*, 15 vols. For further information on publications, contact Marian L. Nash, editor, *Digest of U.S. Practice in International Law* (202/632-2628).

FOREIGN SERVICE INSTITUTE (FSI)
1400 Key Boulevard
Arlington, Virginia 22209
John T. Sprott, Acting Director
(703) 235-8750

The FSI is responsible for area and language training and the instruction of foreign service and other personnel of the department, as well as personnel of other government departments and agencies involved in foreign affairs. The FSI library is described in entry A16.

OFFICE OF ACADEMIC AFFAIRS
J. Brian Atwood, Deputy Director
(703) 235-8714

This office develops and maintains close relations with the academic community and with learned and professional societies and coordinates assignments of foreign-service officers to universities, armed-services training institutions, colleges, and other educational institutions.

SCHOOL OF LANGUAGE STUDIES
Pierre Shostal, Dean
(703) 235-8816

The School of Language Studies provides intensive and part-time language instruction in support of the department's policies on language proficiency among its personnel, and to meet the needs of other government agencies with similar language requirements. The Asian and African Languages Department currently teaches several Southeast Asian languages including Burmese, Indonesian, Lao, Malay, Tagalog, and Thai. Each intensive class is conducted by a native-speaking language instructor and is supervised by a scientific linguist.

The school has developed techniques and standards, which are widely used throughout the federal government, for testing language competence. An active program of research and development has resulted in published courses for more than thirty languages, plus a wealth of as-yet unpublished and experimental material. The school maintains extensive recordings and language-laboratory facilities. Complementary tape recordings of the courses are obtainable from the National Audiovisual Center (301/763-1896) of the National Archives and Records Service.

SCHOOL OF AREA STUDIES
Dwight R. Ambach, Dean
(703) 235-8839

The School of Area Studies is a focal point for promotion of area and country knowledge within the executive branch of the U.S. government. It provides training to personnel from the department and other foreign-service agencies to meet their requirements for broad, interdisciplinary knowledge of a geographic region or country. The Southeast Asian Studies Branch (Eugene Brunn, chairman, 703/235-8843) of the school is responsible for organizing and administering several introductory and advanced courses on the area. The center prepares annual, unannotated, area bibliographies of mainly commercially published monographs for use in its training programs.

SCHOOL OF PROFESSIONAL STUDIES
J. Brian Atwood, Dean
(703) 235-8779

This school provides general courses in economics, science, human rights, political analysis, politico-military affairs, multilateral diplomacy, and other related fields. The school also conducts the Foreign Affairs Interdepartmental Seminar attended by senior mid-career officers from the departments and agencies concerned with foreign affairs. The seminar provides an advanced, intensive look at the major elements of U.S. foreign policy, including its formulation and conduct. Emphasis is placed on domestic factors affecting policy, current major foreign and national security problems, and such critical international issues as food, population, and energy.

EXECUTIVE SEMINAR IN NATIONAL AND INTERNATIONAL AFFAIRS
Jack Perry, Coordinator
(703) 235-8753

This ten-month program provides senior U.S. government officials with the most advanced training available on the topic of contemporary political, economic, social, and cultural trends in the U.S. and the ways these domestic trends interact with U.S. interests abroad.

K35 Transportation Department (DOT)

1. a. *400 7th Street, S.W.*
    Washington, D.C. 20590
    (202) 426-4000

    b. Open to the public.

2. Southeast Asia–related international activities of the Transportation Department are described below.

3. The Transportation Department library is described in entry A39.

4. The Information Management Division (James L. Duda, chief, 202/426-0957) of the Office of Policy, Plans and Program Management (202/426-9676) has developed—in conjunction with the Transportation Research Board (TRB) of the National Academy of Science's National Research Council and numerous other organizations—a computerized bibliographic data base known by the acronym TRISNET (Transportation Research Information Services Network). Indexed by country and transportation mode, the system is accessible to private researchers on a cost basis through the TRB computer terminal. TRB's Special Technical Activities Office (Paul E. Irick, 202/334-3255) may be contacted for further information. Two useful brochures describing the system are *TRISNET: Directory to Transportation Research Information Service* (1976) and *TRISNET: A Network of Transportation Information Services and Activities* (1978).

    The department sponsors the annual *World Survey of Current Research and Development on Roads and Road Transport* prepared and distributed by the International Road Federation. The department's collection of more than 700,000 abstracts and annotated index entries to the periodical literature on the subject of transportation is available on 140 reels of microfilm. The *Transportation Master File, 1921– 1970*, and a hard cover volume, *Transportation Serials*, published by the U.S. Historical Documents Institute, as well as *Investment Strategies for Developing Areas: Highway Cost Model Operating Instructions and Program Documentation* (1973), prepared under DOT contract by the Massachusetts Institute of Technology, may be of interest to Southeast Asianists. The department's Freedom of Information officer is Rebecca Lima Daley (202/426-4542).

POLICY AND INTERNATIONAL AFFAIRS
Judith T. Conner, Assistant Secretary
(202) 426-4544

Policy and International Affairs coordinates U.S. interests in international transportation. Activities include analysis, development, and review of department-wide policies and programs for domestic and international transportation; analysis of social, economic, and energy aspects of transport systems; promotion and coordination of international research cooperation; and technical assistance to developing countries.

OFFICE OF INTERNATIONAL POLICY AND PROGRAMS
Vance Fort, Director
(202) 426-4368

International Trade Division
Arnold Levine, Chief
(202) 755-7684

In cooperation with the Agency for International Development (AID), this division provides technical-assistance support for planning management and evaluation of foreign transportation projects sponsored and funded by AID or host countries. In 1982 the division had several projects in the Philippines including: a 56-million-dollar rural roads project, and a 40-million-dollar project for feeder-road and river-basin-road construction. For further information, contact the division chief or Charles Vandervoort (202/426-4196).

FEDERAL AVIATION ADMINISTRATION (FAA)
800 Independence Avenue, S.W.
Washington, D.C. 20591
J. Lynn Helms, Administrator
(202) 426-3111

The FAA is primarily charged with regulating air commerce to foster aviation safety; however, it is also called on to make air transport studies in foreign countries.

POLICY AND INTERNATIONAL AVIATION
Donald Segner, Associate Administrator
(202) 426-3030

Office of International Aviation
Quentin Taylor, Director
(202) 426-3213

The Analysis and Evaluation Branch (Jane Stolar, 202/426-3231) of the International Analysis and Coordination Division (Cathleen W. Gorman, chief, 202/426-3230) maintains file books known as "country profiles," which contain general and statistical information on current aviation activities in all countries of Southeast Asia. The branch also has internal document files of memos, correspondence, and in-house research papers for many foreign countries. Interested researchers should contact the Office of International Aviation.

Within the International Analysis and Coordination Division is the Interagency Group of International Aviation (IGIA) (202/426-3180). IGIA monitors and coordinates international aviation for all U.S. government agencies, and it is the U.S. depository for all International Civil Aviation Organization (ICAO) documents, which are available to serious researchers, as is a small reference library.

The Technical Assistance Division (J. Stuart Jamison, chief, 202/426-3173), of the Office of International Aviation, provides technical experts to AID–sponsored projects. In 1981 and 1982 the division conducted a national airport and airway system study for the Republic of the Philippines. Gerald Mahdik (202/426-3175) was the program manager.

International Liaison and Policy Division (Romney Pattison, chief, 202/426-3057), within the International Aviation Office, deals with operational matters related to U.S. airmen and aircraft in foreign countries, and foreign airmen and aircraft in the U.S. The division acts as liaison for the agency in coordinating the technical aspects of international civil aviation policy.

The FAA maintains a reference library (Dorothy Poehlman, librarian,

202/426-3611) that contains 50,000 monographs, 50,000 technical reports, 150,000 microforms, and 700 periodical subscriptions. The primary focus of the collection is on aeronautics, aviation safety, and various facets of civil aviation, such as navigation, airports, air-traffic control, air transportation, aviation medicine, and aviation law. This collection is open to the public for on-site use, except for documents restricted to agency use. Interlibrary loan and limited photoduplication services are available. The library is open from 10:00 A.M. to 3:00 P.M., Monday through Friday. A card index serves the collection, and the library issues bibliographies and other announcements from time to time.

The FAA's Freedom of Information officer is Suzanne Holloway (202/426-3893). The FAA's Office of the Historian (Nick A. Komons, 202/755-7234), in the Public Affairs Bureau, maintains a small archive of indexed key documents that reflect the evolution of U.S. civil aviation policy from 1926 to the present, and may include some materials of interest. The office is currently compiling a three-volume narrative history of federal civil aviation policies. A catalog of FAA publications is available free on request.

FEDERAL HIGHWAY ADMINISTRATION (FHWA)
400 7th Street, S.W.
Washington, D.C. 20590
Ray A. Barnhart, Administrator
(202) 426-0650

A component of DOT since 1966, the FHWA carries out the highway transportation programs of the department, including some limited international activities. The Foreign Project Division (Joseph DeMarco, chief, 202/426-0380) provides technical-assistance advisors for AID–sponsored projects. In 1982 there were no activities in Southeast Asia.

MARITIME ADMINISTRATION
Harold E. Shear, Administrator
(202) 426-5812

The Maritime Administration, which was transferred to the Transportation Department from the Commerce Department in 1981, administers programs to aid in the development, promotion, and operation of the U.S. merchant marine, and to organize and direct emergency merchant-ship operations. The administration manages U.S. maritime relations with foreign countries. Researchers may confer with the staff of the International Activities Office (Reginald A. Bourdon, 202/426-5772) about the administration's activities such as commercial shipment of grains and other commodities in Southeast Asia, trade studies, and participation in international programs with the ASEAN countries—Indonesia, Malaysia, the Philippines, Singapore, and Thailand.

OFFICE OF TRADE STUDIES AND STATISTICS
William Ebersold, Director
(202) 382-0376

This office compiles statistical data on U.S. waterborne trade with foreign countries and foreign merchant shipping with the U.S. Data is available in hard copy or computer printout to scholars. Publications of the office include *New Ship Construction, Merchant Fleets of the World, A Statistical Analysis of the World's Merchant Fleets,* and *Essential U.S. Trade Routes.*

K36 Treasury Department

1. a. *15th Street and Pennsylvania Avenue, N.W.*
   Washington, D.C. 20220
   (202) 566-5252

   b. Open to the public on the basis of advanced appointment.

2. The Department of the Treasury's primary responsibilities include formulating and recommending domestic and international financial, economic, and tax policies. Most research is conducted in-house although, from time to time, contract research opportunities develop.

OFFICE OF ECONOMIC POLICY
Manuel H. Johnson, Acting Assistant Secretary
(202) 566-2551

Within the Office of Economic Policy, the Deputy Assistant Secretary for International Economic Analysis is responsible for international economic issues, which include: developing forecasts of U.S. trade and current account balances for use by the officials of the department in formulating international economic policy; conducting research and analysis of major policy issues in the international trade, monetary, and energy areas; and producing information on flows of banking and corporate capital into and out of the U.S. and on the extent of portfolio investment by foreigners in the U.S. and by U.S. residents abroad. This unit also maintains the Developing Countries Data Bank, which contains information from 1960 on national income, balance of payments, and foreign debts of developing nations. This data bank, however, is not accessible to the public.

OFFICE OF INTERNATIONAL AFFAIRS
Mark E. Leland, Assistant Secretary
(202) 566-5363

The Office of International Affairs advises and assists the department in the formulation and execution of international monetary, financial, commercial, energy, and trade policies and programs. The office staff is organized into groups responsible for developing nations, monetary affairs, trade and investment policy, and commodities and natural resources.

DEVELOPING NATIONS
Thomas Dawson, Deputy Assistant Secretary
(202) 566-8243

Office of International Development Bank
Frank Maresca, Director
(202) 566-8171

This office engages in financial diplomacy with the developing nations, monitors the operations of the Asian Development Bank and the World Bank Group, and makes recommendations for U.S. policy. Researchers may confer with office staff members for information relating to Southeast Asia.

Office of Developing Nations Finance
Donald C. Templeman, Director
(202) 566-2373

Organized on a geographical basis, the office monitors Southeast Asian monetary and financial conditions, including balance of payments, debt levels, and general fiscal and development conditions. The Southeast Asia desk officers in the Middle East/Asia Division are the best contact persons for researchers seeking information on Southeast Asian countries. William McFadden (202/566-2896) is responsible for Burma and the Philippines; Steven Tvardek (202/566-2638) handles Indonesia, Malaysia, and Singapore; and Robert Anderson (202/566-2637) monitors Thailand.

3.   The Treasury Department Library (Elizabeth Knauff, chief, 202/566-2069) is open to the public from 9:00 A.M. to 5:00 P.M., Monday through Friday. Interlibrary loan and photoduplication services are available. The collection consists of 125,000 monographs, 200,000 microfiche, and 8,000 microfilms. The areas of emphasis include taxation and public finance, money and banking, and international law and economics. The library is also a depository of congressional records and documents. The holdings contain a large number of government statistical publications from Southeast Asia, as well as documents and records produced by the Asian Development Bank. *Treasury Notes*, a monthly review of current literature, lists the library's new acquisitions and abstracts selected books and periodical articles of interest to department employees.

4.   Publications of interest include: *Foreign Credit by the United States Government: Status of Active Foreign Credits of the United States Government and of International Organizations* (semiannual), which records the debts owed to the government of the United States and international organizations; *Annual Report of the National Advisory Council on International Monetary Policies*; *Report on Developing Countries External Debt and Debt Relief Provided by the United States* (annual); and *Treasury Bulletin*, a monthly that provides statistical data on receipts and expenditures, public debt, and capital movements between the U.S. and foreign countries. A *Selected List of Treasury Publications* is revised periodically and can be obtained free from the Office of Public Affairs (Steven Hayes, chief, International Affairs, 202/566-2041).

Inactive and retired records and documents of the department are managed by the Record Management Branch (Sarah J. Allen, chief, 202/376-1571). All Freedom of Information requests should be addressed to the Disclosure Operation's Freedom of Information Branch (Phyllis DePiazza, chief, 202/376-1577).

L Southeast Asian Embassies and International Organizations

Southeast Asian Embassies and International Organizations Entry Format (L)

1. General Information
   a. *address; telephone numbers*
   b. hours/conditions of access
   c. names and titles of chief officials

2. Organization Functions, Programs, Research Activities (including in-house research, contract research, research grants, and employment of outside consultants)

3. Libraries and Reference Facilities

4. Publications and Internal Records (including unpublished research projects)

Introductory Note

The Southeast Asian embassies in Washington vary in staff size and available information. In some cases, however, a press or public-affairs officer will be able to answer general reference questions, provide social and economic statistics, furnish information on political and legal matters, and answer questions about the country's participation in international agreements and its position on international issues. In the more highly differentiated embassies, such as those of Indonesia (entry L2), Malaysia (entry L4), the Philippines (entry L5), Singapore (entry L6), and Thailand (entry L7), commercial, military, and cultural attachés are usually available. The embassies also host specific cultural events, film showings, music or dance troupes, and lecture programs to which the public may be invited.

In the entries below, each embassy is identified by its official name as presented in the *Diplomatic List* (February 1982), but is listed alphabetically according to its geographical designation. It should be noted that, at the time of this writing, the countries of Cambodia (Khmer Republic) and Vietnam are without diplomatic representation in Washington.

The personnel of the international organizations described here can also provide valuable Southeast Asia–related information within limits imposed by their schedules and official regulations.

L1 Embassy of the Socialist Republic of the Union of Burma

1.   a. *2300 S Street, N.W.*
Washington, D.C. 20008
(202) 332-9044

    b. 9:00 A.M.–5:00 P.M. Monday–Friday

    c. His Excellency, U Kyaw Khaing, Ambassador

3.   The embassy has a small number of general references on Burma, including a collection of current magazines, which interested persons may see. There is no library or reading room facility at present.

L2 Embassy of the Republic of Indonesia

1.   a. *2020 Massachusetts Avenue, N.W.*
Washington, D.C. 20036
(202) 293-1745

    b. 9:00 A.M.–5:00 P.M. Monday–Friday

    c. His Excellency, D. Ashari, Ambassador

3.   The Indonesian Embassy does not maintain a library or reading room facility, as such, for the public. However, the Information Office at the embassy does have a small collection of materials on Indonesia, including the *Indonesia Handbook*. Persons interested in general information about the country are encouraged to contact the Information Office. The embassy film collection is described in entry F5.

4.   The embassy publishes *Indonesia News and Views* (See entry Q13).

L3 Embassy of the Lao People's Democratic Republic

1.   a. *2222 S Street, N.W.*
Washington, D.C. 20008
(202) 332-6416 and 332-6417

    b. 9:00 A.M.–noon and 2:00 P.M.–5:00 P.M. Monday–Friday

    c. Mr. Khamtan Ratanavong, Counselor, Chargé d'Affaires, ad Interim

3.   The embassy does not as yet have a library facility for public use.

L4 Embassy of Malaysia

1.   a. *2401 Massachusetts Avenue, N.W.*
Washington, D.C. 20008
(202) 328-2700

    b. 9:30 A.M.–5:00 P.M. Monday–Friday

    c. His Excellency, Zain Azraai, Ambassador

3.   The Malaysian Embassy has several hundred books and official government publications that may be used on the premises by serious scholars. Included in the collection are back issues of the *Malaysia Yearbook* and the *Malaysia Budget*. The embassy film collection is described in Entry F6.

4.   The *Malaysia Digest*, available from the embassy, is described in entry Q15.

L5 Embassy of the Philippines

1.   a. *1617 Massachusetts Avenue, N.W.*
     Washington, D.C. 20036
     (202) 483-1414

     b. 9:00 A.M.–noon and 2:00 P.M.–5:00 P.M.   Monday–Friday (except holidays)

     c. His Excellency, Eduardo Z. Romualdez, Ambassador

3.   The embassy maintains a small library that contains general reference materials on the Philippines and includes official government publications. Also available are a few films and slides for loan in the Washington, D.C., metropolitan area. Contact the Cultural Section for additional information.

L6 Embassy of the Republic of Singapore

1.   a. *1824 R Street, N.W.*
     Washington, D.C. 20009
     (202) 667-7555

     b. 9:00 A.M.–5:00 P.M.   Monday–Friday

     c. His Excellency, Punch Coomaraswamy, Ambassador

3.   The embassy has a small general collection of Singapore–related references that may be used on the premises. Also available is a small collection of films that may be lent (See entry F7).

L7 Embassy of Thailand

1.   a. *2300 Kalorama Road N.W.*
     Washington, D.C. 20008
     (202) 667-1446

     b. 10:00 A.M.–5:00 P.M.   Monday–Friday

     c. His Excellency, Prok Amaranand, Ambassador

3.   The embassy does not have facilities to accommodate research by outside persons, but a few materials may be available from the Information Section. The Embassy film collection is described in Entry F8.

4.   The embassy publishes *News from Thailand* (monthly) in English, and in Thai (weekly). This publication is available on request (see entry Q20).

L8 Food and Agriculture Organization (FAO)—Liaison Office of North America (United Nations)

1. a. *1776 F Street, N.W.*
   Washington, D.C. 20437
   (202) 376-2306

   b. Open to the public.

   c. Don C. Kimmel, Director

2. An autonomous specialized agency of the U.N., the FAO works to raise the levels of nutrition and standard of living of the peoples in the Third World, securing improvements in the efficiency of the production and distribution of all food and agricultural products, bettering the condition of rural populations, and thus contributing toward an expanding economy. The FAO administers its own technical cooperation program for agricultural development and works closely with a number of international and national financing institutions, including the World Bank, regional development banks, and national development banks, for the purpose of securing capital for agricultural projects in the developing countries. With 144 nations as members, FAO activities touch most nations in the Third World. FAO's regional office for Asia and the Far East is located in Bangkok, Thailand.

   FAO's Washington office serves as a liaison for coordinating FAO-administered programs in the U.S. and Canada. This includes administering a fellowship program (Theresa Clark, 202/376-2226) in North America for trainees from developing countries. Several participants are selected each year from Southeast Asian countries.

3. The FAO's Washington office maintains a small reference collection, which is open to the public weekdays, and offers interlibrary loan and photoduplicating services. This collection contains selected FAO documents and publications, including budgets and conference reports, FAO statistical yearbooks on world agriculture production and trade, fisheries, forest products, animal health, world agricultural commodity reviews and projections, and FAO nutritional and agricultural studies. The collection also includes FAO's international *Food and Agricultural Legislation* series, the *Monthly Bulletin of Agricultural and Economic Statistics*, the bimonthly *Ceres: FAO Review on Agriculture and Development*, and the Washington office's *Notes for North America*.

4. FAO is a central point for studies of agricultural questions on a world scale. FAO collects the latest information on food, agriculture, forestry, and fisheries from all over the world and makes it available to all its member countries for the use by the government planners, research workers, businessmen, students, and the general public. In addition to the statistical yearbooks and regular reviews of the situation and outlook for world food supplies and agriculture, scientific monographs bring together the result of research carried out in many countries. Special international catalogs list such information as manufacturers of tractors, institutes of agricultural engineering, genetic stocks of cereal available to plan breeders and forest seed supplies. Every ten years, FAO coordinates and publishes the results

of a census of world agricultural resources. Two publications, *FAO Books in Print* and *FAO Periodicals*, are available on request.

Note: See also entry F10.

L9 International Bank for Reconstruction and Development (IBRD) (World Bank)

1. a. *1818 H Street, N.W.*
    Washington, D.C. 20433
    (202) 477-1234

    b. Visitors are received by appointment.

    c. A. W. Clausen, President

2.   For Southeast Asian scholars, the World Bank provides valuable and extensive research resources. Established in 1945, and having a current membership of 134 countries, the World Bank is a group of three institutions: the International Bank for Reconstruction and Development (IBRD), the International Development Association (IDA), and the International Finance Corporation (see entry L10). The common objective of these institutions is to help raise standards of living in developing countries by channeling financial resources to them. World Bank capital is subscribed by its member countries. The bank finances its lending operations primarily from its own borrowings in world money markets. As spelled out in its charter, the bank must lend only for productive purposes and must stimulate economic growth in the developing countries where it lends. In fiscal year 1981, the World Bank, with its affiliates, made lending and investment commitments totaling $12.3 billion.

    While the bank has traditionally financed all kinds of capital infrastructure, such as roads, railways, telecommunications, ports, and power facilities, its present development strategy places increased emphasis on investments that directly affect the well-being of the masses of poor people in developing countries. This new strategy is reflected in the increasing number of bank funded projects in agriculture, rural development, education, family planning, nutrition, water, sewerage, and low-cost housing. In addition to projects funded independently, the bank also cofinances a number of other projects with other national or multinational development-assistance agencies.

    Credit terms differentiate the IBRD from its affiliate, the IDA, which came into existance in 1960 with membership open to all member countries of the IBRD. IDA's resources consist of subscriptions and supplementary resources in the form of general replenishments mostly from its twenty-one industrialized and developed members; special contributions by its wealthier members; and transfers from the net earnings of the IBRD. The IDA provides funds to developing nations on concessionary terms, which are more flexible and bear less heavily on the balance of payments than those of conventional loans.

    Outside scholars are frequently contracted as research consultants. Increasingly, World Bank research is conducted in collaboration with researchers and research institutions in developing countries. The objective is to develop a network of mutually supportive studies dealing with general issues of development policy as well as with specific sectoral problems of particular concern to the bank's operations in developing countries. Two free brief publications, *World Bank Research Program Abstracts of Current Studies* (1980) and *Uses of Consultants by the World Bank and its Borrowers* (1974), provide additional information on the research activities and the availability of consultancy assignments in the World Bank.

EAST ASIA AND PACIFIC REGIONAL OFFICE
Shahid S. Husain, Vice President
(202) 477-2283

This office is the focal point for planning and coordinating all Southeast Asia–related activities. Burma, however, is under the South Asia Regional Office (David Hopper, vice president, 202/477-2395). Alphonse Shibasawa (202/477-3568) heads the Burma Division in the South Asia Regional Office.

Administratively, the East Asia and Pacific office is divided along sectoral lines (Projects Department) and geographically (Country Program Department).

PROJECTS DEPARTMENT
S. Kirmani, Director
(202) 477-4258

Technical experts in this department's sectoral divisions work with borrowers to identify priority projects and analyze their economic and technical feasibility. The Technical Assistance and Special Studies Staff, under the department, takes the lead on technical-assistance projects in Southeast Asia.

Agricultural Division 4
M. Altaf Hussain, Chief
(202) 477-2145

The Agricultural Division 4 is responsible for all the bank's agricultural projects, with the exception of those in the field of irrigation. The on-going Transmigration Project, with the government of Indonesia, is under the division. This project is a massive population relocation effort, which encourages people on the crowded island of Java to relocate to the less-populated island of Kalimantan. Gloria Davis (202/477-4215) is the mission leader for the Transmigration Project.

COUNTRY PROGRAM DEPARTMENT
Edward Jaycox, Director
(202) 477-2103

The Country Program Department acts as project liaison between the World Bank and the appropriate government ministry—usually the ministries of finance and planning. Within this department, several divisions oversee activities in the countries of Southeast Asia.

Philippine Division
Steve O'Brien, Director
(202) 477-2433
Sarshar Khan, Economist
(202) 477-2137

For fiscal year 1981, IBRD–lending to the Philippines totaled $533 million. Projects in the Philippines included: rural development, fisheries-training, Manila sewage and sanitation, rain-fed agriculture, urban development, ports development, and rural roads improvement.

Indonesian Division
Richard Stern, Director
(202) 477-4274
Armene Chokai, Economist
(202) 477-3619

In 1981, IBRD loans to Indonesia totaled $673 million. This was the first year in which Indonesia was no longer eligible for IDA loans, due to the rise in the country's standard of living. Projects for which these funds were used include swamp reclamation, small-holders coconut development, urban development, university education, small enterprise development, and power facilities.

Malaysia, Singapore Division
Andreas Tsantis, Director
(202) 477-2271
Farid Thanji, Economist
(202) 477-4225

In fiscal year 1982, IBRD had one rural electrification project in Malaysia with a loan value of $85 million. Two agricultural and one rural electrification project are under consideration for fiscal year 1983.

Thailand, Laos, Cambodia, Vietnam Division
Nicholas Gibbs, Director
(202) 477-3571
Johannes Linn, Economist
(202) 477-4254

For fiscal year 1981, IBRD loans to Thailand totaled $325.9 million. Projects included inland waterway and coastal ports, power subsector loan, irrigation, Bangkok and Sattahip ports, potash engineering, and a loan for the Industrial Finance Corporation of Thailand. There were no IBRD projects for Laos, Cambodia, or Vietnam in 1981.

INFORMATION AND PUBLIC AFFAIRS DEPARTMENT
Frank Vogl, Director
(202) 477-2468

Regional specialists in the department can assist scholars seeking information concerning World Bank activities in Southeast Asia. They may direct the scholars to the appropriate functional and geographic offices or departments. S. Sankaran (202/477-3962) is the public affairs specialist for East Asia and Pacific.

This department also maintains an extensive collection of still photographs, slides, and motion pictures of projects supported by the bank in the member countries. For further information, contact the Audio-Visual Unit (Pastor B. Sison, 202/676-1632).

ECONOMIC DEVELOPMENT INSTITUTE (EDI)
Ajit Mozoomdar, Director
(202) 477-2203

The EDI trains officials from developing countries in economic management, development programs, and projects. A recently initiated EDI five-
year program (1979–1983) envisages: increased support for training institutions overseas through teaching, advice on training methods, course planning and administration, and the supply of training materials prepared by
EDI staff; an increased number of national and regional courses; and the
introduction, testing, and development of new courses and short innovative
seminars in its Washington teaching program.

During fiscal year 1979, EDI offered 11 courses and 3 seminars for about
400 participants in Washington, and supported 33 overseas courses and
seminars given to about 850 participants. Some of the courses offered through
the Washington program include population and development; preparation,
evaluation, and management of railway projects; development banking;
and rural development projects. The EDI also participates with the United
Nations Institute for Training and Research in conducting seminars for the
staff of diplomatic missions to the U.N.

EDI overseas activities in Southeast Asia include a number of regional
seminars held in several countries. Regional seminars were held in the
Philippines (winter 1981 and summer 1982) on small-scale industries, development banking, and rural-project organization and management. The
above courses were taught in Manila. A transportation course, emphasizing
inland waterway transport, was offered in the spring of 1982, in Bangkok.

3.   For the Joint Bank Fund Library, see entry A26.

4.   The World Bank publishes numerous reports and studies listed in the pe-
riodically updated *Catalog: World Bank Publications.* To obtain the bank's
free publications, contact the Publications Unit (202/477-2403). Some recent
publications of interest include: Kevin Young et al., *Malaysia: Growth and
Equity in a Multiracial Society* (1980); Russell J. Cheetham et al., *The
Philippines: Priorities and Prospects for Development* (1976); Michael M.
Cernea and Benjamin J. Tepping, *A System of Monitoring and Evaluating
Agricultural Extension Projects* (includes data from Burma and Indonesia)
(1977); Alan A. Walters, *Costs and Scale of Bus Services* (an eight-country
study, including Malaysia, the Philippines, and Thailand) (1979); Dipak
Mazumdar, *Urban Labor Markets and Income Distribution in Malaysia*
(1980); and Orville John McDiarmid, *Unskilled Labor for Development:
Its Economic Cost* (a four-country study, including Indonesia and the Philippines) (1977).

Other useful publications are *World Bank Annual Report*; *World De-
velopment Report* (annual); *Finance and Development* (quarterly); *World
Economic and Social Indicators* (quarterly); *World Debt Tables: External
Public Debt of Developing Countries* (annual); *Borrowing in International
Capital Markets* (quarterly); *Commodity Trends and Price Trends* (annual);
and *World Bank Atlas* (annual).

While most bank publications are publicly available, some special studies
are restricted to official use only. All bank documents and records are
ultimately deposited into the custody of the Records Management Office
(Donald K. Bloomfield, 202/477-2711) of the Administrative Services Department, which maintains an index of documentation available to staff.

Note: See also entries A26, E7, E22.

L10 International Finance Corporation (IFC)

1. a. *1818 H Street, N.W.*
   Washington, D.C. 20433
   (202) 676-0391

   b. An appointment is required.

   c. Judhvir Parmar, Vice President, Asia, Europe and the Middle East
   (202) 676-0385
   Torstein Stephansen, Director, Department of Investment, Asia
   (202) 676-0601
   W. E. Kaffenberger, Divisional Manager, South Asia (Indonesia and Burma)
   (202) 676-0607
   Carlos Tan, Divisional Manager, East Asia and Pacific (Malaysia, the Philippines, and Thailand)
   (202) 676-0620

2. The IFC, established in 1956, is affiliated with the International Bank for Reconstruction and Development (IBRD). The corporation seeks to further economic development by encouraging the growth of productive private enterprise in member countries, particularly in the less-developed states. IFC's principal tasks are to provide and bring together financing, technical assistance, and management needed to develop productive investment opportunities in the less-developed member states, whether from private, mixed or government enterprises. IFC capital is provided by its 109 member countries, of which 88 are developing countries. Indonesia, Malaysia, the Philippines, and Thailand are members. IFC occasionally contracts outside consultants for specific research and policy development.

   In fiscal 1980, IFC loan and equity investment in Southeast Asia supported 37 projects. Total commitments to Indonesia in 1980 equaled $61.3 million and included support for such businesses as textiles, glass-dish dinnerware, tourism, money markets, development finance, cement, and construction. Loans and equity in Malaysia totaled $1.1 million. The IFC commitment to the Philippines totaled $51.7 million and included loans for mining, ship-building, chemicals, textiles, fibers, food, utilities, iron, steel, plywood, coconut oil, and copra. In Thailand, loans totaled $32 million for glass, cement, food, and money markets.

4. *IFC Annual Report* summarizes the highlights of its activities for the year. An informative brochure, *IFC General Policies,* is also available from the IFC Information Office (Carl T. Bell, chief, 202/676-0391).

International Labor Organization (ILO) See entries A24 and F11

L11 International Monetary Fund (IMF)

1. a. *700 19th Street, N.W.*
   Washington, D.C. 20431
   (202) 477-3011

   b. Visitors are received by appointment only.

   c. J. deLarosiere, Managing Director and Chairman of the Executive Board.

2. The International Monetary Fund is an organization of 140 countries that seeks to promote international monetary cooperation and facilitate the expansion of trade. It makes financing available to members in balance-of-payment difficulties and provides them with technical assistance to improve their economic management. All Southeast Asian countries except Brunei are members of the IMF and participate in the Special Drawing Rights (SDR). Opportunities for contract research are limited. The fund maintains a pool of private, international fiscal and central banking specialists to act as advisors to foreign governments.

Membership in the fund is a prerequisite to membership in the World Bank (see entry L9), and a close working relationship exists between the two organizations, as well as between the fund and other international and U.N. agencies.

ASIAN DEPARTMENT
Tun Thim, Director
(202) 477-2991

This department is divided into a number of divisions, several of which cover the Southeast Asia region: Division A (Bruce Smith, chief, 202/477-2923), Singapore; Division B (Kunio Saito, chief, 202/477-5661), Malaysia, Thailand, and Burma; Division C (Ranji Salgado, chief, 202/477-5672), Indonesia and the Philippines; and Division D (George Szatary, chief, 202/477-5975, Cambodia, Laos, and Vietnam.

The Asian Department is the principal IMF subdivision concerned with Southeast Asia. The department advises the IMF's management and executive board on all matters concerning the economics and economic policies of Southeast Asian countries, assists in the formulation of IMF policies in relation to these countries, and—along with other departments of the IMF—provides technical assistance and financial advice on many subjects related to improving the management of the economies in our region. Division personnel make periodic trips to Southeast Asia to collect data, analyze financial trends and policies, and hold policy consultations with national authorities responsible for economic affairs. The Asian Department compiles annual reports on recent economic development in each country under its charge. Country staff reports, prepared on the basis of field consultations, are not accessible to researchers.

IMF INSTITUTE
Gerard M. Teyssier, Director
(202) 477-3727

The IMF Institute was established in 1964 to broaden and coordinate the increasing technical assistance given by the IMF. A department of the IMF fund, the institute's purpose is to improve the expertise of officials from member countries in the use of modern tools of economic analysis, in the management of economies, and in IMF procedures and policies. Training courses on financial analysis and policy, balance-of-payments methodology, and public finance are conducted at the institute. Some 2,500 officials from nearly every member country have completed such courses since the founding of the institute, which also provides assistance in its areas of competence to regional and national training centers.

RESEARCH DEPARTMENT
William C. Hood, Director
(202) 477-2981

IMF's research activities are primarily the responsibility of the Research Department. Although most research is concerned with questions of financial, theoretical, and internal policy, Southeast Asia–related issues are also examined occasionally. Researchers may consult the specialists within the department: Commodities Division (Nihad Kaibni, 202/477-4162); Current Studies Division (Michael Deppler, 202/477-2893); External Adjustment Division (Jacques Artus, 202/477-7158); Financial Studies Division (George von Furstenberg, 202/477-4316); and Special Studies Division (Anthony Lanyi, 202/477-2941).

BUREAU OF STATISTICS
Werner Dannemann, Director
(202) 477-3395

The bureau's component units are: Balance of Payments Division (Arie C. Bouter, 202/676-9600); Data Fund Division (Robert L. Kline, 202/477-3206); Financial Statistics Division A (Jai B. Gupta, 202/477-4133); Financial Statistics Division B (Muthusswami Swaminathan, 202/477-4135); General Statistics Division (Chandrakant A. Patel, 202/477-3130); and Government Finance Statistics Division (Jonathan V. Levin, 202/676-0811).

The IMF is a principal source of internationally comparable statistics on national economies, including financial and economic data relevant to the analysis of countries' monetary and payment problems. Compilations and publications of these vital statistics is the responsibility of the Bureau of Statistics. In addition to each country's transactions and operations with the fund, the statistics published by the bureau include data on exchange rates, international reserves, money and banking, prices, production, external trade, wages and employment, balance of payments, government finance, and national accounts. These are all covered in the issues of *International Financial Statistics* (monthly), *Balance of Payments Yearbook, Government Finance Statistics Yearbook, Direction of Trade* (monthly), and similar other publications prepared by the bureau. Magnetic tapes with data from these statistical publications are available on subscriptions.

3.   For Joint Bank—Fund Library, see entry A26.

4.   A booklet, *The International Monetary Fund Purposes: Structure and Activities,* and a brochure, *Publications, International Monetary Fund* (1979), provide descriptions of all major fund publications. Requests for IMF publications should be addressed to the Publications Section (Amparo Masakayan, supervisor, 202/477-2945).

IMF publications include the following. The annual report reviews the fund's activities and analyzes developments in the world economy and in the international monetary system. The *Annual Report on Exchange Arrangements and Exchange Restrictions* includes country-by-country descriptions of most of the exchange systems in the world.

The results of IMF's research on economic and financial problems are published in *Staff Papers*, a quarterly economic journal of the fund. Some examples of staff papers are: Duncan Ridler and Christopher A. Yandle, "Changes in Patterns and Policies in the International Trade in Rice" (Vol.

19, No. I, 1972); Omotundle Johnson and Joanne Salop, "Distributional Aspects of Stabilization Programs in Developing Countries" (Vol. 27, No. I, 1980); and Bijan B. Aghevli et al., "Monetary Policy in Selected Asian Countries" (Vol. 26, No. 4, 1979).

The fortnightly *IMF Survey* reports developments in the fund and the international monetary system in the broader context of world economic and financial news—including changes in countries' policies. A quarterly magazine, *Finance and Development*, published jointly by the IMF and the World Bank carries articles on topics related to the interests of the two institutions. *Technical Assistance Service of the International Monetary Fund* (1979) is an informative publication of the Pamphlet Series. Other publications include the three-volume history of the fund, *The International Monetary Fund, 1945–1965: Twenty Years of International Monetary Cooperation*; and its two-volume sequel, *The International Monetary Fund, 1966–1971: the System Under Stress*.

All inactive files are held by the Records Management Unit (K. Kyung-Hoy Cho, chief, 202/477-6024). Most IMF records are confidential.

Note: See also entries A26 and G8.

L12 UNESCO Liaison Office

1.   a. *918 16th Street, N.W.*
     Washington, D.C. 20006
     (202) 457-0770

     b. Open to the public.

     c. Herschelle Challenor, Director

2–4.   The United Nations Educational, Scientific, and Cultural Organization (UNESCO) promotes international cooperation in the fields of education, science, mass communication, and culture. This recently established small office acts as liaison with the intergovernmental organizations headquartered in Washington, the World Bank group, the Inter-American Development Bank and the Organization of American States, the U.S. government, and other United Nations agencies. A small collection of UNESCO documents is maintained. Researchers desiring to use the library are advised to call in advance. Some UNESCO publications are available in the State Department's U.S. National Commission for UNESCO, located at 515 22nd Street, N.W., Washington, D.C. 20520 (Sally Cutting, 202/632-2767).

L13 United Nation's Development Program (UNDP)—Washington Office

1.   a. *2101 L Street, N.W., Suite 209*
     Washington, D.C. 20037
     (202) 296-5074

     b. Open to the public. Appointments recommended.

     c. Charles L. Perry, Director

2–4.   The Washington Office of the UNDP maintains a small collection of country program reports relating to U.N.–assisted development programs in Southeast Asia. Most of these documents are accessible to researchers. Researchers may request staff assistance in obtaining any records not available at the D.C. office from the UNDP headquarters in New York (One United Nations Plaza, New York, New York 10017).

M Associations (Academic, Professional, and Cultural)

Associations Entry Format (M)

1. *Address; telephone numbers*

2. Name and Title of Chief Official

3. Programs and Activities Pertaining to Southeast Asia

4. Libraries and Reference Collections

5. Publications

Introductory Note

The wide variety of organizations listed in this section should prove useful to scholars of Southeast Asia in two basic ways. First, many of these organizations administer Southeast Asia–related programs, which generate valuable information in and of themselves. Second—and possibly more important—many of these associations serve as clearinghouses for information and can put scholars in touch with a variety of persons having research or active work experience in Southeast Asia. The cultural organizations are valuable as meeting places where people with area expertise, ties, and knowledge gather to share information and experiences or to enjoy Southeast Asia–related cultural programs.

Groups that meet infrequently or have no permanent headquarters—such as the Friends of Malaysia—have been excluded from the main text, but are listed in Appendix I, Southeast Asia Ethnic, Social, Cultural, and Recreational Organizations.

M1 American Anthropological Association (AAA)

1. *1703 New Hampshire Avenue, N.W.*
    Washington, D.C. 20009
    (202) 232-8800

2. Edward J. Lehman, Executive Director

3. The American Anthropological Association is a professional society of anthropologists, students, educators, and others interested in advancing the

discipline of anthropology. The AAA also serves as the administrative headquarters for a number of affiliated professional associations and may be of assistance to scholars in establishing contacts with specialists in the American universities across the country. The society also sponsors lectures and conferences and maintains a speaker's bureau.

5. In addition to *Anthropology Newsletter*, the association publishes a quarterly journal, *American Anthropologist*, and various special publications. A publications list, as well as information about the various journals of affiliated professional associations, are available on request.

M2 American Association for the Advancement of Science (AAAS)

1. *1515 Massachusetts Avenue, N.W.*
    Washington, D.C. 20005
    (202) 467-4400

2. William D. Carey, Executive Officer

3. The world's largest federation of scientific and engineering societies is the AAAS. In fulfilling its mission of providing a more systematic direction to scientific research, and in securing for scientists increased facilities and wider usefulness, the AAAS recognizes that the application of science and technology has global consequences. Largely through its Office of International Science (Denise Weiner, program associate, 202/467-5230), AAAS coordinates many activities of an international scope.

    In preparation for the 1979 U.N. Conference on Science and Technology for Development (UNCSTD), AAAS cosponsored—with the Indian National Science Academy and the Indian Science Congress Association—a major seminar in New Delhi (October 1978) on the "Contribution of Science and Technology to National Development." The AAAS also sponsored a global seminar (December 1980) in New Delhi on the "Role of Scientific and Engineering Societies in Development." The ASEAN states participated in both seminars. The AAAS maintains contact with its sister associations in Indonesia, Malaysia, the Philippines, Singapore, and Thailand and extends invitations to them to attend its annual meetings in the U.S.A.

    AAAS is now administering a Science, Engineering, and Diplomacy Fellows Program. Fellows receive one year appointments to work in the State Department's Bureau of Oceans and International Environmental and Scientific Affairs. A major goal of the program is more effective utilization of scientific and technical expertise in shaping foreign policy.

5. AAAS publications include a weekly magazine, *Science*; a monthly magazine, *Science 82*; and two quarterly newsletters, *The Consortium Notes*, and *Scientific and Engineering Societies in Development*. An information booklet, *American Association for the Advancement of Science* (1981) is available without cost as is a list of AAAS publications.

American Association of Collegiate Registrars and Admissions Officers (AACRAO) See entry N3

M3 American Association of Museums (AAM)

1. *1055 Thomas Jefferson Street, N.W., Suite 428*
   Washington, D.C. 20007
   (202) 338-5300

2. Lawrence L. Reger, Director

3-5 The AAM has been a service organization for museums and museum professionals since 1906. The International Council of Museums Committee (ICMC) of the AAM (Maria I. Papageorge, coordinator) receives foreign museum personnel including those from Southeast Asia. The council also publishes a quarterly newsletter, which lists current international exhibitions across the U.S. Other AAM publications include the bimonthly *Museum News*, and the monthly newsletter *Aviso*. A published list, *Books and Reprints* (1979), is available free.

M4 American Association of University Women (AAUW)

1. *2401 Virginia Avenue, N.W.*
   Washington, D.C. 20037
   (202) 785-7700

2. Q. Brown, Executive Director

3. A national organization for the advancement of women, the AAUW promotes understanding and friendship among university women, encourages international cooperation, furthers the development of education, and encourages the full application of members' skills to cultural and community affairs. The AAUW's Educational Foundation Program offers international fellowships for advanced study in the United States for outstanding women in foreign countries. For the period 1981–1982 the AAUW has fellows from Indonesia, Malaysia, and the Philippines. AAUW is an affiliate of the International Federation of University Women (IFUW) (Geneva, Switzerland). Through the IFUW, the AAUW maintains contact with its sister organizations in Indonesia, the Philippines, and Thailand. The association sponsors the annual AAUW United Nations Seminar and other conferences on issues involving women's interests.

4. The association has a small library and archival collection on women. Nonmembers may visit the collection through prior arrangements.

5. A bimonthly magazine, *Graduate Women*, is circulated to members only. The *Resource Catalog* lists all AAUW current publications and is available free.

M5 American Catholic Historical Association

1. *The Catholic University of America*
   Washington, D.C. 20064
   (202) 635-5079

2. Robert Trisco, Secretary

3. The American Catholic Historical Association was established in 1919 to promote a deeper and more widespread knowledge of the history of the Catholic Church in the U.S.A. and abroad. Members may include specialists on the Catholic Church in French Indochina.

5. The association publishes a quarterly, *Catholic Historical Review*, which occasionally contains reviews of books on Southeast Asian subjects.

M6 American Council on Education

1. *1 Dupont Circle, N.W.*
    Washington, D.C. 20036
    (202) 833-4700

2. J. W. Peltason, President

3. The American Council on Education, which includes among its membership most U.S. colleges, universities, and professional educational organizations, serves as the chief liaison between U.S. higher education and the U.S. government. The council's Division of International Educational Relations (Becky Owens, director, 202/833-4672) fosters improved relations between educational institutions and the federal government and aims at increasing the funding of federal programs for international education. Through its Council for the International Exchange of Scholars (see entry N15) the division administers the International Communication Agency's senior scholars program under the provision of the Fulbright Hays Act.

4. The council's small reference library is available for on-site use by educational researchers. This collection of approximately 4,000 volumes is strong in the history of higher education, educational management, and finance.

M7 American Film Institute (AFI)

1. *John F. Kennedy Center for the Performing Arts*
    Washington, D.C. 20566
    (202) 828-4000

2. Jean Firstenberg, Director

3. AFI is an independent, nonprofit organization established by the National Endowment for the Arts to preserve the heritage and advance the art of film and television in the U.S. The institute preserves and catalogs films; conducts an advanced conservatory for filmmakers; gives assistance to new American filmmakers through grants and internships with major film educators; distributes film books, periodicals, and reference works; supports basic research in motion-picture areas; operates a motion-picture theater in the Kennedy Center; and provides assistance to organizations that present film programs across the country. AFI has screened a few Southeast Asian films.

4. The Institute's Resource Center (202/828-4088) maintains a collection of some 2,500 books and 270 periodical titles devoted to film and television. It also maintains vertical files on film and film-making in foreign countries and a "Theatre File" series that deals with information on films shown by

the AFI. The Resource Center is open by appointment from 10:00 A.M. to 5:30 P.M., Monday through Friday.

5. Publications include: *The Education of the Film-Maker: An International View*; the monthly *American Film*; and the *Factfile* series, volume 10 of which focuses on the *Third World Cinema*; annual report; *AFI Guide to College Courses in Film and Television; Preview*; and the *AFI Education Newsletter*.

M8 American Foreign Service Association (AFSA)

1. *2101 E Street, N.W.*
    Washington, D.C. 20037
    (202) 338-4045

2. Robert Beers, Executive Director

3. The American Foreign Service Association is a professional organization of active and retired U.S. foreign service officers. It holds an annual meeting each June in Washington.

5. The AFSA publishes the monthly *Foreign Service Journal*.

M9 American Friends Service Committee (AFSC)—Washington Office

1. *1822 R Street, N.W.*
    Washington, D.C. 20009
    (202) 232-3196

2. Tartt Bell, Director

3. Headquartered in Philadelphia, the AFSC is a nonprofit, Quaker organization that carries on a variety of services, development, reconciliation, and social-change programs in the U.S. and overseas. In 1981, AFSC was active in the Indochina states of Southeast Asia, trying to ease the causes of the massive migrations from Vietnam, Laos and Cambodia. They did this through relief and reconstruction efforts in the refugees' home countries and by efforts toward peacemaking and international reconciliation. The AFSC is also providing aid to refugees in the camps and encouraging Quakers and others in the U.S. to sponsor refugee families coming to America. The AFSC has worked with Vietnamese refugees at the Malaysian Island camp of Pulau Bidong and continues to work with Laotians and Kampucheans in Thailand.

    In addition, AFSC has sponsored a Southeast Asia Seminars Program for a number of years. In March 1981, AFSC organized a small seminar that brought together academicians, opinion-makers, and development specialists to discuss Southeast Asia in the 1980s, with special emphasis on ASEAN–Indochina relations.

5. Southeast Asia project reports are available on request from the committee's Philadelphia office (1501 Cherry Street, Philadelphia, Pennsylvania 19102).

M10 American Historical Association (AHA)

1. *400 A Street, S.E.*
   Washington, D.C. 20003
   (202) 544-2422

2. Samuel Gammon, Executive Director

3. The American Historical Association is a nonprofit, membership corporation founded in 1884 for the promotion of historical studies, the collection and preservation of historical manuscripts, and the dissemination of historical research. As the largest historical society in the U.S., the AHA conducts an active scholarly and professional program for historians interested in every period and geographic area. The AHA also promotes liaison with historical societies throughout the world, sponsors joint colloquia with foreign historians, and exchanges publications with foreign historical societies. As part of its commitment to promoting historical research, the AHA publishes a variety of research materials and offers prizes and fellowships to scholars. AHA has also become involved with the status and rights of historians and their grievances. At the AHA's annual meeting, there are usually several panels devoted to Southeast Asia.

5. The AHA has traditionally undertaken bibliographic projects to promote historical scholarship. One such bibliography is the *Recently Published Articles*, published three times a year, on the basis of surveys of some 3,000 journals from around the world. It is the most current bibliography of periodical literature available to historians in all fields. The *American Historical Review*, published five times a year, includes scholarly articles and critical reviews of current publications in all fields of history. Through its now discontinued Service Center for Teachers of History, the AHA published a series of highly successful pamphlets intended primarily for school teachers. Among the pamphlets was *Asian Religions: An Introduction to the Study of Hinduism, Buddhism, Islam, Confucianism and Taoism* (1967). Other AHA publications of interest include: the *AHA Newsletter; Discussions on Teaching; Employment Information Bulletin; Grants and Fellowships of Interest to Historians; Doctoral Dissertations in History*; and *Guide to Departments of History*.

American Home Economics Association See entry N7

American Petroleum Institute See entry A3

M11 American Political Science Association (APSA)

1. *1527 New Hampshire Avenue, N.W.*
   Washington, D.C. 20036
   (202) 483-2512

2. Thomas E. Mann, Executive Director

3. The APSA is a national professional association of political scientists, seeking to promote and improve the study and teaching of political science. The association endeavors to realize its objectives largely through publications and conferences. APSA annual conferences often include panels or papers on Southeast Asia–related subjects.

5. APSA offers the following publications of interest: *The American Political Science Review*, a quarterly journal of scholarly articles and book reviews in political science; *PS*, a quarterly journal of association news and articles of professional concern; *APSA Annual Meeting Proceedings; Guide to Graduate Study in Political Science*; and *Research Support for Political Scientists*.

M12 American Psychiatric Association (APA)

1. *1700 18th Street, N.W.*
Washington, D.C. 20009
(202) 797-4900

2. Daniel X. Freedman, M.D., President

3. APA is a professional organization of practicing psychiatrists. Its Council on International Affairs (Jack Weinberg, chairperson) is responsible for dealing with international questions and problems pertaining to psychiatry and mental health, and for planning all international congresses and conferences sponsored or cosponsored by APA. In May 1980, the APA sponsored the Pacific Congress of Psychiatry held in Manila, the Philippines, at which many papers of interest to Southeast Asianists were presented. Scholars may be able to obtain copies of these and other papers from the association.

5. A *Catalog of Publications* (1981) lists all major APA publications. A 1978 report, *Culturally Relevant Training for Asian Psychiatric Trainees*, focuses on the particular needs and concerns of Asian physicians participating in psychiatric training programs in the United States. The APA also publishes the quarterly *American Journal of Psychiatry*; the fortnightly *Psychiatric News*; and the monthly *Hospital and Community Psychiatry*.

M13 American Psychological Association (APA)

1. *1200 17th Street, N.W.*
Washington, D.C. 20036
(202) 833-7600

2. Michael Pallak, Executive Director

3. A major professional organization of qualified psychologists, the APA aims at advancing psychology as a science, as a profession, and as a means of promoting human welfare. APA's International Affairs Office (202/833-3560) has occasional contact with Southeast Asian sister associations in Malaysia, the Philippines, Singapore, and Thailand, and provides information on international conferences and meetings dealing with psychology.

4. APA maintains a small research collection of books and journals on psychology. The library is open to scholars for on-site use by appointment. APA's Psychological Information Services maintains a computerized data base of abstracts scanned from periodicals, technical reports, and monographs world wide. For further information, call Lois Granick (202-833-7624).

5. APA publishes some twenty-two psychological journals; a monthly newspaper, *APA Monitor*; and the monthly *Psychological Abstracts*, which compiles noncritical summaries of the world's scientific literature in psychology and related disciplines. Abstracts accumulated since 1967 are also available on magnetic tape for search and retrieval purposes.

M14 American Public Health Association (APHA)

1. *1015 15th Street, N.W.*
    Washington, D.C. 20005
    (202) 789-5600

2. William H. McBeath, Executive Director

3. A professional organization of health-care specialists and others interested in the field of community health, the APHA has most recently expanded its expertise to assist the developing nations of the world develop sound programs for the delivery of health services. Currently, APHA interest extends to sixty developing countries, including Indonesia, the Philippines, Singapore, and Thailand, where consultant services are being provided through AID in such areas as nutrition, rural health, family planning, water supply, and sanitation.

    At the invitation of the national governments in many developing countries, teams of APHA experts are studying health programs intensively to evaluate activities and advise on program methods and priorities. APHA assists educational institutions in improving their curriculum for teaching health and family-planning techniques and program methodology. For further information, contact Technical Advisory Services for International Health Programs (Myrna Seidman, chief, 202/789-5699). The APHA serves as the secretariat for the World Federation of Public Health Associations (WFPHA), of which several Southeast Asian states are members.

4. The APHA Resource Center (Maria McMurtry, Manager, 202/789-5771) maintains a vertical file of miscellaneous materials on health-care delivery systems of different countries of the world. The center is open to the public from 8:30 A.M. to 5:00 P.M., weekdays.

5. A list of American Public Health Association publications is available free on request. *Salubritas*, a quarterly newsletter on problems of basic health services in the developing world, is distributed free to persons or institutions involved in the delivery or support of public health services in developing countries. Other publications of interest are the monthly *American Journal of Public Health*, the quarterly *Mothers and Children, Health Care Financing in Developing Countries* (1979), and *Environmental Sanitation and Integrated Health Delivery Programs* (1981).

M15 American Society for Public Administration (ASPA)

1. *1225 Connecticut Avenue, N.W.*
    Washington, D.C. 20036
    (202) 785-3255

2. Keith Mulrooney, Executive Director

3. The ASPA is a nationwide, nonprofit, educational and professional organization dedicated to improved management in public service through exchange, development, and dissemination of information about public administration. The ASPA program includes publications, conferences, education, research, and various special services—all aimed at improved understanding and strengthened administration of public service.

    Within the general framework of ASPA goals, the Section on International and Comparative Administration (SICA) (Larry Graham, chairperson, 512/471-5121) seeks to improve the understanding of the "science, processes, and art" of public administration by bringing to the discourse an international and comparative perspective regarding problems and issues of public administration. SICA conducts programs, activities, research, and studies in the areas of international and comparative public administration, and makes the results available to interested ASPA members. The targets of concern include the structure, processes, and outcomes of public policy making and implementation in different economic, political, and social cultural settings. Within SICA, separate committees on development administration, international organizations, and international professional exchanges may assist researchers interested in Southeast Asian studies.

5. The *ASPA Publications Price List* is available on request. Of particular interest is the *SICA Newsletter, Global Network*, and the series of *Occasional Papers*. ASPA also publishes a bimonthly journal, *Public Administration Review*, and a fortnightly newspaper, *Public Administration Times*.

M16 American Society of International Law (ASIL)

1. *2223 Massachusetts Avenue, N.W.*
    Washington, D.C. 20008
    (202) 265-4313

2. Seymour J. Rubin, Executive Director

3. A professional association with membership in some 100 countries, the ASIL is devoted to fostering the study of international law and promoting international relations based on law and justice. Among the many subjects recently dealt with in the society's Research and Study programs are: international terrorism; a number of issues in the field of international human rights; the U.S. Constitution and the conduct of foreign policy; international trade institutions; ocean law and management; comparative national treaty law and practice; management of international river basins; the law of state responsibility; and various international environmental problems.

    The society has undertaken extensive in-house research on the international regulation of activities of a highly scientific or technological nature, covering such diverse fields as food standards, trade in pharmaceuticals or pesticides, and earth-resource satellites, and has recently extended this work into an assessment of the effectiveness of certain United Nations programs. The society also holds ad hoc meetings and conferences in the United States and elsewhere, to examine specific problems of current interest. For further information, contact the society's director of studies (John Lawrence Hargrove, 202/265-4313).

4. The society's library (Helen Philos, librarian) contains over 22,000 items. It is a collection of treatises and other books, documents, briefs, pamphlets, and periodicals—both foreign and domestic—on all aspects of public international law. The library includes basic reference works plus specialized materials, not easily obtainable elsewhere. The library is open to the public, 9:00 A.M. to 5:00 P.M., weekdays, on the basis of prior appointment. Interlibrary loan and photoduplication services are available.

5. Publications of the society include: *The American Journal of International Law* (quarterly); the society's annual meeting *Proceedings*, which contain discussions by leading authorities on important topics of international concern; the bimonthly *International Legal Materials*, which reproduces current treaties and agreements, legislation and regulations of states, judicial and arbitral decisions, official reports, and resolutions of international organizations; the *Occasional Papers* series, covering subjects of great variety and interest in transnational legal policy; and the *ASIL Newsletter*, which reports on pending international litigation and other newsworthy developments in the world of international law. A descriptive brochure, *The American Society of International Law*, is available free.

M17 American Sociological Association (ASA)

1. *1722 N Street, N.W.*
   Washington, D.C. 20036
   (202) 833-3410

2. Russell Dynes, Executive Officer

3. A national association of sociologists and professional social workers, the ASA was established in 1905 to further research and teaching in sociology. Southeast Asian scholars may contact the ASA Committee on World Sociology for establishing scholarly contacts.

5. ASA publications include: *American Sociological Review* (bimonthly); *The American Sociologist* (quarterly); *Sociology of Education* (quarterly); the *Journal of Health and Social Behavior* (quarterly); *ASA Footnotes* (nine issues per year); *Sociological Methodology* (annual); and *Guide to Graduate Departments in Sociology*.

M18 Amnesty International U.S.A.—Washington Office

1. *705 G Street, S.E.*
   Washington, D.C. 20003
   (202) 544-0200

2. Patricia L. Rengel, Director—Washington Office

3.   Amnesty International (AI) is a worldwide, human-rights organization, which works for the release of prisoners of conscience—men and women detained anywhere for their beliefs, color, ethnic origin, sex, religion or language—provided they have neither used nor advocated violence. Independent of all governments, political factions, ideologies, economic interests, and religious creeds, AI opposes torture and the death penalty in all cases, without reservation, and advocates fair and prompt trials for all political prisoners.

Recipient of the 1977 Nobel Prize for Peace, the organization has a consultative status with the United Nations. AI's International Secretariat, based in London, pursues news of arrests, investigates cases of prisoners, and follows the political and legal activities in over 100 countries of every political persuasion. The AI also sends fact-finding missions to countries where human rights are believed to have been violated. In 1980, Amnesty International was active in all of the countries of Southeast Asia.

In Brunei, AI continued to work for the release of nine prisoners who have been held without trial between 15 and 18½ years. From Burma, AI received reports of the imprisonment and torture of both actual and alleged members of the political opposition. AI was investigating this and other allegations of human rights violations in the country.

In Indonesia, AI welcomed the Indonesian government's further implementation of its plan to release political prisoners held without trial after their alleged involvement in the 1965 coup; however, the organization expressed concern about reports of severe human-rights violations in Indonesia-occupied East Timor.

In Kampuchea (Cambodia) AI concerns centered on the forcible repatriation of Kampuchean refugees to the country when there was danger of their being imprisoned, ill-treated, or executed for political reasons. AI was concerned also about the detention of people by the authorities of the People's Republic of Kampuchea (PRK) for purposes of "re-education."

In Laos, AI welcomed the release of a significant number of people in late 1980 and early 1981, although precise figures and details were unavailable. However, the organization was concerned by new arrests and the lack of legal safeguards for those detained on political grounds. Those in detention without charge or trial since 1975 continue to be of concern to AI.

In Malaysia, a number of prisoners have been released since the beginning of 1980, but AI has continued to work on the problem of arrests and indefinite detention without trial of several hundred Malaysians under the Internal Security Act of 1960 (ISA). Under the ISA, a person may be held if the minister of home affairs decides detention is "necessary with a view to preventing him from acting in any manner prejudicial to the security of Malaysia." AI is also concerned about the sudden resumption of executions in February and March 1981.

In the Philippines, President Marcos lifted the state of martial law on January 17, 1981. AI has been concerned that the pattern of human rights violations established during the period of martial law did not end with its lifting. The grounds for such concern were the wide-ranging emergency powers retained by the president, particularly concerning arrest and detention, the prominent role still assigned to the armed forces, and continuing reports of human-rights violations. AI has been particularly concerned about the continuing evidence of torture and ill-treatment, "disappearances," and extrajudicial killings. Military units—irregular units believed to be acting as agents of the armed forces—or other officials are reported to be involved in the extrajudicial killings, known as "salvaging."

In Singapore, AI was concerned with the arrests—and indefinite detention without trial under the Internal Security Act (ISA)—of individuals alleged to have acted in a manner prejudicial to Singapore's security. In Thailand, political imprisonment, the prison conditions of political prisoners, the death penalty, and the *refoulement* of Kampuchean refugees were problems to which AI addressed itself. In Vietnam the main problem for AI was the detention without charge or trial of thousands of people held in "re-education" camps since 1975.

5. Amnesty International publishes the annual *Amnesty International Report* and a monthly newsletter. The U.S. Section of AI publishes a monthly newsletter, *Amnesty Action*, and a quarterly bulletin, *Matchbox*. A number of AI publications deal specifically with Southeast Asia, including: *Indonesia—An AI Report* (1977); *Report of an AI Mission to the Federation of Malaysia* (1970); *Report of AI Mission to the Republic of the Philippines* (1977); *Singapore Briefing Paper* (1976), and *Report of an AI Mission to the Socialist Republic of Vietnam* (1981).

M19 Arms Control Association

1. *11 Dupont Circle, N.W.*
   Washington, D.C. 20036
   (202) 797-6450

2. William H. Kincade, Executive Director

3. The Arms Control Association is a nonpartisan, membership organization formed in 1971 by a group of concerned individuals to promote understanding of arms control and its contribution to national security.

4. The association's Research and Information Service contains books, periodical literature, and newspaper clippings on international arms control and related subjects including items on Southeast Asia. The service answers requests for documentation information, consultation, referral, and other research assistance.

5. The association publishes *Arms Control Today* (eleven issues a year), which occasionally includes materials on Southeast Asia and contains current bibliographies on Southeast Asian regional security issues. In addition, the association participates in or sponsors the publication of a variety of arms-control materials, such as topical bibliographies and the annual *World Military and Social Expenditures*.

M20 Asia Society—Washington Center

1. *1785 Massachusetts Avenue, N.W.*
   Washington, D.C. 20036
   (202) 387-6500

2. William H. Gleysteen, Jr., Director

3. A regional branch of the New York–based educational organization, the Asia Society provides a forum for diverse views of the countries of East,

Southeast, and South Asia, their cultural traditions, contemporary affairs, and relations with the U.S. The center's programs and services include public lectures and films for general audiences, thematic seminars and topical briefings for more specialized audiences, and small meetings where Asians and Americans can share information and views. In 1981 the center sponsored a number of Southeast Asia–related events including a talk by the Malaysian Minister of Home Affairs, Ghazali Shafie, and two programs, *Focus on Indonesia* and *Focus on the Philippines: What is America's Interest?*

4. A small reading room of books and periodicals is available to Asia Society members for reference purposes.

5. A free monthly calendar of events, *Asia In Washington*, lists Washington Center programs and hundreds of Asia–related events and activities in the Washington area. The center has compiled a guide to Asian resources in the greater Washington area; scholars may consult the guide at the Washington Center.

M21 Asian Benevolent Corporation (ABC)

1. *2142 F Street, N.W.*
    Washington, D.C. 20037
    (202) 332-0129

2. Rita O'Donnell, Vice President

3. ABC is a public, nonprofit organization devoted to the promotion of the arts in the Asian community in the metropolitan Washington area. ABC maintains a regular gallery of Amerasian art, organizes exhibitions, educational workshops and seminars on different cultural topics, and holds demonstration classes on various techniques of art. Southeast Asia–related subjects, including Indonesian art, have been occasionally featured.

M22 Association for Academic Travel Abroad

1. *1346 Connecticut Avenue, N.W.*
    Washington, D.C. 20036
    (202) 785-3412

2. David Perry, Executive Director

3. The association assists academic institutions, museums, and professional organizations in planning and conducting educational travel programs. Tours to Southeast Asia are occasionally arranged by the association.

5. Various information brochures regarding travel programs are available on request.

M23 Association for Childhood Education International (ACEI)

1. *3615 Wisconsin Avenue, N.W.*
    Washington, D.C. 20016
    (202) 363-6963

2. James S. Packer, Executive Director

3.　ACEI is a nonprofit membership organization of those concerned with promoting the welfare of children from infancy to early adolescence. The association maintains an international Childhood Education Center, to which leading educators, foreign visitors, members, and others come for meetings, research, exhibitions, and personal interchange. Currently the association has 350 affiliates, including ten foreign affiliates.

5.　An *ACEI Publications* list is available free. *Children and International Education* (1974) is a kit of three booklets developing appreciation for cultural diversity and for sensitizing teachers to ethnicity. Also available is a 1972 portfolio of ten leaflets on ways of developing international understanding and fellowship in children and those who work with them. ACEI's educational journal, *Childhood Education*, contains occasional features and information about our region.

M24　Association of American Colleges (AAC)

1.　*1818 R Street, N.W.*
Washington, D.C. 20009
(202) 387-3760

2.　Mark H. Curtis, President

3.　Established in 1915, the AAC is committed to improving quality in higher education by enhancing and promoting humans and liberating learning. In 1980, the association sponsored the AAC National Assembly on Foreign Language and International Studies (1980) to assist colleges and universities in finding ways to overcome current weaknesses in academic programs in foreign language and international studies. A follow-up National Conference was held in 1981.

5.　In addition to several newsletters and magazines, the association's publications include *Asian Studies in Liberal Arts Colleges* (1961) and *Asian Studies in Liberal Education* (1959). Also of interest may be *College Education with a Global Perspective* (1981).

M25　Association of American Geographers (AAG)

1.　*1710 16th Street, N.W.*
Washington, D.C. 20009
(202) 234-1450

2.　Patricia McWethy, Executive Director

3.　AAG is the national professional association of geographers. The association may be helpful to Southeast Asianists in establishing contacts with specialists in academic as well as nonacademic professions. AAG provides small grants to members for research and field work. At the annual meeting of the association, several Southeast Asia–related panels or papers are often presented.

5.　AAG publications include: two quarterly journals, the *Annals* and the *Professional Geographer*; the *AAG Newsletter*; an annual, *Guide to Graduate Departments of Geography in the United States and Canada*; and an annual-meeting *Abstract* volume. Four papers appear annually in AAG's *Resource Publication Series for College Geography*. Recent issues include: "The Underdevelopment and Modernization of the Third World," "The Geography of the Third World," "The Geography of International Tourism," and "Triumph or Triage? The World Food Problem in Geographical Perspective." Maps can be purchased directly from the Geography Map Fund, Program Director in Geography, George Mason University, Fairfax, Virginia 22030.

M26 Association of Former Intelligence Officers (AFIO)

1. *6723 Whittier Avenue*
    McLean, Virginia, 22101
    (703) 790-0320

2. John M. Maury, President

3. The AFIO is a private, nonpartisan and nonprofit organization founded in 1975 by the intelligence professionals concerned with the future of the U.S. intelligence community in the wake of the revelations and allegations emanating from the media, Congress, and other sources. The AFIO serves as a clearinghouse for the media and has been invited to testify before committees of Congress, and association representatives have also appeared as individual witnesses. AFIO monitors media-reporting on intelligence matters and assists authors and scholars by providing assistance from the AFIO and its members in preparing books and monographs on matters related to intelligence. The association may assist scholars in contacting former U.S. intelligence officers knowledgeable about Southeast Asian affairs.

4. The AFIO is endeavoring to develop a library of works on national security matters for use by members and legitimate researchers. The collection was not yet ready for use at the time of this writing.

5. A periodic publication with limited circulation, *Periscope*, provides news of association activities and useful information on intelligence matters. The association also publishes a *Membership Directory*, which is not released to nonmembers.

M27 Association on Third World Affairs (ATWA)

1. *2011 Kalorama Road, N.W.*
    Washington, D.C. 20009
    (202) 265-7929

2. Lorna Hann, Executive Director

3. A membership organization established in 1961, the ATWA is composed of educators, lawyers, diplomats, and others who share a common interest in promoting cooperation between Americans and the peoples of developing countries. The organization sponsors ad hoc lectures and panel discussions on subjects of current interest with guest speakers at various sites, including foreign embassies, in Washington.

5.   The association publishes a bimonthly newsletter, *Third World Forum*—which often contains material of interest on Southeast Asia—and a series of occasional papers focusing on current issues.

M28 Cambodian Relief and Rehabilitation Committee

1.   *1806 North Harrison Street*
Arlington, Virginia 22205
(703) 536-2796

2.   Ronald T. Seguin, Executive Director

3.   The committee is a private, nonprofit organization that attempts to promote the entry into, and resettlement in, the United States by Cambodian refugees, primarily, but also by other Indochinese emigres. The committee is affiliated with the Hebrew Immigrant Aid Society.

M29 Center of Concern

1.   *3700 13th Street, N.E.*
Washington, D.C. 20017
(202) 635-2757

2.   Peter J. Henriot, Director

3.   In response to an invitation of the United States Catholic Bishops to the International Jesuit Order, the Center of Concern was opened in 1971 as an independent, interdisciplinary team with outreach into the policy-making religious and civic communities in the United States and overseas. The center collaborates with a network of social action and reflection centers in the United States and throughout the world. Holding consultative status with the Economic and Social Council of the United Nations, the center has participated in many international conferences on population, food, women, trade, development, housing, employment, and technology. It also cooperates with the International Labor Organization (ILC) and seeks to build links with international trade union structures.

     The center also serves as the secretariat of the Interreligious Peace Colloquium (IRPC), a nonprofit, educational, charitable, and religious body incorporated in 1976 to bring together members of the major faiths—Muslims, Jews, Christians, Hindus, and Buddhists—who are policy- and decision-makers on transnational issues in the fields of politics, economics, media, and education. The colloquium sponsored a symposium on "Changing World Economic Order: Challenge to the Five World Faiths" (Lisbon, 1977), which was participated in by delegates from Indonesia and Thailand. The colloquium wishes to establish interfaith groups for peace and justice in different parts of the world.

5.   In addition to IRPC occasional papers—*Food/Energy and Major Faiths* (1978), which is principally a report and interpretation of the IRPC meeting held in Bellagio, Italy, and the *World Faiths and the New World Order* (1977), which is a summary of papers and discussion notes of IRPC's second conference held in Lisbon in 1977—the center publishes a free, bimonthly newsletter, *Center Focus*.

M30 Chamber of Commerce of the United States—International Division

1. *1615 H Street, N.W.*
    Washington, D.C. 20062
    (202) 659-6111

2. Michael A. Samuls, Vice President, International Division

3. The world's largest, volunteer business federation, the Chamber of Commerce of the United States seeks, through its policies and programs, to advance human progress, private initiative, and international interdependence. The International Division works to achieve a freer international flow of goods, services, capital technology, and people. While the division's International Economic Policy Section develops the chamber's positions on all aspects of international economic policy, the International Economic Affairs Section develops and conducts the foreign relations of the national chamber.

    Chamber activities with the ASEAN states of Southeast Asia include several conferences and programs. In 1979, the ASEAN–U.S. Business Council was established to address trade and economic problems, with the objective of making recommendations to the members' respective governments. The second plenary session of the council met in October 1980 in Singapore. The third plenary session was held in Kuala Lumpur, Malaysia, in November 1981, and was preceded by the ASEAN–U.S. Finance Conference.

    A recent project, June 1981, was the ASEAN–U.S. Automotive Seminar, which was held in Detroit, and which brought together officials from the Automotive Federation of Asia and the auto manufacturers in Detroit. This seminar was cosponsored by the National Bank of Detroit.

    The Chamber of Commerce has recently completed a market profile on rattan furniture for the Philippines, analyzing the potential for export of this product to the U.S. A guide has also been prepared on the U.S. Generalized System of Preferences (GSP) for use by ASEAN exporters. For further information, interested scholars should contact Oakley Johnson, director of Asia/Pacific Affairs at the U.S. Chamber of Commerce. Mr. Johnson is also the executive secretary of the ASEAN–U.S. Business Council.

5. International Division publications include: *International Report* and *Trade Policy Review*, monthly newsletters; *Foreign Commerce Handbook; International Digest; Guide to Foreign Information Sources;* and *Foreign Investment in the Third World: A Comparative Study of Selected Developing Country Investment Promotion Programs.*

M31 Coalition for a New Foreign and Military Policy

1. *120 Maryland Avenue, N.E.*
    Washington, D.C. 20002
    (202) 546-8400

2. Betty Bono, Co-Director
    Cynthia M. Buhl, Human Rights Coordinator and Co-Director

3.   A coordinating organization of forty-nine national labor, peace, religious, social-change, and research groups, the coalition, through lobbying and dissemination of information, seeks to develop a peaceful, noninterventionist and humanitarian U.S. foreign and military policy.

5.   Publications include the quarterly newsletter *Close-Up*, periodic *Action Alerts*, and an updated *Human Rights Guide*. Of more specific interest to Southeast Asianists are: *U.S. Policy and the Indochina Crisis* (1980) and *The Refugees of Indochina: The U.S. Response* (1980).

M32 Council for International Urban Liaison (CIUL)

1.   *818 18th Street, N.W.*
      Washington, D.C. 20006
      (202) 223-1434

2.   John Garvey, President

3.   The CIUL is probably the best source in Washington for information on developing countries' urban affairs. The council serves as a clearinghouse for information on coping with problems common to urban areas throughout the world. The CIUL monitors developments abroad and reports on them to its member organizations in the United States and Canada. It follows innovations in urban conservation, transportation, finance, planning, and waste management. The council's collection of documents and vertical files may be examined by scholars who have made an appointment.

5.   CIUL publications include *Urban Innovation Abroad, Urban Transit Abroad*, the *Urban Edge*, and various international *Urban Reports. Urban Edge* features some informative articles on Southeast Asia.

M33 Diplomatic and Consular Officers Retired (DACOR)

1.   1718 H Street, N.W.
      Washington, D.C. 20006
      (202) 298-7848

2.   Allen B. Moreland, Executive Director

3.   DACOR is a membership association of retired foreign service officers, former ambassadors, and other officials involved in the field of foreign affairs. The organization can be of assistance to scholars interested in contacting former U.S. diplomats who have served in Southeast Asia.

5.   The association publishes a monthly newsletter, the *DACOR Bulletin*.

M34 Federation of Cambodian Associations

1.   *P.O. Box 943*
      Alexandria, Virginia 22313
      (703) 379-7296

2.   Chun Chen, President

3. The federation is affiliated with Cambodian organizations both in the U.S. and Canada. The federation attempts to bring together Cambodians in the U.S. and Canada and seeks to assist in the reorganization of the Cambodian community by actively supporting and sponsoring refugees from Indochina who resettle in the U.S.. The federation supports any program of action—initiated by either government or private-sector organizations—which helps the plight of Cambodian people.

5. The Federation publishes the weekly *Voice of the Federation* (in Khmer) and a monthly bulletin, *Cambodian Appeal* (in Khmer and English). An informational brochure is available on request.

M35 Foreign Policy Association (FPA)—Washington Office

1. *1800 K Street, N.W.*
   Washington, D.C. 20006
   (202) 833-2030

2. M. Jon Vondracek, Coordinator

3. Founded in 1918, the New York–based FPA is a private, nonprofit, non-partisan organization, whose purpose is to develop an informed, thoughtful, and articulate public opinion on international affairs. The association provides educational and informational materials and sponsors meetings designed to increase American interest in, and knowledge of, foreign policy issues. FPA annually conducts approximately thirty seminars and major events and provides a podium for outstanding speakers at meetings that are open to all interested individuals. FPA prepares reprints of key addresses and makes them available to interested citizens and organizations. Through its "Great Decisions" public-opinion survey, FPA solicits and disseminates public views on major international questions each year.

5. In addition to the *Great Decisions* program book, FPA publishes an annual series of five, short, topical booklets, the *Headline Series*. The only Southeast Asia publication in this series was written by Richard Butnell in 1968. Every four years, FPA also produces *Foreign Policy Briefs*—kits with briefing materials on current world problems—which are extensively used by voter groups and political candidates. Final reports on "Great Decision" opinion ballots are circulated through a bulletin, the *Outreacher*.

International Road Federation (IRF) See entry N22

M36 Foreign Policy Discussion Group

1. *815 Connecticut Avenue, N.W.*
   Washington, D.C. 20006
   (202) 298-8290

2. Charles T. Mayer, President

3. A small membership organization of government officials, academicians, and attorneys, the group holds monthly meetings that feature distinguished

speakers from the realm of foreign policy. Meetings are off the record and closed to nonmembers.

M37 Indochina Refugee Action Center (IRAC)

1. *1424 16th Street, N.W., Suite 404*
    Washington, D.C. 20036
    (202) 667-7810

2. Jesse Bunch, Director

3. The IRAC, created in July 1979, is a private, nonprofit organization, which receives foundation funds, primarily, and some government grants and contracts to provide information and program-development assistance to public and private agencies involved in the resettlement of Indochinese refugees. By October 1979, the center staff had expanded and was involved in research and information services and the planning of specific projects to meet the needs of local resettlement workers.

    The IRAC's program activities to date can be categorized into three primary groups: convening role, information services, and program-development assistance. In its convening role, IRAC facilitated three "Working Group Meetings" (Washington, D.C., area and Chicago) in which representatives of voluntary organizations and agencies—federal, state, local, public, and private—worked closely together to design implementation plans on various topics related to refugee resettlement. IRAC also sponsored a' conference for twenty-six Indochinese people from five ethnic groups in Santa Ana, California, to obtain their active involvement in the Domestic Resettlement Planning Project.

    IRAC's information services include: production of a series of color-coded, national maps from INS registration forms of Indochinese refugee populations in Washington state; publication of five *Cambodian Action Updates*; publication of several *Statistical Updates* on the Indochinese refugee situation; conducting a survey and writing an analysis of the technical-assistance needs of refugee-program service providers.

    Program development includes: preparing seven specific project proposals to respond to the most important needs of the domestic refugee program; working closely with the Department of Housing and Urban Development and the Federal Interagency Task Force to identify housing problems related to refugees; working with the Cambodian Association of America to develop a proposal and obtain funding from the Department of Health and Human Services (HHS) for a significant Khmer cluster project; and advising the Center for Applied Linguistics on the IARC proposal to create an orientation resource center funded by HHS.

5. IRAC publications include the following papers and special reports: *Crying for Life, Cambodia: The Desperate Plight of a Starving People* (1979); *Cambodian Action Update*, five issues published between October 29, 1979, and January 7, 1980; *The Indochinese Mutual Assistance Association* (1980); *Special Report: Physical and Emotional Health Care of Indochinese Refugees* (1980); and *Statistical Update on Indochina Refugee Situation* (1980). In addition, the IRAC can also make available various "Practitioner Workshop" documents all published in 1981, including: *Refugee Orientation, Health-Related Services, Social Adjustment Services, Employment Services,*

Outreach Information and Referral, and *Refugee Resettlement: An Outline for Service Planning and Delivery*. The center also has published a bibliography, *The Resettlement of Indochinese Refugees in the United States: A Selected Bibliography* (1980). Interested scholars should write the IRAC for a complete list of publications.

M38 Indochinese Community Center

1. *1628 16th Street, N.W.*
    Washington, D.C. 20009
    (202) 462-4330

2. Vily Chaleunrath, Executive Director

3. A membership organization, the center seeks sponsors for, and conducts orientation sessions for, new refugees arriving in the Washington, D.C. area, and works in the areas of health education, distribution of educational materals, and counseling. In addition, the center distributes clothing to refugees in need.
    Music and dance festivals and other social-cultural activities are also sponsored. Various public meetings are held at the center and relate to its varied activities.

5. The Indochinese Community Center does not have its own publication, but does make announcements in the publications of other ethnic organizations and relevant agencies.

M39 Institute of Public Administration (IPA)

1. *1717 Massachusetts Avenue, N.W.*
    Washington, D.C. 20036
    (202) 667-6551

2. Annmarie Hauck Walsh, President

3. The Institute of Public Administration is a nonprofit, educational, research, and consultative organization founded in 1906, for the promotion of scientific management in government. IPA has offices in New York and Washington, the latter of which is the operational base for overseas programs.
    IPA's international division was established in 1961. Since that time, this organization has provided technical assistance in research, consultative services, and training in public management, governmental organizations and finance, and urban planning, development, and transportation. Clients have included the governments of South Vietnam, the Philippines, and Indonesia.
    In the Philippines, IPA participated in the January 1981 Manila seminar on metropolitan management in Asia, which was sponsored by the Asia Development Bank and the Economic Development Institute of the World Bank. Dr. Leslie Green, international program advisor, presented a paper and assisted in organizing the seminar. In South Vietnam, IPA provided general technical assistance to the South Vietnamese Institute of Administration. This program was terminated in 1975.
    The continuing Indonesian project has been IPA's largest Southeast Asia project, one for which it is providing technical assistance for a four-year

program, ($5.3 million) for the development of professional resources for development, planning, and administration. The program, financed by a USAID loan to the government of Indonesia, emphasizes both short-term and long-term management training.

M40 International Association of Chiefs of Police (IACP)

1. *13 Firstfield Road*
   Gaithersburg, Maryland 20878
   (301) 948-0922

2. Norman Darwick, Executive Director

3. IACP is the world's leading association of police executives, representing more than sixty-three nations of the world including: the Philippines, Indonesia, Singapore, and Thailand. IACP works for the professionalization of police service in all parts of the world.

   In 1955, IACP created a Training Division for police officers for the International Cooperation Administration (now the Agency for International Development). The culmination of that effort was the creation of the International Police Academy in Washington (closed in 1973), from which police and intelligence officers from Vietnam, the Philippines, and— to a lesser extent—Singapore and Thailand received specialized training.

4. IACP maintains an extensive research library of law enforcement materials for use by members, scholars, journalists, and others who need research assistance in police problems.

5. IACP produces a monthly publication, *The Police Chief*; a quarterly, *The Journal of Police Science and Administration*; and the *Police Yearbook*, which contains the proceedings of the association's annual conference.

M41 International Religious Liberty Association (IRLA)

1. *6840 Eastern Avenue, N.W.*
   Washington, D.C. 20012
   (202) 723-0800

2. B. B. Beach, Secretary General

3. The IRLA spreads the principles of religious liberty throughout the world and safeguards, by all legitimate means, the right of all men to worship or not to worship as each shall individually choose. The IRLA, together with the Geneva–based *par la Defense de la Liberté Religieuse,* sponsored the "First World Congress on Religious Liberty" held in Amsterdam in 1977. A second congress was held in 1981.

4. The IRLA maintains a small library of books and other material pertaining to its mission. Its journal collection includes *Conscience et Liberté* which includes many articles on Islam.

5. A bimonthly magazine, *Liberty*—published by the Religious Liberty Association of America (an affiliate of the IRLA) and by the Seventh Day Adventists—occasionally carries articles of interest on Southeast Asia.

M42 Islamic Center

1. *2551 Massachusetts Avenue, N.W.*
    Washington, D.C. 20008
    (202) 332-3451

2. Mustafa Abulghaith-El Balghita, Acting Director

3. Founded in 1949, and governed by a board composed of thirty-five chiefs
    of missions from countries with predominately Muslim populations (in-
    cluding Indonesia and Malaysia), the Islamic Center is a place of worship
    for the Muslim community as well as a cultural institution for the dissem-
    ination of information on Islam, its history, and culture (see entry P8). It
    also seeks to enlighten American public opinion on Islamic countries and
    peoples and to promote friendly relations between the Muslim world and
    the Americas.
    In order to foster greater interest in and understanding of Islam, the
    center sponsors a number of programs and activities, including lectures,
    symposia, film presentations, and Arabic language classes. The Islamic
    Center is also one of the principal sponsors of the National Committee to
    Honor the Fourteenth Centennial of Islam—a presidentially mandated or-
    ganization devoting its efforts over the 1980–82 period to promoting an
    American awareness and knowledge of the world of Islam.

4. The center maintains a small library of some 4,600 titles of standard works
    on Islam and important commentaries on Islamic law, history, philosophy,
    traditions, and bibliographies. Numerous copies of the *Qur'an*, including
    a number of old copies, are available in the library, which also receives
    vernacular newspaper from the Washington embassies of the Muslim coun-
    tries. The library is open daily from 10:00 A.M. to 4:00 P.M. for on-site use
    only.

5. A bulletin of the Islamic Center appears quarterly, and the center distributes
    English and Arabic editions of the *Qur'an* and a number of titles on *al-
    Hadith*, the life of the Prophet Muhammad, Islamic beliefs and practices,
    law and society, and other educational materials. See also entry P8.

Note: Activities were temporarily suspended in November 1981.

M43 Malaysian Rubber Bureau (MRB)

1. *1925 K Street, N.W.*
    Washington, D.C. 20006
    (202) 452-0544

2. Paul E. Hurley, President

3. The Malaysian Rubber Bureau is an organization established and supported
    by the Malaysian Rubber Research and Development Board to promote
    the use of natural rubber. Founded in 1946 as an information unit of the
    British Rubber Development Board in the United States, it has evolved to
    become more than just an information outlet to provide technical advisory
    service facilities to consumers of natural Malaysian rubber. This technical

advisory service provides a link between the producers and consumers of natural rubber. It is staffed with experienced personnel from the rubber industry. Through this service, manufacturers are made aware of the latest developments in research, updated compounding and processing methods, and new applications and types of natural rubber.

5.   Some publications of the MRB are: *Natural Rubber News*, MBR's own monthly news bulletin that presents topical developments in the rubber scene and industry statistics; *Rubber Developments*, a quarterly periodical that describes current developments in natural rubber research, technology, and use; *Map of Malaysia*, with pictures and facts about Malaysia and natural rubber; and *Natural Rubber Technical Bulletins*, which are issued periodically and describe major advances in raw rubber, processing, and applications. The bureau also publishes an introductory pamphlet, *Natural Malaysian Rubber: Technical Advisory/Information*.

M44 Muslim Women's Association

1.   *Islamic Center*
2551 Massachusetts Avenue, N.W.
Washington, D.C. 20008
(202) 332-3451

2.   Nouha Alhegelan, President
(202) 265-2068

3.   The Muslim Women's Association, founded in 1960 under the auspices of the Islamic Center, is an independent, nonpolitical organization of Muslim women drawn from the local community and the diplomatic corps. The objective of the association is to promote cultural, educational, and social activities and services for the Muslim community and to cooperate with other women's groups. The association organizes monthly meetings, bazaars, and occasional panel presentations on aspects of Islamic culture and status of women in Islamic countries.

5.   A brief mimeographed history of the association, prepared by Sevine Carlson, is available on request.

M45 National Academy of Sciences (NAS)

1.   *2101 Constitution Avenue, N.W.*
Washington, D.C. 20418
(202) 334-2000

2.   Dr. Frank Press, President

3.   The NAS is a private, nonprofit organization of scientists and engineers dedicated to the furtherance of science and its use for the general welfare of all. NAS, through its operating arm, the National Research Council (NRC), serves as the official advisor to the federal government on matters of science and technology. The Board on Science and Technology for International Development (BOSTID), a division of the NRC's Commission on International Relations, is responsible for programs in developing countries.

NAS has on-going activities with Indonesia and has had cooperative projects in the past with scientific and technical institutions in the Philippines, Singapore, and Thailand, and with regional organizations such as the Asian Institute of Technology in Bangkok. Activities in Indonesia have been primarily long-term, cooperative arrangements but have included a variety of workshops and seminars in such areas as management and organization of industrial research, water resources, and food technology. For specific project information contact John G. Hurley, deputy director of the Board on Science and Technology for International Development.

4. BOSTID maintains a working library of resource materials related to scientific and technological aspects of economic development.

5. The Fellowship Office of the NRC's Commission on Human Resources has prepared two useful booklets: *A Selected List of Major Fellowship Opportunities and Aids to Advanced Education for United States' Citizens* and *A Selected List of Major Fellowship Opportunities and Aids to Advanced Education for Foreign Nationals.*

Also of interest are these BOSTID publications: *The Water Buffalo: An Underexploited Resource* (1981), *Supplement, Energy for Rural Development: Renewable Resources and Alternative Technologies for Developing Countries* (1981), and *Proceedings, International Workshop on Energy Survey Methodologies for Developing Countries* (1980). A list of NAS and BOSTID publications is available on request, without charge.

M46 National Association for Foreign Students Affairs (NAFSA)

1. *1860 19th Street, N.W.*
   Washington, D.C. 20009
   (202) 462-4811

2. John F. Reichard, Executive Vice President

3. NAFSA was founded in 1948 to develop the knowledge and competence of persons concerned with international education. Its goal is the most effective operation of international, educational interchange in an effort to assure maximum benefits for individuals, institutions, and society. To achieve these ends, NAFSA provides professional training and information through national and regional conferences, workshops, publications, and consultations. It also maintains communication with governmental agencies and with public and private organizations, both domestic and foreign, in the international education field; supports research and development projects; and conducts an employment registry for students and scholars seeking employment in their home countries.

4. The association's small collection of books on international student affairs may be used by researchers who have made prior arrangements.

5. NAFSA issues numerous publications and reports in the field of educational exchange, including the *NAFSA Newsletter*, the *NAFSA Directory* of institutions enrolling foreign students, and such studies as *The Needs of Students from Developing Countries* and *Learning Across Cultures*. A publication list is available.

M47 National Association of State Universities and Landgrant Colleges (NASULGC)

1. *One Dupont Circle, N.W.*
   Washington, D.C. 20036
   (202) 293-7120

2. James W. Cowan, Director, International Program and Studies Office

3. The oldest higher-education association in the U.S., the NASULGC is the catalyst through which the collective strength of its entire membership is brought to bear on educational and scientific issues of common concern. Its International Programs and Studies Office is a center for information on legislation and governmental and nongovernmental programs related to international education, research, and development. It also serves as a liaison between the universities, government agencies, private organizations, and educational associations concerned with international programs and studies. The International Programs and Studies Office (IPSO) works closely with international program officials at NASULGC member institutions and consortia to help establish and strengthen relationships with developing countries.

5. The IPSO publishes a newsletter, *International Letter*, which is distributed to officers at member institutions who are concerned with international affairs. It reports proposed legislation in the international field as well as international program activities and achievements of member institutions.

M48 National Geographic Society

1. *1146 16th Street, N.W.*
   Washington, D.C. 20036
   (202) 857-7000

2. Gilbert Grosvenor, President

3. A nonprofit, scientific and educational organization established in 1890, the National Geographic Society conducts explorations and research to expand man's knowledge of earth, sea, and sky. The society sends researchers and photographers throughout the world and diffuses the knowledge thus gathered through magazines, maps, books, monographs, lectures, filmstrips, records, and media services.

4. The society's library is described in entry A31, and its map collection, in entry E6.

5. The monthly *National Geographic* (Q18) has carried articles on several Southeast Asian states. A publication list of the society's books, maps, and atlases is available on request.

M49 National Strategy Information Center—Washington Office (NSIC)

1. *1730 Rhode Island Avenue, N.W.*
   Washington, D.C. 20036
   (202) 296-6406

2.   Roy Godson, Program Director

3.   This New York–based center is a nonprofit institution organized in 1962 to conduct educational programs in international security affairs. NSIC seeks to encourage civilian-military partnership on the grounds that, in a democracy, informed public opinion is necessary for a viable U.S. defense system—a system capable of protecting the nation's vital interests and assisting allies and other free nations, who are determined to maintain their core values of freedom and independence. The center occasionally schedules policy workshops in Washington on resource strategy, geopolitics, military reform, comparative defense budgets, and alternatives to détente, and commissions *Agenda Papers* on these topics.

5.   Publications of interest include: George G. Thomson, *Problems of Strategy in the Pacific and Indian Oceans* (1970); Alvin Cottrell and Walter Hahn, *Naval Race for Arms Control in the Indian Ocean* (1978); Harold Hinton, *The China Sea: The American Stake in the Future* (1980); and Joyce Larson, ed., *New Foundation for Asian and Pacific Security* (New Brunswisk, N.J.: Transaction Books, 1980).

M50 Overseas Writers

1.   *National Press Building*
14th and F Streets, N.W.
Washington, D.C. 20045
(202) 737-2934

2.   James Anderson, President

3.   Overseas Writers is a luncheon club that meets once a month and is composed of U.S. and foreign newspaper and broadcast correspondents with overseas experience. A membership list is available. The club can put researchers in touch with members who are currently working in Washington and who may have Southeast Asia experience.

M51 Population Association of America (PAA)

1.   *806 15th Street, N.W., Suite 640*
Washington, D.C. 20005
(202) 393-3253

2.   Edgar M. Bisgyer, Business Manager

3.   PAA is a nonprofit, scientific, professional organization, established to promote research on problems of human population, in both its qualitative and quantitative aspects, and to publish and disseminate results of such research. PAA members are interested in all aspects of population and related subjects, such as general demography, family-planning, fertility, trends in population size, marriage, divorce, the family, internal and international migration, population, and economic and social development. At its annual conference, papers focus on the different regions of the world.

5.   PAA publishes a newsletter, *PAA Affairs*, and the quarterly *Demography*, which contains articles related to current research, including selected papers

presented at the most recent PAA annual meeting; and *Population Index*, which contains items of current demographic interest, an extensive bibliography of books and scientific articles on population from all over the world, and summary tables of population statistics.

M52 Population Crisis Committee (PCC)

1. *1120 19th Street, N.W.*
   Washington, D.C. 20036
   (202) 659-1833

2. Fred O. Pinkham, President

3. A nonprofit, educational organization, the PCC develops worldwide support for international population and family programs through public education, policy analysis, and liaison with international leaders and organizations, as well as through direct funding of private family-planning projects overseas. Currently, such projects are in operation in Indonesia, the Philippines, and Thailand. For specific information on these projects and PCC's role in them, contact PCC's Special Projects Fund (202/659-1833).

5. PCC publications include *Draper Fund* reports and *Population Crisis* sheets.

M53 St. Thomas' Episcopal Church

1. *1772 Church Street, N.W.*
   Washington, D.C. 20036
   (202) 332-0607

2. Hayden Wetzel, Program Coordinator
   (202) 377-4493

3. In 1981, St. Thomas' Parish offered free classes in beginning and advanced English for newly arrived people from Laos, Cambodia, and Vietnam. Students attended three 2-hours classes a week to study the English language. This program was discontinued in 1982.

M54 Society for International Development (SID)—Washington Office

1. *1834 Jefferson Place, N.W.*
   Washington, D.C. 20036
   (202) 293-2903

2. Alfred Van Huyck, Director

3. SID is a Rome–based, nonprofit, nonpolitical, membership organization, founded in 1957 to provide a forum for the exchange of ideas, views, and experiences among persons involved with, or seriously interested in, the vital problems of global, social, and economic development. The society has consultative status with the United Nations Economic and Social Council, and its institutional supporters include the World Bank and the International Monetary Fund.

Members of the association represent 130 countries and territories and are affiliated with more than 800 different organizations. SID chapters have been opened in Indonesia, Malaysia, the Philippines, Singapore, and Thailand. SID's nineteenth "International Conference" (1982) was held in Baltimore. The Washington Office sponsors "work groups" on various development themes and other special events, including briefings by senior officials from Washington–based development institutions.

5. The society publishes the quarterly *International Development Review*, which includes the supplement entitled *Focus-Technical Corporation*; the bimonthly *Survey of International Development*; and the *International Roster on Development Skills*.

M55 United States National Committee (USNC)—World Energy Conference

1. *1620 Eye Street, N.W., Suite 615*
    Washington, D.C. 20006
    (202) 331-0415

2. C. D. Everhart, Executive Director

3. The USNC was organized in connection with the first World Power Conference held in 1924 in London. The USNC is concerned with energy resources and their use, policy, management, technology, and conservation—and how these relate to the total energy picture of the United States and the world. Membership in the World Energy Conference totals eighty-one countries, including Indonesia, Malaysia, the Philippines, Singapore, and Thailand.

M56 World Population Society (WPS)

1. *1337 Connecticut Avenue, N.W.*
    Washington, D.C. 20036
    (202) 833-2440

2. Philander P. Claxton, President

3. A nonprofit, membership organization of professional populationists dedicated to finding solutions to world-population problems, the WPS has members in over six countries, including the ASEAN states of Southeast Asia. WPS organizes international conferences, symposia, and workshops related to action programs to advance the World Population Plan of Action, adopted by 136 countries at the 1974 World Population Conference in Bucharest. A WPS conference was held in Manila in the summer of 1978.

5. WPS publications include: the *WPS Newsletter*; the monthly *World Population News; World Population Growth and Response; Twenty-two Dimensions to the Population Problem*; and the proceedings of its international conferences. WPS plans the creation of a worldwide directory of populationists, with descriptions of their institutions and programs.

M57 World Wildlife Fund—U.S. (WWF–US)

1. *1601 Connecticut Avenue, N.W.*
   Washington, D.C. 20009
   (202) 387-0800

2. Russell Train, President

3. A private, international organization, the WWF–US is dedicated to preserving endangered wildlife and wilderness areas throughout the world, and to protecting the biological resources upon which human well-being depends. Its priorities and programs are designed to be relevant to the socioeconomic needs of peoples everywhere. The fund is represented in twenty-seven countries, including Malaysia.

5. Publications include a newletter, *Focus*, and annual reports.

N Cultural-Exchange and Technical-Assistance Organizations

Cultural-Exchange and Technical-Assistance Organizations Entry Format (N)

1. *Address; Telephone Numbers*

2. Name and Title of Chief Official

3. Programs and Activities Pertaining to Southeast Asia

4. Libraries and Reference Facilities

5. Publications

Introductory Note

As with the numerous associations and research centers listed in sections H and M, many of the cultural-exchange and technical-assistance organizations described below have specialized in a particular type of activity (e.g., management training, rural development, and electrification, among others) and have acquired a certain level of Southeast Asia expertise as a result of current or recently completed contracts in the area. Both private counsultants and nonprofit organizations are included in this section, although the list of consultants presented here—as in Section H (see the introductory note for Section H)—is intended to be representative rather than exhaustive. Several hundred such firms have established themselves in and around Washington due to the extensive contract work available with the U.S. government, particularly with the International Communication Agency (entry K21), the Agency for International Development (entry K1), and the Department of Defense (entry K11). The more extensive ties developed by these groups in Southeast Asia are currently with Indonesia, the Philippines, and Thailand.

N1 Academy for Educational Development (AED)—International Division

1. *1414 22nd Street, N.W.*
   Washington, D. C. 20037
   (202) 862-1900

2. Stephen S. Moseley, Executive Vice President

3. This New York—based academy, which was founded in 1961 to help U.S. colleges and universities solve some of their long-range educational, administrative, and financial problems, has expanded steadily over the past years into an international planning and research organization that is currently conducting 53 projects in the developing countries of the world. The primary concern of the International Division is development of human resources.

   Under U.S. trade and development (TDP) funding, the academy, in conjunction with the Vocational and Industrial Training Board (VITB) of Singapore, held a three-week seminar (April 1981) to acquaint professional job trainers and employers with self-paced, competency-based training techniques. The VITB was in charge of local arrangements. The academy, through its contract, provided training experts and arranged for transportation of equipment and learning packages to Singapore. Lou Thornton (202/862-1940) can provide additional information on this and other past Southeast Asia activities.

   The academy is currently active in Indonesia with its development of a software system for a planned educational-radio project, its software development production and training center, and its feasibility study of satellite applications in the health and education sectors. Peter Boynton (202/862-1950) can provide additional information on the Indonesian activities.

4. The division maintains a clearinghouse on development communication, which is designed to serve planners in developing countries and international agencies. The clearinghouse responds to requests for information, provides referral services, and welcomes visitors to use its extensive collection of evaluation and research materials about projects using communication media.

5. The clearinghouse publishes a quarterly newsletter, *Development Communication Report*, which is circulated internationally, a series of succinct project files, and a series of information bulletins, which treat in some depth the application of communications media to major development problems.

N2 Agricultural Cooperative Development International (ACDI)

1. *1012 14th Street, N.W.*
   Washington, D. C. 20005
   (202) 638-4661

2. Donald H. Thomas, President

3. ACDI, a nonprofit organization, works under contract, funded by the Agency for International Development or other agencies, such as the Asian Development Bank, in providing technical assistance to agricultural cooperatives and farm credit systems in developing countries. ACDI assistance includes advisory and training services in the fields of agricultural credit, cooperative banking, agricultural marketing, supply, education, and policy planning. ACDI has been active in the Philippines for over a decade and, since 1979, has had a major cooperative marketing project there, admin-

istered by two full-time staff members. ACDI has also provided recent short-term support services in Indonesia, Thailand, and Burma.

5. ACDI publications include an annual report and the bimonthly *News of Cooperative Development.*

N3 American Association of Collegiate Registrars and Admissions Officers (AACRAO)

1. *One Dupont Circle, N.W.*
   Washington, D. C. 20036
   (202) 293-9161

2. J. Douglas Conner, Executive Director

3. A nonprofit national professional association, the AACRAO's International Education Activities Group assists the academic placement offices in U.S. institutions with the credentials of foreign students. It also sponsors workshops on the evaluation of foreign-student credentials, provides credential analysts and consultant sources, and conducts studies designed to improve the selection and admission of AID participants to study in U.S. academic institutions.

5. AACRAO publishes the *World Education Series* booklets that describe the educational systems of foreign countries and provide guides to the academic placement of foreign students. The booklets are produced with the help of a special grant from the International Communication Agency. Booklets are now for sale on Indonesia, Thailand, and Vietnam (out of date). A publications brochure is available.

N4 American Council of Young Political Leaders (ACYPL)

1. *426 C Street, N.E.*
   Washington, D. C. 20002
   (202) 546-6010

2. Thomas H. Hutson, Executive Director

3. The council, which is a private, nonprofit organization, provides opportunities for young American and foreign political leaders to gain insight into the vital areas of international affairs and American political processes, respectively, and fosters personal relationships among the young political leaders. With assistance from the International Communication Agency, the ACYPL sends a U.S. delegation overseas and receives foreign delegations to the U.S. Delegations from this country have not visited any Southeast Asian states in the last two years, nor have delegations from these countries visited the U.S. Such visits are, however, possible in the future. Other ACYPL programs include foreign policy conferences at the State Department, seminars, and workshops participated in by both American and foreign delegates.

5. Program information is available on request.

N5 American Council on International Sports (ACIS)

1. *817 23rd Street, N.W.*
   Washington, D.C. 20052
   (202) 676-7246

2. Carl A. Troester, Jr., Executive Director

3. A nonprofit organization, ACIS attempts to enhance international cooperation and understanding through physical education and sport. It administers international sports-exchange programs in cooperation with the State
   Department, the U.S. Olympic Committee, and numerous international
   sports federations. The twenty-fourth Annual Congress of the International
   Council on Health, Phsyical Education, and Recreation was held in Manila,
   July 1981.

5. The council publishes a monthly bulletin, *News Briefs*, which is available
   on request.

N6 American Federation of Labor and Congress of Industrial Organizations (AFL-CIO)—Department of International Affairs

1. *815 16th Street, N.W., Room 705*
   Washington, D. C. 20006
   (202) 637-5000 (Information)
   (202) 637-5063 (International Affairs)

2. Ernest Lee, Director Department of International Affairs
   James Ellenberger, Representative, Asian Specialist

3. The AFL-CIO Department of International Affairs serves as a liaison office
   for the various international contacts and activities of the union. Direct,
   bilateral trade-union relations are maintained with labor organizations in
   the Philippines, Indonesia, Singapore, and Maylasia.
   This office assists foreign visits in arranging meetings with representatives
   of AFL-CIO member unions and aids U.S. trade unionists visiting their
   counterparts overseas. The International Affairs Department also provides
   liaison and technical support of AFL-CIO sponsored institutes involved in
   providing technical assistance to foreign trade unions and U.S. government
   agencies involved in labor affairs. Responsibility for AFL-CIO, Southeast
   Asia technical-assistance programs is divided between two institution (see
   entries N9 and N16).

4. The AFL-CIO library (202/637-5297), located in Room 102 of the headquarters building, is open to the public weekdays from 9:00 A.M. to 4:30
   P.M.. The library maintains a vertical file of clippings, pamphlets, and correspondence that contain a limited amount of information on Southeast
   Asian labor movements and U.S.–Southeast Asian labor relations. Librarian Jean Webber can assist scholars interested in this collection.
   AFL-CIO archival material, including the union's international records,
   1950s–1970s, is maintained separately from the library. Logan Kimmel (202/
   637-5138) can provide further information on these items.

5.   The international programs of the AFL-CIO are outlined in the semi-annual *Executive Council Report to the Convention*, which is available on request.

American Friends Service Committee–Washington Office See entry M9

N7 American Home Economics Association—International Family Planning Project

1.   *2010 Massachusetts Avenue, N.W.*
Washington, D. C. 20036
(202) 862-8300

2.   Elizabeth W. Brabble, Director

3.   The International Family Planning Project of the American Home Economics Association is funded by the U.S. Agency for International Development. Its goal is to reduce population expansion through a program of information, education, and communication. The mission of the project is to assist the developing countries' home-economics education systems to integrate family planning and population information into their curricula. Project activities include: consultation visits; country surveys; the in-country workshops and seminars; in-depth training fellowships; publications, research, and pilot projects; an international committee of key home economics in developing countries to act as contacts, advisors, and leaders for on-going activities of the project; and cooperation with international agencies such as the International Federation for Home Economics, FAO, UNESCO, and the International Planned Parenthood Federation. IFPP currently has on-going projects in the Philippines, with the ministry of Agrarian Reform, and in Thailand, where rural extension personnel are being trained to use family-planning information for dissemination to the public.

5.   A quarterly newsletter of the International Family Planning Project, *The Link*, serves as an information exchange for its activities, new resources, and research. Project resource materials include: *Resource Catalog: Family Planning and Population Education in Home Economics; Sourcebook for Teachers*; and *Working with Villagers*, a training kit for field workers. A list of project publications is available free.

Note: The International Family Planning Project was terminated on March 29, 1982.

American Public Health Association See entry M14

N8 American Red Cross—Office of International Services

1.   *17th and D Streets, N.W.*
Washington, D.C. 20006
(202) 737-8300

2.   Joseph Carniglia, Director

3.   Operating under congressional charter and fulfilling U.S. obligations under certain international treaties, the American Red Cross is a humanitarian disaster-relief and health-education organization. The American Red Cross is affiliated with the worldwide federation of the Geneva–based League of Red Cross Societies. The Office of International Services supervises the donation of supplies, funds, and technical assistance for relief in major, natural calamities and man-made disasters abroad. In the past the American Red Cross has participated in technical assistance and international disaster-relief operations in Southeast Asia and can provide information on these activities.

4.   The American Red Cross National Headquarters Library (Roberta F. Biles, Library Director, 202/857-3491) is open to the public weekdays from 8:30 A.M. to 4:45 P.M. Photoduplicating facilities and interlibrary loan are available. The collection contains approximately 17,000 books and bound periodicals, and, in addition, the library maintains numerous records, reports, documents, pamphlets, and periodicals covering the history and current activities of the American Red Cross, the International Committee of the Red Cross, and the League of Red Cross Societies. A card index to Red Cross periodicals and reports, and an extensive vertical file collection of reports and publications of major national and international voluntary organizations are also available.

5.   Publications include the annual report, which describes the domestic and international activities of the American Red Cross; a bi-monthly periodical, *The Good Neighbor*, and occasional press releases.

Note: See also entries B2 and F3.

N9 Asian-American Free Labor Institute (AAFLI)

1.   *1125 15th Street, N.W.*
Washington, D.C. 20005
(202) 737-3000

2.   Morris Paladino, Executive Director

3.   The AAFLI was established in 1968 by the American Federation of Labor and Congress of Industrial Organization (AFL-CIO) to encourage and advance the development of strong, independent trade unions throughout Asia. Educational, social, and impact programs, designed to serve the needs of Asian workers, are administered by the institute in 16 countries including: Indonesia, Malaysia, the Philippines, Thailand, and Vietnam (discontinued in 1975).

In Indonesia, some 2,000 people have participated in AAFLI–sponsored education seminars. Other AAFLI social projects in this country include: construction of a trade-union library, establishment of a revolving loan fund for workers' co-ops, and construction of a school in Bali. In Malaysia there have been 33 participants in the educational seminars, while in Thailand almost 5,000 have participated. Also in Thailand, AAFLI has provided typewriters and mimeograph machines to eight national unions, constructed a prototype union community center for use by nine unions in Sriracha, and translated and published basic union education texts. In the Philippines, some 17,000 persons have participated in AAFLI–sponsored education seminars.

The AAFLI has inoculated over 1,000 workers' children against contagious diseases, sent capital loans to the National Mines and Allied Workers Union consumer cooperative, and subsidized the basic operating costs of the Trade Union Congress of the Philippines research center. The AAFLI also gives grants to Asian trade unionists for study abroad as part of the program development in their countries. Recipients, who are nominated by their unions, receive grants to study and work with labor organizations in the United States, where they attend labor courses at Harvard University or the University Center for Cooperatives at the University of Wisconsin.

5.   The institute has produced some 50 pamphlets, manuals, books and other published materials for use in its own programs as well as those of the unions with which it cooperates. These materials have appeared in several Asian languages, including Indonesian. Among the institute's publications, the following two publications may be of special interest: *Building Unions in Asia—A Unique Task* (1972); and *Asia: A Study in Emerging Unions*. The institute also publishes the monthly *AAFLI News*, which includes reports on projects and activities supported by the institute. Its annual *Progress Report* provides a brief summary of its activities in Southeast Asian countries. The AAFLI slide-tape cassette, *American Labor in Asia*, is available without charge for loan to educational organizations.

N10 Baptist World Aid (Baptist World Alliance)

1.   *1628 16th Street, N.W.*
Washington, D.C. 20009
(202) 265-5027

2.   Erna Redlich, Assistant Secretary for Aid and Development

3.   Baptist World Relief administers the Baptist World Alliance's Relief Fund program. It provides funds to Baptist groups in the Third World for the purchase of equipment needed in local development projects related to schools, clinics, and irrigation projects. In recent years, the Baptist World Relief has been active with Indochinese refugees in Cambodia, working with Oxfam America. It has also been helping refugees in Northern Thailand and along the Thai–Cambodian border. In the Philippines, activities have included Indochinese refugee relief, chicken-farming projects, technical education, and flood relief in Mindinao.

5.   The Baptist World Alliance publishes a monthly magazine, the *Baptist World*.

Business Council for International Understanding See entry H10

Chamber of Commerce of the United States–International Division See entry M30

N11 Checchi and Company

1. *1730 Rhode Island Avenue, N.W.*
   Washington, D.C. 20036
   (202) 452-9700

2. Mary Culbertson, Coordinator of International Programs

3. Checchi is a private international consulting and research corporation that specializes in development and management services and works under contract for U.S. government agencies, the World Bank, and other organizations. Checchi and Company has been extensively involved in numerous projects in the countries of Southeast Asia. In Indonesia, Checchi has undertaken a Nusa Dua transportation study for the Bali Tourism Development Corporation, designed a marketing strategy for a proposed consortium of small hotels on the Island of Bali, carried out a feasibility study of a pilot, brackish-water fisheries project proposed for Lampung Province in Sumatra, produced a study on the nature and problems of the cooperative movement in Indonesia—and the political and economic settings in which it operates—and has provided technical assistance to the government of Indonesia in planning and executing a comprehensive development strategy for the Luwu area of South Sulawesi.

   Other representative projects include a study for the Asian Development Bank of the Laotian economic situation; an analysis of present and future private consumption in Malaysia; an analysis of the financial conditions and operations of a group of companies in the Philippines, which were involved in industrial manufacturing and shipping activities; assistance in the development of market outlets for Philippine plywood, as well as the training and recruitment of personnel for that industry; an assessment for the Nationwide Insurance Company of Columbus, Ohio, of the feasibility of investing in the Philippines; a cost-benefit analysis of tourism in Southeast Asia, using the multiplier theory; and a report to the Advanced Research Projects Agency (ARPA) of the U.S. Department of Defense, assessing the relationship of economic development to rural security in Northeast Thailand.

5. The reports and studies generated by the company are the property of the clients and are available only with the permission of the clients. However, reports produced under contract from U.S. government agencies are available from the National Technical Information Service (entry Q19).

N12 Chemonics—International Consulting Division

1. *1120 19th Street, N.W.*
   Washington, D.C. 20036
   (202) 466-5340

2. Thurston F. Teele, Director

3. A conglomerate based in Phoenix, Arizona, the International Consulting Division provides a wide range of management and consulting services overseas under contracts from the Agency for International Development

(AID). In 1982, Chemonics provided an agronomist extension specialist for a provincial development program in Indonesia.

5. A pamphlet describing the division's programs is available on request.

N13 Cooperative for American Relief Everywhere (CARE)— Washington Field Office

1. *1016 16th Street, N.W.*
   Washington, D.C. 20036
   (202) 296-5696

2. Ronwyn Ingraham, Director

3. With its World Headquarters in New York (660 First Avenue, New York, N.Y. 10016, 212/686-3110), CARE is a voluntary, nonprofit and nongovernmental, technical-assistance and disaster-relief agency. This organization has been involved in Cambodian relief efforts since September 1980. Activities include rice distribution in Cambodia, food relief and distribution of rice in Thailand for Cambodian refugees, and distribution of seed grain in Cambodia. CARE also distributed, on a one-time basis, hospitality kits to Indochinese "boat people" in Indonesia. In the late 1960s and early 1970s, CARE also had a medical-assistance program in Malaysia.

5. CARE's annual report and its quarterly newsletter, *CARE World Report*, are available at the Washington Field Office.

N14 Cooperative Housing Foundation (CHF)

1. *2501 M Street, N.W.*
   Washington, D.C. 20037
   (202) 887-0700

2. Charles Dean, President

3. The Cooperative Housing Foundation works to develop innovative and fresh approaches for the shelter needs of moderate- and low-income families in the United States and developing countries. In the U.S., CHF sponsors the development of cooperative housing—60,000 units since 1952. In developing countries, CHF provides consulting services in both technical and policy-development fields at the invitation of local governments and cooperative organizations. Specifically, CHF provides expertise in such areas as: training and collaboration with local technicians in the development of self-help cooperative housing, disaster-relief shelters, rural housing, and special programs for refugees. Funding for this international program is derived from the U.S. Agency for International Development, the United Nations, the World Bank, and others. CHF has been involved in housing projects in Thailand, Indonesia, and the Philippines, and in 1981 was awaiting approval of a pending proposal for additional services in the Philippines.

5. Publications include *CHF International Program*, which describes the organizations goals and activities.

N15 Council for International Exchange of Scholars (CIES)

1.   *11 Dupont Circle, N.W.*
      Washington, D.C. 20036
      (202) 833-4950

2.   Cassandra A. Pyle, Director

3.   CIES was established in 1947 as a private, nonprofit organization to facilitate international exchange in higher education. Under arrangements with the U.S. International Communication Agency, the council cooperates in the administration of the Fulbright program, which was established in 1961 to increase mutual understanding between the people of the United States and the people of other cultures. Each year, 650–700 foreign scholars and 550 American scholars, under the Fulbright program, receive various awards, which the council is responsible for arranging and confirming, in addition to administering grants. CIES has aided in the exchange of more than 14,000 scholars from the U.S. and other countries for research, lecturing and consultation at the university level. The council currently administers exchange programs in the ASEAN states of Southeast Asia.

5.   The council publishes several information leaflets, including the annual *Fulbright Awards Abroad; Fulbright Opportunities Abroad;* a *Directory of Visiting Fulbright Lecturers and Researchers in the U.S.;* and *Visiting Fulbright Scholars Available for Occasional Lecture Programs.*

N16 Credit Union National Association (CUNA)—Global Projects Office

1.   *1120 19th Street, N.W.*
      Washington, D.C. 20036
      (202) 659-4571

2.   Thomas R. Carter, Director of Programs

3.   An affiliate of the World Council of Credit Unions (WOCCU), CUNA's Global Projects Office provides technical assistance and advisory services to aid in the development of credit unions abroad. In 1980 CUNA had a short-term project with the Credit Union National Organization of Indonesia. CUNA has also been involved in the region indirectly through the Asian Confederation of Credit Unions.

4.   The Global Projects Office receives copies of some of the publications of the World Council of Credit Unions, namely, the *Annual Report, WOCCU Newsletter* (monthly), and *World Reporter* (quarterly).

N17 Development Alternatives, Incorporated (DAI)

1.   *624 9th Street, N.W.*
      Washington, D.C. 20001
      (202) 783-9110

2.   Donald R. Mickelwait, President

3. DAI is a private consulting firm that designs and implements development and technical-assistance projects in the fields of agriculture (farmer training, livestock marketing, and seed multiplication), rural health, manpower development and rehabilitation in various Third World countries, including Indonesia. Much of DAI's work is undertaken on a contract basis for the U.S. Agency for International Development (USAID) the World Bank, and other international organizations.

4. The office maintains a reference library for the staff.

5. A number of DAI studies, reports, and occasional papers can be obtained through USAID.

N18 Experiment in International Living—Washington Office

1. *1346 Connecticut Avenue, N.W., Suite 802*
   Washington, D.C. 20036
   (202) 872-1330

2. Penny Linn, Director—Washington Office

3. The Experiment in International Living is a private, nonprofit, educational organization that sponsors international "homestay" exchange programs and cross-cultural education programs for high-school students, college students, and adults from the United States and foreign countries. Currently, there are no programs for the countries of Southeast Asia. The organization is headquartered in Brattleboro, Vermont.

5. The organization publishes a quarterly newsletter, *Odyssey*. Program literature is also available.

N19 General Federation of Women's Clubs (GFWC)

1. *1734 N Street, N.W.*
   Washington, D.C. 20036
   (202) 347-3168

2. Marijo Shide, President

3. An international organization with membership in 37 countries including the Philippines and Thailand, GFWC's International Affairs Program, with cooperation from the Cooperative for American Relief Everywhere (CARE), emphasizes a wide range of educational programs in developing countries in the fields of nutrition, health-care training, vocational skills, agricultural development, fish production, reforestation, and school construction.

5. *GF Clubwoman Magazine* is published nine times a year.

N20 Institute of International Education (IIE)—Washington Office

1. *918 16th Street, N.W.*
   Washington, D.C. 20006
   (202) 775-0600

2.   Sherry Mueller Norton, Director of Washington Office

3.   The Institute of International Education (IIE) is the largest and most active educational exchange agency in the United States. IIE administers exchange programs with over 120 countries, provides services to technical-assistance programs overseas, and offers scholarships for study in the U.S. The agency has had working relationships with the ASEAN states and Burma in recent years through sponsored programs. The Washington office provides information and counseling services on all aspects of international education exchange, and assists in the U.S. government's International Visitors Program.

5.   Institute Publications are standard references on international exchange. IIE produces both comprehensive reference works and specialized study guides.

Institute of Public Administration See entry M39

International Association of Chiefs of Police See entry M40

N21 International Center for Dynamics of Development

1.   *4201 South 31st Street*
      Arlington, Virginia 22206
      (703) 578-4627

2.   Dana D. Reynolds, President

3.   The center focuses attention and crystallizes action on policies and programs in the international, national, public, and independent sectors to broaden participation in political, economic, and social development. It fosters strategies to promote unity and cooperation among, and within, nations. Major Southeast Asia related activities of the center include an International Conference on Country Strategies to Involve Peoples in Development (1975), which included several panels and papers on Southeast Asia, and the International Symposium on National Strategies to Build Support for Development in the Context of the New International Economic Order (1971). The latter conference also included panels and papers on Southeast Asia and was attended by scholars from the region. The center's advisory committee has representatives from several ASEAN states.

5.   Some conference programs and papers are available.

N22 International Road Federation (IRF)

1.   *Washington Building*
      15th Street and New York Avenue, N.W.
      Washington, D.C. 20005
      (202) 783-6722

2.   W. Gerald Wilson, President

3.   Established in 1948, the IRF is an international federation consisting of some 74 foreign national associates in 67 countries including Burma, Indonesia, Malaysia, the Philippines, and Thailand. The federation's purpose is two-fold: to be of service to the people responsible for planning, building, maintaining, and managing of, and those benefiting from use of, the world's roads and road systems; and to create understanding of the social and economic benefits that good roads provide. IRF also serves as a link between those who have need of, and those who can provide, expertise. The IRF Fellowship Program, begun in 1948 for graduate engineers from abroad, is tailored to the special transport problems and requirements of the participating fellows' countries. IRF fellowships have been awarded to engineers from Indonesia, Malaysia, Burma, the Philippines, Thailand, and Vietnam. An *IRF Fellowship Directory* is published at regular intervals.

5.   Each year IRF publishes the *World Survey of Current Research and Development on Roads and Roads Transport*, an extensive inventory of highway research and development in 77 countries, including Indonesia, the Philippines, and Thailand. IRF also publishes *IRF World Highways* nine times a year and the annual *Road and Motor Vehicle Statistics*, which includes data on the number of automobiles, trucks, buses, and motorcycles, highway mileage, and estimated highway expenditures for the countries of Southeast Asia, excluding the Indochinese states. *Limits of Motor Vehicle Sizes and Weights* also covers most countries of Southeast Asia. The IRF annual report also contains useful information concerning Southeast Asia.

N23 International Voluntary Services (IVS)

1.   *1717 Massachusetts Avenue, N.W.*
      Washington, D.C. 20036
      (202) 387-5533

2.   John T. Rigby, Executive Director

3.   International Voluntary Services is a private, nonprofit, independent organization that recruits skilled volunteer technicians from around the world to work on rural development projects in developing countries. Funding for its activities has come from various sources including the U.S. Agency for International Development, Catholic Relief Services, OXFAM, the United Presbyterian Church, and other organizations. Currently, IVS has no Southeast Asian activities. IVS was, however, active in Indonesia in the early 1970s.

5.   IVA annual reports are available on request.

N24 Jesuit Missions

1.   *1717 Massachusetts Avenue, N.W.*
      Washington, D.C. 20036
      (202) 387-3720

2.   Simon E. Smith, Executive Secretary

3.   The Jesuit involvement in Southeast Asia has been considerable and of long duration. Currently there are 322 Jesuits in Indonesia, working in the

fields of education and social work. The Jesuit community in Indonesia is of Dutch and indigenous origin. In 1981, the Jesuits celebrated their four-hundredth anniversary in the Philippines, where today 339 Jesuits (mostly native born) work in secondary and higher education. The Jesuits are currently active to a much lesser degree in Thailand and Singapore, and were expelled, like many other groups, from Burma some years ago.

This office does not have archival materials but may be able to direct serious scholars to other sources.

5.   Publications include the *JM Newsletter* and *Studies in the International Apostolate of Jesuits*, both of which are irregular.

N25 Meridian House International (MHI)

1.   *1630 Crescent Place, N.W.*
Washington, D.C. 20009
(202) 667-6800 or (202) 332-1025

2.   Joseph John Jova, President

3.   Meridian House International, a nonprofit corporation in the field of international affairs, is dedicated to supporting international exchange programs. MHI is financed by government contracts and grants, foundation support, and corporate and individual gifts. In addition to providing visitors with reception, orientation, and programming, the MHI conducts a lecture series on world affairs, organizes topical seminars for members of the Washington diplomatic community, and sponsors other educational and cultural programs. The MHI can provide assistance in some 48 foreign languages, including several Southeast Asian languages. Its programs include the Visitors Program Service (202/822-8688) and the Washington International Center (202/332-1025); its affiliates are the National Council for International Visitors (202/332-1028), the International Visitors Information Service (202/872-8747), and the Hospitality and Information Service for Diplomats (202/232-3002).

5.   Publications include *MHI Newsletter*, a quarterly development magazine entitled *International Exchange News*, and specialized works devoted to aspects of intercultural exchanges. MHI also publishes catalogs devoted to its art exhibitions and proceedings of its major seminars.

National Academy of Sciences See entry M45

N26 National Education Association (NEA)

1.   *1201 16th Street, N.W.*
Washington, D.C. 20036
(202) 833-4000

2.   Terry Herndon, Executive Director

3.   NEA, a nonprofit membership organization of public school teachers in the U.S., promotes public education in the nation. International programs

of the NEA are coordinated by the Committee on International Relations (Braulio Alonso, 202/833-4105). NEA maintains cooperative relationships with teacher organizations in countries around the world, including Indonesia, Malaysia, the Philippines, Singapore, and Thailand. In Singapore, where teachers are well organized into five separate, ethnically based organizations, and in Malaysia, where members of the profession are also well organized, NEA's role is primarily to exchange information. In the other three Southeast Asian states, teachers are less well organized and, in the case of the Philippines, under somewhat stricter control. NEA attempts to help these organizations by sponsoring teacher seminars and related activities.

4. NEA publications include *Today's Education* (issued 4 times during academic year), *NEA News Service* (weekly), *NEA Reporter* (8 times a year), and *Higher Education Newspaper* (4 times a year).

N27 National 4-H Council

1. *7100 Connecticut Avenue*
    Chevy Chase, Maryland 20815
    (301) 656-9000

2. Melvin J. Thompson, Coordinator, International Relations

3. The National 4-H Council, a private, not-for-profit educational institution, was incorporated to strengthen the 4-H program by providing educational experiences that complement the work of the Cooperative Extension Service of the U.S. Department of Agriculture. The Council's international exchange programs are designed to promote international understanding and develop better-informed youth leaders by providing an opportunity to learn about 4-H and youth development programs as well as by providing a crosscultural experience. Over 18,000 individuals, representing the U.S. and 89 cooperating countries, have participated in 4-H international exchange programs since they began in 1948. Participating countries in recent years included the Philippines and Thailand. The international programs arc supported by private funds and limited public grants available for use with some countries.

5. Program literature is available on request.

N28 National Rural Electric Cooperative Association (NRECA)

1. *1800 Massachusetts Avenue, N.W.*
    Washington, D.C. 20036
    (202) 857-9500

2. Samuel Bunker, Administrator, International Programs Division

3. The International Programs Division of NRECA provides technical assistance to foreign government agencies, utility companies, and cooperatives in the development and operation of rural electric systems and electricity cooperatives. Activities include advisory, consulting, and training services, along with preparation of country surveys and feasibility studies. In some projects the association is involved from the planning stages through im-

plementation. Since 1978, NRECA has had a staff of seven persons working on a rural electrification project in Indonesia. A ten-year rural electrification project in the Philippines was completed in 1979.

5.   Publications include *NRECA Overseas Report* and *Rural Electrification Magazine* (a monthly). The numerous studies and reports prepared by the association are for the use of their clients. However, the staff can direct researchers to the appropriate agency to gain access to these materials.

N29 Overseas Education Fund (OEF)

1.   *2101 L Street, N.W., Suite 916*
Washington, D.C. 20037
(202) 466-3430

2.   Emily Dicicco, Program Development
Suzanne Kindervatter, Program Implementation

3.   OEF is a project- and task-oriented organization working with organizations in foreign countries on programs in community- and human-resources development within their own cultural framework. In particular, OEF assistance is directed to the underutilized potential of women to strengthen the true partnership between women and men in societies where women have been forgotten by the economic system. OEF has been offering technical assistance in nearly fifty countries throughout the world. IN 1981, OEF was working on a project on nonformal education for women with the North-East Regional Training Center, Division of Land Settlement, in North-East Thailand.

5.   An OEF newsletter, *OEF Focus on Development*, is published twice yearly.

N30 Practical Concepts Incorporated (PCI)

1.   *604 Clear Spring Road*
Great Falls, Virginia 22066
(703) 430-4141

2.   Leon Rosenberg, Vice President

3.   PCI is a management consulting firm that is committed to helping health managers serve the people. It has provided management services for over 200 projects in some 55 countries including Thailand, where a training program was completed in 1977, and a 1980 project to design a management training program in the area of rural development has been completed. Contact Jane Hersee for additional information.

5.   Some project reports are available for a charge.

N31 Project HOPE (The People-to-People Health Foundation, Inc.)

1.   *Project HOPE Health Sciences Education Center*
Millwood, Virginia 22646
(703) 837-2100

2.　Dr. William B. Walsh, President

3.　The People-to-People Health Foundation, Inc. is an independent, nonprofit corporation that was formed in 1958 to carry out programs of cooperation in the field of health education between professionals in the U.S. and those in developing countries. Project HOPE brings skills and techniques developed by U.S. medical, dental, and allied health professions to the people of other nations. The Project's International book program is currently operating in Indonesia and has received requests from the Philippines and Thailand.

5.　Publications include *HOPE News* (a quarterly newsletter); *Health Affairs* (a quarterly); reports; papers following conferences coordinated by the Project HOPE Institute for Health Policy; monographs; bulletins; and reports issued by the HOPE Press.

N32 Public Administration Service (PAS)

1.　*1497 Chain Bridge Road*
McLean, Virginia 22101
(703) 734-8970

2.　Theodore Sitkoff, President

3.　A nonprofit, private management consulting firm, PAS works for the improvement of public administration through research, publishing, and consultation services. PAS has been working on projects in Indonesia since the 1960s in such areas as finance administration, agricultural credit studies; and, more recently, on the government's transmigration project. PAS recently concluded a number of projects in the financial and agriculture credit fields in Malaysia. The firm has also done project monitoring in the Philippines and is currently working on budgeting studies for rural governments in Thailand. For additional information, contact Julia Grottola, Administrative Assistant for International Programs.

N33 Resources Management International, Inc.

1.　*2000 L Street, N.W., Suite 200*
Washington, D.C. 20036
(202) 223-1020

2.　Walter Flinn, Director of U.S. Operations

3.　RMI provides a wide range of technical assistance and consulting services to the countries of Southeast Asia. The organization is unique in that all principal staff are headquartered in Djakarta, Indonesia, while the Washington, D.C., office provides U.S. and European support services including some recruitment. RMI is currently involved in a number of projects in Indonesia, including a management advisory project for the Ministry of Transmigration; the Provincial Development Projects II and III, for which it is principal contractor; and a large road-building project in Sumatra. An Agriculture Research Program is underway, as is a major irrigation/flood control project in Citanduy.
　　In the Philippines, RMI is under contract to the Ministry of Education,

to upgrade twenty engineering schools, and to the Public Works Ministry, to establish forty regional road-maintenance, equipment-repair stations. Operations in Thailand have been limited to providing support services to U.S. oil company drilling operations. An agriculture and an irrigation project are anticipated in the near future. RMI also has an on-going, low-income housing project in Malaysia.

5.   Publications include various descriptive brochures available as appropriate.

N34 Secretariat for Women in Development (New Transcentury Foundation)

1.   *1789 Columbia Road, N.W.*
      Washington, D.C. 20009
      (202) 328-4422

2.   May Rihani, Director

3.   The Secretariat for Women in Development was created in 1977 to provide services and materials that help integrate women into development programs and processes. The secretariat provides technical assistance to organizations involved in development efforts in the Third World including Southeast Asia. In addition, the secretariat organizes a variety of workshops on the role of women in development. A roster of qualified Third World women, who are available for consulting work, is maintained by the secretariat.

4.   The secretariat has a documentation center (Patricia Harlan McClure, Director, 202/328-4438), which is open Monday through Friday from 9:00 A.M. to 5:30 P.M. The center's collection of over 1,300 documents specifically relating to women in development, focuses on the Third World. The center also collects published and unpublished documents written by women in the Third World. The collection is divided by region and major subject areas and is accessible by country. Documents do not circulate, but photoduplication facilities are available.

5.   *Women in Development: A Resource List*, a listing of some 700 documents in the collection, is available. An additional 287 documents are listed in *Development as if Women Mattered: An Annotated Bibliography with a Third World Focus*. The secretariat also compiles and publishes information about 110 field projects from nearly 70 Third World countries, including Indonesia, the Philippines, and Malaysia.

N35 Seventh-Day Adventist World Service (SAWS)

1.   *6840 Eastern Avenue, N.W.*
      Washington, D.C. 20012
      (202) 722-6000

2.   Richard Offill, Executive Director

3.   The Seventh-Day Adventist World Service is a volunteer relief agency of the General Conference of Seventh-Day Adventists. SAWS has had extensive operations in Thailand and Cambodia since October 1979, with

some 300 volunteers presently involved in its various programs. SAWS involvement was medically oriented initially and included the operation of field hospitals. Operations now include nutrition, optometry, surgery, and dentistry; the latter boasts a large number of dentists and a mobile clinic. Plans are underway to send a team of opthamologists to Southeast Asia in the near future.

N36 Sister Cities International (Town Affiliation Association of the U.S.)

1. *1625 Eye Street, N.W.*
    Washington, D.C. 20006
    (202) 293-5504

2. Thomas Gittins, Executive Vice President

3. Sister Cities International is a nonprofit, membership organization of city governments and their sister-city communities. It was established to further international cooperation and understanding through links between cities in the U.S. and other nations. The program currently works with nearly 700 American cities and numerous cities in 80 countries in all parts of the world. The program receives grant assistance from the U.S. International Communication Agency. Sister-city links have been established with 21 cities in the Philippines, one in Burma, and one in Thailand.

5. The organization publishes the bimonthly *Sister City News*.

N37 United States Catholic Conference (USCC)

1. *1312 Massachusetts Avenue, N.W.*
    Washington, D.C. 20005
    (202) 659-6600

2. The Reverand J. Bryan Hehir, Director, Office of International Justice and Peace
    John E. McCarthy, Director, Migration and Refugee Services

3. USCC's Office of International Justice and Peace deals with policy matters regarding human rights, foreign aid for food, and military and political affairs in various regions of the world, including Southeast Asia. The office maintains files on most of the Southeast Asian states.
    Migration and Refugee Services currently has a program for refugee resettlement in the Washington area. For specific information, contact Mr. Vu Thu, administrative assistant (202/659-6646). For information concerning overseas relief activities, contact Catholic Relief Services, 1011 First Avenue, New York, New York 10022 (212/838-4700).

4. The Office of International Justice and Peace maintains a small reference library open to scholars during regular hours.

5. Publications include a *Publications List*, a monthly newsletter, and a brochure describing refugee resettlement operations.

N38 Volunteer Development Corps

1. *1629 K Street, N.W.*
    Washington, D.C. 20006
    (202) 223-2072

2. David W. Angevine, President

3. The Volunteer Development Corps is a private, nonprofit organization that recruits specialists primarily from U.S. cooperatives to provide short-term, voluntary technical assistance to cooperatives and government agencies in developing countries. It is funded mainly by the U.S. Agency for International Development. Corp volunteers have been involved in projects in Indonesia, Malaysia, the Philippines, and Thailand.

5. Project summaries and annual reports are available on request.

N39 Volunteers in Technical Assistance (VITA)

1. *3706 Rhode Island Avenue*
    Mt. Rainier, Maryland 20712
    (301) 277-7000

2. Henry Norman, Executive Director

3. A private, nonprofit organization, VITA recruits volunteer consultants to advise on appropriate technology in overseas development projects. Consultants are available in the fields of agriculture, food processing, water resources, renewable energy resources, housing and construction, and small-business management. The organization is partially funded by the U.S. Agency for International Development, contributions from private industry, and contracts with bilateral and international development agencies. VITA maintains a regional office in Bangkok and provides on-site consultation in the Southeast Asia region.

4. VITA operates a documentation center, which is open to the public for on-site use. Researchers may use the collection on the basis of prior appointment.

5. In addition to the quarterly *VITA News*, other publications include various technical manuals, bulletins, and project handbooks. Particularly useful is the *Village Technology Handbook*, which is updated periodically. *A Catalog of Books, Bulletins and Manuals* is available free on request.

Woodrow Wilson International Center for Scholars See entry H37

P Religious Organizations

Religious Organizations Entry Format (P)

1. *Address; Telephone Numbers*

2. Name and Title of Chief Official

3. Programs Pertaining to Southeast Asia

4. Publications

Introductory Note

Southeast Asian religions—as well as Western religious organizations with Southeast Asia–related activities—are represented in the Washington Area and are described below. Many of the Christian, Muslim, and Buddhist groups have become increasingly American in character, although the first-generation immigrant community continues to grow and thus remains significant for most of them. This is particularly true in the case of the Indochinese community, which has undergone tremendous growth in the Washington area since 1975.

Baptist World Aid See entry N10

P1 Buddhist Congregational Church of America

1. *5401 16th Street, N.W.*
   Washington D.C. 20011
   (202) 829-2423

2. The Venerable Dr. Thich Giac Duc, President

3. The church seeks to meet the spiritual and cultural needs of the rapidly increasing Vietnamese–American community in the Washington area. Membership is optional for anyone using the organization's facilities.

4. The church distributes a Vietnamese–English–language newsletter, monthly, without charge. Articles in other Southeast Asian languages are occasionally featured.

P2 Buddhist Vihara Society

1. *5017 16th Street, N.W.*
   Washington, D.C. 20011
   (202) 723-0773

2. The Venerable Dr. H. Gunaratana, President

3. A vihara of the Theravada order of Buddhism, with membership drawn from several countries including Burma and Thailand, the society's objective is to spread the teachings of Gautama Buddha. Devotional services and *dharma* discussions are held on Sundays. A religious class for children is conducted on Sundays.

4. The *Washington Buddhist*, a quarterly publication, is distributed by the society.

P3 Cambodian Buddhist Society, Inc.

1. *6301 Westbrook Drive*
   New Carrollton, Maryland 20784
   (301) 577-7596

2. The Venerable Oung Mean, President

3. The society operates exclusively for religious, educational, cultural, and charitable purposes, and is not affiliated with any other organizations in the U.S. or abroad. The society has over 400 active members. Religious activities, such as the *Magha Puja* celebration, the *Visakha Puja* celebration, the New Year celebration, memorial services (*Phhachum Ben*), and the robe offering ceremony (*Kathina*), are periodically coordinated. All religious activities related to Buddhism and to Cambodian traditions are celebrated once a year. Any person who is interested in Buddhist studies, in practicing Buddhist meditation, or in seeking spiritual comfort is welcome, irrespective of national origin, color, creed, or religion.

4. The society publishes a quarterly newsletter and a monthly brochure, which are available without charge. The society is currently considering the possibility of reproducing several books on Cambodian Buddhism and culture.

P4 Chinese Community Church

1. *1011 L Street, N.W.*
   Washington, D.C. 20001
   (202) 289-3611

2. The Reverend Man-King Tso, Pastor

3. The Chinese Community Church, in its present location since 1957, serves the Chinatown community and many Chinese now living in the suburban Washington, D.C., area. A weekly service is conducted each Sunday at 11:00 A.M. This church has for years provided a place of worship for the community. At present, a substantial number of Chinese immigrants from the Indochinese states of Southeast Asia participate in church activities,

including English–language classes. Through its Chinese Service Center, the church also assists refugees with housing searches and other needs.

P5 Church of the Vietnamese Blessed Martyrs

1. *3464 Annandale Road*
    Falls Church, Virginia 22042
    (703) 560-5997

2. Father Tran Duy Nhat

3. This church was the first Vietnamese–run Catholic church in the United States and the first local church to embrace the 5,000 Roman Catholics among the Washington area's growing Vietnamese refugee population. The church holds services on Saturday afternoon and Sunday.

P6 Dharmadhatu Buddhist Meditation and Study Center

1. *1424 Wisconsin Avenue, N.W.*
    Washington, D.C. 20007
    (202) 338-7090

2. David Sable, Director

3. A meditation and study center, Dharmadhatu contains a shrine room and provides classes in Buddhism and sitting practice. The center is mostly patronized by the followers of The Venerable Chögyam Trungpa Rinpoche, leader of the Kagyu Order of Tibetan Buddhism in the west. Some followers of the order have settled in parts of Southeast Asia.

4. A monthly newsletter and a brochure of class schedules are distributed free.

P7 Friends of Buddhism of Washington, D.C.

1. *306 Caroline Street*
    Fredericksburg, Virginia 22401
    (703) 373-2370

2. Kurt F. Leidecker, President
    Suzanne N. Doğruyol, (703) 620-9830

3. Founded in 1952, the Friends of Buddhism is a free association of men and women who are interested in Buddhism and Buddhist communities throughout the world. The association presents opportunities for the study of Buddhist philosophy, art, and way of life. To the Friends of Buddhism, understanding Buddhism is a way of understanding Asia. The society does not commit itself to any particular form of Buddhism, nor does it make the acceptance of Buddhism as a personal way of life, or the holdings of any particular philosophy or creed, a criterion for admission to membership or participation in meetings. The society organizes monthly lectures, film presentations, and other functions at which scholars, travelers, and lay and clerical Buddhist leaders present their contribution to Buddhism in all its phases.

4. An irregular newsletter, *Friends of Buddhism*, is circulated to members.

P8 Islamic Center

1. *2551 Massachusetts Avenue, N.W.*
   Washington, D.C. 20008
   (202) 332-3451

2. Mustafa Abulghaith-El Balghita, Acting Director

3. A place of worship for the Muslims, the mosque is open for the five daily prayers, the congregational prayer on Friday, and the *Eid al Fitr* and the *Eid al Adha* prayers. The mosque is also open to visitors during the normal working hours of the Islamic Center, 10:00 A.M. to 4:00 P.M., daily (see entry M42).

4. A *Bulletin of the Islamic Center* appears twice a year.

Note: Activities were temporarily suspended in November 1981.

Jesuit Missions See entry N24

P9 Muslim Community Center

1. *15200 New Hampshire Avenue*
   Silver Spring, Maryland 20904
   (301) 384-3454

2. N. S. Dajani, Chairman

3. The Muslim Community Center was established in 1976 to hold religious ceremonies, impart religious education to the children, and promote cultural activities. The center's master plan includes the construction of a Muslim community center equipped with a mosque, a school, a social building, and a residence for the staff. A phase of the construction has already commenced. The center runs a weekend school, organizes *Eid* prayers, and sponsors other social and cultural events.

4. The center issues its *MCC Bulletin*, bimonthly.

P10 Muslim Development Corporation

1. *P.O. Box 3252*
   Alexandria, Virginia 22302
   (703) 971-2020

2. Miraj H. Siddiqi, President

3. The center was established in 1976 to build an Islamic community in Northern Virginia, to promote good will and to build a bridge of understanding between different communities and religious inside and outside the USA. The project includes the development of a complex consisting of mosque, school, day-care center, shopping mall, and housing units on a self-supporting and self-sustaining basis. The corporation is currently trying to

acquire 100-plus acres of land for building the complex. The corporation sponsors religious, cultural, educational, and recreational activities.

Seventh-Day Adventist World Service See entry N35

United States Catholic Conference See entry N37

Q Publications and Media

Publications and Media Entry Format (Q)

1. *Address; Telephone Numbers*

2. Name and Title of Chief Official

3. Programs and Publications Pertaining to Southeast Asia.

Introductory Note

This section lists Southeast Asia–related publications and media not discussed in other sections of the *Guide*. Included here are various newsletters, journals, magazines, and newspapers, some of which are devoted exclusively to Southeast Asian subjects, while others are general publications with some pertinence to the region. Also included in this section are area publishing houses that produce titles on Southeast Asia or having relevance to Southeast Asian studies. All publications listed are from the Washington area and are in addition to publications listed elsewhere in this volume.

Q1 *Air Force Magazine*

1. *1750 Pennsylvania Avenue, N.W.
   Washington, D.C. 20006
   (202) 637-3362*

2. F. Clifton Berry, Jr., Editor

3. A monthly publication of the Air Force Association, *Air Force Magazine* began publication in 1948. Particularly useful to the Southeast Asian scholars is the December military-balance issue of the magazine, which provides comprehensive data on the armed forces of all countries, including the states of Southeast Asia.

Q2 American Broadcasting Company (ABC)—Washington Bureau

1. *1717 De Sales Street, N.W.
   Washington, D.C. 20036
   (202) 887-7777*

2. William Knowles, Vice President and Bureau Chief

3. Headquartered in New York, ABC is a major commercial television network. Its evening newscasts are videotaped by the Vanderbilt University Library (Nashville, Tennessee 37203, 615/322-2927), which also produces the *Television News Index and Abstracts*—available commercially.

Q3 *Armed Forces Journal*

1. *1414 22nd Street, N.W.*
   Washington, D.C. 20037
   (202) 296-0450

2. Benjamin F. Schemmer, Editor

3. The monthly *Armed Forces Journal*, which began publishing in 1863, occasionally features articles concerning Southeast Asian affairs.

Q4 *Asia Mail*

1. *128 South Royal Street*
   Alexandria, Virginia 22314
   (703) 548-2881

2. Donna Gays, Managing Editor

3. *Asia Mail* presents diverse opinions and ideas about Asia to executives, businessmen, academicians, and others interested in Asian affairs in the United States. The monthly publication presents essentially American perspectives on Asia and the Pacific. *Asia Mail* features not only in-depth analyses of major issues by Southeast Asia specialists, but also timely information on business trends and travel tips for Americans interested in Asia. The paper has a circulation of over 30,000 subscribers, worldwide.

Q5 *Asian–American Journal of Commerce*

1. *P.O. Box 1933*
   Washington, D.C. 20013
   (202) 638-5595

2. Norman Caron, Editor

3. A publication of the Association of Asian–American Chambers of Commerce, established in 1962, the journal is issued quarterly, supplemented by eight newsletters. With its main focus on the trade and commerce of Asia, the *Asian–American Journal of Commerce* reports changes in import and export regulations, joint ventures, living costs, patents, and business climates of various nations. In addition, it provides information on travel, culture, and other subjects.

Note: This publication was discontinued in March 1982.

Q6 Carrollton Press—Declassified Documents Reference System

1.   *1911 Fort Myer Drive*
     Arlington, Virginia 22209
     (703) 525-5940

2.   Elizabeth Jones, Executive Editor

3.   The Carrollton Press compiles declassified United States government documents and distributes hard and microfiche copies on a subscription basis. Its *Declassified Documents Reference System*, which is published four times a year, to date has disseminated some 19,000 documents from the State Department, Central Intelligence Agency, Defense Department, National Security Council, White House, Treasury Department, Federal Bureau of Investigation, and other government agencies. The collection is growing at the rate of 2,000 documents per year.

     Many of the declassified documents cover important aspects of the United States' relations with Southeast Asia. Finding aids include quarterly, cumulative subject indexes and abstracts of the declassified documents. An irregular newsletter, *Declassified Document News*, may be obtained free on request. Local subscribers of the *Declassified Documents Reference System* include the Department of State Library, Georgetown University Library, and the Library of Congress.

     Other useful Carrollton Press publications include: *Cumulative Index to Her Majesty's Stationery Office Annual Catalogues of Publications, 1922–1972: Combined Retrospective Indexes to Journals in History* (1838–1974); *Political Science* (1886–1974); *Sociology* (1895–1974); and *Cumulative Subject Index to the Monthly Catalog of United States Government Publications*. Several information brochures and publications lists are available on request.

Note: In 1981 Carrollton Press was acquired by Research Publications, Inc., at the same address.

Q7 Columbia Broadcasting System (CBS)—Washington Bureau

1.   *2020 M Street, N.W.*
     Washington, D.C. 20036
     (202) 457-4321

2.   Jack Smith, Vice President and Bureau Chief

3.   A national television and radio broadcasting network, CBS news coverage of Southeast Asia is best accessed through the annual *CBS News Index: Key to the Television News Broadcasting*, produced by the Microfilm Corporation of America (21 Harristown Road, Green Rock, New Jersey 07452, 201/447-3000). This index provides comprehensive access to the transcripts of CBS television broadcasts. Every entry consists of a subject heading, a descriptive phrase, and a locator, which guides readers to verbatim news transcripts.

     Television News Index and Abstracts, produced by the Vanderbilt University Library (Nashville, Tennessee 37203), is another excellent guide to the videotape collection of the network's evening news program. The Vanderbilt videotape collection of the three major, commercial-television networks is available for use by scholars on a loan basis. Scholars may also contact the CBS information services manager (Frances Foley Stone) for assistance in retrieving news transcripts and newscast tapes.

Q8 Congressional Quarterly Inc.

1. *1414 22nd Street, N.W.*
   Washington, D.C. 20037
   (202) 887-8500

2. Eugene C. Patterson, Editor and President

3. An editorial research service and publishing company, the Congressional Quarterly Inc. (founded in 1945) serves clients in the fields of news, education, business, and government. It combines specific coverage of Congress, government, and politics. Its basic periodical publication is the *Weekly Report*, which highlights legislation on military, diplomatic, and economic issues, including some relating to Southeast Asia. Editorial Research Reports, an affiliated service of the quarterly, publishes reference materials on foreign policy, national security, and other topics of news interest.

Q9 Foreign Broadcast Information Service (FBIS)—*Daily Report*

1. *P.O. Box 2604*
   Washington, D.C. 20013
   (202) 351-3577 (Information)
   (202) 351-2051 (Asia–Pacific and China)

2. The U.S. government's Foreign Broadcasting Information Service publishes a series called *Daily Reports*, containing current news and commentary monitored by FBIS from foreign broadcasts, news-agency transmissions, newspapers, and periodicals. Items from foreign-language sources are translated by FBIS: those from English–language sources are transcribed, with original phrasing and other characteristics retained. Users of this publication may cite FBIS, provided they do so in a manner clearly identifying it as the secondary source.

   Volume IV (Asia Pacific) of the *Daily Report* includes all the countries of Southeast Asia. Edited versions of the *Daily Report*, both in hard cover and microfiche, are made available to the public on a subscription basis through the National Technical Information Service (see entry Q19). Effective use of this source has, in the past, been hampered by lack of indexing. Beginning in 1975, however, the Newsbank (P.O. Box 645, 135 East Putnam Avenue, Greenwich, Connecticut 06830, 203/966-1100) began producing an *Index to the Daily Reports*, which is divided into major subject categories, such as, agriculture-environment, commerce-industry-finance, government-politics, international relations, and society-culture. Geographic indicators and name indexes make it even more useful. An FBIS reference publication, *Broadcast Stations of the World* is available from the Government Printing Office (see entry Q11).

Q10 *Foreign Policy*

1. *11 Dupont Circle, N.W.*
   Washington, D.C. 20036
   (202) 797-6420

2. Charles W. Maynes, Editor

3. A quarterly journal, *Foreign Policy* is published by the Carnegie Endowment for International Peace. With its general focus on international affairs, the journal covers the whole range of political, economic, military, and human issues of concern to policymakers and laymen alike. Articles on Southeast Asian subjects appear from time to time.

Q11 Government Printing Office (GPO)

1. *North Capitol and H Streets, N.W.*
   Washington, D.C. 20401
   (202) 275-2051

2. Danford L. Sawyer, Jr., Public Printer

3. The GPO prints and binds documents for Congress and the departments and agencies of the federal government; distributes and maintains catalogs and a library of government publications; and sells nonconfidential documents to the public. The GPO sells over 25,000 different publications through mail orders and government bookstores, and administers the depository library program, through which selected government publications are made available to libraries throughout the country.

   Orders and inquiries concerning publications for sale should be directed to the Assistant Public Printers/Superintendent of Documents (Carl A. LaBarre, 202/783-3238). An information brochure, *Consumers Guide to Federal Publications*, is available free and describes the services provided by the Superintendent of Documents and gives some sources for certain categories of publications not distributed through that office. Also available free from the Superintendent of Documents is a list of depository libraries.

   The *Monthly Catalog of United States Government Publications*, which has semiannual indexes and annual cumulations, lists about 3,000 new titles that enter the sales inventory annually. A sales catalog, *The GPO Sales Publication Reference File*, is issued bimonthly on microfiche. A useful set of some 270 *Subject Bibliographies* is also available for a wide range of topics, including foreign affairs, foreign languages, foreign trade, annual reports, *Country Studies*, *Background Notes*, maps, national defense and security, and statistics and treaties. The quarterly *Price List 36* is available free on request.

Q12 *I & NS Reporter*

1. *U.S. Immigration and Naturalization Service*
   425 Eye Street, N.W. (Room 7021)
   Washington, D.C. 20536
   (202) 633-2648

2. Janet R. Graham, Editor

3. A quarterly magazine of the U.S. Immigration and Naturalization Service, the *I&NS Reporter* contains articles on immigration and naturalization topics, recent court and administrative decisions, statistical data, and other relevant materials on immigration. The magazine is of considerable value in ethnic studies.

Q13 *Indonesian News and Views*

1. *Embassy of Indonesia*
    2020 Massachusetts Avenue, N.W.
    Washington, D.C. 20036
    (202) 293-1745

2. Information Division

3. *Indonesian News and Views* is published biweekly, with occasional, additional special issues. This publication contains current information on Indonesian politics, economics, culture, education, sports, tourism, and a variety of other topics of interest to those following events in Indonesia. The ten- to twenty-page publication is available from the embassy on request, without charge.

Q14 Joint Publications Research Service (JPRS)

1. *1000 North Glebe Road*
    Arlington, Virginia 22201
    (703) 841-1050

2. C. P. Braegelmann, Chief

3. The JPRS provides translations and abstracts of foreign-language, political and technical publications to various federal departments and agencies. In providing its services, JPRS contracts with freelance translators from a variety of language backgrounds, including many from Southeast Asia. JPRS publishes, approximately once a week, the *South and East Asia Report*, which covers socio-economic, government, political, and technical developments in Southeast Asia. JPRS ad hoc publications are announced in the *Monthly Catalog* (GPO) and the *Government Reports Announcements and Index* (NTIS).

    The National Technical Information Service (NTIS) (see entry Q19) sells an annual *Reference Aid Directory of JPRS Ad Hoc Publications*. A monthly and annual cumulation of the *Transdex Index*, to translations issued by the JPRS, is available from the Micro Photo Division of Bell and Howell (Old Mansfield Road, Wooster, Ohio 44691). While the monthly index is available in paper form, the annual cumulation may be obtained in either 16-mm microform or 105-mm microfiche. Subscriptions are available on a calendar-year basis. The index is organized through title, bibliographic, keyword, and personal-names sections. JPRS publications are available at the Library of Congress and in the JPRS reading room, which is open from 8:00 A.M. to 4:30 P.M., Monday through Friday. All JPRS publications in the public domain are sold by NTIS.

Q15 *Malaysia Digest*

1. *Embassy of Malaysia*
   2401 Massachusetts Avenue, N.W.
   Washington, D.C. 20008
   (202) 328-2700

2. External Information Division, Ministry of Foreign Affairs

3. *Malaysia Digest*, available through the Malaysian Embassy, is published biweekly and features news items on politics, economics, culture, education, and other topics. Both domestic and international subjects related to Malaysia are covered. The *Digest* features a "Learn Bahasa Malaysia" column on the back page of each issue.

Q16 National Archives and Records Service—Office of the Federal Register (General Services Administration)

1. *1100 L Street, N.W., Room 8401*
   Washington, D.C. 20408
   (202) 523-5240

2. John E. Byrne, Director

3. The Office of the Federal Register publishes a number of important publications concerned, primarily, with the operations of the United States government: *United States Government Manual* (annual); *Weekly Compilation of Presidential Documents*; *Public Papers of the Presidents of the United States*; *Federal Register* (daily except weekends and holidays); and *Code of Regulations*. These publications may be ordered from the Government Printing Office (see entry Q11).

Q17 National Broadcasting Company (NBC)—Washington Bureau

1. *4001 Nebraska Avenue, N.W.*
   Washington, D.C. 20016
   (202) 686-4000

2. Sid Davis, Vice President, News

3. Scholars may obtain transcripts of newscasts from the NBC headquarters in New York (212/664-4444). Videotapes of the evening newscasts may be accessed through the *Television News Index and Abstracts*, prepared by Vanderbilt University Library (Nashville, Tennessee 37203).

Q18 *National Geographic*

1. *National Geographic Society*
   17th and M Streets, N.W.
   Washington, D.C. 20036
   (202) 857-7000

2.   Wilbur E. Garrett, Editor

3.   *National Geographic* is the monthly journal of the National Geographic Society, a nonprofit, scientific and educational organization (see entry M48). The journal occasionally publishes articles on Southeast Asia–related subjects, such as "A Sumatran Journey" (March 1981).

Q19 National Technical Information Service (NTIS)

1.   *Sills Building*
5285 Port Royal Road
Springfield, Virginia 22161
(703) 487-4600

2.   Joseph Caponio, Acting Director

3.   The NTIS, which is open from 7:45 A.M. to 4:15 P.M., Monday through Friday, aims at simplifying and improving public access to Department of Commerce publications, and to data files and scientific and technical reports sponsored by federal agencies. The NTIS is the central point in the United States for the public sale of government-funded research and development reports and other analysis prepared by federal agencies, their contractors, or their grantees.

    Through agreements with more than 300 organizations, NTIS adds about 70,000 new reports a year to its collection, now exceeding one million titles. The agency also coordinates the publishing and technical-inquiry functions of various special technology groups.

    Researchers may conveniently locate abstracts of interest, from among the 680,000 federally sponsored research reports completed and published from 1964, by using the agency's on-line computer search service (NTISearch, 703/487-4640). Copies of the research reports are sold in paper form or on microfiche. The NTIS Bibliographic Data File on magnetic tape, which includes published and unpublished abstracts, is available for lease. A *Reference Guide* to the *NTIS Bibliographic Data File* (1978) is available on request.

    Current abstracts of new research reports and other specialized technical information in various categories of interest are published in some thirty-three weekly *Abstract Newsletters*. A comprehensive biweekly journal, *Government Reports Announcements and Index*, is published for libraries, technical information specialists, and those requiring such all-inclusive volumes. A standard-order microfiche service (SRIM) automatically provides subscribers with the full texts of research reports selected to satisfy individual requirements. Scholars may also note that over 1,000 *Published Searches* on various topics are available from computer searches already conducted by the NTIS. The *NTIS Search Catalog* provides a subject index to the materials. The staff will perform, for a fee, an on-line custom search for topics requested by individual researchers.

    NTIS publications of interest include monthly foreign trade reports, such as *Foreign Market Reports*, *Foreign Market Airgrams*, and the Foreign Broadcasting Information Service's *Daily Reports*, of which volume IV includes those on Southeast Asia. NTIS also distributes various reports, abstracts, and translations of the Joint Publication Research Service (JPRS) (see entry 814), some of which are listed in the annual *Reference Aid*

Directory of JPRS Ad Hoc Publications and in the biweekly *Government Reports Announcement and Index.* For general information of the services and resources of NTIS, researchers may consult *NTIS Information Services* (1979) and *Subject Guide to NTIS Information Collection.* The Information and Sales Center for the NTIS services and publications is located at 425 13th Street, N.W., Washington, D.C. (202/724-3509).

Q20 *News from Thailand*

1. *Embassy of Thailand*
   2300 Kalorama Road, N.W.
   Washington, D.C. 20008
   (202) 667-1446

2. Public Relations Office

3. *News from Thailand* is published monthly in English, weekly in Thai, and is distributed without cost to persons interested in Thailand. This publication features current news from Thailand on cultural, economic, and political affairs. Other topics commonly featured are education, sports, tourism, and Thai foreign relations.

Q21 *Strategic Review*

1. *1612 K Street, N.W.*
   Washington, D.C. 20006
   (202) 331-1776

2. Walter F. Hahn, Editor-in-Chief

3. *Strategic Review*, the quarterly publication of the United States Strategic Institute, provides a forum for the discussion of matters of current significance in the politico-military field. It occasionally carries articles relating to Southeast Asia.

Note: For subscriptions and submission of manuscripts, contact the main office of the *Review*, at 20 Memorial Drive, Cambridge, Massachusetts 02142 (617/661-1240).

Q22 *Strategy Week*

1. *1777 T Street, N.W.*
   Washington, D.C. 20009
   (202) 223-4934

2. Gregory R. Copley, Editor and Publisher

3. This new weekly periodical reviews military and political developments abroad, including those relating to Southeast Asia, and supplies defense-industry information on transfer of arms. The same publisher also produces *Defense and Foreign Affairs*, a monthly magazine examining military and defense-related issues on a worldwide basis. In addition, a newsletter, the

Defense and Foreign Affairs Daily, and the annual *Defense and Foreign Affairs Handbook* are published.

Q23 *Tien Phong*

1. *2809 Columbia Pike*
    Arlington, Virginia 22204
    (703) 979-2393

2. Hoang Nguyen, Editor

3. *Tien Phong* is a biweekly publication featuring news of the Vietnamese community in the Washington area and items of general interest to Washington–area Vietnamese. The subscription fee is currently $2.00 an issue or $45.00 per year.

Q24 **Time-Life Books**

1. *777 Duke Street*
    Alexandria, Virginia 22314
    (703) 960-5000

2. Carl Jaeger, President

3. A division of Time Incorporated of New York, the Time-Life illustrative, documentation publications include two volumes on Southeast Asia, "China-Burma-India Theater of War" (1978) and "Return to the Philippines" (1979) in the *World War II Series*, and a volume on the city of "Bangkok" (1979) in the *Great City Series*. In addition to its research staff, outside scholars are hired on a consulting basis. Brochures describing publication programs are available on request.

Q25 *U.S. News & World Report*

1. *2300 N Street, N.W.*
    Washington, D.C. 20037
    (202) 861-2000

2. Marvin L. Stone, Editor

3. *U.S. News & World Report* is an independent weekly newsmagazine that reports and analyzes national and international affairs. Its various stringer bureaus, and the bureaus in Peking and Tokyo, contribute news and analysis on Southeast Asian affairs. A biennial *U.S. News & World Report Index* includes country and subject headings.

Q26 **University Press of America**

1. *4720 Boston Way*
    Lanham, Maryland 20706
    (301) 459-3366

2. James Lyons, Managing Editor and Vice President

3.   The University Press of America publishes books intended for the academic community covering a wide range of topics, including anthropology, history, religion, political science, philosophy, and international studies. The press uses a cost-efficient approach, employing a lithographic process to print typewritten manuscripts provided by the authors. A list of publications is available on request. A few Southeast Asia–related scholarly titles have been published, including *Ideas and Reality: An Analysis of the Debate Over Vietnam*, by Stephen A. Garrett (1978).

Q27 University Publications of America (UPA)

1.   *44 North Market Street*
      Frederick, Maryland 21701
      (301) 694-0100

2.   John Mosacato, President

3.   University Publications of America publishes both printed and microfilm copies of original works, as well as reprints and collections of government documents. UPA publications are designed for the scholarly community and cover a wide range of subjects, including law, history, economics, foreign affairs, and the sciences. A list of publications is available on request.
      Of particular interest to Southeast Asian scholars are the *OSS State Department Intelligence and Research Reports on Asia, Japan, Korea, and Southeast Asia, 1941–49*; and *Japan, Korea, Southeast Asia and Far East, 1950–1961*. Also of interest are: *Transcripts and Files of the Paris Peace Talks, 1968–1973*; *Records of the Joint Chiefs of Staff, Part I, 1942–1945: Pacific Theater*, and *Part II, 1946–1953: The Far East*. Of equal interest is *The War in Vietnam: Classified History* (National Security Council); and the new *Special Studies Series: Vietnam and Southeast Asia, 1960–1980*. A publications list is available on request.

Q28 Voice of America (VOA)

1.   *HEW Building*
      330 Independence Avenue, S.W.
      Washington, D.C. 20547
      (202) 755-4180

2.   John Hughes, Director

3.   The Voice of America is the global radio network of the U.S. International Communication Agency, which seeks to promote understanding abroad of the United States, its people, culture, and policies. VOA currently broadcasts some 865 hours per week in 39 languages, including Burmese, Indonesian, Khmer, Lao, Thai, and Vietnamese. VOA has overseas transmitters located in Sri Lanka and Thailand. Satellite circuits are used to feed VOA overseas relay stations that are beaming programs to Southeast Asia. The VOA *Broadcasts Schedule* is available on request.

Note: See also entry K21.

Q29 WPFW-FM

1. *700 H Street, N.W.*
   Washington, D.C. 20001
   (202) 783-3100

3. WPFW-FM (89.3) is a noncommercial, community-supported radio station, which sponsors *Gold Mountain*, a monthly program dealing with material of interest to and about Asian–Pacific Americans. The program occasionally covers Southeast Asia–related topics.

Q30 Washington Monitor

1. *499 National Press Building*
   1529 14th Street, N.W.
   Washington, D.C. 20045
   (202) 347-7757

2. James Marsh, Executive Editor

3. The Washington Monitor publishes five serials that provide useful reference tools for researchers interested in utilizing the personnel and published resources of the federal government. The *Daily Congressional Monitor* and *Weekly Congressional Monitor* list and report on legislative activities, while the biweekly *Congress in Print* lists all committee publications of both houses of Congress and the General Accounting Office and supplies addresses and phone numbers to be used in ordering listed items.

   The Washington Monitor also publishes the *Congressional Record Scanner Daily*, which indexes the *Congressional Record*, and the *Weekly Regulatory Monitor*, which indexes the *Federal Register*. The Monitor also issues two telephone books—the *Congressional Yellow Book* (quarterly) and the *Federal Yellow Book* (bimonthly)—for Capitol Hill and the top 27,000 federal employees.

   In addition to its publications, Washington Monitor conducts seminars on "Understanding Congress," "Understanding the Federal Regulatory Process," and "Understanding the News Media." All of these publications and activities may be useful for scholars following congressional and federal activities and publications on Southeast Asia.

Q31 *Washington Post*

1. *1150 15th Street, N.W.*
   Washington, D.C. 20071
   (202) 334-6000 (Foreign News)

2. Benjamin Bradlee, Executive Director

3. A daily newspaper, *The Washington Post* provides extensive coverage of international affairs. Its Southeast Asia Bureau, located in Bangkok (William Brannigin, chief), reports frequently on the political, economic, and diplomatic aspects of Southeast Asian countries, as well as on regional developments. The Washington Post Library (Mark Hannan, librarian)

contains over 9 million newspaper clippings, 600,000 photographs, and 20,000 books, as well as cuts, maps, and roll and card microfilm. The newspaper clippings and photographs are arranged alphabetically by names and subject headings. Interlibrary loan and photoduplication services are available. The library is restricted to the use of staff members only.

Q32 *World Affairs*

1. *American Peace Society*
    4000 Albemarle Street, N.W.
    Washington, D.C. 20016
    (202) 362-6445

2. Frank Turley, Managing Editor

3. *World Affairs* is a quarterly journal devoted to international relations and world affairs. Book reviews and articles related to Southeast Asian affairs are occasionally published.

APPENDIXES

Appendix I. Southeast Asian Ethnic, Social, Cultural, and Recreational Organizations

Buddhist Social Services
5401 16th Street, N.W.
Washington, D.C. 20011
Hip Lowman, director, (202) 291-7799

Cambodian Federation Association
7930 Ashbrook Drive
Alexandria, Virginia 22309
Pheach Srey, director, (703) 360-5647

Friends of Malaysia
c/o Center for Asian Studies
American University
Washington, D.C. 20015
Llewellyn D. Howell, (202) 686-2000

Friends of the Philippine People
100 Maryland Avenue, N.E.
Washington, D.C. 20002
Boone Schumer, national coordinator, (202) 543-1093

Indonesian–American Friendship Society
8725 Piccadilly Place
Springfield, Virginia 22151
Howard Maynard, (703) 425-5080

Lao Association of Greater Washington Metro Area
3413 Carlyn Springs Road, #202
Falls Church, Virginia 22041
Mr. Nachapassak, president, (703) 820-3688

Lao Buddhist Society
5903 Camberly Avenue
Springfield, Virginia 22150
Pouatsamy Naughton, president, (703) 769-6048

Philippine Heritage Federation
6345 South Kings Highway
Alexandria, Virginia 22306
Alex Peralta Yadao, president, (703) 765-7252

Thai Committee of Washington
100 5th Street, N.E.
Washington, D.C. 20002
Susan A. Greene, chairperson, (202) 387-8883

Vietnam Foundation
6713 Lumsden Street
McLean, Virginia 22101
Pho Ba Long, president, (703) 893-7458

Vietnamese–American Buddhist Association
c/o Mrs. Le Thi Bai
7060 Wyndale Street, N.W.
Washington, D.C. 20015
(202) 966-0015

Vietnamese Association for Freedom
6825 Dyer Court
Springfield, Virginia 22170
Mr. Tran Van Bien, (202) 971-3763

Vietnamese Association in Washington
3526 Pinetree Terrace
Falls Church, Virginia 22041
Dr. Tran Dinh De, (703) 671-8687

Vietnamese Buddhist Association
30 South Old Glebe Road, Building E, #201
Arlington, Virginia 22204
Professor Tang Xuan An, (703) 521-3945

The Vietnamese Catholic Students Association in America
8659 Dallway Lane
Vienna, Virginia 22180
Ha Ton Vinh, (703) 573-0073

Vietnamese Cultural Association
6713 Lumsden Street
McLean, Virginia 22101
Professor Pho Ba Long, (703) 893-7458

Vietnamese Lawyers Association
1200 North Courthouse Road, #727
Arlington, Virginia 22201
Mr. Nguyen Huu Phu, (703) 525-6135

Vietnamese Refugee Fund, Inc.
6103 Amherst Avenue
Springfield, Virginia 22150
Nguyen Ngoc Bich, (703) 569-9289

Vietnamese Senior Citizens Association
4129 Wadsworth Court, #201
Annandale, Virginia 22003
Chu Ngoc Lien, (703) 354-8431

Vietnamese Veterans
14643 Bauer Drive, #107
Rockville, Maryland 20853
Mr. Truong Nhu Phung

Washington–Bangkok Women's Club
7300 Burroughs Lane
Falls Church, Virginia 22043
Dorris Borland, president, (703) 893-9084

Appendix II.   Library Collections: A Listing by Size of Southeast Asian Holdings

The size of Southeast Asia holdings in the Washington, D.C., area library collections is difficult to determine. The following table provides estimates only.

Size Categories/Libraries

More than 100,000 volumes
  Library of Congress (A27)

8,000 to 15,00 volumes
  National Agricultural Library (A30)

5,000 to 8,000 volumes
  Howard University Founders Library, Bernard B
    Fall Collection (A21)
  National Library of Medicine (A33)
  State Department Library (A37)

3,500 to 5,000 volumes
  Agency for International Development-
    Development Information Center (A2)
  American University Library (A4)
  Joint Bank-Fund Library (A26)

2,000 to 3,500 volumes
  Army Department Library (A6)
  Foreign Service Institute (A16)
  Georgetown University Library (A19)
  Maryland University Library (A29)

Appendix III. Vietnam War Archives

Within the Washington, D.C., area are a number of large and significant collections of archival material relating to the Vietnam War. These materials consist of documents, films, photographs, paintings, and recordings. This vast collection of Vietnam–related material will provide scholars with inestimable research opportunities for one of the most significant periods of recent U.S. foreign relations.

Air Force Art Museum   C1
Air Force History Office   B1
Air Force Still Photographic Depository   F2
Army Audiovisual Center   F4
Army Center of Military History   B3
Army Library   A6

Defense Department, Historical Staff   K11
Defense Technical Information Center   G5, K11

House of Representatives Library   A20
Howard University, Bernard B. Fall Collection   A21

Joint Publication Research Service (JPRS)   Q14

Library of Congress   B5, D4, D5, F12, F13

Marine Corps Archives   B6
Marine Corps Historical Center—Art Collection   C4
Marine Corps Still Photographic Archives   F14

National Archives and Records Service (NARS)   B7, D5, E5, F16, F17, G10
Naval Historical Center   A34, B9, C8, F19
Navy Motion Media Depository   F20

Appendix IV. Bookstores

Very few bookstores in the Washington, D.C., area carry a good selection on Southeast Asia. The following is a selected list of bookstores that may have a few Southeast Asia–related materials and may assist scholars in obtaining materials through special orders. The bookstores of local universities that offer courses on Southeast Asian themes may carry reference works on the area in addition to textbooks. Researchers may contact individual bookstores for information on service, hours, discount rates, and related matters. Scholars will note that several book sales are held in the Washington area each year including those of the Association of American Foreign Service Wives, Brandeis University, and Vassar College. Information concerning these sales is generally announced in the local newspapers.

American University Book Store
Anderson Hall
Massachusetts and Nebraska Avenues, N.W.
Washington, D.C. 20016
(202) 686-2660

Asia Books and Periodicals
2409 18th Street, N.W.
Washington, D.C. 20009
(202) 462-9137

Catholic University Bookstore
McMahon Hall
4th Street and Michigan Avenue, N.E.
Washington, D.C. 20064
(202) 635-5232

Book Annex and Record and Tape Annex
1340 Connecticut Avenue, N.W.
Washington, D.C. 20036
(202) 785-1133 (Books)
(202) 785-2662 (Records)

This store has a good collection of international records, including a few from Southeast Asia.

George Mason University Bookstore
Student Union
4400 University Drive
Fairfax, Virginia 22030
(703) 323-2696

George Washington University Bookstore
21st and H Streets, N.W.
Washington, D.C. 20052
(202) 676-6870

Georgetown University Bookstore
37th and Prospect Streets, N.W.
Washington, D.C. 20057
(202) 625-4068

Globe Book Shop
1700 Pennsylvania Avenue, N.W.
Washington, D.C. 20006
(202) 393-1490

Howard University Bookstore
2801 Georgia Avenue, N.W.
Washington, D.C. 20059
(202) 636-6656

Institute of Modern Languages Bookstore
2622 Pittman Drive
Silver Spring, Maryland 20910
(301) 565-2580

International Learning Center Bookstore
1715 Connecticut Avenue, N.W.
Washington, D.C. 20009
(202) 232-4111

Kramer Books
1347 Connecticut Avenue, N.W.
Washington, D.C. 20036
(202) 293-2072

Other locations of this store are 1722 H Street, N.W., (202) 298-8010; 1919
Pennsylvania Avenue, N.W., (202) 466-3111; 1517 Connecticut Avenue,
N.W., (202) 387-1400; and 336 Pennsylvania Avenue, S.E., (202) 547-
5990.

The Map Store
1636 Eye Street, N.W.
Washington, D.C. 20006
(202) 628-2608

Maryland Book Exchange
4500 College Avenue
College Park, Maryland 20740
(301) 927-2510

Modern Language Book and Record Store
3160 O Street, N.W.
Washington, D.C. 20007
(202) 338-8963

National Technical Information Service Bookstore
425 13th Street, N.W.
Washington, D.C. 20004
(202) 724-3382

Newman Bookstore of Washington
3329 8th Street, N.E.
Washington, D.C. 20017
(202) 526-1036

Second Story Books
3236 P Street, N.W.
Washington, D.C. 20007
(202) 338-6860

Sidney Kramer Books
1722 H Street, N.W.
Washington, D.C. 20006
(202) 298-8010

Smithsonian Institution Museum Shops
Director of Museum Shops
Natural History Building
12th Street and Constitution Avenue, N.W.
Washington, D.C. 20560
(202) 357-1805

Trover Shop Books
277 Pennsylvania Avenue, S.E.
Washington, D.C. 20005
(202) 543-8006

Other locations of this store are: 800 15th Street, N.W., (202) 347-2177; 1031 Connecticut Avenue, N.W., (202) 659-8138; 1715 Pennsylvania Avenue, N.W., (202) 833-2855.

U.S. Government Printing Office (GPO)
Main Bookstore
710 North Capitol Street, N.W.
Washington, D.C. 20402
(202) 783-3238

Other locations are:

GPO Bookstore, Commerce Department
14th and E Streets, N.W.
Washington, D.C. 20230
(202) 377-3527

GPO Bookstore, Health and Human Services Department
330 Independence Avenue, S.W.
Washington, D.C. 20201
(202) 472-7899

GPO Bookstore, International Communication Agency
1776 Pennsylvania Avenue, N.W.
Washington, D.C. 20547
(202) 724-9928

GPO State Department Bookstore
23rd and D Streets, N.W.
Washington, D.C. 20520
(202) 632-1437

University of the District of Columbia Bookstore—Mount Vernon Campus Bookstore
929 E Street, N.W.
Washington, D.C. 20004
(202) 727-2517

University of Maryland Bookstore
Student Union Building
Campus Drive
College Park, Maryland 20742
(301) 454-3222

Appendix V.   Housing, Transportation, and Other Services

This section is prepared to help outside scholars who come to Washington, D.C., for short-term research, to find suitable housing. It also contains data on local transportation facilities and information services. Prices quoted are current as of March 1982 and are subject to change.

Housing Information and Referral Service

For anyone interested in leasing an apartment or house, *Apartment Shoppers' Guide and Housing Directory* (ASGHD) (updated every 3 motnhs) is a valuable source of information. The directory, which quotes current rental prices, terms of leases, and directions to each of the facilities listed, is available at People's Drug Stores in the Washington area. It is published by ASGHD (202/363-8016), located at 3301 New Mexico Avenue, N.W., Suite 310, Washington, D.C. 20016. The staff provides a housing-referral service, for a fee, from 9:00 A.M. to 5:00 P.M., Monday through Friday.

Scholars can also get help from the following local university housing offices:

George Washington University Off-Campus Housing Resources Center
Rice Hall
2121 I Street, N.W., 4th Floor
Washington, D.C. 20052
(202) 676-6688
Summer: 9:00 A.M.–7:00 P.M.   Monday–Friday
Winter: 9:00 A.M.–5:00 P.M.   Monday–Friday

This office has listings of apartments and other housing in the Washington area. Open to the public, the office also distributes the *Apartment Shoppers' Guide and Housing Directory* (see above), maps of Washington, D.C., and a *Guide to Off-Campus Housing* (annual), prepared for students by the office.

Georgetown University Off-Campus Housing Office
Healy Building Basement
37th and O Streets, N.W., Room G08
Washington, D.C. 20057
(202) 625-3026
1:00 P.M.–4:30 P.M.   Monday–Friday

Open to the public, this office offers services similar to those at the George Washington University Off-Campus Housing Resource Center.

Catholic University of America Off-Campus Housing Office
St. Bonaventure Hall, Room 106
Washington, D.C. 20064
(202) 635-5618
9:00 A.M.–5:00 P.M.   Monday–Friday (Call until 2:00 P.M.)

Open to the public, this office provides services similar to those of George Washington University.

Northern Virginia Community College
Annandale Campus Housing Board
Student Activities Center
Science Building, Room 225-A
8333 Little River Turnpike
Annandale, Virginia 22003
(703) 523-3147
8:30 A.M.–5:00 P.M.   Monday–Friday

The board maintains a listing of rooms available in private homes.

Note: The off-campus housing offices of American University, Howard University, and the University of Maryland handle inquiries and requests from their own students and faculty members only.

Short-term Housing

For those scholars who intend to stay for a short period of time—a few weeks to several months—the following facilities may be useful:

International Guest House
1441 Kennedy Street, N.W.
Washington, D.C.
(202) 726-5808

Rates: $12.28 per bed, per day, or $74.08 per week (breakfast and evening tea with shared rooms); $6.34 for a child under ten years of age.

International Student House
1825 R Street, N.W.
Washington, D.C. 20009
(202) 232-4007

Rates: $350.00 to $450.00 per month (minimum, one-semester stay) for room and board (2 meals, 7 days). Single rooms and shared double or triple rooms are available. The house maintains a nationality quota policy that permits no more than ten Americans or three citizens from any one foreign country at any time.

The Woodner Hotel
3636 16th Street, N.W.
Washington, D.C. 20010
(202) 328-2800

The hotel has furnished efficiency and one-bedroom apartments. Rates $550.00 and up for efficiencies; $685.00 and up for one-bedrooms.

The Capitol Park
800 4th Street, S.W.
Washington, D.C. 20024
(202) 479-6800
(Near the Library of Congress)

Rates: Furnished one-bedroom apartments, by the week, $49.00 per day; by the month, starting at $500.00.

Long-term Housing

Those wishing to rent an apartment or house for one year or more should consult not only the *Apartment Shoppers' Guide and Housing Directory* and the local university housing offices, but also the following rental agencies:

Millicent Chatel	(202) 338-0500
Lynch Realty	(202) 232-4100
Nyman Realty Co.	(301) 474-5700
Edmund Flynn Co.	(202) 554-4800
	or (202) 537-1800
H. A. Gill	(202) 338-5000
Shannon & Luchs	(202) 659-7000
Norman Bernstein	(202) 331-7500

Home and apartment rents vary greatly from area to area around Washington. Normally, rents are lower in suburban Virginia and Maryland than in Washington, D.C. One should also remember that it is difficult to find furnished apartments in the Washington area through regular real estate agents. People who need furnished quarters may have to take unfurnished apartments and rent furniture. Such an arrangement can be negotiated with the real estate brokers. Even under such an arrangement, linen, blankets, dishes, silverware, and cooking utensils must be furnished by the tenant.

Transportation in the Washington Area

Scholars should be advised that parking space in the nation's capital is limited and it is relatively expensive (around $1.75 per hour) to park at commercial lots. It may be preferable, therefore, to use either Metro bus, Metro subway, or taxicab to get around the downtown Washington area.

To National Airport

Metro bus numbers 11A and 11E leave every ten minutes (more frequently in rush hour) from 10th Street and Pennsylvania Avenue, N.W. There is also a Metro subway train that leaves every seven minutes from downtown stations for National Airport.

To Dulles International Airport

An airport bus leaves from the Capital Hilton Hotel, 16th and K Streets, N.W., every hour on the hour, from 6:00 A.M. until 10:00 P.M. (fare: $7.75). Also, there is a daily limousine service to National Airport until 11:15 P.M. and to Dulles Airport until noon. For further information call Airport Limo, Inc. at (703) 532-1000.

To Baltimore–Washington (Friendship) International Airport

All buses leave from 16th and K Streets, N.W., downtown Washington, making one stop at Greenbelt Station, Maryland. For further information, call (301) 441-2345. The tickets are $7.50 for a single trip, and $14.00 for a round trip.

Taxicabs

Fares in Washington, D.C., are based on a zone system and are reasonable when compared with other large cities in the United States; however, taxi fares for crossing state lines into and out of Virginia and Maryland are fairly expensive.

Metro Subway System

Although the subway system is still under construction, parts of it have been completed, with the remainder to be operational within the next few years. It is a reasonably economical and efficient means of transportation in the Washington, D.C., area. Maps of the subway can be obtained at most subway stations.

Metro Buses

In order to get around town by Metrobus, which links almost every major corner of metropolitan Washington, scholars should get a copy of *Getting About by Metro Bus,* which is available at the Metro Headquarters, 600 5th Street, N.W., Washington, D.C. 20001. For routes and schedule information call (202) 637-2437.

Train

Union Station, 50 Massachusetts Avenue, N.E., is the terminal for all trains serving Washington, D.C. Located near the Capitol, it is within minutes of the downtown hotel area.

International Visitors Information Service (IVIS)

IVIS is a private, nonprofit, community organization that offers a diversified program of services to international visitors to Washington. Its programs are operated with the support of over 1,200 volunteers living in the Washington area. IVIS has 2 locations: the Main Information and Reception Center, 801 19th Street, N.W., Washington, D.C. 20006, (202) 872-8747, and the information booth at Dulles International Airport.

Multilingual staff and volunteers are available to help the visitor with sightseeing arrangements, hotel accommodations, and bilingual medical assistance. IVIS also provides tour brochures, maps and information, and telephone assistance in 55 languages (operating 24 hours a day, 7 days a week). Persons in need of language assistance may call (202) 872-8747.

For the foreign student enrolled in U.S. institutions of higher education, it may be useful to contact the Foreign Student Service Council of Greater Washington (FSSC), located at 1623 Belmont Street, N.W., Washington, D.C. 20009 (202/232-4979). The council's staff and volunteers provide home hospitality, sightseeing, and other services to the foreign students (local and transient).

Other Sources of Information

Dated somewhat, but still useful, is *"The Washington Post" Guide to Washington,* Laura L. Babb, ed. (New York: McGraw-Hill Book Co., 1976).

Free copies of the metropolitan Washington area map are available from the District of Columbia Department of Transportation's Map Office, 415 12th Street, N.W., Room 519, Washington, D.C. 20004 (202/727-6562). Mail orders must include a stamped, self-addressed, 8″ x 10″ envelope. The office is open from 8:15 A.M. to 4:45 P.M., Monday through Friday.

A Final Word

In general, it would cost you more to live in Washington, D.C., than in neighboring Virginia or Maryland. However, for those intending to do research primarily in Washington, especially along the Metro "blue line" (i.e., Foggy Bottom to Capitol Hill), the time lost commuting to and from Washington, and the transportation expense, may well make up the difference in rental costs.

For those intending to have their family accompany them, there are other considerations. Southwest D.C. is an excellent area in which to live. Apartments are within two or three blocks of the metro system, and the Mall can be reached on foot in ten to fifteen minutes. It is also worth noting that the D.C. public-school system is presently undergoing an academic revival. Thus far, this program has reached up into the lower grades. There are very good public elementary school programs in new Southwest and the Capitol Hill areas of the District.

One caution, the D.C. Department of Transportation is to be avoided at all costs; therefore, since parking tickets fall like the leaves, it pays to pay to keep your car off the street. Permits are required for street parking and these can only be had with the local registration of your vehicle, which can be very expensive.

Appendix VI. Federal Government Holidays

Federal government offices are closed on the following holidays:

New Year's Day	January 1
Washington's Birthday	Third Monday in February
Memorial Day	Last Monday in May
Independence Day	July 4*
Labor Day	First Monday in September
Columbus Day	Second Monday in October
Veterans' Day	November 11*
Thanksgiving	Fourth Thursday in November
Christmas	December 25*

*If this date falls on a Saturday, the holiday is on Friday; if the date falls on a Sunday, the holiday is on Monday.

The public areas of the Smithsonian Institution and the General Reading Rooms of the Library of Congress are open on most holidays.

Appendix VII.   Standard Entry Formats

A. Libraries Entry Format

1.   General Information
   a. *address; telephone numbers*
   b. hours of service
   c. conditions of access (including availability of interlibrary loan and repro-
      duction facilities)
   d. name/title of director and heads of relevant divisions

2.   Size of Collection
   a. general
   b. Southeast Asia

3.   Description and Evaluation of Collection
   a. narrative assessment of Southeast Asian holding—subject and area strengths/
      weaknesses
   b. tabular evaluation of subject strengths for holdings on Brunei, Burma,
      Cambodia, Indonesia, Laos, Malaysia, the Philippines, Singapore, Thai-
      land, Vietnam, and Southeast Asia, giving the number of titles and a rating
      of A-D,* in the following subject categories:

   Philosophy and Religion
   History and Auxiliary Sciences of History
   Geography and Anthropology
   Economics
   Sociology

---

*A—comprehensive collection of primary and secondary sources (Library
   of Congress collection to serve as standard of evaluation).
   B—substantial collection of primary and secondary sources sufficient for
      some original research (holdings equivalent to roughly one-tenth of
      those of the Library of Congress).
   C—substantial collection of secondary sources with some primary mate-
      rials, sufficient to support graduate instruction (holdings of roughly
      one-half those of the B collection).
   D—collection of secondary sources, mostly in English, sufficient to support
      undergraduate instruction (holdings of roughly one-half those of C
      collection); collections rated below D are indicated by "D − ."

Politics and Government
International Relations
Law
Education
Art and Music
Language and Literature
Military Affairs
Bibliography and Reference

4.   Special Collections
   a. periodicals
   b. newspapers
   c. government documents
   d. miscellaneous vertical files
   e. archives and manuscripts
   f. maps
   g. films
   h. tapes

5.   Bibliographic Aids (catalogs, guides, etc.) Facilitating Use of Collection

---

B. Archives and Manuscript Repositories Entry Format

1.   General Information
   a. *address; telephone numbers*
   b. hours of service
   c. conditions of access
   d. reproduction services
   e. name/title of director and heads of relevant divisions

2.   Size of Holdings Pertaining to Southeast Asia

3.   Description of Holdings Pertaining to Southeast Asia

4.   Bibliographic Aids (inventories, calendars, etc.) Facilitating Use of Collection

---

C. Museums, Galleries, and Art Collections Entry Format

1.   General Information
   a. *address; telephone numbers*
   b. hours of service
   c. conditions of access
   d. reproduction services
   e. name/title of director and heads of relevant divisions

2.   Size of Holdings Pertaining to Southeast Asia

3.   Description of Holdings Pertaining to Southeast Asia

4.   Bibliographic Aids (Inventories, calendars, etc.) Facilitating Use of Collection

D. Collections of Music and Other Sound Recordings Entry Format

1.   General Information
   a. *address; telephone numbers*
   b. hours of service
   c. conditions of access
   d. name/title of director and key staff members

2.   Size of Holdings Pertaining to Southeast Asia

3.   Description of Holdings Pertaining to Southeast Asia

4.   Facilities for Study and Use
   a. availability of audio equipment
   b. reservation requirements
   c. fees charged
   d. reproduction services

5.   Bibliographic Aids Facilitating the Use of Collection

E. Map Collections Entry Format

1.   General Information
   a. *address; telephone numbers*
   b. hours of service
   c. conditions of access
   d. reproduction services
   e. name/title of director and heads of relevant divisions

2.   Size of Holdings Pertaining to Southeast Asia

3.   Description of Holdings Pertaining to Southeast Asia

4.   Bibliographic Aids (inventories, calendars, etc.) Facilitating Use of Collection

F. Film Collections Entry Format

1.   General Information
   a. *address; telephone numbers*
   b. hours of service
   c. conditions of access
   d. name/title of director and key staff members

2.   Size of Holdings Pertaining to Southeast Asia

3.   Description of Holdings Pertaining to Southeast Asia

4.   Facilities for Study and Use
   a. availability of audiovisual equipment

    b. reservation requirements
    c. fees charged
    d. reproduction services

5. Bibliographic Aids Facilitiating Use of Collection

G. Data Banks Entry Format

1. General Information
    a. *address; telephone numbers*
    b. hours of service
    c. conditions of access (including fees charged for information retrieval)
    d. name/title of director and key staff members

2. Description of Data Files (hard data and bibliographic references) Pertaining to Southeast Asia

3. Bibliographic Aids Facilitating Use of Storage Media

H. Research Centers Entry Format

1. *Address; Telephone Numbers*

2. Name and Title of Chief Official

3. Programs and Research Activities Pertaining to Southeast Asia

4. Libraries and Research Facilities

5. Publications

J. Academic Programs and Departments Entry Format

1. *Address; Telephone Numbers*

2. Name and Title of Chief Official

3. Degrees and Subjects Offered; Program Activities Related to Southeast Asia

4. Libraries and Research Facilities

K. United States Government Agencies Entry Format*

1. General Information
    a. *address; telephone numbers*
    b. conditions of access
    c. name/title of director and heads of relevant divisions

2. Functions, Programs, and Research Activities (including in-house research, contract programs, research grants, employment of outside consultants, and international exchange programs)

3. Libraries and Reference Facilities

4. Publications and Records (including unpublished materials, indexes, and vertical files, among other data)

> *In the case of large, structurally complex agencies, each relevant division or bureau is described separately in accordance with the above entry format.

L. Southeast Asian Embassies and International Organizations Entry Format

1. General Information
   a. *address; telephone numbers*
   b. hours/conditions of access
   c. names and titles of chief officials

2. Organization Functions, Programs, Research Activities (including in-house research, contract research, research grants, and employment of outside consultants)

3. Libraries and Reference Facilities

4. Publications and Internal Records (including unpublished research projects)

M. Associations Entry Format

1. *Address; Telephone Numbers*

2. Name and Title of Chief Official

3. Programs and Activities Pertaining to Southeast Asia

4. Libraries and Reference Collections

5. Publications

N. Cultural-Exchange and Technical-Assistance Organizations Entry Format

1. *Address; Telephone Numbers*

2. Name and Title of Chief Official

3. Programs and Activities Pertaining to Southeast Asia

4. Libraries and Reference Facilities

5. Publications

P. Religious Organizations Entry Format

1. *Address; Telephone Numbers*
2. Name and Title of Chief Official
3. Programs Pertaining to Southeast Asia
4. Publications

Q. Publications and Media Entry Format

1. *Address; Telephone Numbers*
2. Name and Title of Chief Official
3. Programs and Publications Pertaining to Southeast Asia

BIBLIOGRAPHY

Bibliography

Reference sources consulted for identification of collections and organizations included in this *Scholars' Guide.*

Akey, Denise, ed. *Encyclopedia of Associations,* 2 vols., 16th ed. Detroit: Gale, 1981.

American Association of Museums. *Official Museum Directory.* Washington, D.C.: American Association of Museums, 1981.

American Council of Voluntary Agencies for Foreign Service, Inc. *U.S. Non-Profit Organizations in Development Assistance Abroad Including Voluntary Agencies, Missions, and Foundations.* New York: Technical Assistance Information Clearing House of the American Council of Voluntary Agencies for Foreign Service, Inc., 1971.

American Library Directory. 34th ed., 1981. New York: Jacques Cattell Press, 1981.

Androit, John L., ed. *Guide to U.S. Government Publications,* 2 vols. McLean, Va.: Documents Index, 1980.

Ayer Press. *'82 Ayer Directory of Publications.* Philadelphia: Ayer Press, 1982.

Bhatt, Purnima M. *Scholars' Guide to Washington, D.C. for African Studies.* Washington, D.C.: Smithsonian Institution Press, 1980.

Brown, Allison, ed. *Organizations Serving International Visitors in the National Capital Area,* 4th ed. Washington, D.C.: International Visitors Information Service, 1973.

Brownson, Charles B., comp. *1981 Congressional Staff Directory,* Mount Vernon, Va.: Congressional Staff Directory, 1981.

Chamberlain, Jim, and Ann Hammond. *Directory of the Population Related Community of the Washington, D.C. Area.* Washington, D.C.: World Population Society, D.C. Chapter, April 1978.

Congressional Quarterly, Inc. *Washington Information Directory, 1982–83.* Washington, D.C.: Congressional Quarterly, Inc., 1982.

Dillon, Kenneth J. *Scholars' Guide to Washington, D.C. for Central and East European Studies,* Washington, D.C.: Smithsonian Institution Press, 1980.

Diplomatic List. Washington, D.C.: U.S. Department of State, February 1982.

Dorr, Steven R. *Scholars' Guide to Washington, D.C. for Middle Eastern Studies.* Washington, D.C.: Smithsonian Institution Press, 1981.

Downey, James A. *U.S. Federal Official Publications: The International Di mension.* Oxford: Pergamon Press, 1978.

Grant, Steven A. *Scholars' Guide to Washington, D.C. for Russian/Soviet Studies.* Washington, D.C.: Smithsonian Institution Press, 1977.

Green, Shirley L. *Pictorial Resources in the Washington, D.C. Area.* Washington, D.C.: Library of Congress, 1976.

Grow, Michael. *Scholars' Guide to Washington, D.C. for Latin American and Caribbean Studies.* Washington, D.C.: Smithsonian Institution Press, 1979.

Hamer, Philip M., ed. *A Guide to Archives and Manuscripts in the United States.* New Haven, Conn.: Yale University Press, 1961.

Jennings, Margaret S., ed. *Library and Reference Facilities in the Area of the District of Columbia,* 10th ed. Washington, D.C.: American Society for Information Science, 1979.

Joyner, Nelson T., Jr. *Doing Business Abroad: Joyner's Guide to Official Washington,* 4th ed. Reston, Va.: Joyner and Associates, 1978.

Kim, Hong N. *Scholars' Guide to Washington, D.C. for East Asian Studies.* Washington, D.C.: Smithsonian Institution Press, 1979.

Kruzas, Anthony T., ed. *Encyclopedia of Information Systems and Services,* 1st ed. Ann Arbor: Edward Brothers, 1971.

Martin, Thomas J., comp. *North American Collections of Islamic Manuscripts.* Boston: G. K. Hall, 1978.

Mason, John Brown, ed. *Research Resources: Annotated Guide to the Social Sciences,* 2 vols. Santa Barbara, Calif.: American Bibliographical Center, 1968–71.

Metropolitan Bookstore Guide. Washington, D.C.: Washington Booksellers Association, 1975.

Padolsky, Arthur, and Carolyn R. Smith. *Education Directory: Colleges and Universities, 1978–79.* Washington, D.C.: National Center for Education, Education Division, U.S. Department of Health, Education and Welfare, n.d.

Palmer, Archie M., ed. *Research Centers Directory,* 6th ed. Detroit: Gale Research Co., 1979.

Pearson, J. D., comp. *Oriental Manuscripts in Europe and North America: A Survey.* Bibliotheca Asiatica, No. 7. Zug, Switzerland: Interdocumentation Co., 1971.

Rahim, Enayetur. *Scholars' Guide to Washington, D.C. for South Asian Studies.* Washington, D.C.: Smithsonian Institution Press, 1981.

Rowan, Bonnie G. *Scholars' Guide to Washington, D.C. for Film and Video Collections.* Washington, D.C.: Smithsonian Institution Press, 1980.

Schmeckebier, Laurence Frederick, and Roy B. Eastin, *Government Publications and Their Use,* 2nd rev. ed. Washington, D.C.: Brookings Institution, 1969.

Schneider, John H., Marvin Gechman, and Stephen E. Furth, eds. *Survey of Commercially Available Computer-Readable Bibliographic Data Bases.* Washington, D.C.: American Society for Information Science, 1973.

Sessions, Vivian S., ed. *Directory of Data Bases in the Social and Behavioral Sciences.* New York: Science Associates/International, 1974.

Smith, David Horton, ed. *Voluntary Transnational Cultural Exchange Organizations of the U.S.: A Selective List.* Washington, D.C.: Center for a Voluntary Society, 1974.

U.S. Congress. *Official Congressional Directory.* Washington, D.C.: Government Printing Office, 1981.

U.S. Department of State, Office of External Research. *Foreign Affairs Research: A Directory of Governmental Resources.* Washington, D.C.: Government Printing Office, 1969.

————. *Government Supported Research on Foreign Affairs: Current Project Information.* Washington, D.C.: Government Printing Office, 1981.

U.S. General Services Administration, National Archives and Records Service, Office of the Federal Register. *United States Government Manual, 1981–82.* Washington, D.C.: Government Printing Office, 1981.

U.S. National Historical Publications and Records Commission. *Directory of Archives and Manuscript Repositories.* Washington, D.C.: National Archives and Record Service, 1978.

U.S. Library of Congress. National Referral Center for Science and Technology. *A Directory of Information Resources in the United States Federal Government.* Washington, D.C.: Government Printing Office, 1974.

————. *A Directory of Information Resources in the United States: Social Sciences,* rev. ed. Washington, D.C.: Government Printing Office, 1973.

Washington V. Washington, D.C.: Potomac Books, 1979.

Wasserman, Paul, ed. *Ethnic Information Sources of the United States.* Detroit: Gale Research Co., 1976.

Weber, Olga S., comp. *North American Film and Video Directory: A Guide to Media Collections and Services.* New York: R. R. Bowker and Co., 1976.

Wynar, Lubomyr Roman. *Encyclopedic Directory of Ethnic Newspapers and Periodicals in the United States,* 2d ed. Littleton, Colo.: Libraries Unlimited, Inc., 1976.

Wynar, Lubomyr Roman, and Lois Buttlar. *Guide to Ethnic Museums, Libraries and Archives in the United States.* Kent, Ohio: The Center for Ethnic Publications, School of Library Science, Kent State University, 1978.

Wynar, Lubomyr Roman, with Lois Buttlar and Anna T. Wynar. *Encyclopedic Directory of Ethnic Organizations in the United States.* Littleton, Colo.: Libraries Unlimited, Inc., 1975.

INDEXES

Personal-Papers Index

Library Subject-Strength Index

This index identifies the most useful library collections in the Washington, D.C., area by subject. The evaluations (A through C) presented here are based on the criteria explained at the beginning of Section A of this *Guide* and summarized below:

>   A—comprehensive collection of primary and secondary sources (Library of Congress collection to serve as a standard of evaluation)
>   B—Substantial collection of primary and secondary sources, sufficient for some original research (holdings roughly one-tenth those of the Library of Congress);
>   C—substantial collection of secondary sources, with some primary sources; sufficient to support graduate instruction (holdings roughly one-half those of a "B" collection).

The standard Library of Congress subject headings have been used for categorization. Some valuable specialized collections have been included here, even though their rating is based on a subcategory of one of the major headings. A listing of library collections according to the size of their Southeast Asia holdings may be found in Appendix II. The table used to rank all the library holdings in this *Guide* is reproduced at the end of this index to indicate the approximate number of items reflected by each ranking for each subject. The subject headings are listed below in the order they appear in Section A.

Philosophy and Religion
A collections: A27
B collections: —
C collections: A21, A41

History and Auxiliary Sciences of History
A collections: A27
B collections: A21, A37
C collections: A4

Geography and Anthropology
A collections: A27
B collections: A31
C collections: A17

Economics
A collections: A27
B collections: A2, A30, A37
C collections: A9, A26

Sociology
A collections: A27
B collections: A2, A33
C collections: A4, A21, A37

Politics and Government
A collections: A27
B collections: A37
C collections: A4, A21

International Relations
A collections: A27, A37
B collections: A4, A18, A19, A21, A23, A29, A35
C collections: A8

Law
A collections: A27
B collections: —
C collections: A25

Education
A collections: A27
B collections: —
C collections: A32

Art and Music
A collections: A27
B collections: A38
C collections: C3

Language and Literature
A collections: A27
B collections: A21
C collections: A19

Military Affairs
A collections: A27
B collections: A37
C collections: A6, A34

Bibliography and Reference
A collections: A27
B collections: A37
C collections: A21, A29

Brunei
A collections: A26, A27
B collections: A4, A17, A19, A29
C collections: —

Burma
A collections: A27
B collections: —
C collections: A37

Cambodia
A collections: A27
B collections: A37
C collections: A21, A26, A30

Indonesia
A collections: A27
B collections: A30
C collections: A4, A37

Laos
A collections: A27
B collections: A37
C collections: A4, A19, A21, A26, A30

Malaysia
A collections: A27
B collections: A4, A26, A30, A37
C collections: —

Philippines
A collections: A27
B collections: A30
C collections: A37

Singapore
A collections: A27
B collections: A26, A37
C collections: A16, A19

Thailand
A collections: A27
B collections: A30
C collections: A26, A37

Vietnam
A collections: A27
B collections: A21, A37
C collections: A4, A6, A19, A34

Indochina
A collections: A27
B collections: A4, A6, A17, A21, A37
C collections: A29

Southeast Asia
A collections: A27
B collections: A16
C collections: A28, A30

Library Ranking Table

This table is based on the holdings of the Library of Congress (see entry A27) and calculated in the following manner:

A = the Library of Congress holdings
B = one-tenth of A
C = one-half of B
D = one-half of C

The evaluation methodology is explained at the beginning of Section A of this *Guide*.

Subject	A	B	C	D
Philosophy and Religion	2,403	240	120	60
History and Auxiliary Sciences of History	26,173	2,617	1,306	653
Geography and Anthropology	3,242	324	162	81
Economics	22,758	2,275	1,137	568
Sociology	2,413	243	121	60
Politics and Government	4,861	496	248	124
International Relations	303	30	15	17
Law	10,263	123	61	30
Education	2,733	273	136	68
Art and Music	1,405	140	70	35
Language and Literature	3,784	378	189	94
Military Affairs	545	54	27	13
Bibliography and Reference	2,294	229	114	57
Brunei	30	3	2	1
Burma	6,011	601	300	150
Cambodia	1,582	158	79	39
Indonesia	17,713	1,771	885	442
Laos	1,073	107	53	26
Malaysia	5,655	565	282	141
Philippines	16,370	1,637	818	409
Singapore	2,028	202	101	50
Thailand	6,896	690	345	172
Vietnam	10,110	1,001	500	250
Indochina	1,507	150	75	37
Southeast Asia	6,010	610	305	152

Subject Index

This subject index incorporates both geographic and topical entries. Entry symbols correspond to the following sections of the *Guide:*

    A — Libraries
    B — Archives and Manuscript Repositories
    C — Museums, Galleries, and Art Collections
    D — Collections of Music and Other Sound Recordings
    E — Map Collections
    F — Film Collections (Still Photographs and Motion Pictures)
    G — Data Banks
    H — Research Centers
    J — Academic Programs and Departments
    K — United States Government Agencies
    L — Southeast Asian Embassies and International Organizations
    M — Associations (Academic, Professional, Cultural)
    N — Cultural-Exchange and Technical-Assistance Organizations
    P — Religious Organizations
    Q — Publications and Media

NAME INDEX

(Organizations and Institutions)

Entry symbols correspond to the following sections of the *Guide:*

A—Libraries
B—Archives and Manuscript Repositories
C—Museums, Galleries, and Art Collections
D—Collections of Music and Other Sound Recordings
E—Map Collections
F—Film Collections (Still Photographs and Motion Pictures)
G—Data Banks
H—Research Centers
J—Academic Programs and Departments
K—United States Government Agencies
L—Southeast Asian Embassies and International Organizations
M—Associations (Academic, Professional, Cultural)
N—Cultural-Exchange and Technical-Assistance Organizations
P—Religious Organizations
Q—Publications and Media

The author, Patrick M. Mayerchak, was born in Covington, Kentucky, in 1943. He attended the University of Kentucky (B.A. in political science, 1965, and M.A. from the Patterson School of Diplomacy, 1967) and received his Ph.D. from the American University, School of International Service, in 1975. The author has conducted research in Malaysia and Singapore and is currently Associate Professor of Political Science at the Virginia Military Institute in Lexington, Virginia, where he teaches courses in Southeast Asian politics and international affairs.

Consultant Louis A. Jacob is the Head of the Southern Asia Section of the Library of Congress.

Consultant Frank Joseph Shulman is the Head of the East Asia Collection in McKeldin Library, University of Maryland.

Series Editor Zdeněk V. David has been Librarian of the Wilson Center since 1974. Previously, he taught history at Princeton and the University of Michigan, Ann Arbor, and library science at Rutgers University. He served as Slavic Bibliographer of the Princeton University Library from 1966 to 1974.

WOODROW WILSON INTERNATIONAL CENTER FOR SCHOLARS

SERIES OF SCHOLARS' GUIDES TO WASHINGTON, D.C. AREA

RUSSIAN/SOVIET STUDIES. By Steven A. Grant (1977)

LATIN AMERICAN AND CARIBBEAN STUDIES. By Michael Grow (1979)

EAST ASIAN STUDIES. By Hong N. Kim (1979)

AFRICAN STUDIES. By Purnima M. Bhatt (1980)

CENTRAL AND EAST EUROPEAN STUDIES. By Kenneth J. Dillon (1980)

FILM AND VIDEO COLLECTIONS. By Bonnie G. Rowan (1980)

MIDDLE EASTERN STUDIES. By Steven R. Dorr (1981)

SOUTH ASIAN STUDIES. By Enayetur Rahim (1981)

SOUTHEAST ASIAN STUDIES. By Patrick M. Mayerchak (1983)

Published by the Smithsonian Institution Press
P.O. Box 1579, Washington, D.C. 20013

Forthcoming:

RUSSIAN/SOVIET STUDIES. By Steven A. Grant (2d rev. ed. 1983)

NORTHWEST EUROPEAN STUDIES. By Louis A. Pitschmann (1984)

AUDIO RESOURCES. By James R. Heintze (1984)

SOUTHWEST EUROPEAN STUDIES. By Joan F. Higbee (1985)